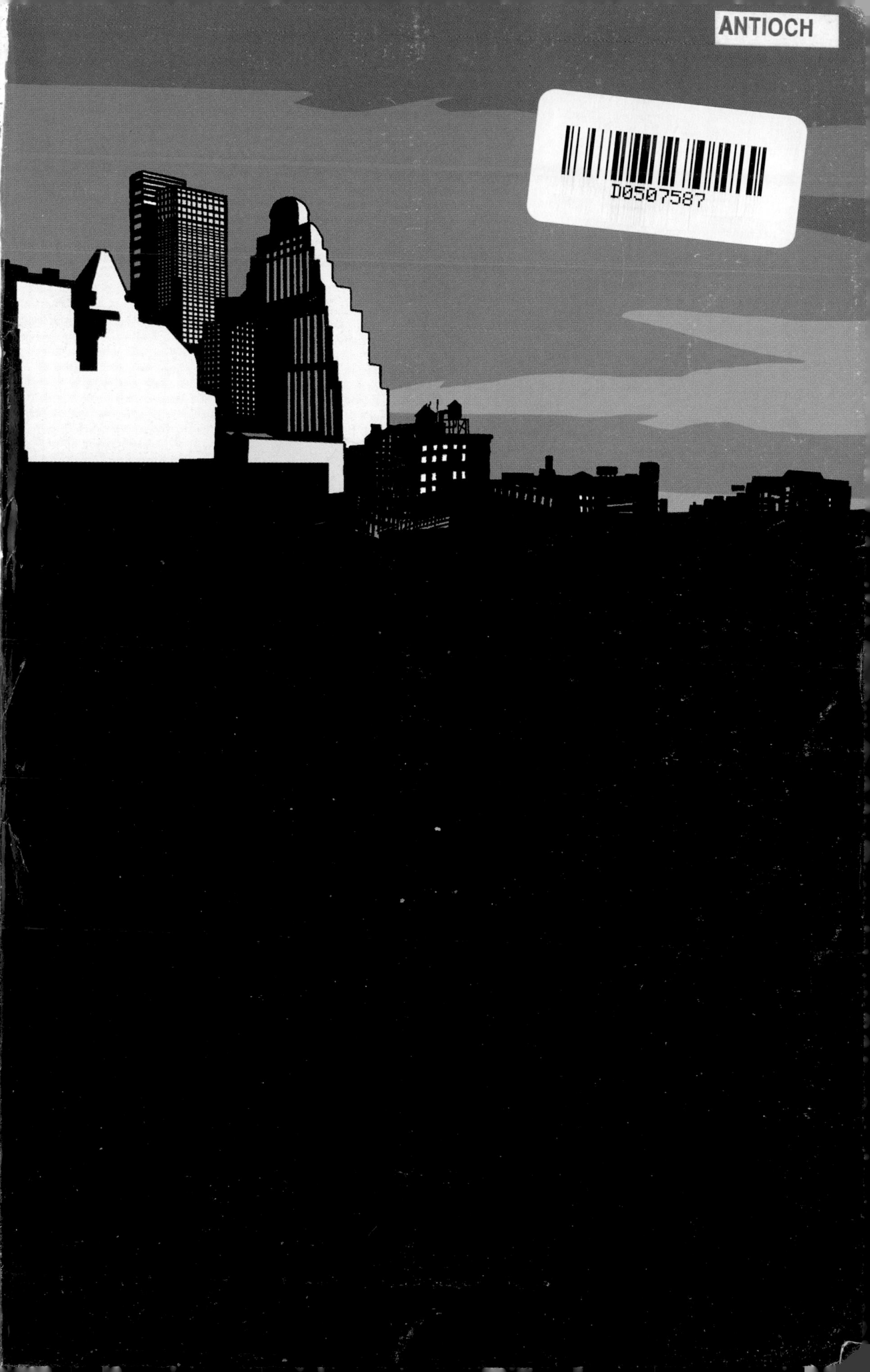

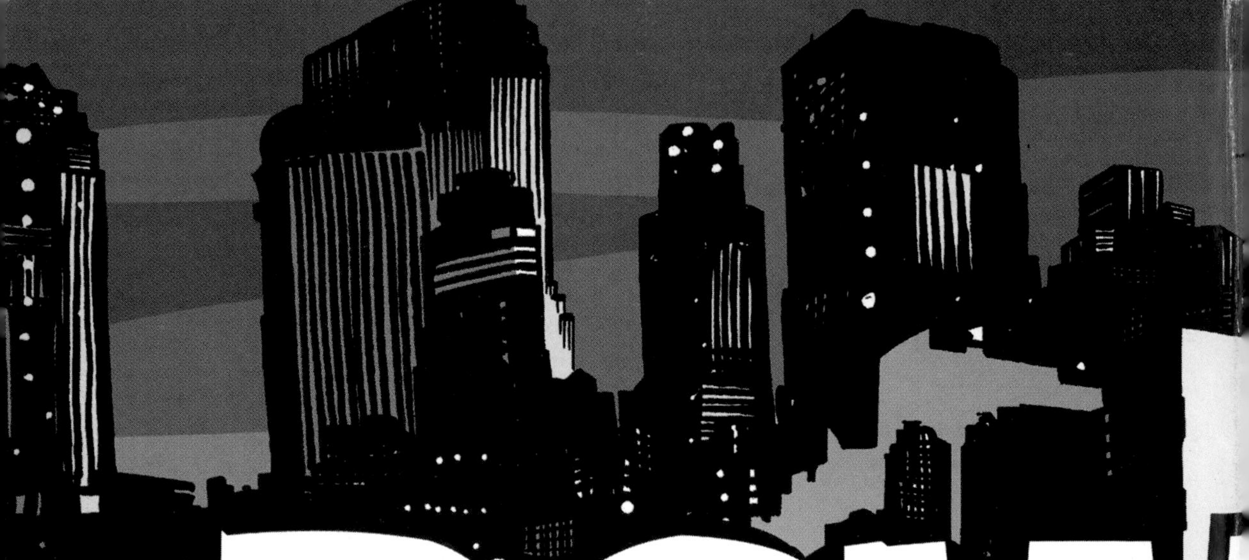

POW

CREATED AND

BRIAN MICHAEL BENDIS

COLOR ART
PETER PENTAZIS
PAT GARRAHY
BRIAN MICHAEL BENDIS

TYPOGRAPHY
KEN BRUZENAK
PAT GARRAHY
BRIAN MICHAEL BENDIS

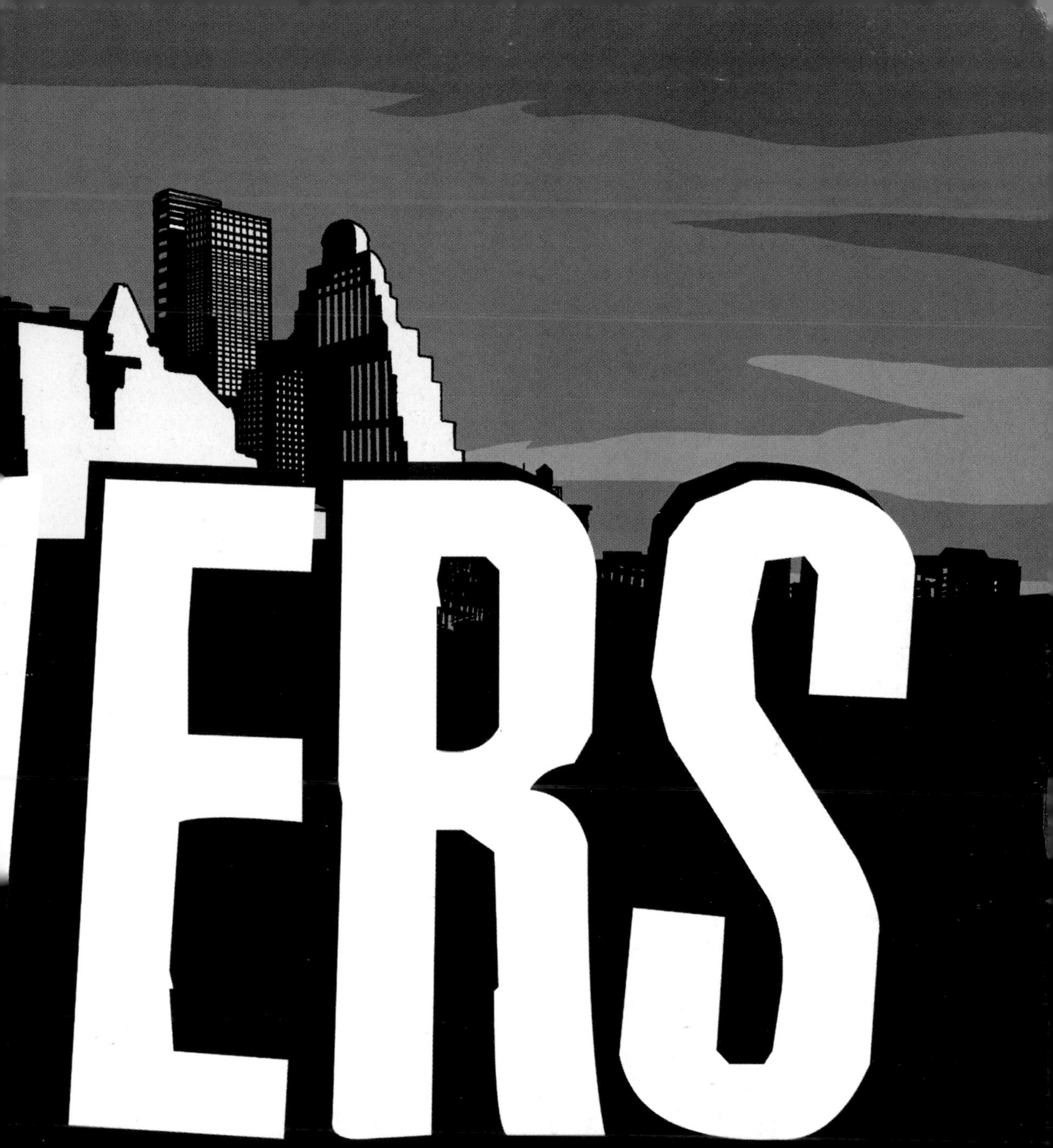
ERS

PRODUCED BY

AND MIKE AVON OEMING

EDITOR

KC MCCRORY

BUSINESS AFFAIRS

ALISA BENDIS

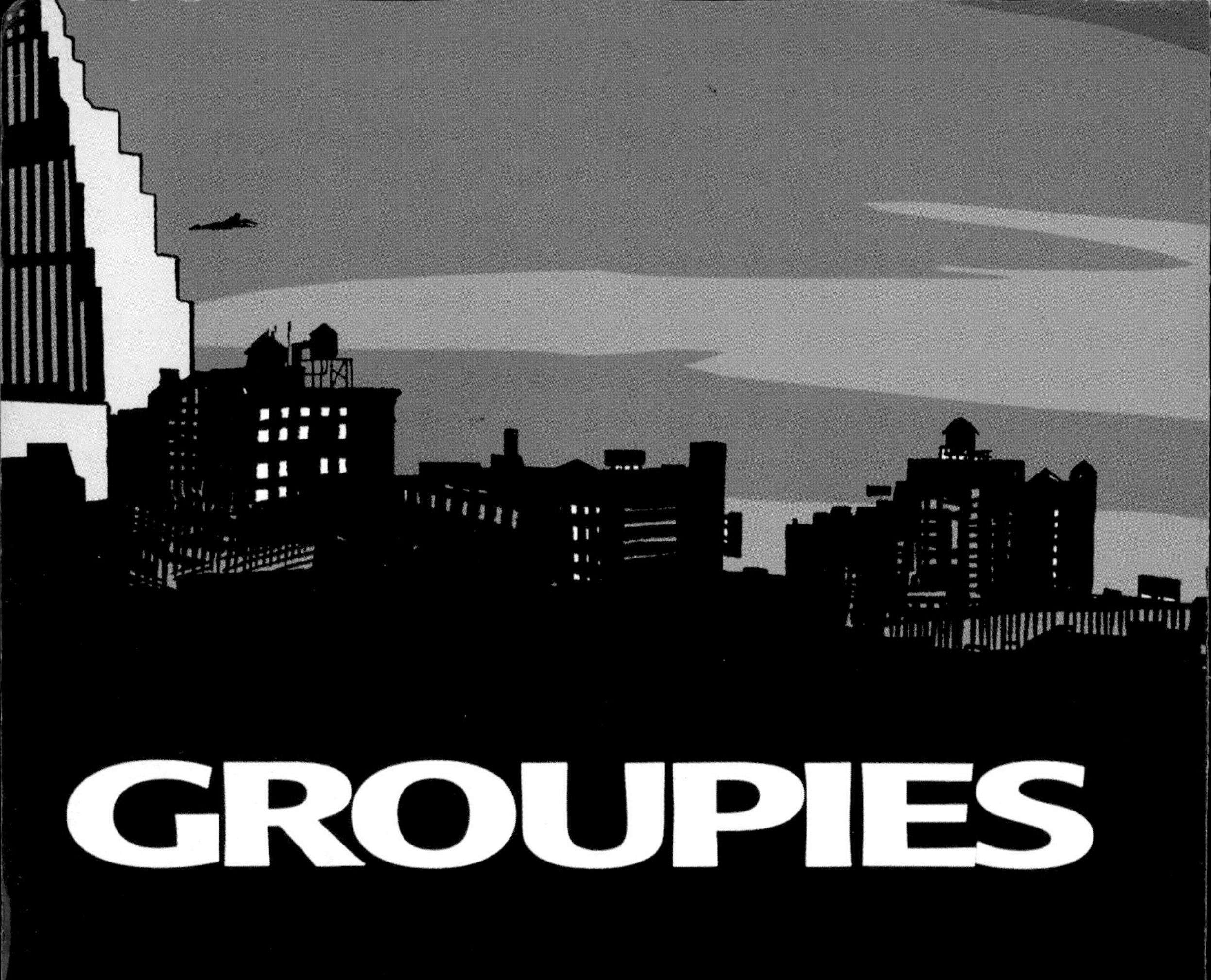

GROUPIES

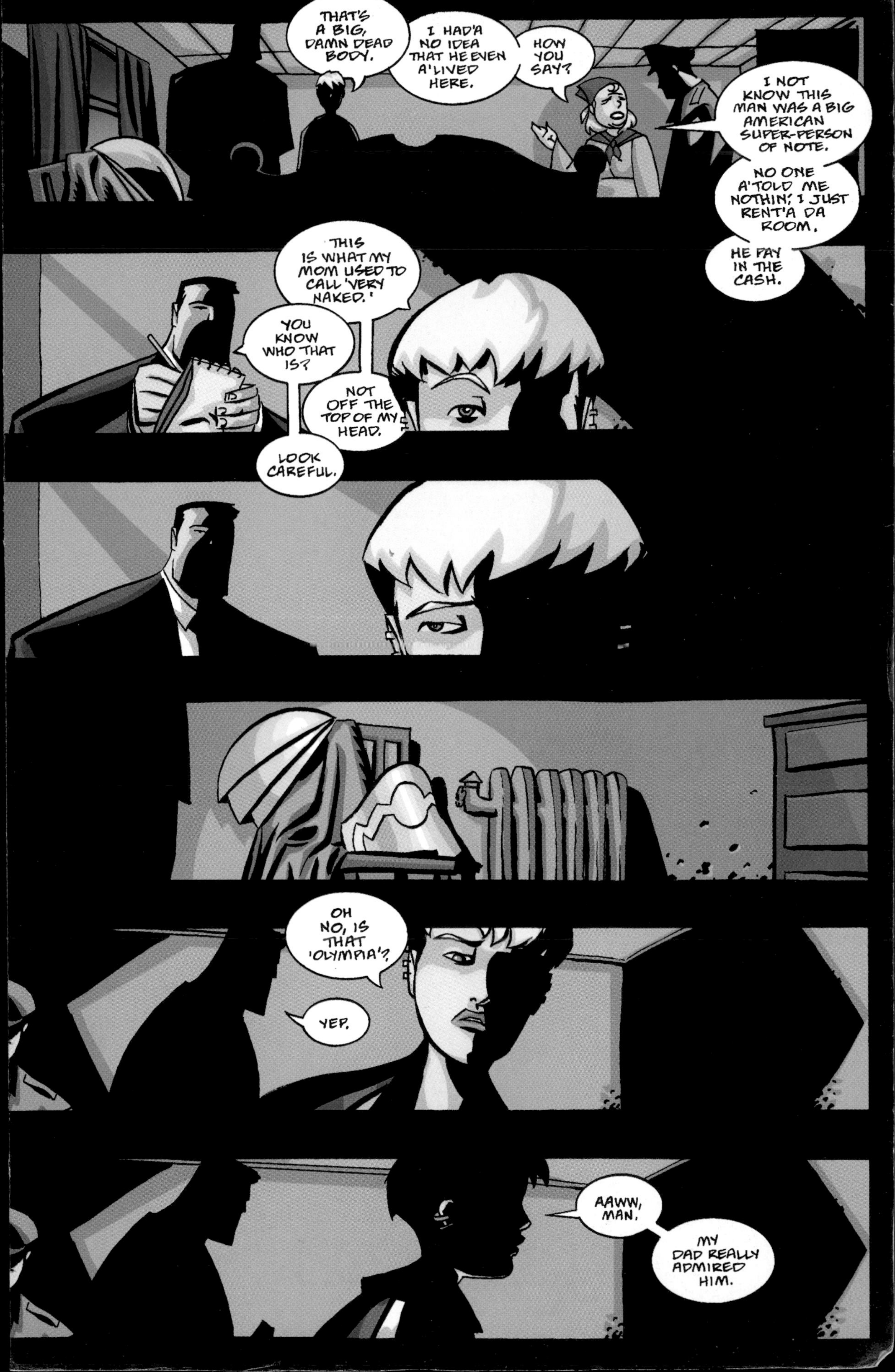
THAT'S A BIG, DAMN DEAD BODY.
I HAD'A NO IDEA THAT HE EVEN A'LIVED HERE.
HOW YOU SAY?
I NOT KNOW THIS MAN WAS A BIG AMERICAN SUPER-PERSON OF NOTE.
NO ONE A'TOLD ME NOTHIN'; I JUST RENT'A DA ROOM.
HE PAY IN THE CASH.
THIS IS WHAT MY MOM USED TO CALL 'VERY NAKED.'
YOU KNOW WHO THAT IS?
NOT OFF THE TOP OF MY HEAD.
LOOK CAREFUL.
OH NO, IS THAT 'OLYMPIA'?
YEP.
AAWW, MAN.
MY DAD REALLY ADMIRED HIM.

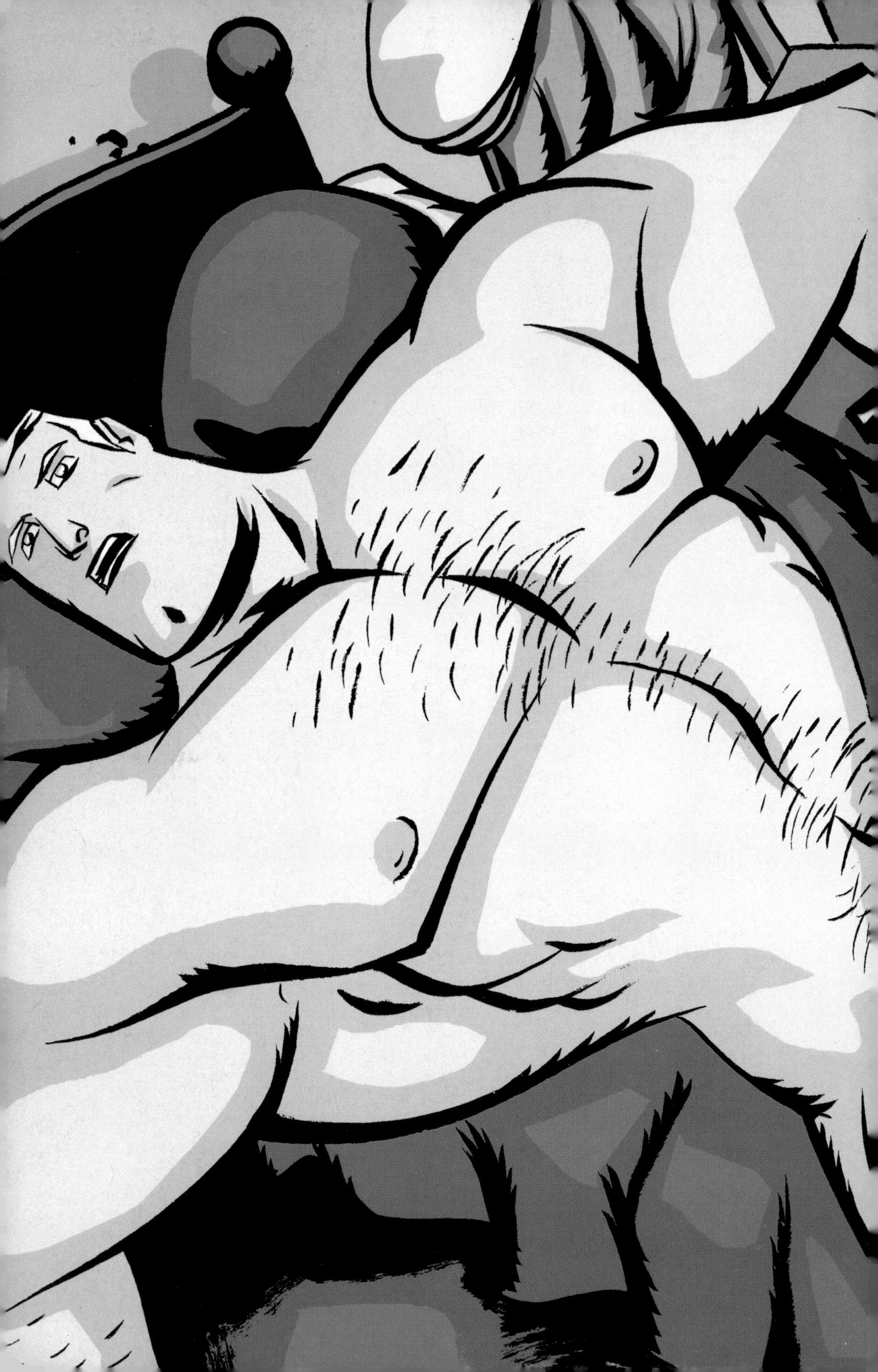

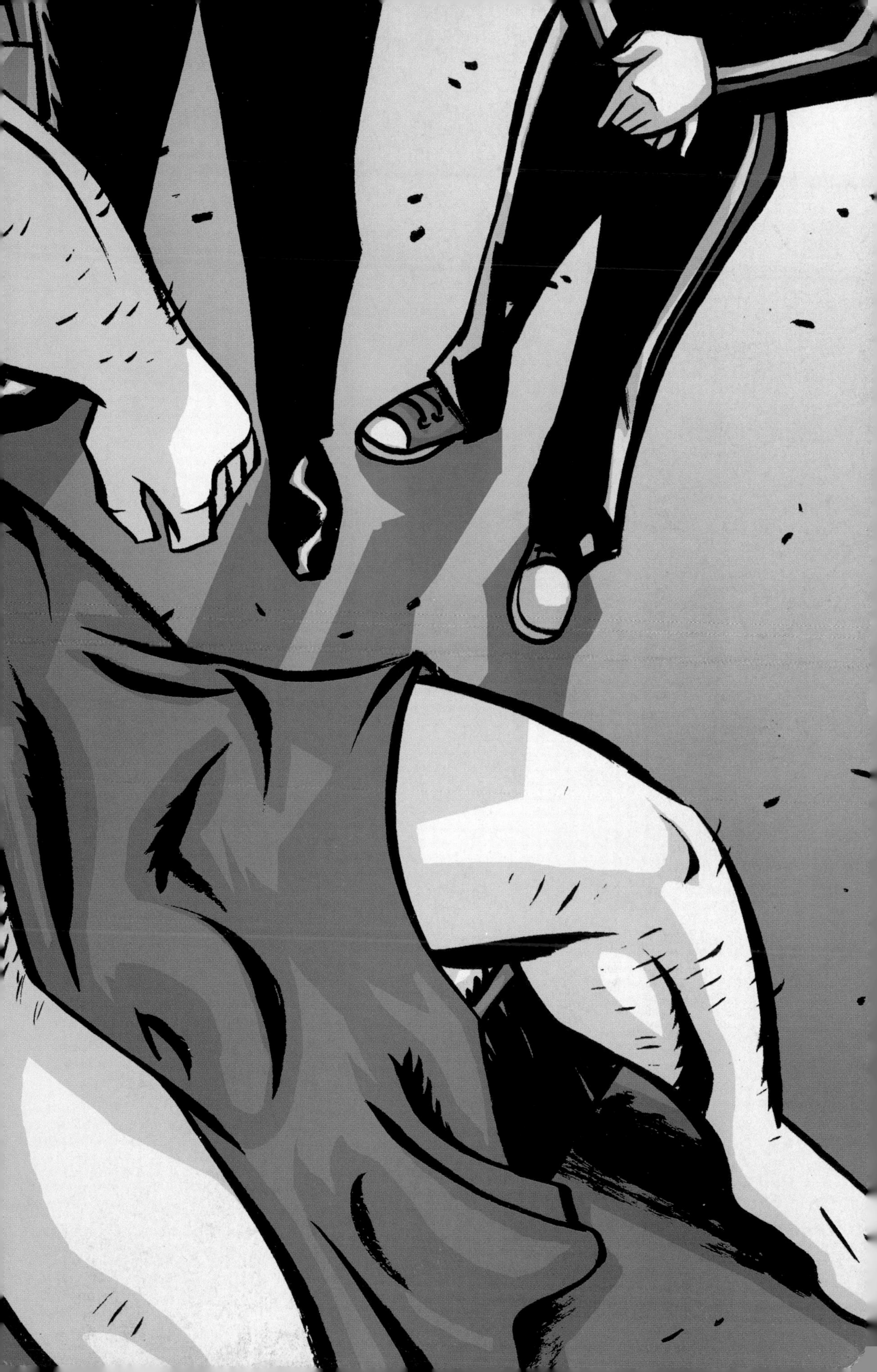

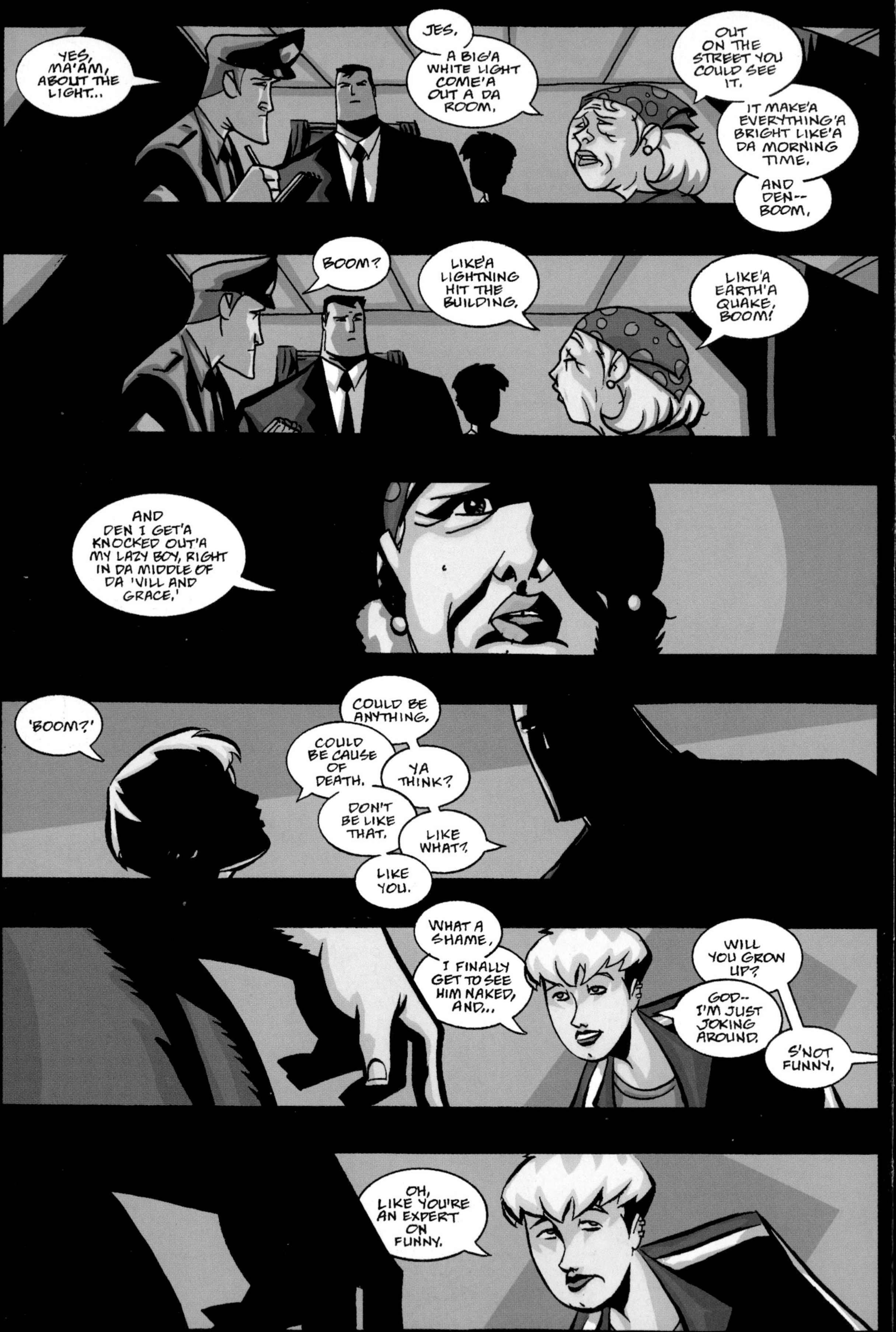
YES, MA'AM, ABOUT THE LIGHT...
JES.
A BIG'A WHITE LIGHT COME'A OUT A DA ROOM.
OUT ON THE STREET YOU COULD SEE IT.
IT MAKE'A EVERYTHING'A BRIGHT LIKE'A DA MORNING TIME.
AND DEN-- BOOM.
BOOM?
LIKE'A LIGHTNING HIT THE BUILDING.
LIKE'A EARTH'A QUAKE, BOOM!
AND DEN I GET'A KNOCKED OUT'A MY LAZY BOY, RIGHT IN DA MIDDLE OF DA 'VILL AND GRACE.'
'BOOM?'
COULD BE ANYTHING.
COULD BE CAUSE OF DEATH.
YA THINK?
DON'T BE LIKE THAT.
LIKE WHAT?
LIKE YOU.
WHAT A SHAME.
I FINALLY GET TO SEE HIM NAKED, AND...
WILL YOU GROW UP?
GOD-- I'M JUST JOKING AROUND.
S'NOT FUNNY.
OH, LIKE YOU'RE AN EXPERT ON FUNNY.

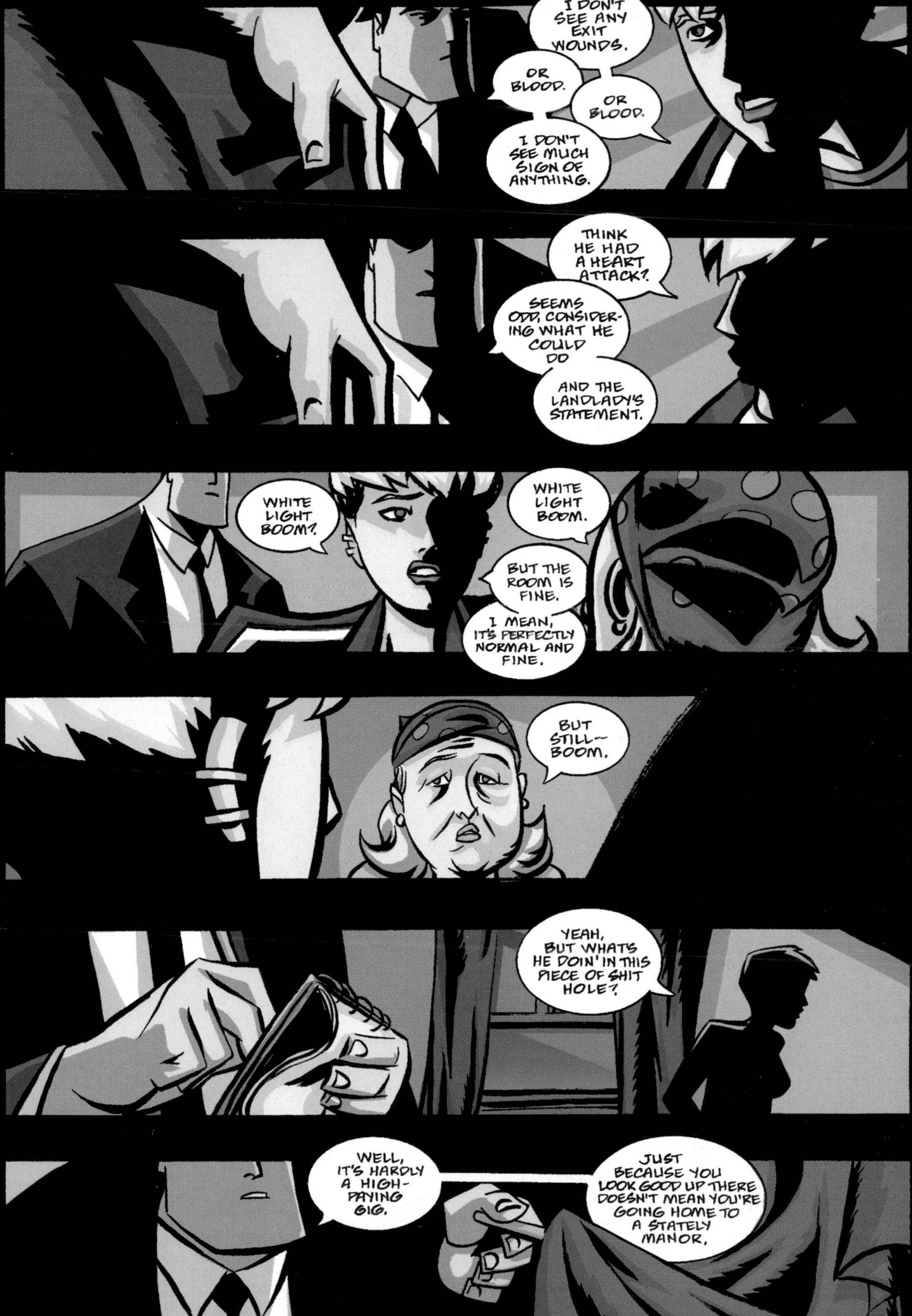
I DON'T SEE ANY EXIT WOUNDS.
OR BLOOD.
OR BLOOD.
I DON'T SEE MUCH SIGN OF ANYTHING.
THINK HE HAD A HEART ATTACK?
SEEMS ODD, CONSIDERING WHAT HE COULD DO
AND THE LANDLADY'S STATEMENT.
WHITE LIGHT BOOM?
WHITE LIGHT BOOM.
BUT THE ROOM IS FINE.
I MEAN, IT'S PERFECTLY NORMAL AND FINE.
BUT STILL-- BOOM.
YEAH, BUT WHAT'S HE DOIN' IN THIS PIECE OF SHIT HOLE?
WELL, IT'S HARDLY A HIGH-PAYING GIG.
JUST BECAUSE YOU LOOK GOOD UP THERE DOESN'T MEAN YOU'RE GOING HOME TO A STATELY MANOR.

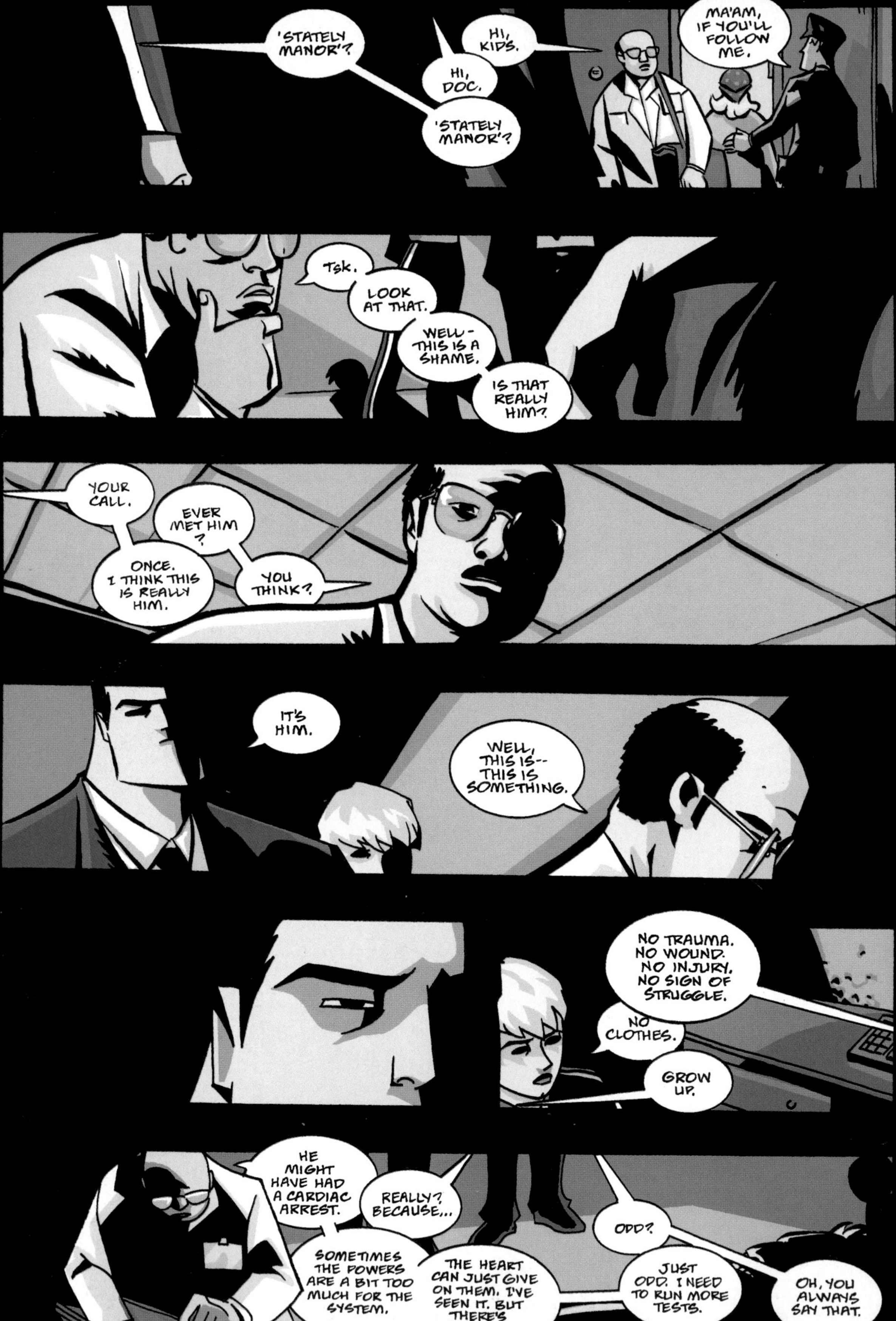
'STATELY MANOR'?
HI, KIDS.
HI, DOC.
'STATELY MANOR'?
MA'AM, IF YOU'LL FOLLOW ME.
Tsk.
LOOK AT THAT.
WELL- THIS IS A SHAME.
IS THAT REALLY HIM?
YOUR CALL.
EVER MET HIM?
ONCE. I THINK THIS IS REALLY HIM.
YOU THINK?
IT'S HIM.
WELL, THIS IS-- THIS IS SOMETHING.
NO TRAUMA. NO WOUND. NO INJURY. NO SIGN OF STRUGGLE.
NO CLOTHES.
GROW UP.
HE MIGHT HAVE HAD A CARDIAC ARREST.
SOMETIMES THE POWERS ARE A BIT TOO MUCH FOR THE SYSTEM.
REALLY? BECAUSE...
THE HEART CAN JUST GIVE ON THEM. I'VE SEEN IT. BUT THERE'S SOMETHING...
ODD?
JUST ODD. I NEED TO RUN MORE TESTS.
OH, YOU ALWAYS SAY THAT.

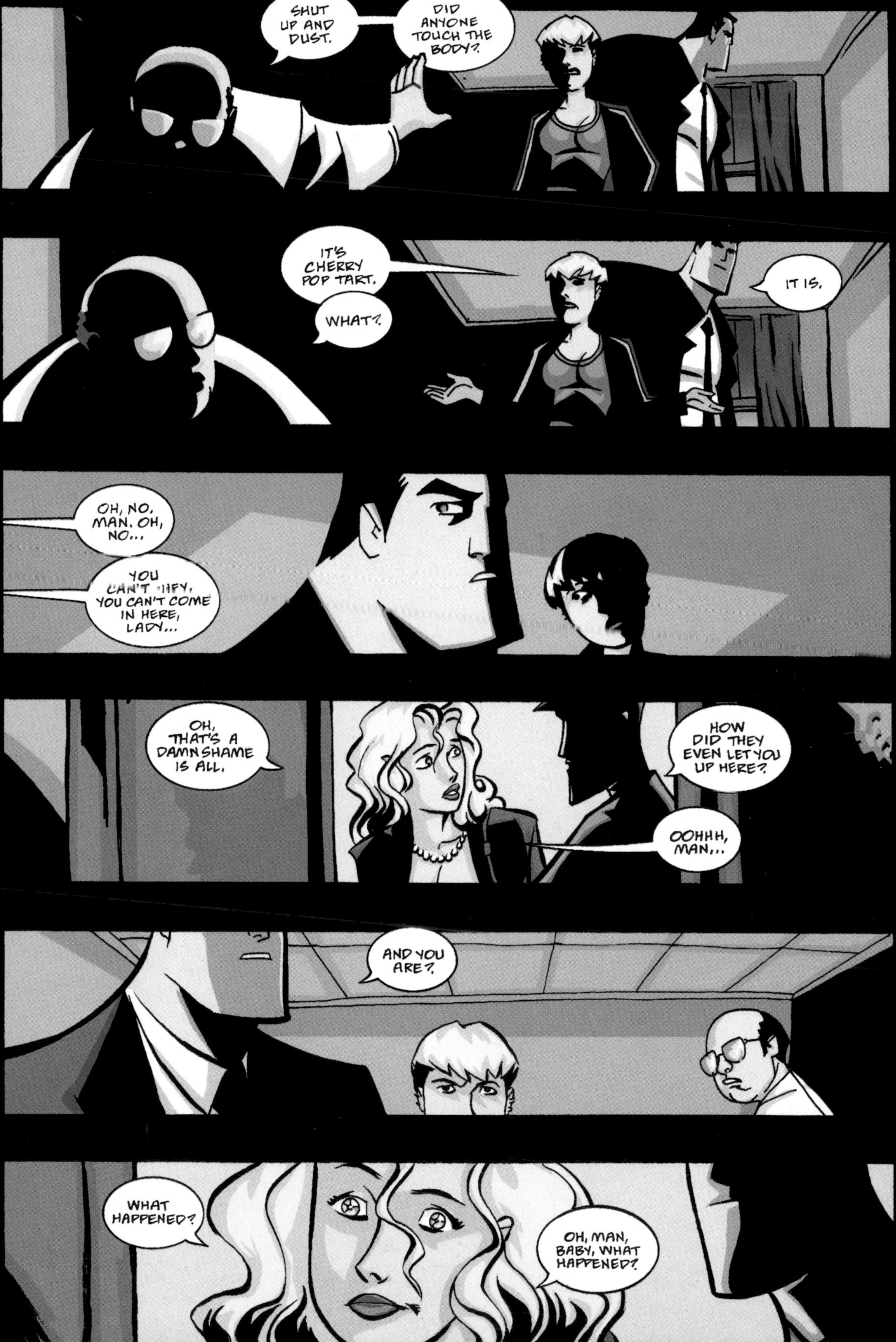
SHUT UP AND DUST.
DID ANYONE TOUCH THE BODY?
IT'S CHERRY POP TART.
WHAT?
IT IS.
OH, NO, MAN. OH, NO...
YOU CAN'T THEY, YOU CAN'T COME IN HERE, LADY...
OH, THAT'S A DAMN SHAME IS ALL.
HOW DID THEY EVEN LET YOU UP HERE?
OOHHH, MAN...
AND YOU ARE?
WHAT HAPPENED?
OH, MAN, BABY, WHAT HAPPENED?

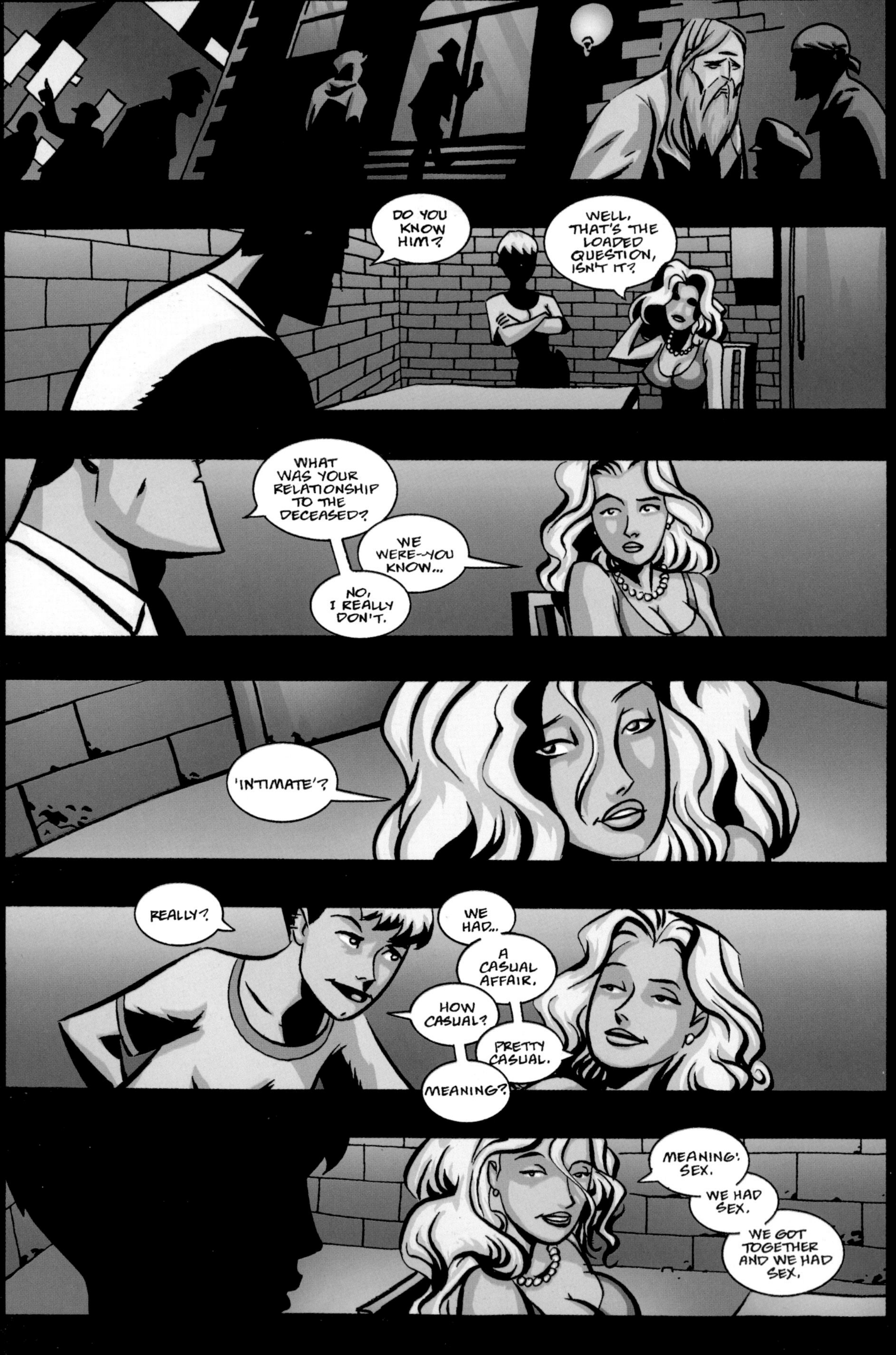
DO YOU KNOW HIM?
WELL, THAT'S THE LOADED QUESTION, ISN'T IT?
WHAT WAS YOUR RELATIONSHIP TO THE DECEASED?
WE WERE--YOU KNOW...
NO, I REALLY DON'T.
'INTIMATE'?
REALLY?
WE HAD...
A CASUAL AFFAIR.
HOW CASUAL?
PRETTY CASUAL.
MEANING?
MEANING: SEX.
WE HAD SEX.
WE GOT TOGETHER AND WE HAD SEX.

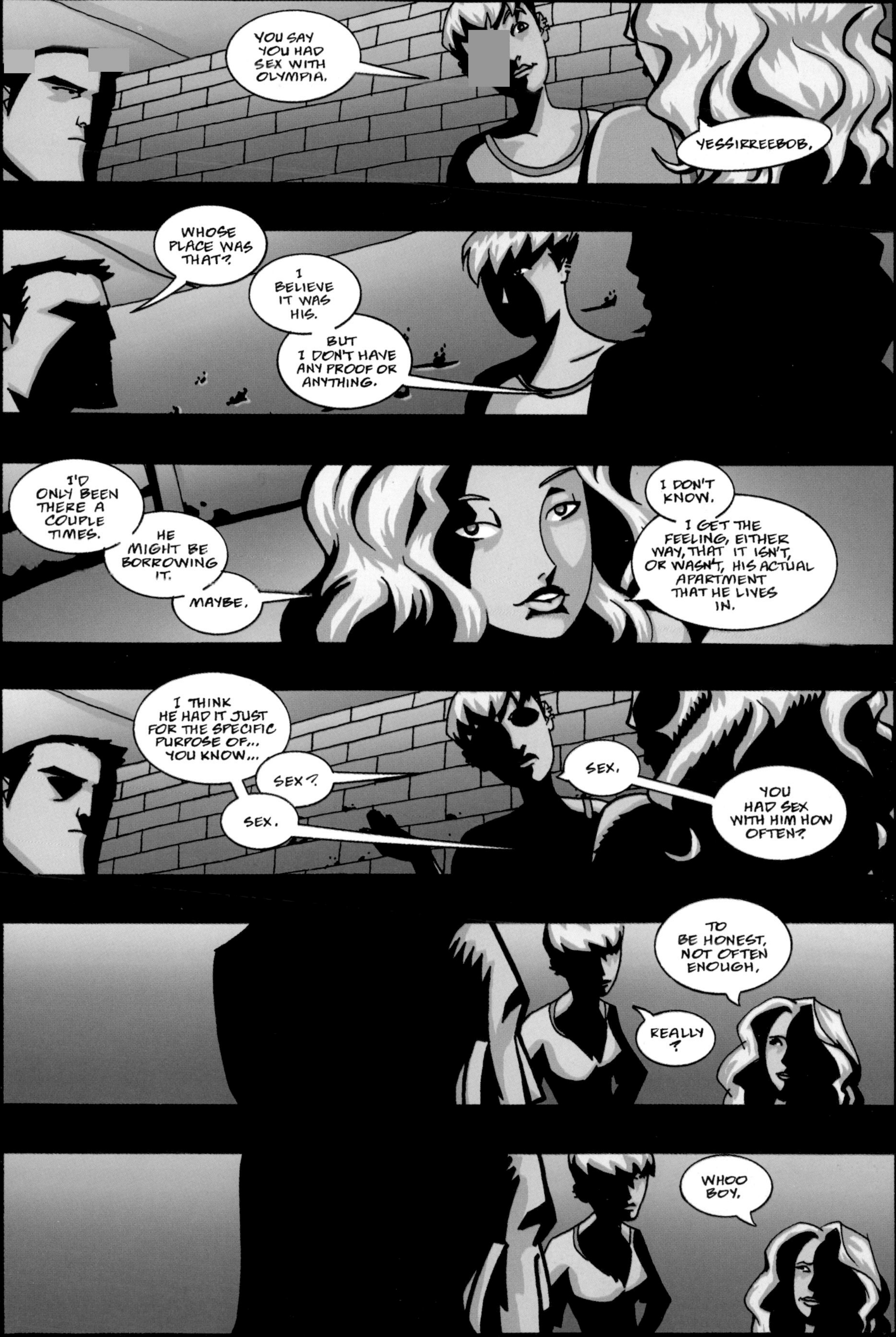

YOU SAY YOU HAD SEX WITH OLYMPIA.
YESSIRREEBOB.
WHOSE PLACE WAS THAT?
I BELIEVE IT WAS HIS.
BUT I DON'T HAVE ANY PROOF OR ANYTHING.
I'D ONLY BEEN THERE A COUPLE TIMES.
HE MIGHT BE BORROWING IT.
MAYBE.
I DON'T KNOW.
I GET THE FEELING, EITHER WAY, THAT IT ISN'T, OR WASN'T, HIS ACTUAL APARTMENT THAT HE LIVES IN.
I THINK HE HAD IT JUST FOR THE SPECIFIC PURPOSE OF... YOU KNOW...
SEX?
SEX.
SEX.
YOU HAD SEX WITH HIM HOW OFTEN?
TO BE HONEST, NOT OFTEN ENOUGH.
REALLY?
WHOO BOY.

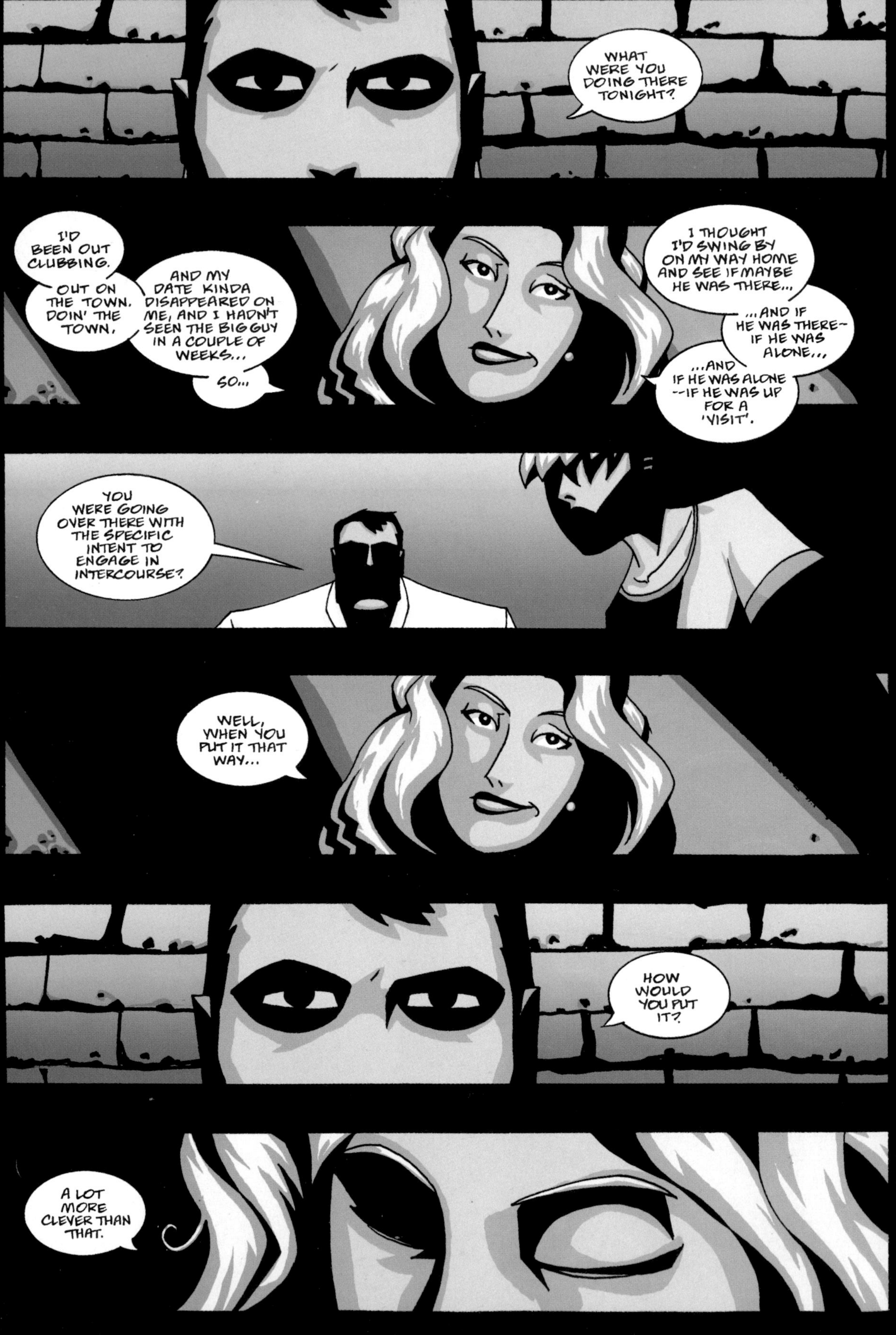
WHAT WERE YOU DOING THERE TONIGHT?
I'D BEEN OUT CLUBBING.
OUT ON THE TOWN. DOIN' THE TOWN.
AND MY DATE KINDA DISAPPEARED ON ME, AND I HADN'T SEEN THE BIG GUY IN A COUPLE OF WEEKS...
SO...
I THOUGHT I'D SWING BY ON MY WAY HOME AND SEE IF MAYBE HE WAS THERE...
...AND IF HE WAS THERE-- IF HE WAS ALONE...
...AND IF HE WAS ALONE --IF HE WAS UP FOR A 'VISIT'.
YOU WERE GOING OVER THERE WITH THE SPECIFIC INTENT TO ENGAGE IN INTERCOURSE?
WELL, WHEN YOU PUT IT THAT WAY...
HOW WOULD YOU PUT IT?
A LOT MORE CLEVER THAN THAT.

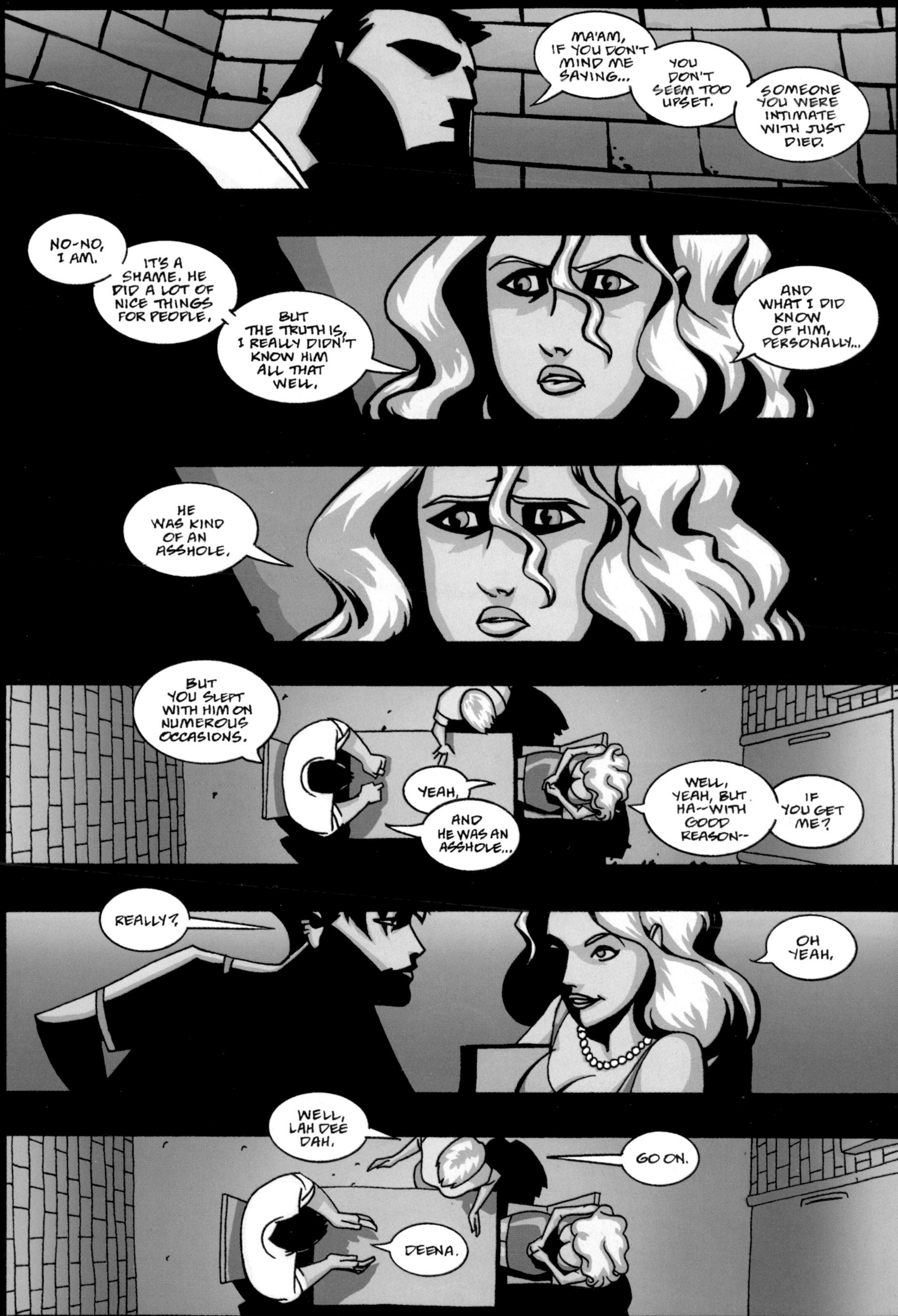
MA'AM, IF YOU DON'T MIND ME SAYING...
YOU DON'T SEEM TOO UPSET.
SOMEONE YOU WERE INTIMATE WITH JUST DIED.
NO-NO, I AM.
IT'S A SHAME. HE DID A LOT OF NICE THINGS FOR PEOPLE.
BUT THE TRUTH IS, I REALLY DIDN'T KNOW HIM ALL THAT WELL.
AND WHAT I DID KNOW OF HIM, PERSONALLY...
HE WAS KIND OF AN ASSHOLE.
BUT YOU SLEPT WITH HIM ON NUMEROUS OCCASIONS.
YEAH.
AND HE WAS AN ASSHOLE...
WELL, YEAH, BUT HA--WITH GOOD REASON--
IF YOU GET ME?
REALLY?
OH YEAH.
WELL, LAH DEE DAH.
GO ON.
DEENA.

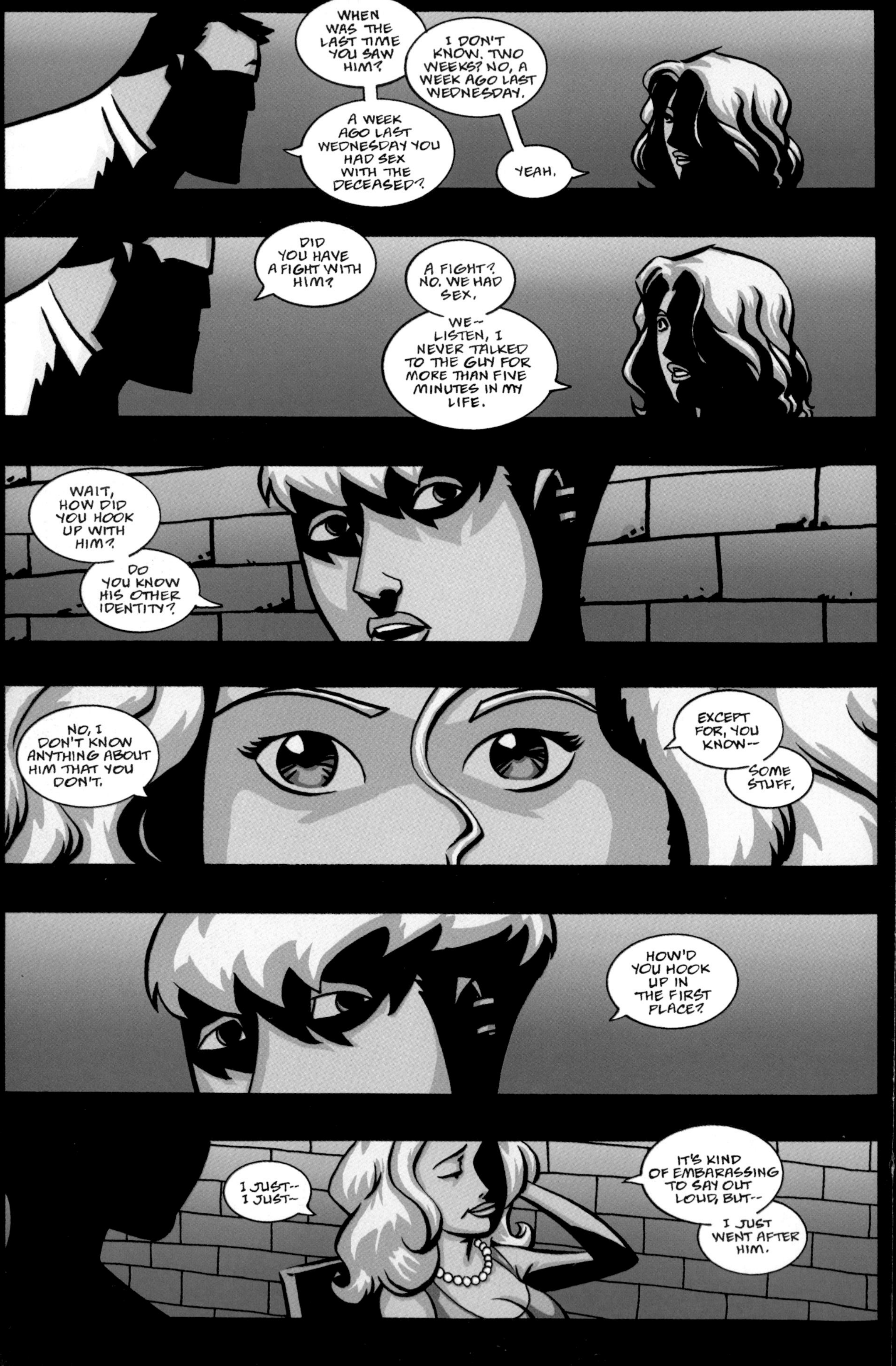

WHEN WAS THE LAST TIME YOU SAW HIM?
I DON'T KNOW. TWO WEEKS? NO, A WEEK AGO LAST WEDNESDAY.
A WEEK AGO LAST WEDNESDAY YOU HAD SEX WITH THE DECEASED?
YEAH.
DID YOU HAVE A FIGHT WITH HIM?
A FIGHT? NO. WE HAD SEX.
WE-- LISTEN, I NEVER TALKED TO THE GUY FOR MORE THAN FIVE MINUTES IN MY LIFE.
WAIT, HOW DID YOU HOOK UP WITH HIM?
DO YOU KNOW HIS OTHER IDENTITY?
NO, I DON'T KNOW ANYTHING ABOUT HIM THAT YOU DON'T.
EXCEPT FOR, YOU KNOW--
SOME STUFF.
HOW'D YOU HOOK UP IN THE FIRST PLACE?
I JUST-- I JUST--
IT'S KIND OF EMBARASSING TO SAY OUT LOUD, BUT--
I JUST WENT AFTER HIM.

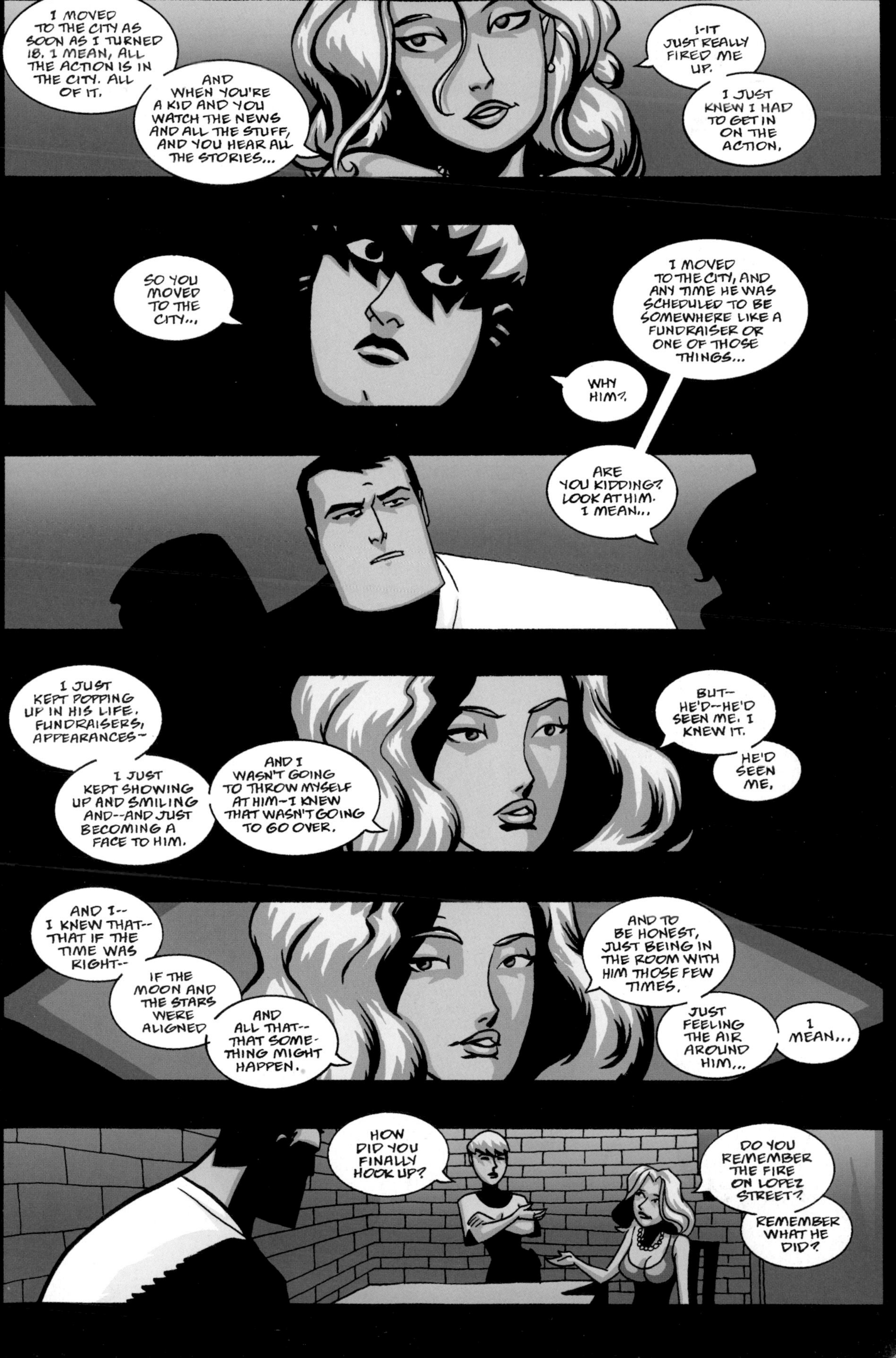
I MOVED TO THE CITY AS SOON AS I TURNED 18. I MEAN, ALL THE ACTION IS IN THE CITY. ALL OF IT.
AND WHEN YOU'RE A KID AND YOU WATCH THE NEWS AND ALL THE STUFF, AND YOU HEAR ALL THE STORIES...
I-IT JUST REALLY FIRED ME UP.
I JUST KNEW I HAD TO GET IN ON THE ACTION.
SO YOU MOVED TO THE CITY...
I MOVED TO THE CITY, AND ANY TIME HE WAS SCHEDULED TO BE SOMEWHERE LIKE A FUNDRAISER OR ONE OF THOSE THINGS...
WHY HIM?
ARE YOU KIDDING? LOOK AT HIM. I MEAN...
I JUST KEPT POPPING UP IN HIS LIFE. FUNDRAISERS, APPEARANCES--
I JUST KEPT SHOWING UP AND SMILING AND--AND JUST BECOMING A FACE TO HIM.
AND I WASN'T GOING TO THROW MYSELF AT HIM--I KNEW THAT WASN'T GOING TO GO OVER.
BUT--HE'D--HE'D SEEN ME. I KNEW IT.
HE'D SEEN ME.
AND I--I KNEW THAT--THAT IF THE TIME WAS RIGHT--
IF THE MOON AND THE STARS WERE ALIGNED
AND ALL THAT--THAT SOMETHING MIGHT HAPPEN.
AND TO BE HONEST, JUST BEING IN THE ROOM WITH HIM THOSE FEW TIMES.
JUST FEELING THE AIR AROUND HIM...
I MEAN...
HOW DID YOU FINALLY HOOK UP?
DO YOU REMEMBER THE FIRE ON LOPEZ STREET?
REMEMBER WHAT HE DID?

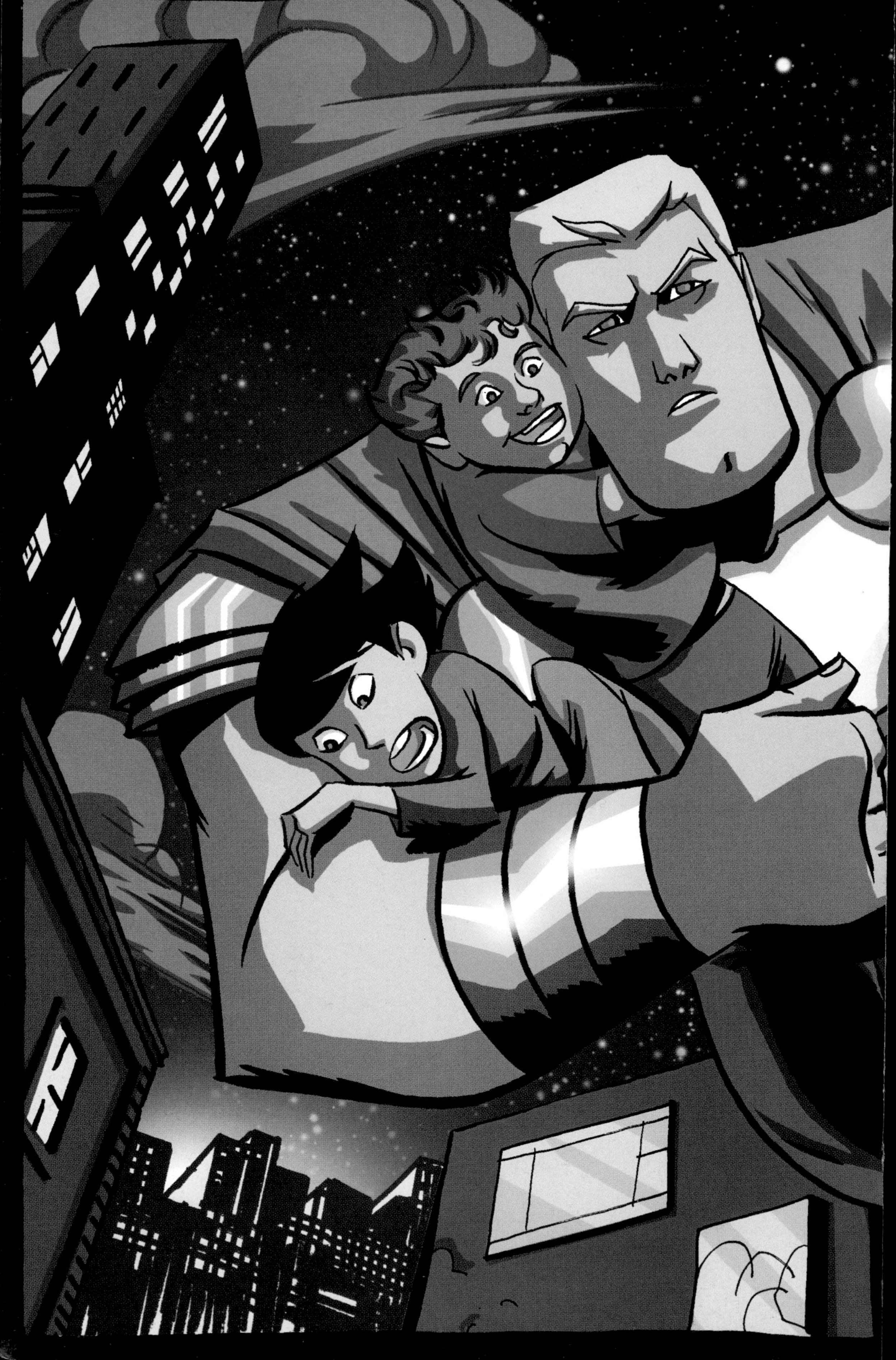

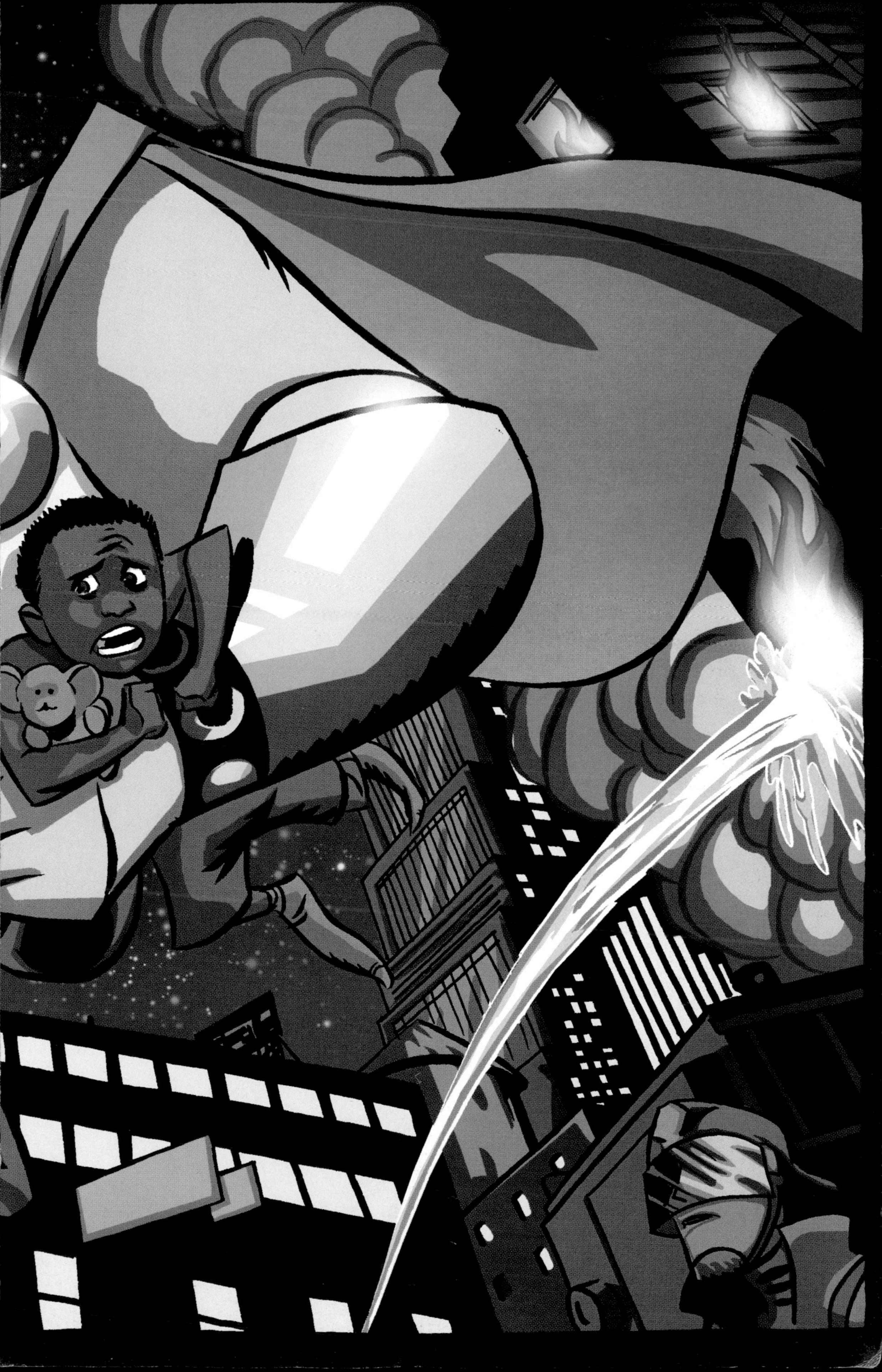

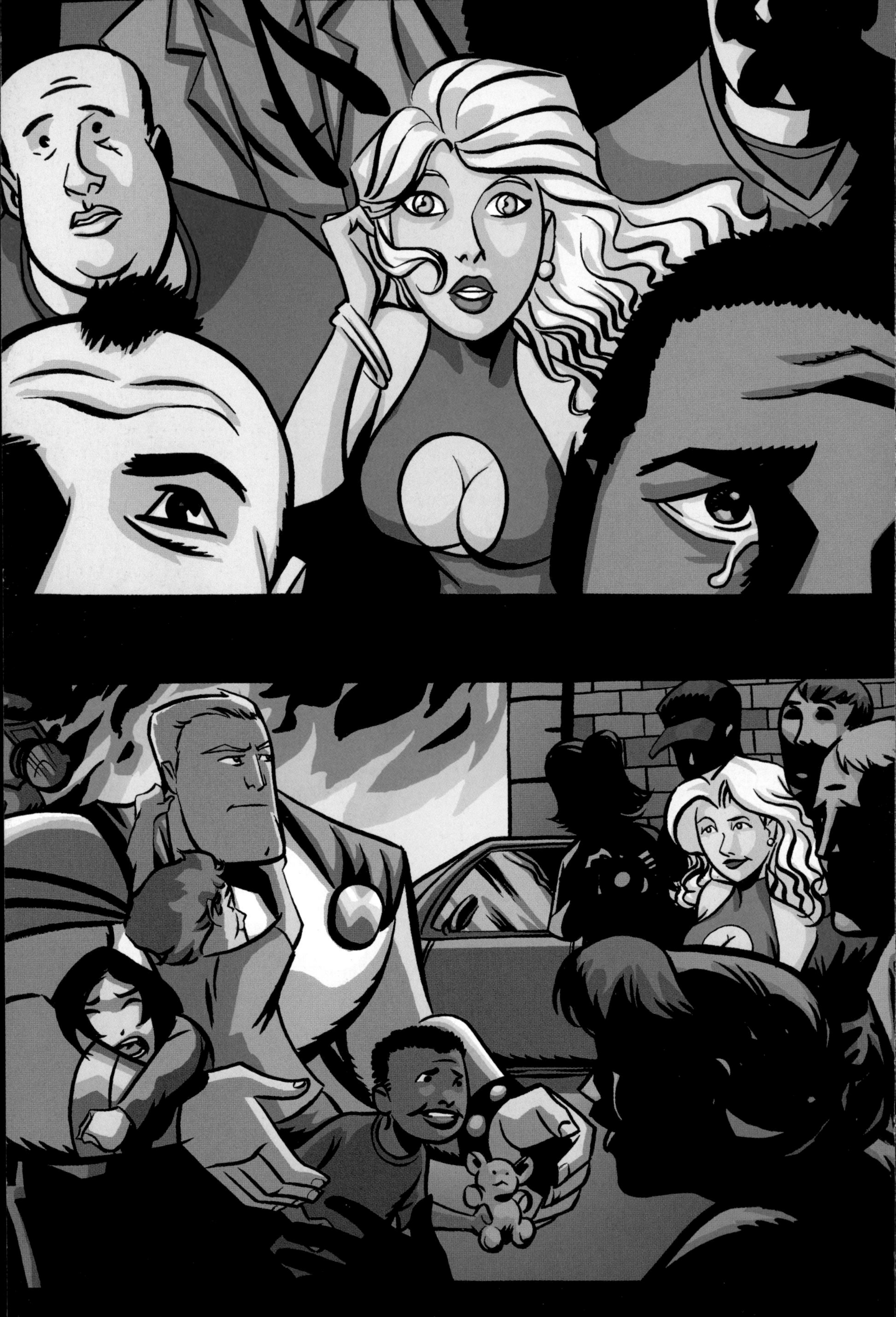

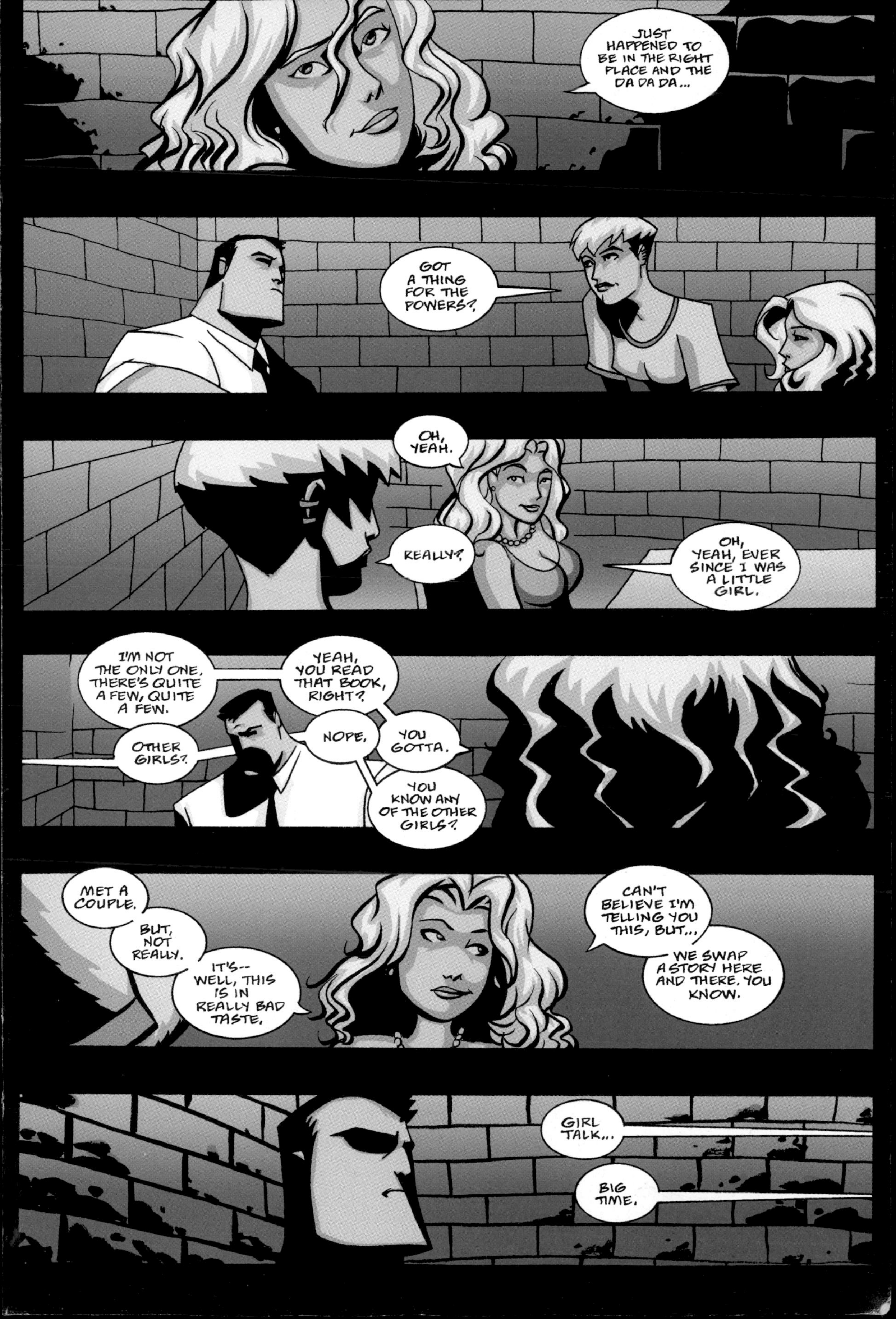
JUST HAPPENED TO BE IN THE RIGHT PLACE AND THE DA DA DA...
GOT A THING FOR THE POWERS?
OH, YEAH.
REALLY?
OH, YEAH, EVER SINCE I WAS A LITTLE GIRL.
I'M NOT THE ONLY ONE. THERE'S QUITE A FEW, QUITE A FEW.
YEAH, YOU READ THAT BOOK, RIGHT?
OTHER GIRLS?
NOPE.
YOU GOTTA.
YOU KNOW ANY OF THE OTHER GIRLS?
MET A COUPLE.
BUT, NOT REALLY.
IT'S-- WELL, THIS IS IN REALLY BAD TASTE.
CAN'T BELIEVE I'M TELLING YOU THIS, BUT...
WE SWAP A STORY HERE AND THERE. YOU KNOW.
GIRL TALK...
BIG TIME.

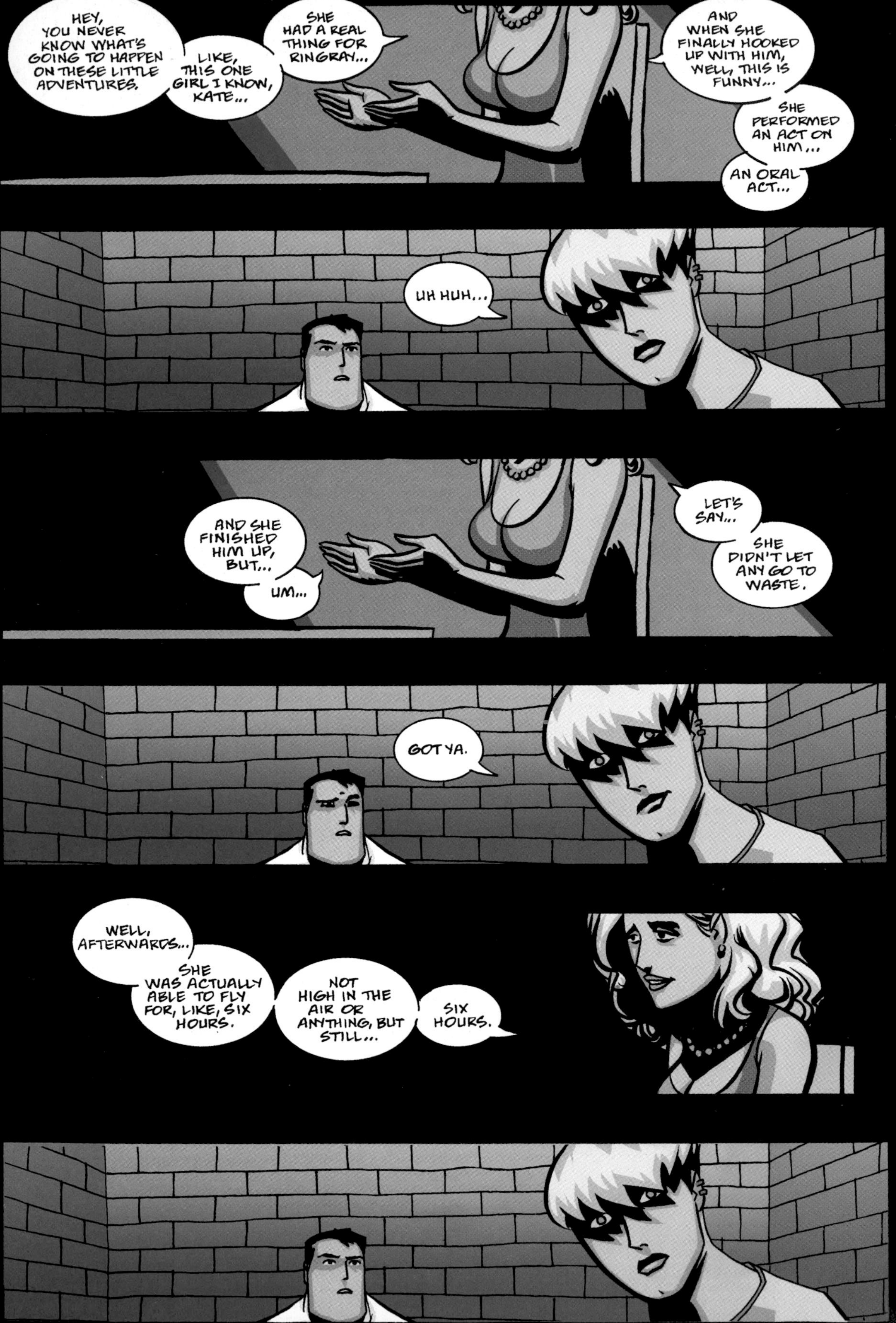
HEY, YOU NEVER KNOW WHAT'S GOING TO HAPPEN ON THESE LITTLE ADVENTURES.
LIKE, THIS ONE GIRL I KNOW, KATE...
SHE HAD A REAL THING FOR RINGRAY...
AND WHEN SHE FINALLY HOOKED UP WITH HIM, WELL, THIS IS FUNNY...
SHE PERFORMED AN ACT ON HIM...
AN ORAL ACT...
UH HUH...
AND SHE FINISHED HIM UP, BUT...
UM...
LET'S SAY...
SHE DIDN'T LET ANY GO TO WASTE.
GOT YA.
WELL, AFTERWARDS...
SHE WAS ACTUALLY ABLE TO FLY FOR, LIKE, SIX HOURS.
NOT HIGH IN THE AIR OR ANYTHING, BUT STILL...
SIX HOURS.

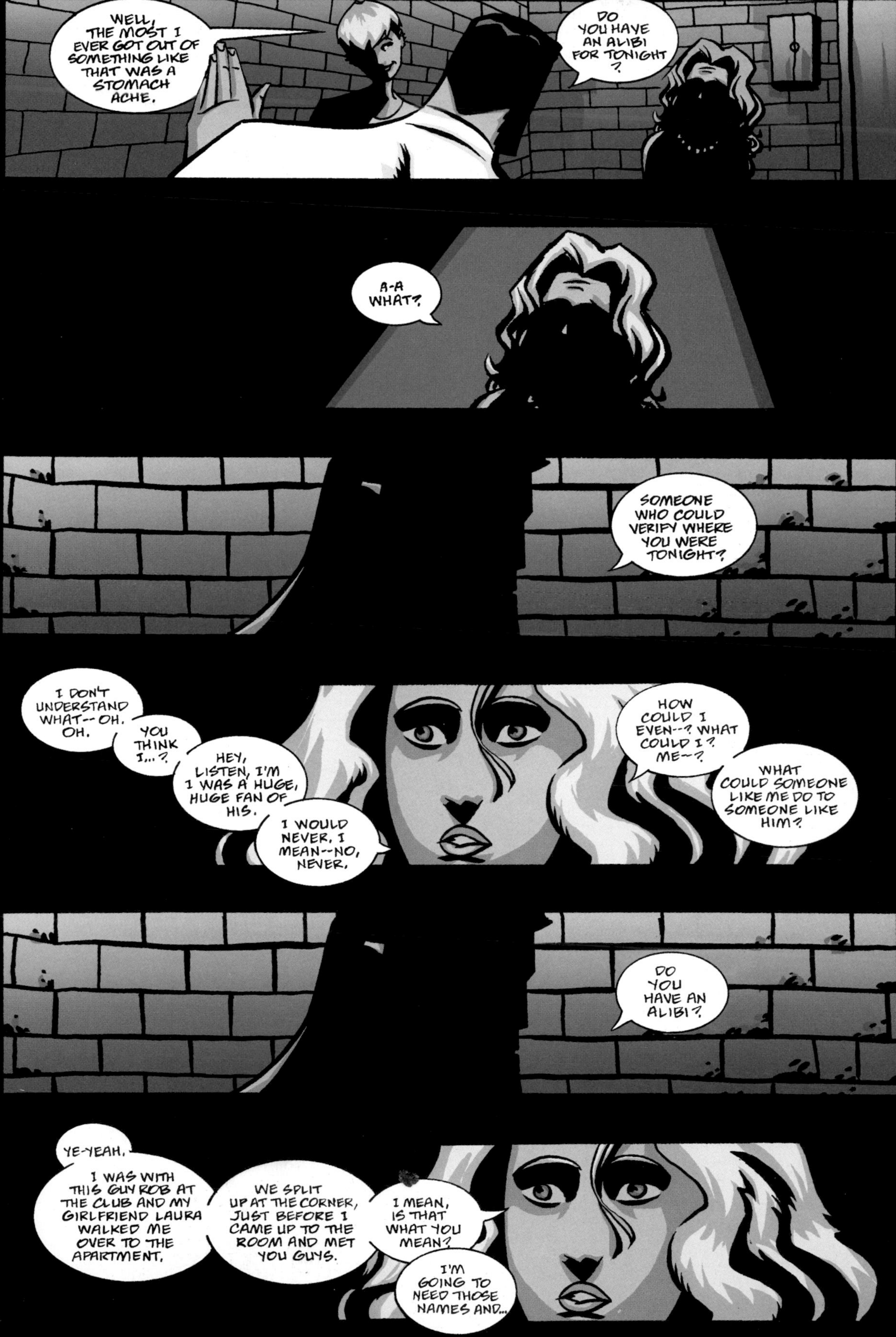
WELL, THE MOST I EVER GOT OUT OF SOMETHING LIKE THAT WAS A STOMACH ACHE.
DO YOU HAVE AN ALIBI FOR TONIGHT ?
A-A WHAT?
SOMEONE WHO COULD VERIFY WHERE YOU WERE TONIGHT?
I DON'T UNDERSTAND WHAT-- OH. OH.
YOU THINK I...?
HEY, LISTEN, I'M I WAS A HUGE, HUGE FAN OF HIS.
I WOULD NEVER. I MEAN--NO, NEVER.
HOW COULD I EVEN--? WHAT COULD I? ME--?
WHAT COULD SOMEONE LIKE ME DO TO SOMEONE LIKE HIM?
DO YOU HAVE AN ALIBI?
YE-YEAH.
I WAS WITH THIS GUY ROB AT THE CLUB AND MY GIRLFRIEND LAURA WALKED ME OVER TO THE APARTMENT.
WE SPLIT UP AT THE CORNER, JUST BEFORE I CAME UP TO THE ROOM AND MET YOU GUYS.
I MEAN, IS THAT WHAT YOU MEAN?
I'M GOING TO NEED THOSE NAMES AND...

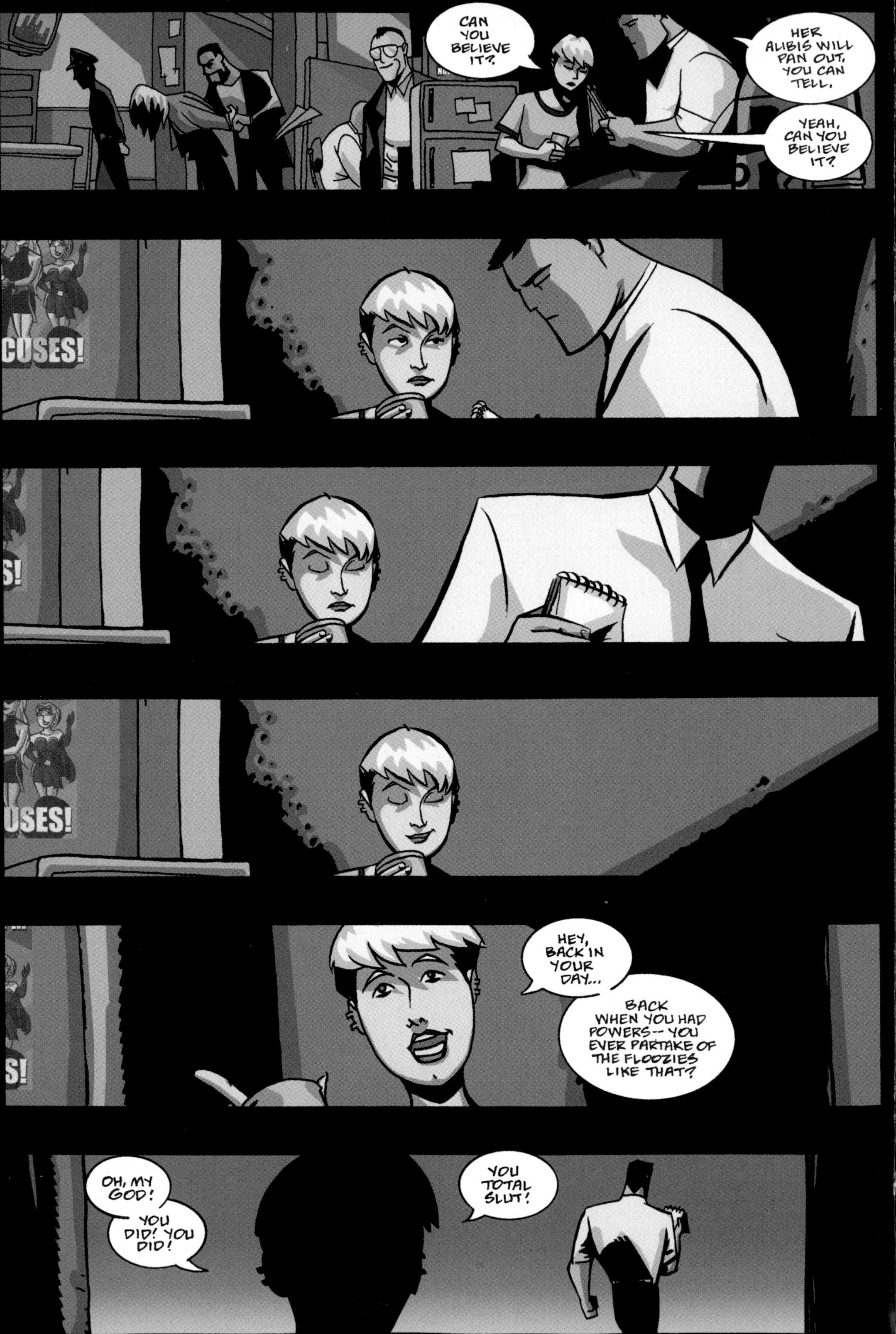
CAN YOU BELIEVE IT?
HER ALIBIS WILL PAN OUT, YOU CAN TELL.
YEAH, CAN YOU BELIEVE IT?
CUSES!
HEY, BACK IN YOUR DAY...
BACK WHEN YOU HAD POWERS-- YOU EVER PARTAKE OF THE FLOOZIES LIKE THAT?
OH, MY GOD!
YOU DID! YOU DID!
YOU TOTAL SLUT!

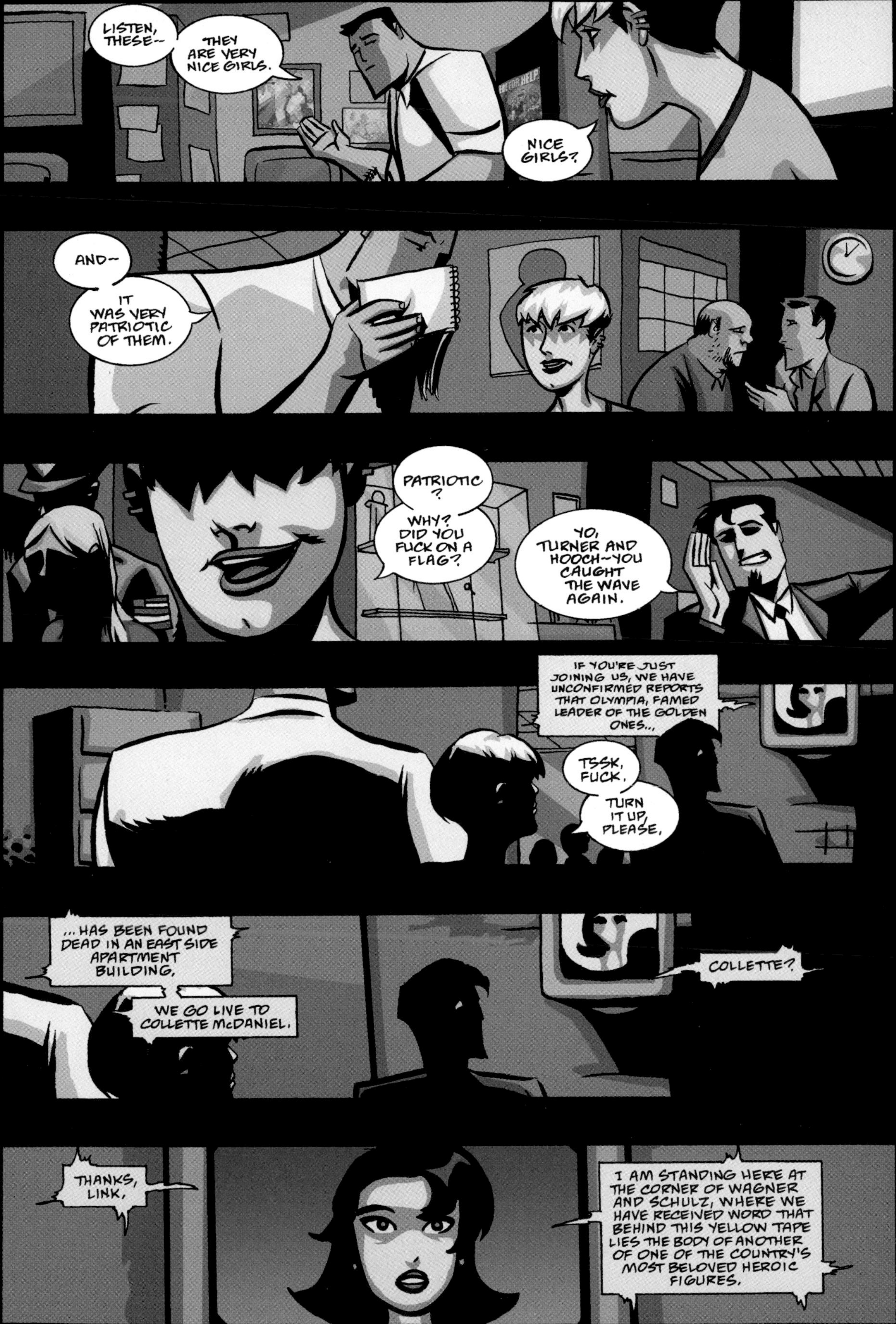

LISTEN, THESE--
THEY ARE VERY NICE GIRLS.
NICE GIRLS?
AND--
IT WAS VERY PATRIOTIC OF THEM.
PATRIOTIC?
WHY? DID YOU FUCK ON A FLAG?
YO, TURNER AND HOOCH--YOU CAUGHT THE WAVE AGAIN.
IF YOU'RE JUST JOINING US, WE HAVE UNCONFIRMED REPORTS THAT OLYMPIA, FAMED LEADER OF THE GOLDEN ONES...
TSSK, FUCK.
TURN IT UP, PLEASE.
...HAS BEEN FOUND DEAD IN AN EAST SIDE APARTMENT BUILDING.
WE GO LIVE TO COLLETTE McDANIEL.
COLLETTE?
THANKS, LINK.
I AM STANDING HERE AT THE CORNER OF WAGNER AND SCHULZ, WHERE WE HAVE RECEIVED WORD THAT BEHIND THIS YELLOW TAPE LIES THE BODY OF ANOTHER OF ONE OF THE COUNTRY'S MOST BELOVED HEROIC FIGURES.

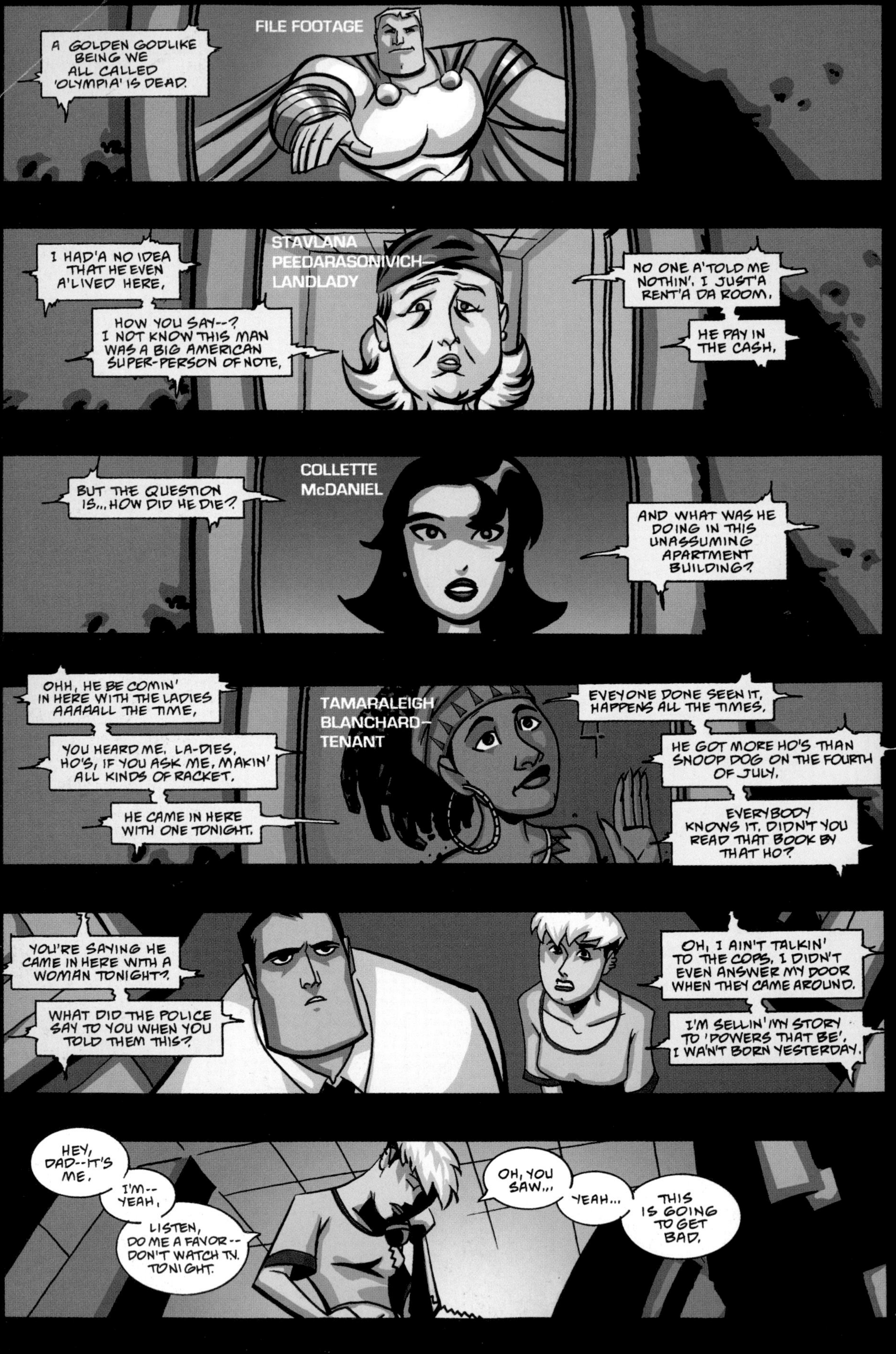
FILE FOOTAGE
A GOLDEN GODLIKE BEING WE ALL CALLED 'OLYMPIA' IS DEAD.
STAVLANA PEEDARASONIVICH—LANDLADY
I HAD'A NO IDEA THAT HE EVEN A'LIVED HERE.
HOW YOU SAY--? I NOT KNOW THIS MAN WAS A BIG AMERICAN SUPER-PERSON OF NOTE.
NO ONE A'TOLD ME NOTHIN'. I JUST'A RENT'A DA ROOM.
HE PAY IN THE CASH.
COLLETTE McDANIEL
BUT THE QUESTION IS... HOW DID HE DIE?
AND WHAT WAS HE DOING IN THIS UNASSUMING APARTMENT BUILDING?
TAMARALEIGH BLANCHARD—TENANT
OHH, HE BE COMIN' IN HERE WITH THE LADIES AAAAALL THE TIME.
YOU HEARD ME. LA-DIES. HO'S, IF YOU ASK ME. MAKIN' ALL KINDS OF RACKET.
HE CAME IN HERE WITH ONE TONIGHT.
EVEYONE DONE SEEN IT. HAPPENS ALL THE TIMES.
HE GOT MORE HO'S THAN SNOOP DOG ON THE FOURTH OF JULY.
EVERYBODY KNOWS IT. DIDN'T YOU READ THAT BOOK BY THAT HO?
YOU'RE SAYING HE CAME IN HERE WITH A WOMAN TONIGHT?
WHAT DID THE POLICE SAY TO YOU WHEN YOU TOLD THEM THIS?
OH, I AIN'T TALKIN' TO THE COPS. I DIDN'T EVEN ANSWER MY DOOR WHEN THEY CAME AROUND.
I'M SELLIN' MY STORY TO 'POWERS THAT BE'. I WA'N'T BORN YESTERDAY.
HEY, DAD--IT'S ME.
I'M--YEAH.
LISTEN, DO ME A FAVOR--DON'T WATCH T.V. TONIGHT.
OH, YOU SAW...
YEAH...
THIS IS GOING TO GET BAD.

GROUPIES
CHAPTER 2

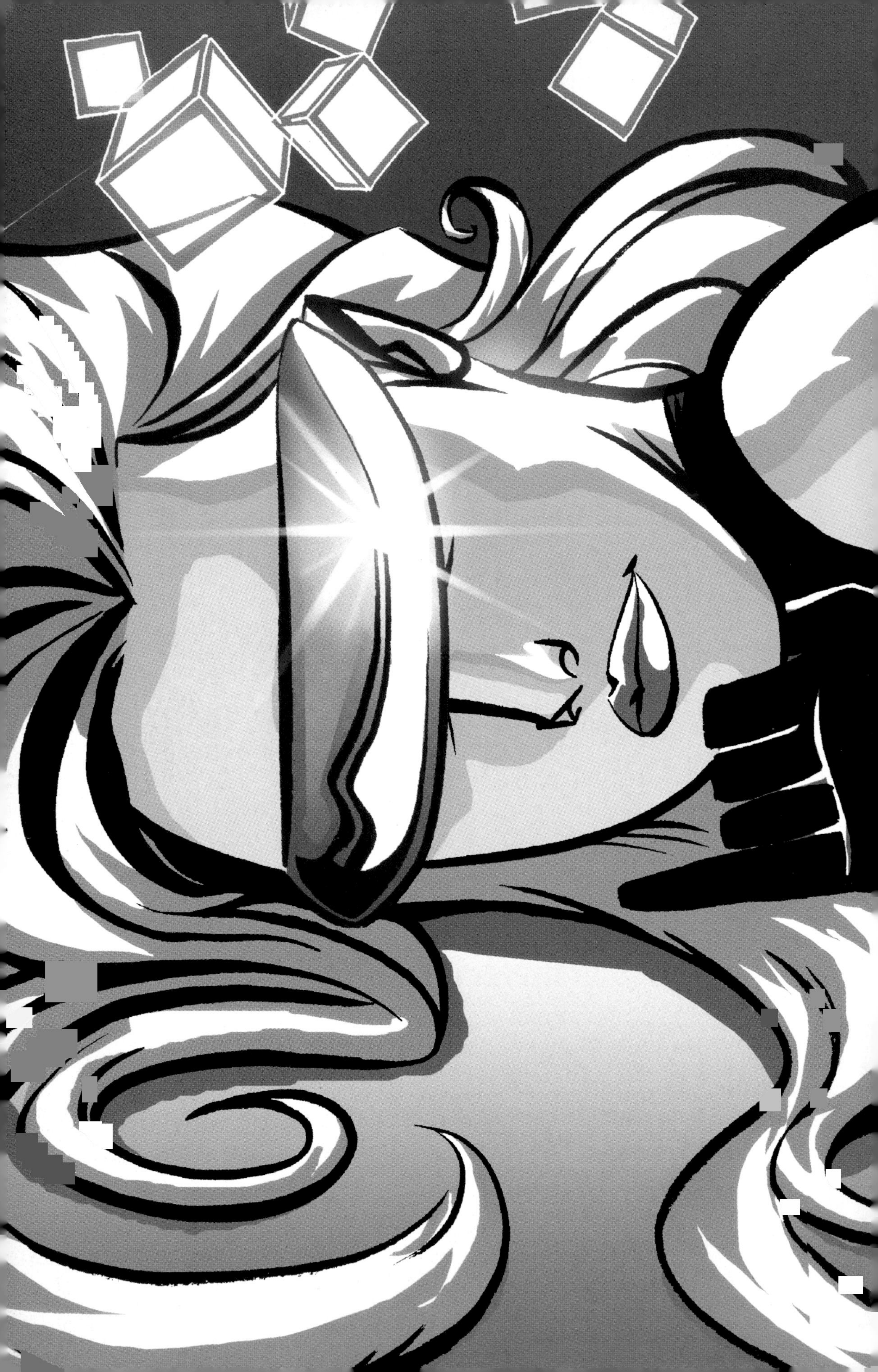

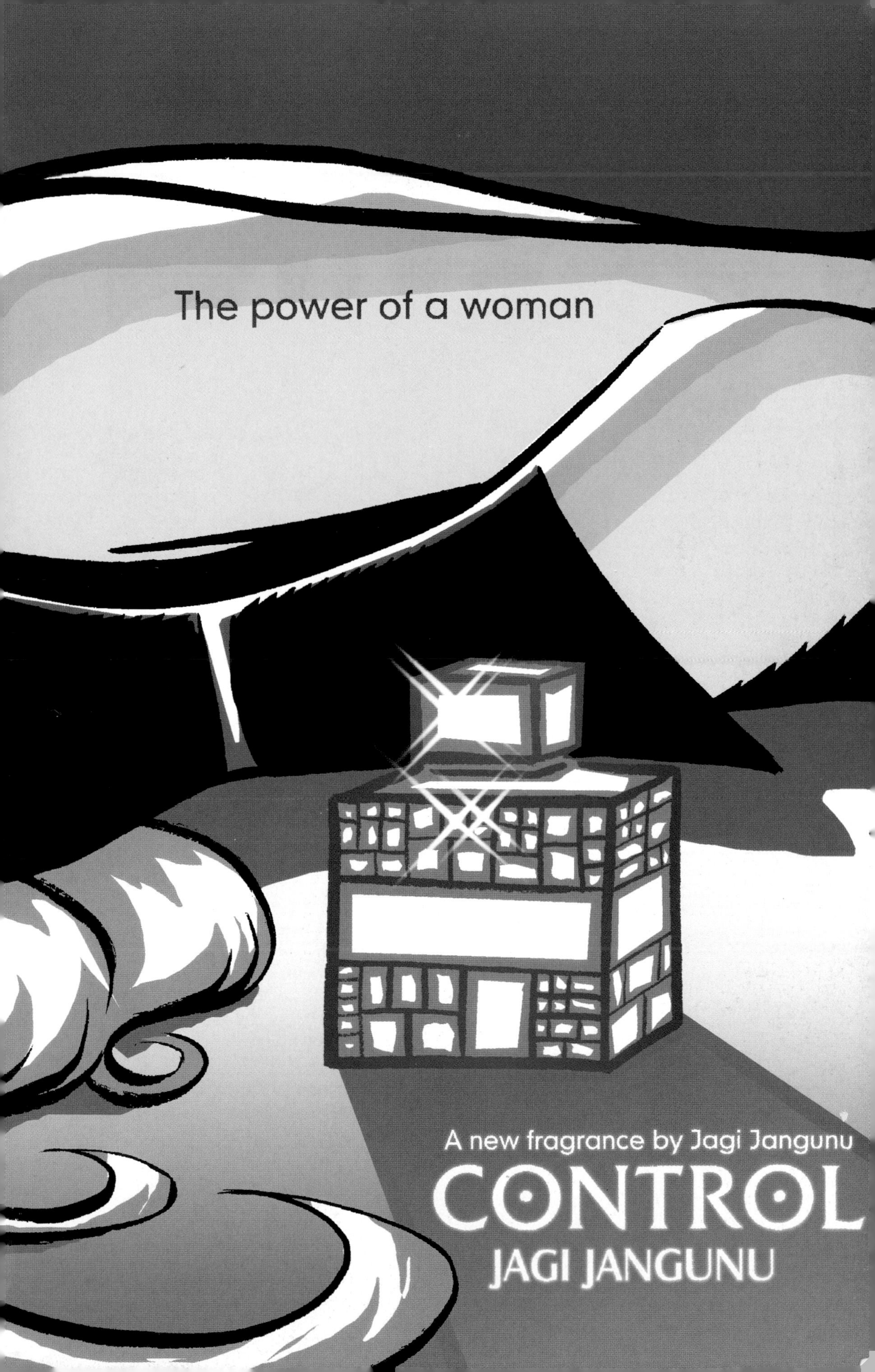
The power of a woman
A new fragrance by Jagi Jangunu
CONTROL
JAGI JANGUNU

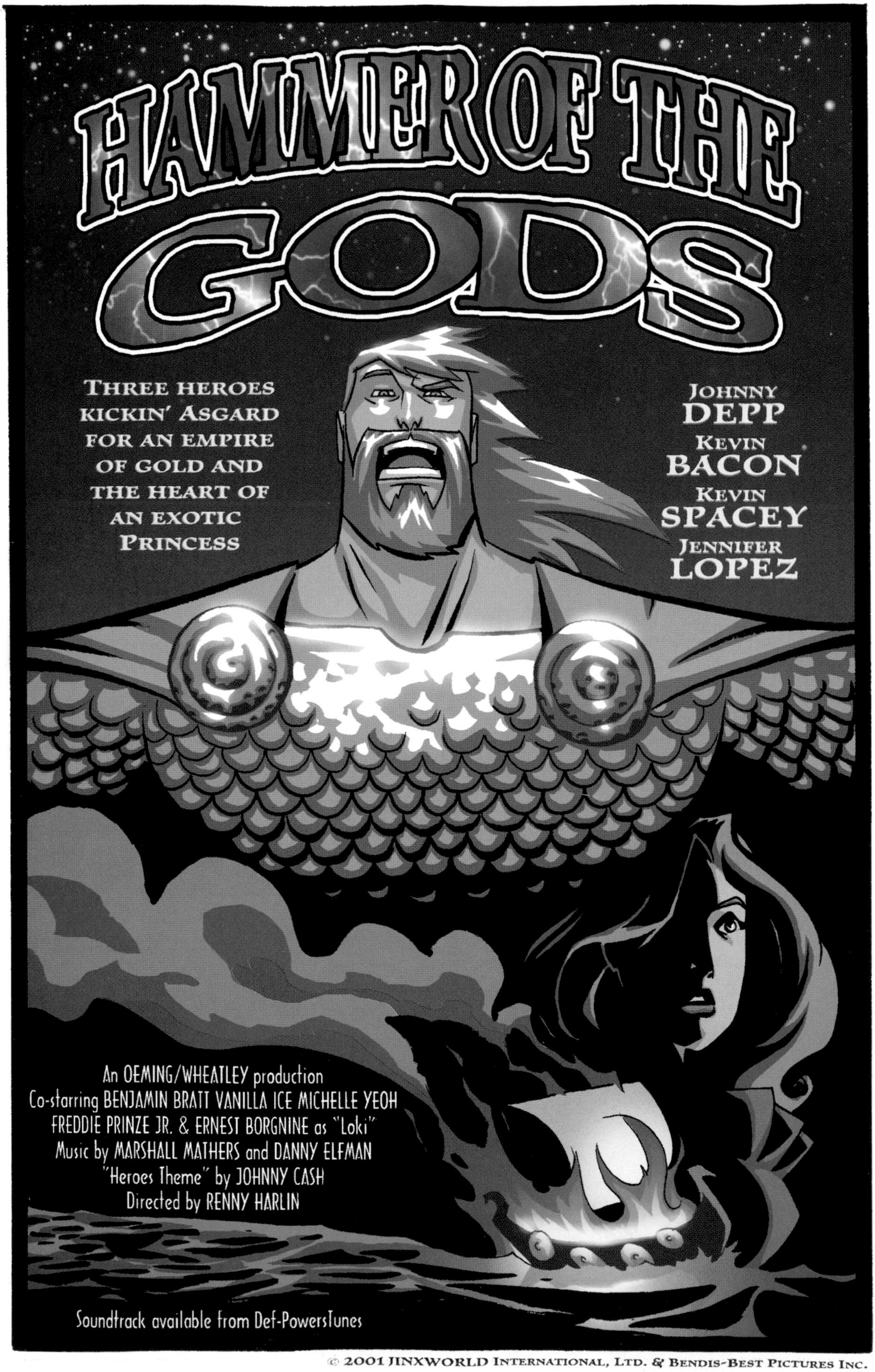
HAMMER OF THE GODS
THREE HEROES KICKIN' ASGARD FOR AN EMPIRE OF GOLD AND THE HEART OF AN EXOTIC PRINCESS
JOHNNY DEPP
KEVIN BACON
KEVIN SPACEY
JENNIFER LOPEZ
An OEMING/WHEATLEY production
Co-starring BENJAMIN BRATT VANILLA ICE MICHELLE YEOH
FREDDIE PRINZE JR. & ERNEST BORGNINE as "Loki"
Music by MARSHALL MATHERS and DANNY ELFMAN
"Heroes Theme" by JOHNNY CASH
Directed by RENNY HARLIN
Soundtrack available from Def-PowersTunes

POWERS! INSIDE INFORMATION

www.jinxworld.com

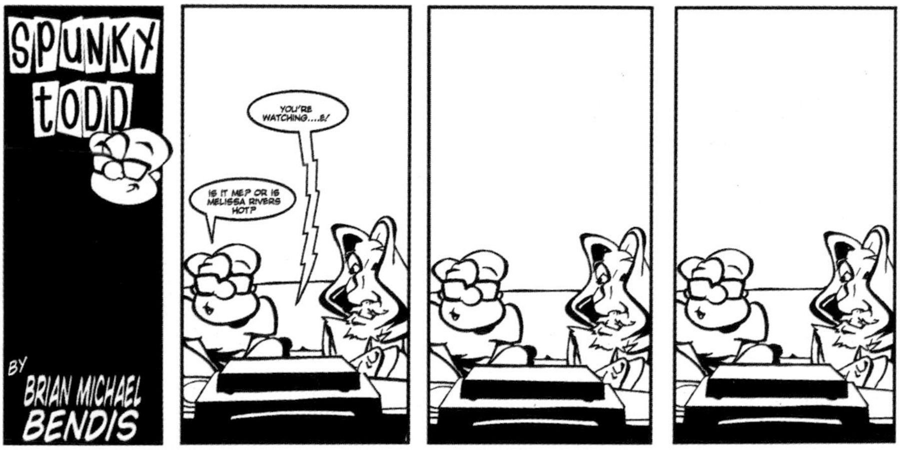

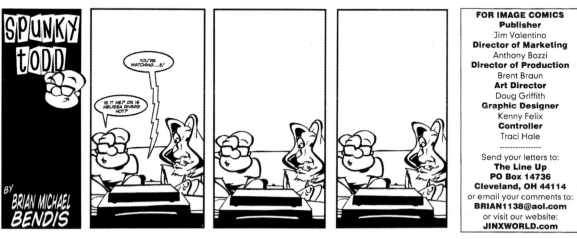

SPUNKY todd
BY BRIAN MICHAEL BENDIS
YOU'RE WATCHING....E!
IS IT ME? OR IS MELISSA RIVERS HOT?

FOR IMAGE COMICS
Publisher
Jim Valentino
Director of Marketing
Anthony Bozzi
Director of Production
Brent Braun
Art Director
Doug Griffith
Graphic Designer
Kenny Felix
Controller
Traci Hale

Send your letters to:
The Line Up
PO Box 14736
Cleveland, OH 44114
or email your comments to:
BRIAN1138@aol.com
or visit our website:
JINXWORLD.com

Image Comics presents POWERS

Created by BRIAN MICHAEL BENDIS & MICHAEL AVON OEMING
Coloring: PETER PANTAZIS—Lettering: KEN BRUZENAK
Copy Editor: K.C. McCRORY—Business Affairs: ALISA BENDIS

DIARY OF THE WEEK

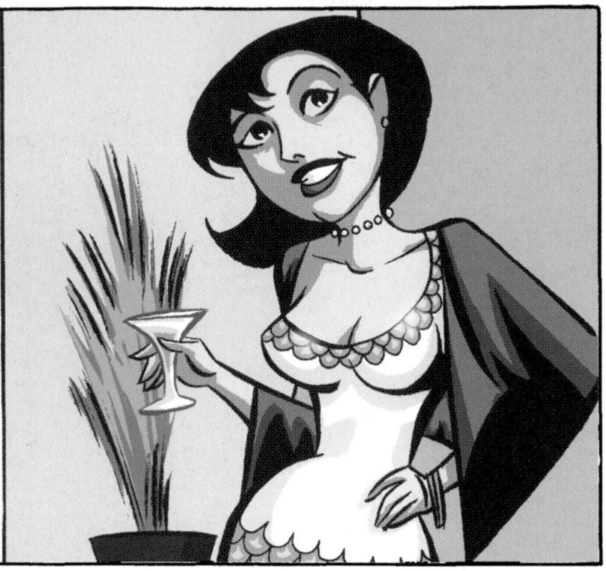

Star reporter Colette McDaniel wowed the crowd with her announcement that portions of the proceeds from her new book: *Who Killed Retro Girl?* Would be going to charity (above). Hunky reporter Rogers Sanders and (Wowsa!) Weather Girl Emma Randle seem awfully chummy for co-workers (above right).

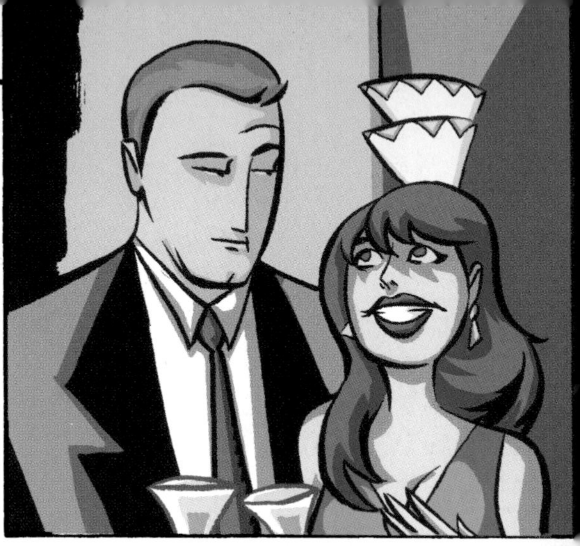

GUESS WHO CAME TO DINNER?

Founders of the Janis Quivers Media Center of the Arts were the brains behind the fund-raising evening at the Broderick Hotel on Benza Island, in aid of the Victims Against Random Super Powered Violence Centre.

Hosted by Channel 5 News many of the cities top chef came out to cook for ninetee separate tables of ten guest each. The main course ranged from jerk chicke pizza to Sashimi salmon torte

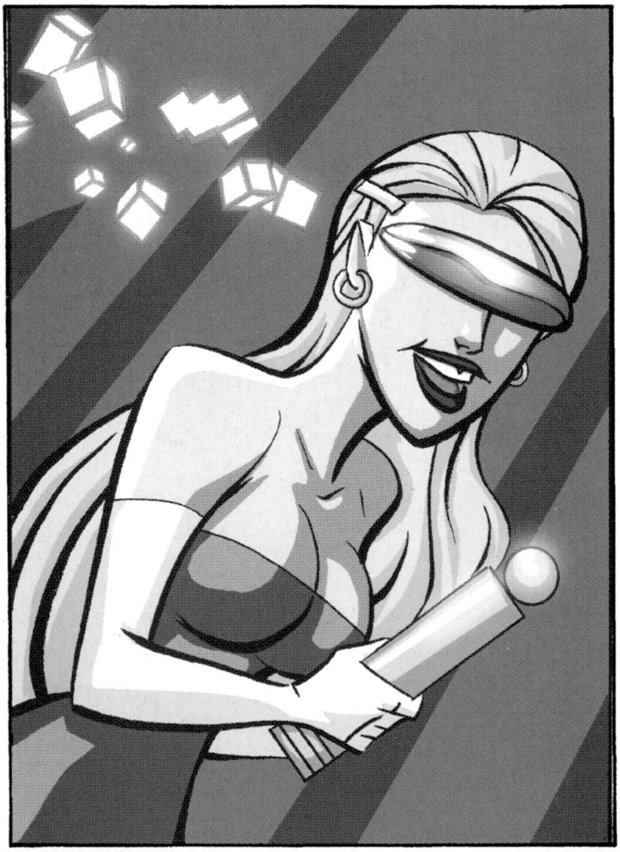

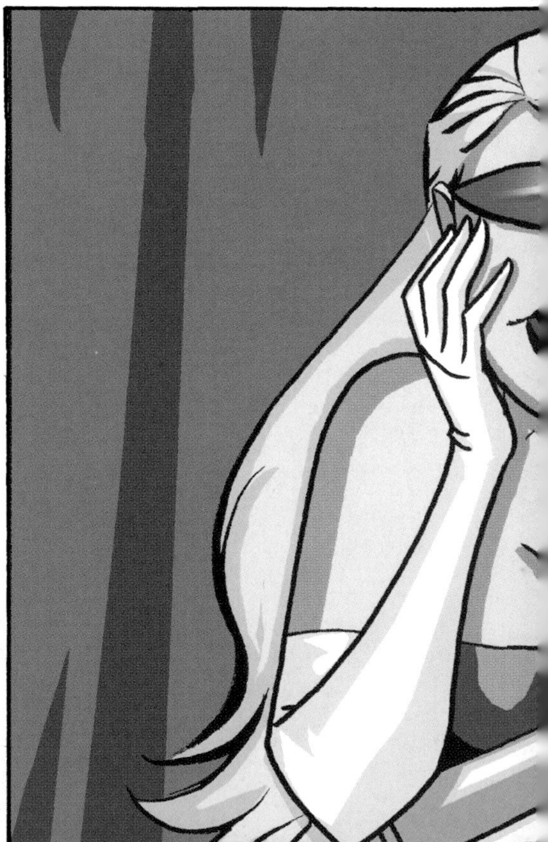

'FIGHT THE MUTATION' FUNDRAISER GALA FETES SUPER STARS

The applause that greeted Zora when she took the stage, in a spectacle of her trademark light, must have reminded her of the enthusiastic response she used to receive with her deceased partner, Retro Girl. But bittersweet memories did not intrude on the festivities did not intru on the evening's festivities.

Zora was in attendance to receive t

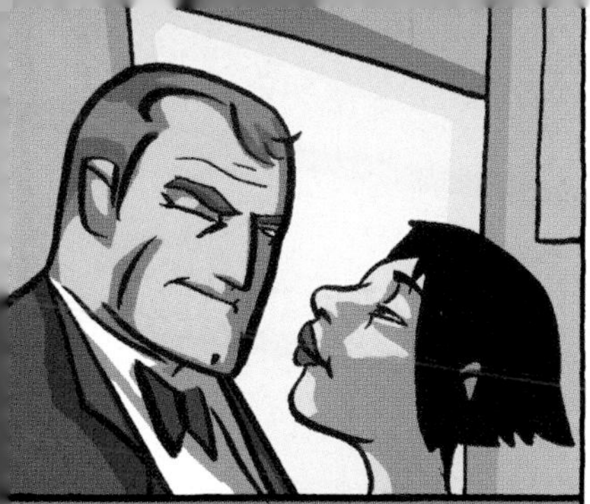

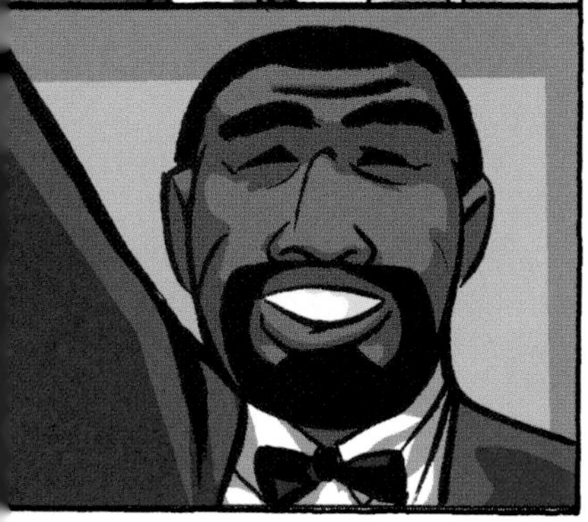

owers That Be **host Ted Henry popped 1 with a mystery date (above top). layor Washington Lee toasts the oom (above).**

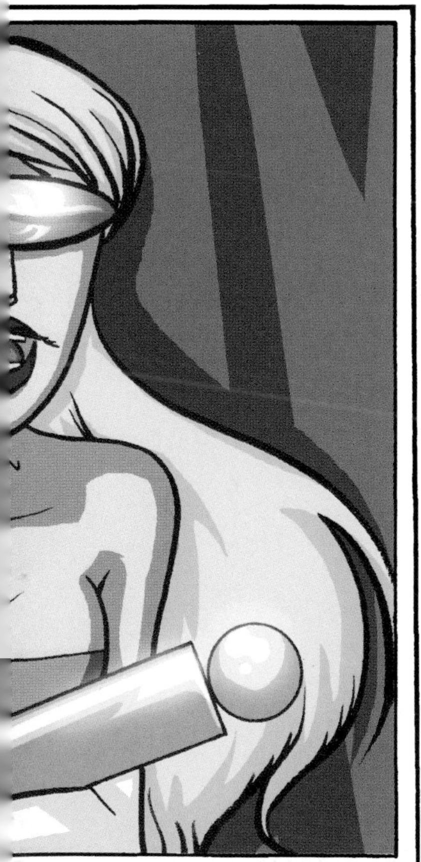

lifetime achievement award for her work against illegal mutation in our city's projects. The gala raised funds to enable children with special abilities to take part in everyday activities with regular children.

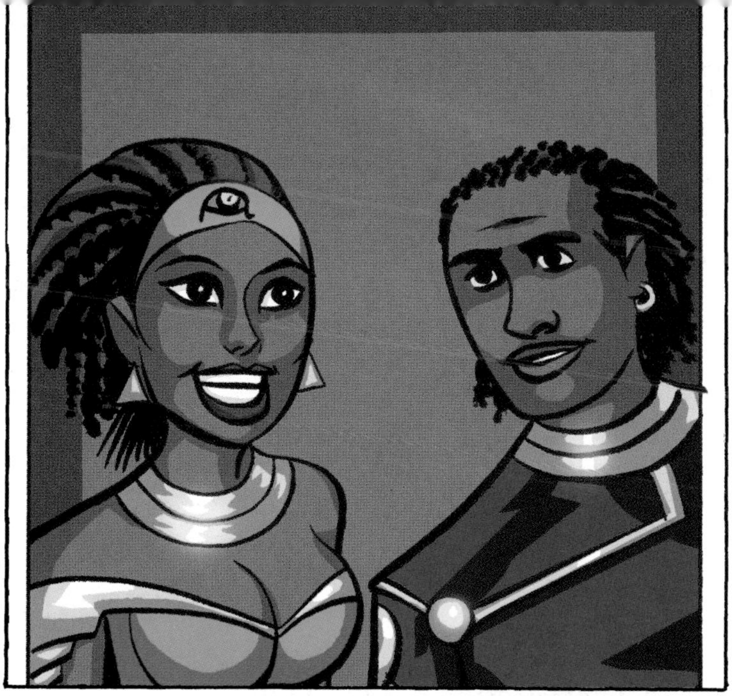

ANNUAL HERO AWARDS HONOR FG-3

Everyone had crossed fingers in hope for the reunion to end all reunions, but it was not to be as Wazz was a no-show when FG-3 teammates Boggiegirl and Benmarley were awarded the Centennial Heroes Award. The gala event was overflowing with Dom Perignon champagne, miniature chocolate Award replicas, and luxury gift baskets for all who attended.

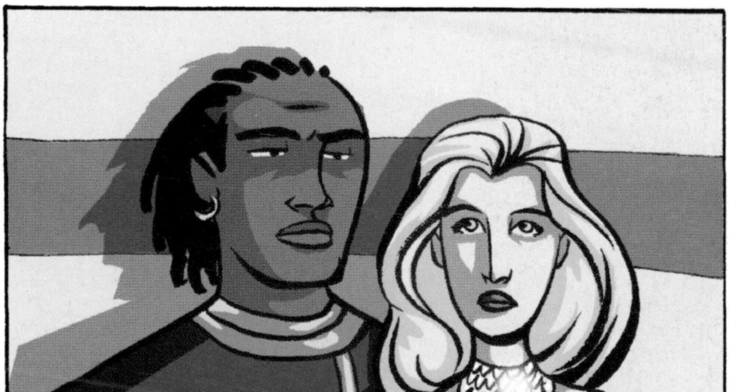

Awards recipients Boggiegirl and Benmarley (top) Benmarly and his date, supermodel Roxanne Plimm (above) Boggie girl and Zora share a hello kiss before the awards (below)

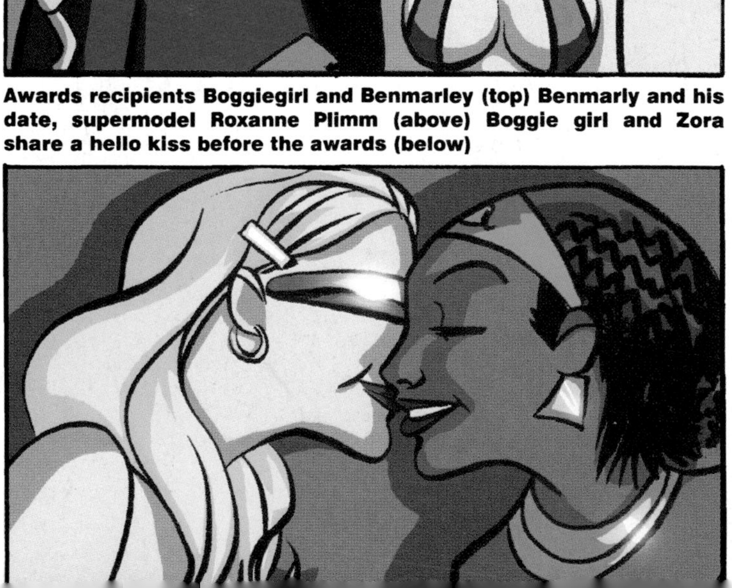

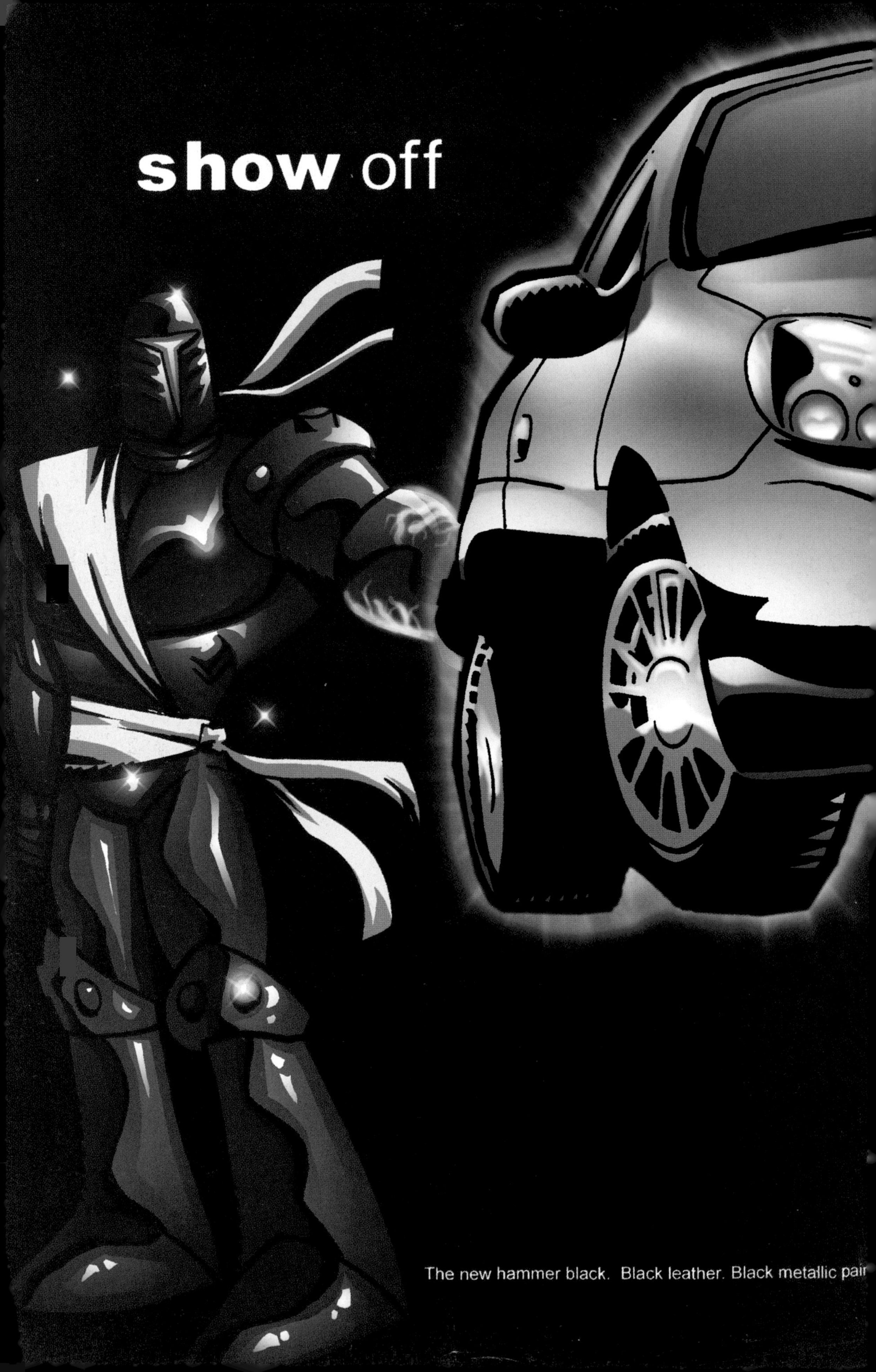
show off
The new hammer black. Black leather. Black metallic pair

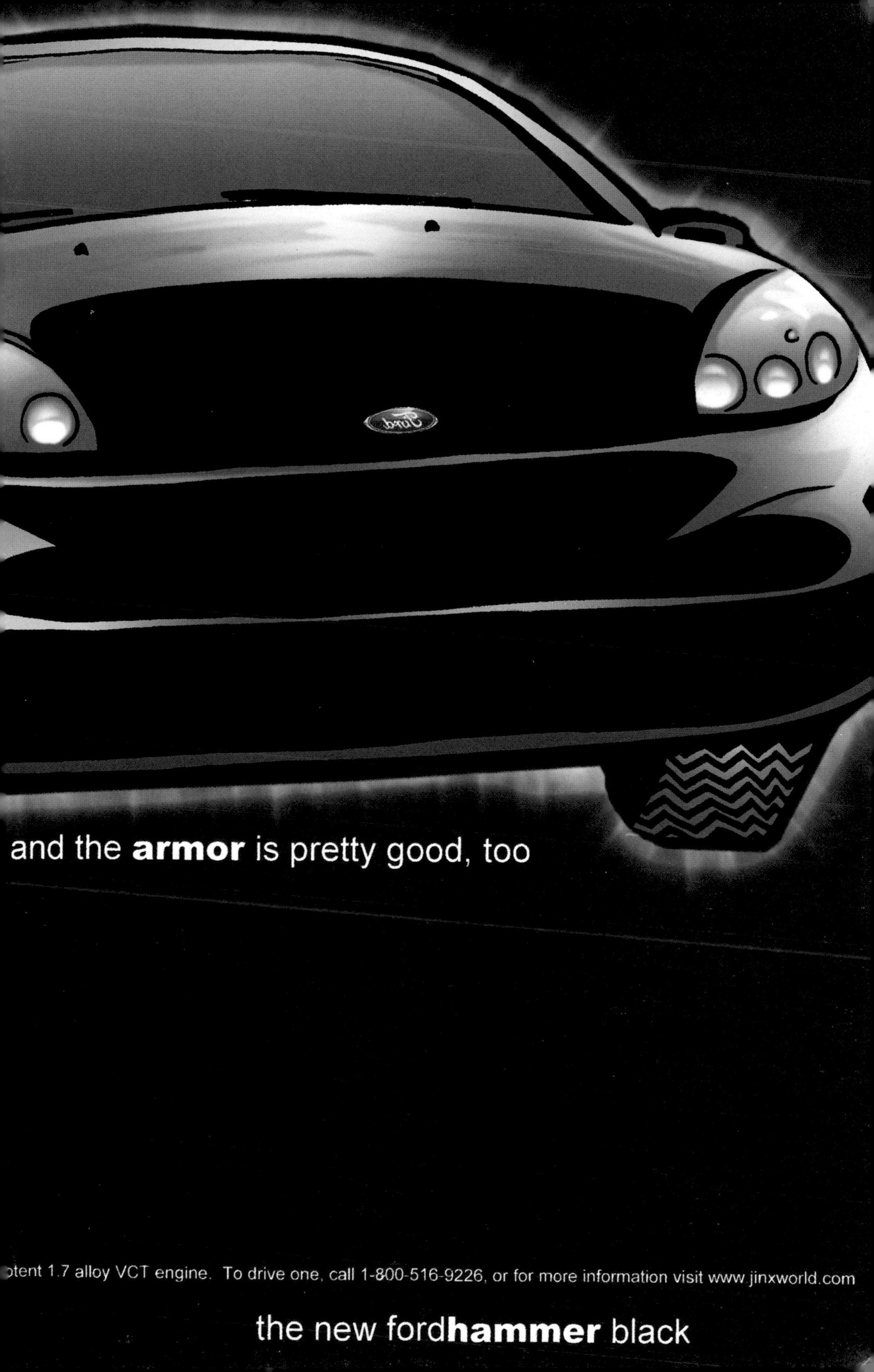
and the armor is pretty good, too
otent 1.7 alloy VCT engine. To drive one, call 1-800-516-9226, or for more information visit www.jinxworld.com
the new fordhammer black

OLYMPIA DEAD
Hero found in apartment

Olympia, widely considered to be one of the city's greatest champions, was found dead Saturday night. The police have not ruled out foul play. Official reports so far indicate the police were called after a 'very bright light' burst forth from an apartment at the corner of W75th and Millar Avenue. Olympia was found in the nude, with no signs of a struggle. Police have offered very little information, but admit the case is still open and suspects are being sought for questioning. (For more information, see main article starting on page 10.)

RETRO GIRL
Vandals in mid-town

The newly erected bronze statue of Retro Girl, located in Chaykin Park was vandalized over the past weekend. The words "KAOTIC CHIC" were spray painted on it. The phrase, made popular by the man who confessed to killing Retro Girl, is now an anthem of anarchistic teen movements on the city's East Side. Police are asking citizens with any information regarding this vandalization of city property to call 443-557-8778.

FG-3
Ex-partner sues in court

The supergroup FG-3, which was recently acquitted of intimidation and bribery, charges following a nightclub battle in which three innocent bystanders were injured, is being sued for four million dollars by ex-member Wazz for royalties he says he is contractually owed for merchandising and other related commercial business ventures when he was with the group.

THIS WEEK
A ROUND-UP OF NEWS REPORTS

QUEEN NOIR
To marry ex-nemesis

Queen Noir, the celebrated cult heroine, is set to marry her one-time archenemy, Strike. The pair met during a hostage crisis at the new Federal Aviation Museum ten years ago. Strike served his time and been a reformed man for over a year and a half. Strike is the son of the late super-villain Katmandu, who died of a self-inflicted gunshot wound 17 years ago at the height of his popularity.

ZORA
Single motherhood

Zora has admitted to being a little scared of facing life as a single mother following recent news reports of her adoption of an 11-month-old girl, Katra. In an interview with the magazine *Cape*, the controversial superheroine said she was always full of admiration for single mothers, but now that she herself was one, "It was scary—a whole new path I am about to venture down."

Wazz, whose real name is Sean Wallace, claims that his former team mates Boggie girl and Benmarley have cheated him out of moneys rightfully owed to him. Wazz left the high profile group after a public argument over the death of their archenemy, Dr. Z.

A member of Wazz's legal team said: "We have no choice but to file suit. FG-3 refuses to address the issue in any other manner."

MOUNTAIN
New career name change

In tune with his new career as spokesperson for Coca-Cola, retired Super Power Mountain has officially changed his street name to " Thirst Quencher." A *Centennial Award* winner, Mountain retired from active status two years ago and has made a name for himself as a spokesman. In a recent interview with *TV Guide*, he stated: "We are all hired monkeys. We all work for as many peanuts as we can. People with powers are no different, and anyone who tells you otherwise is a liar."

SPARKLER
Tops Powers poll

The enduring appeal of Sparkler was proven again last week when the recently deceased hero beat out Retro Girl and Conqueror for the title of "Most Popular Power of the Century." The *Powers of the Century List* was compiled by the BHC Radio2, from the votes of more than 120,000 listeners. Out of the list, only two, Triphammer and Zora, are still alive.

JOHNNY ROYALE
Lawsuit dropped

After months of speculation, the legal firm representing alleged organized crime boss J. "Johnny" Stompinato, a.k.a "Johnny Royale," officially dropped its 150 million dollar lawsuit against the city. Though the murder of Johnny Royale is still under investigation, attorney Robert Evans said that, "further pursuit of the legal action started by our deceased client is at this point a fruitless objective. We hope that this helps the police department find more time to dedicate to our client's mysterious and violent demise."

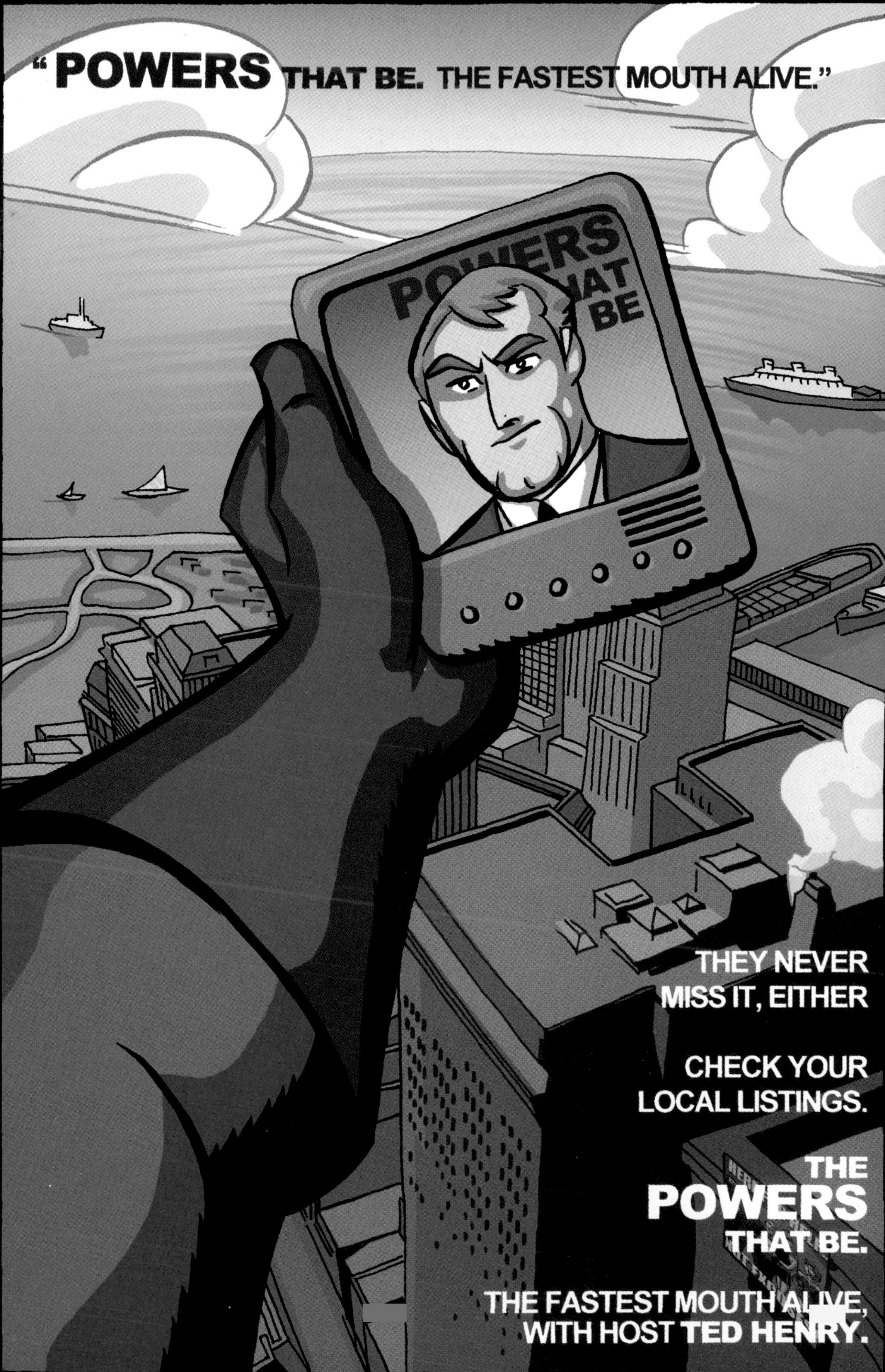
"POWERS THAT BE. THE FASTEST MOUTH ALIVE."
THEY NEVER MISS IT, EITHER
CHECK YOUR LOCAL LISTINGS.
THE POWERS THAT BE.
THE FASTEST MOUTH ALIVE, WITH HOST TED HENRY.

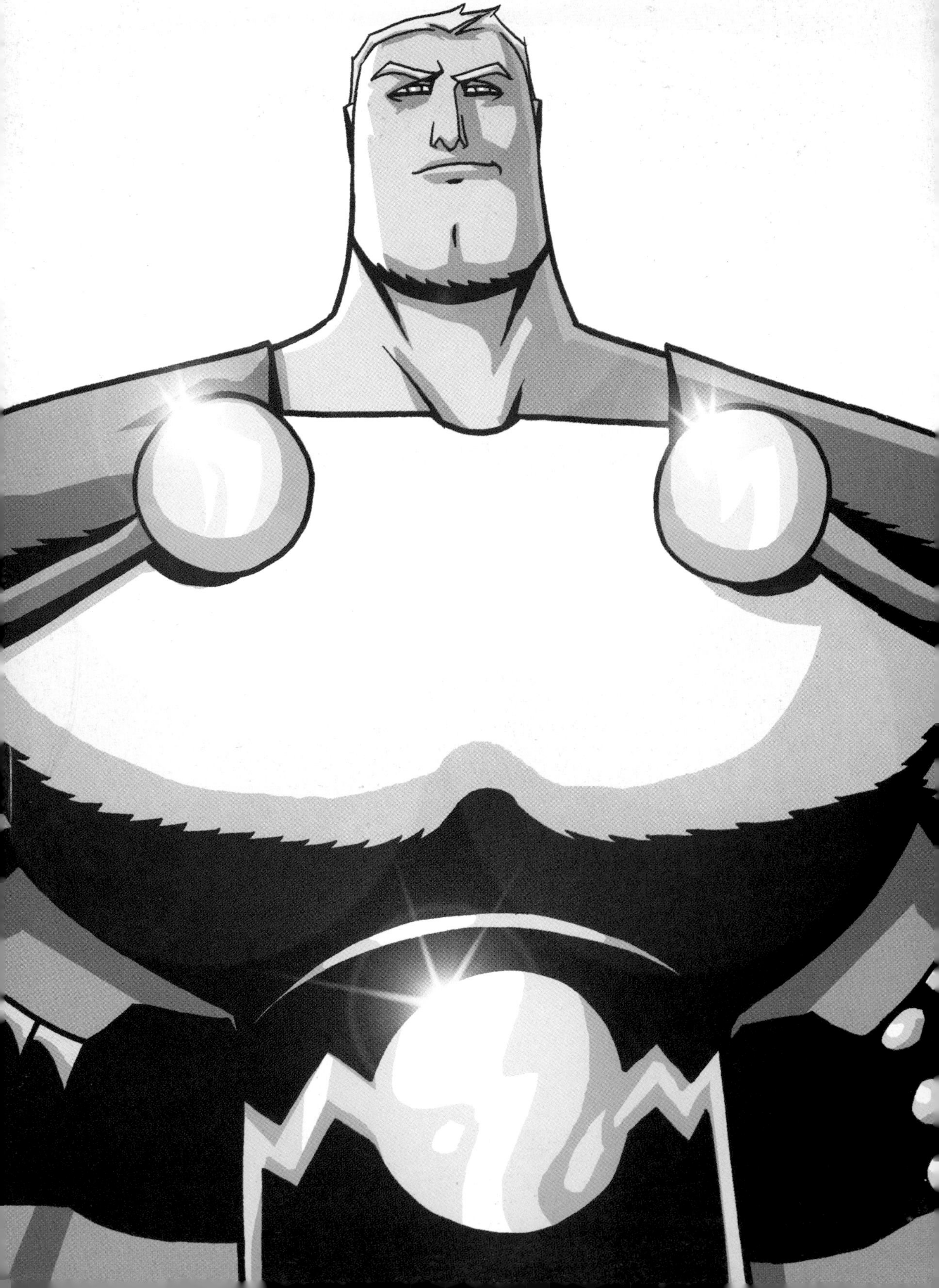

OLYMPIA
LAST INTERVIEW: FACT vs. FICTION

EDITORIAL NOTE: **This interview was conducted two days before the sudden and tragic death of the man known as Olympia. We were going to run an edited version of this interview, but be-cause we believe that this is the last interview he ever gave, we have decided to run it in its entirety. We think this shows a rare glimpse into a man** many admired, but few knew anything about.

Also, legally, we are required to tell you that this rare interview was granted to our magazine in return for us not releasing information that fell into our possession about the man publicly known as Olympia. We will be honoring that agreement.

Olympia. Even his name conjures images of such heroism and self-lessness that immediately fills one's heart with good will towards man, he first came into our lives seven years ago, during the Denver Airport hostage situation--a situation that saved the lives of the President of Mexico and over four hundred civilians.

Olympia then went on to join The Golden Ones, a small band of self-proclaimed heroes that, singly and in groups, have successfully saved the world and mankind from plagues and perils only before imagined in the works of science fiction.

But in recent years, stories have started floating about Olympia alleged sexual transgressions. More than one young woman has come forward with stories of midnight encounters with Olympia. Shocking detail after shock-ing detail has made its way into gossip columns and TV tabloids.

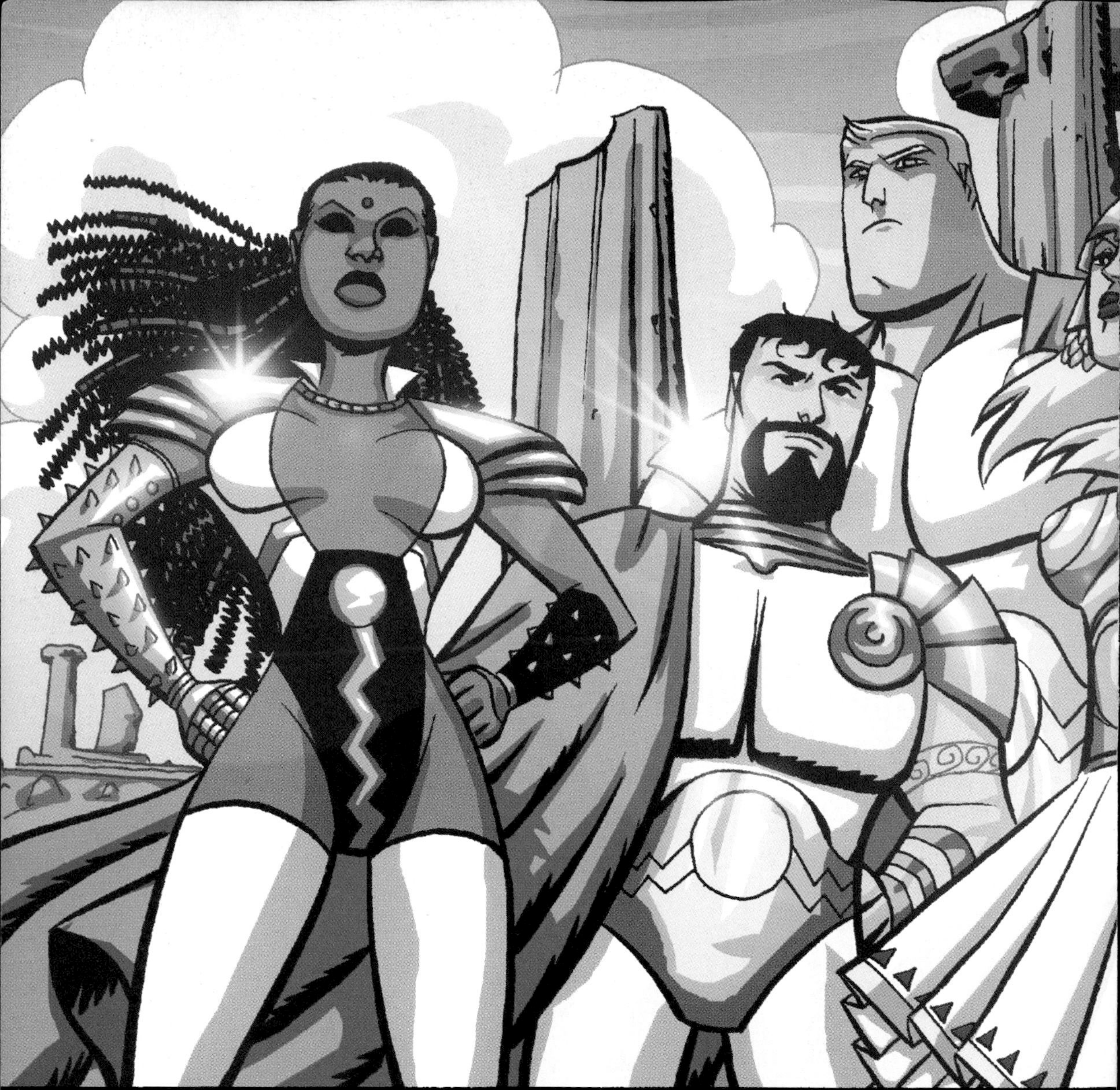

The *New York Times* bestseller: *I'm With the Cape,* by self proclaimed groupie Julia Garrison, detailed a three-year affair with a man she wouldn't name by name, described as a "man of incredible power; a golden god among men," and she went on to describe intimate details of their numerous and daring encounters.

Olympia, the man, has never spoken of such matters publicly. Public opinion polls repeatedly show that most Americans don't care what our powered people do in their free time. A whopping 86 percent. But the rumors have plagued Olympia for years, and here, for the first time, he answers such questions.

POWERS: Did you read the book by Julia Garrison?

OLYMPIA: "Wow, you get right to it, don't you?"

Thought you'd appreciate that.

"And I suppose I do."

And?

"And, no, I didn't read it."

But you heard of it?

"Sure, I have a TV. I saw the press."

You have a TV?

(Laughs) "Yes, a big world exclusive. I have a TV."

So you know of the book.

"Sure."

Never even curious about what it said?

"I'll wait for the movie."

That isn't what I asked.

Good for you. Yes, I was curious, but friends of mine have read certain passages to me. It's a funny book."

Is she talking about you in the book?

"I have no idea."

Really?

"Sure. How do I know what she's doing?"

So, it could be you? You knew her?

"The entire book could be fiction for all we know. She could be having all kinds of fun making up stuff about all kinds of thoughts she's had."

So, you never met her.

"I never said that."

So, you did?

"I didn't say that, either.

Well, either you did or you didn't.

"See, I meet thousands of people every month. I could say I didn't meet her, and then it ends up I did."

But the book details an affair

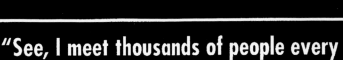

"See, I meet thousands of people every month. I could say I didn't meet her, and then it ends up I did."

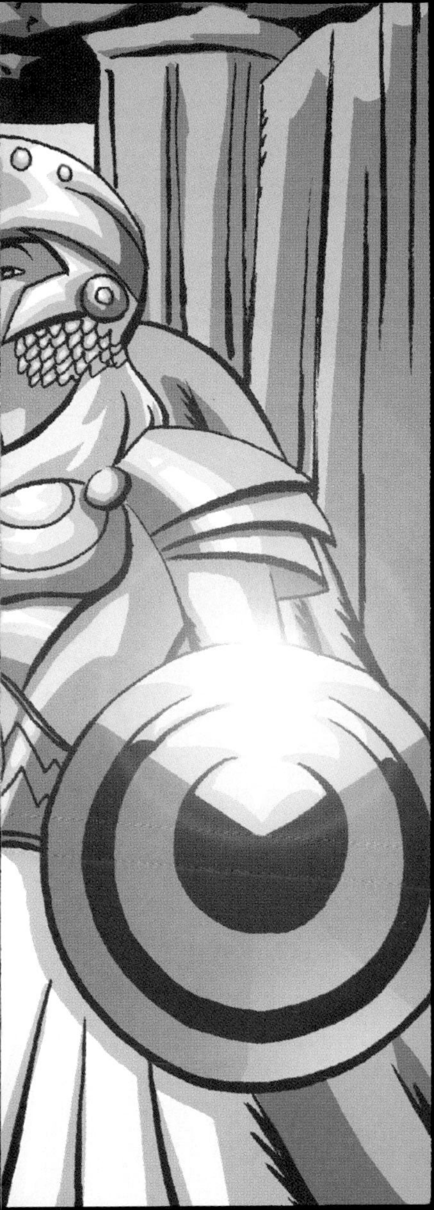

that lasted over three years.
"Wow."
And it's not with you?
"Again, I haven't read the book."
You had no affair with a woman named Julia Garrison?
"Define affair."
Are you serious?
"Sure. What's an affair? If I was having sexual relations with a woman whose name I didn't even know for over three years, I think I would have to call it something other than 'an affair.'"
What, then? What would you call it?
"I don't know. Is there a name for something like that?"
Not really.
"So there you go."
So, you may or may not have met a woman ▶

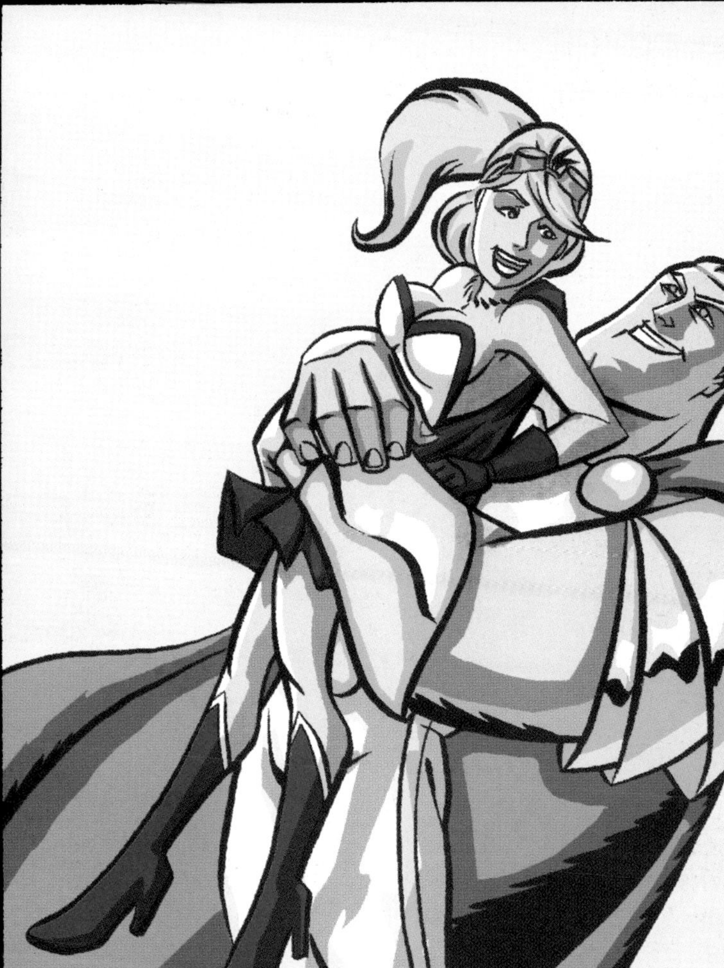

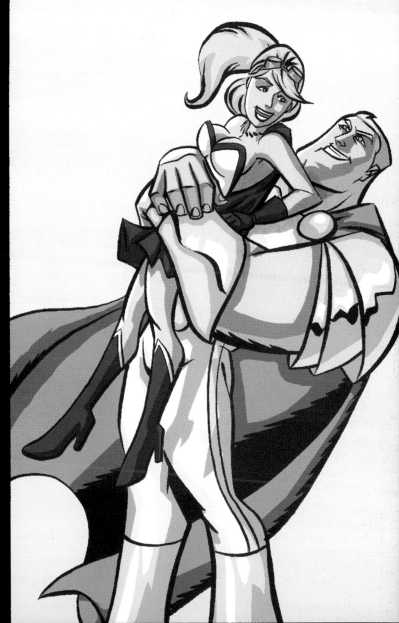

Olympia and the Golden Ones became celebrities thanks to their daring feats, but a cloud of impropriety has shadowed them, and lurid sexual innuendoes abound. Rumors of a relationship between Olympia and Retro Girl have titillated fans, particularly in the wake of the superheroine's mysterious death

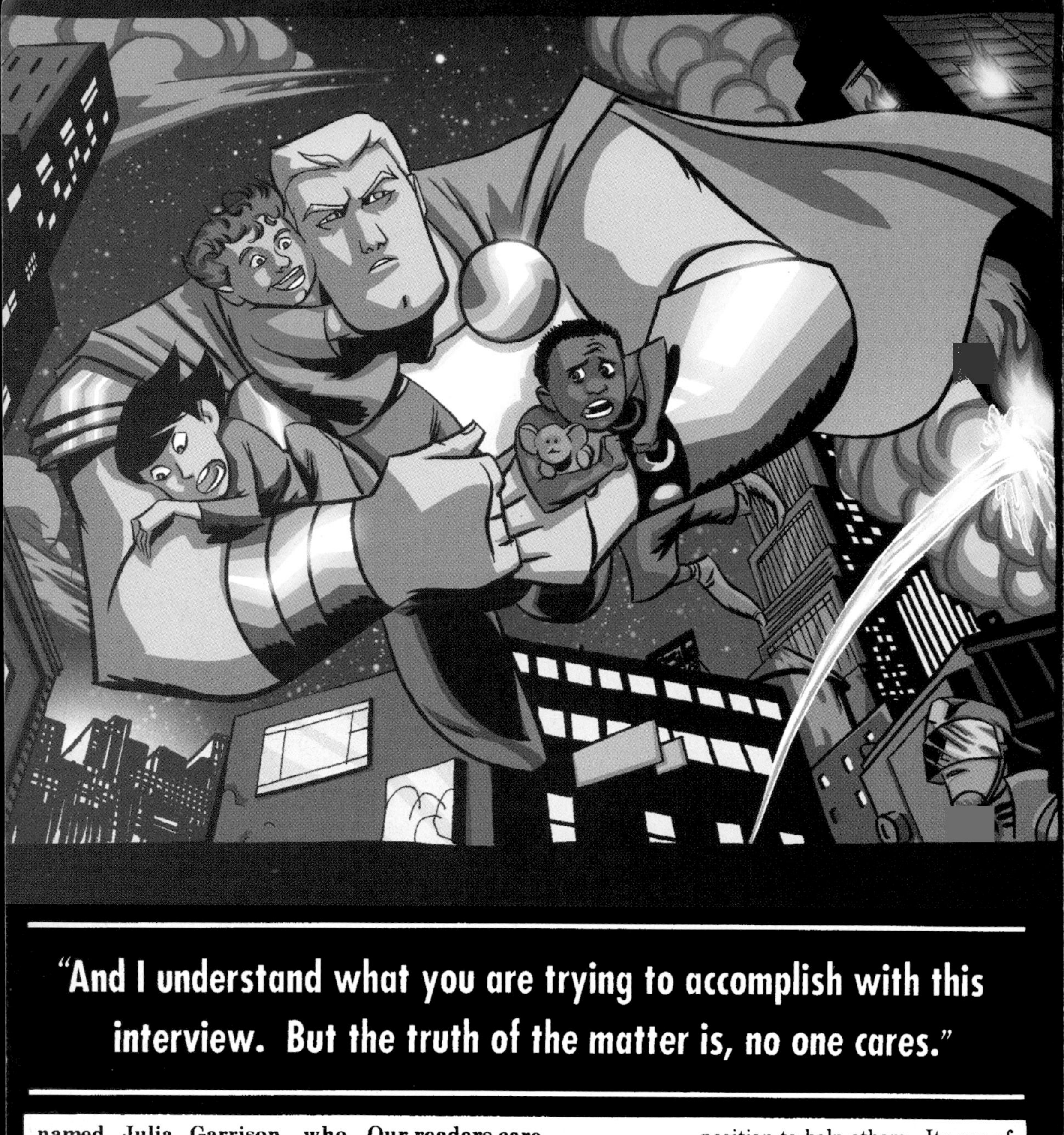

“And I understand what you are trying to accomplish with this interview. But the truth of the matter is, no one cares.”

named Julia Garrison, who you may or may not have had a three year relationship with, who wrote a book about someone who may or may not be you, because you didn’t read it except for some of it.?

“Listen, I understand your job is hard. And I understand what you are trying to accomplish with this interview. But the truth of the matter is, no one cares. First, there's the fact that even if I had a different girlfriend every single night, and engaged in all kinds of who the hell knows what all night long, it’s nobody’s business. It’s not illegal. It’s not hurting anyone. And that’s what really matters to people. So nobody cares.”

Our readers care.

“No, they don’t. You’re trying to make them care. You want them to care in the worst way. And sure, a GOOD sex story is a good sex story, I’m not denying that. But you people run poll after poll and they tell you—‘we don’t care.’ And I think the only reason you care is because you don’t know what is going on. You don’t know what the truth is, and you don’t know why you can’t get to it, and that bothers you.”

We have a pretty good idea what the truth is.

“No, you don’t. And also, I’m not an elected official. I’m just a guy who lucked into a way of life with these abilities that put me in a position to help others. Its one of the greatest things of my life that I’m able to share that gift in a positive way. But, really, I can go on about my business not having to worry about the ‘trust of the people,’ or whatever.

How did you get that gift? Those powers?

(Laughs) “I can’t believe you just asked for my secret origin.”

Had to give it a shot.

“Ha, good for you. (Laughs) Well, that’s not going to happen.”

Can I ask why?

“Um—sure. A friend of mine once gave an interview just like this to a fellow like yourself, and he inadvertently gave some information that helped a

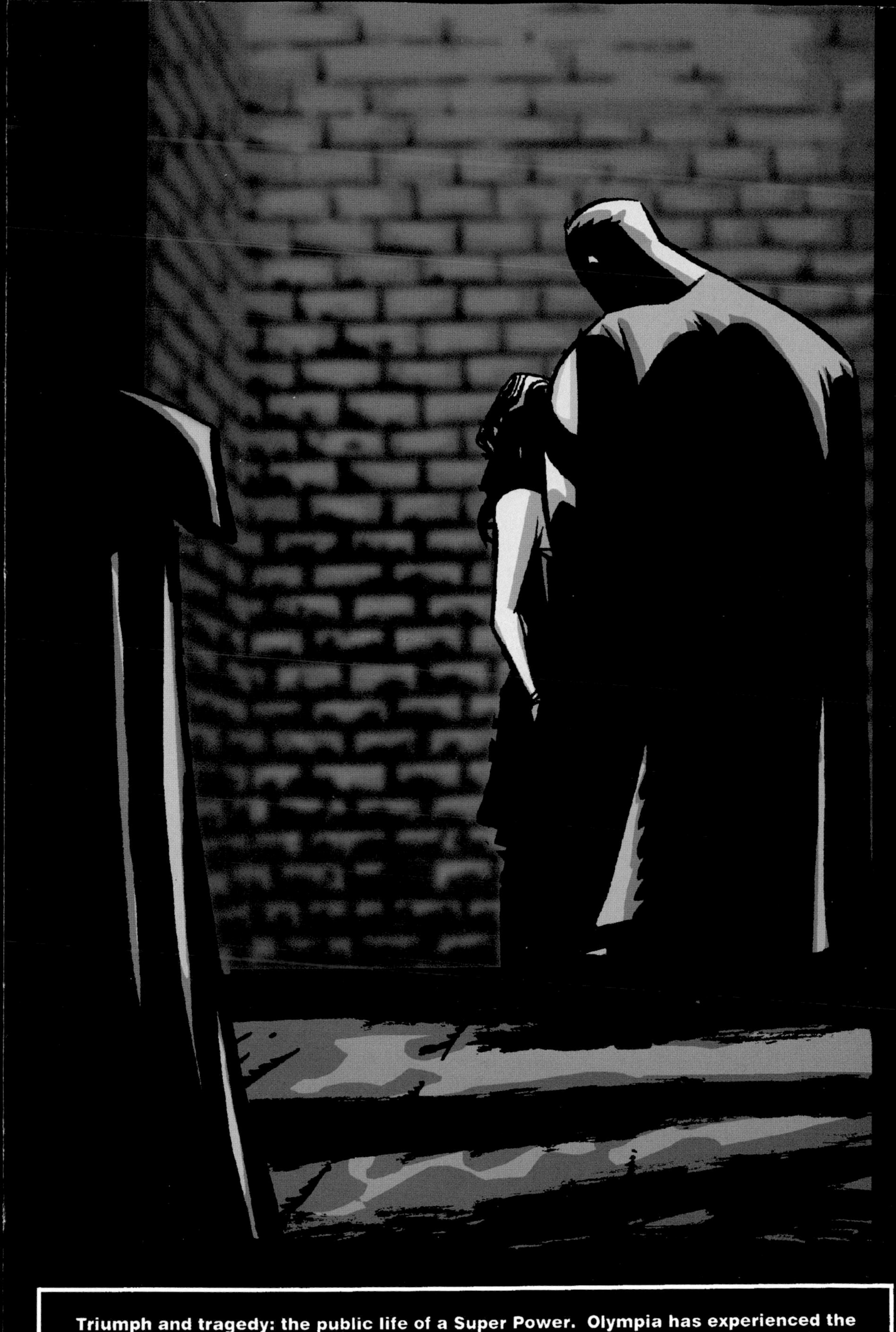

Triumph and tragedy: the public life of a Super Power. Olympia has experienced the full gamut of attention in the press, from heroic adulation to pervasive intrusion during times of sorrow, and now they want to follow him into the bedroom.

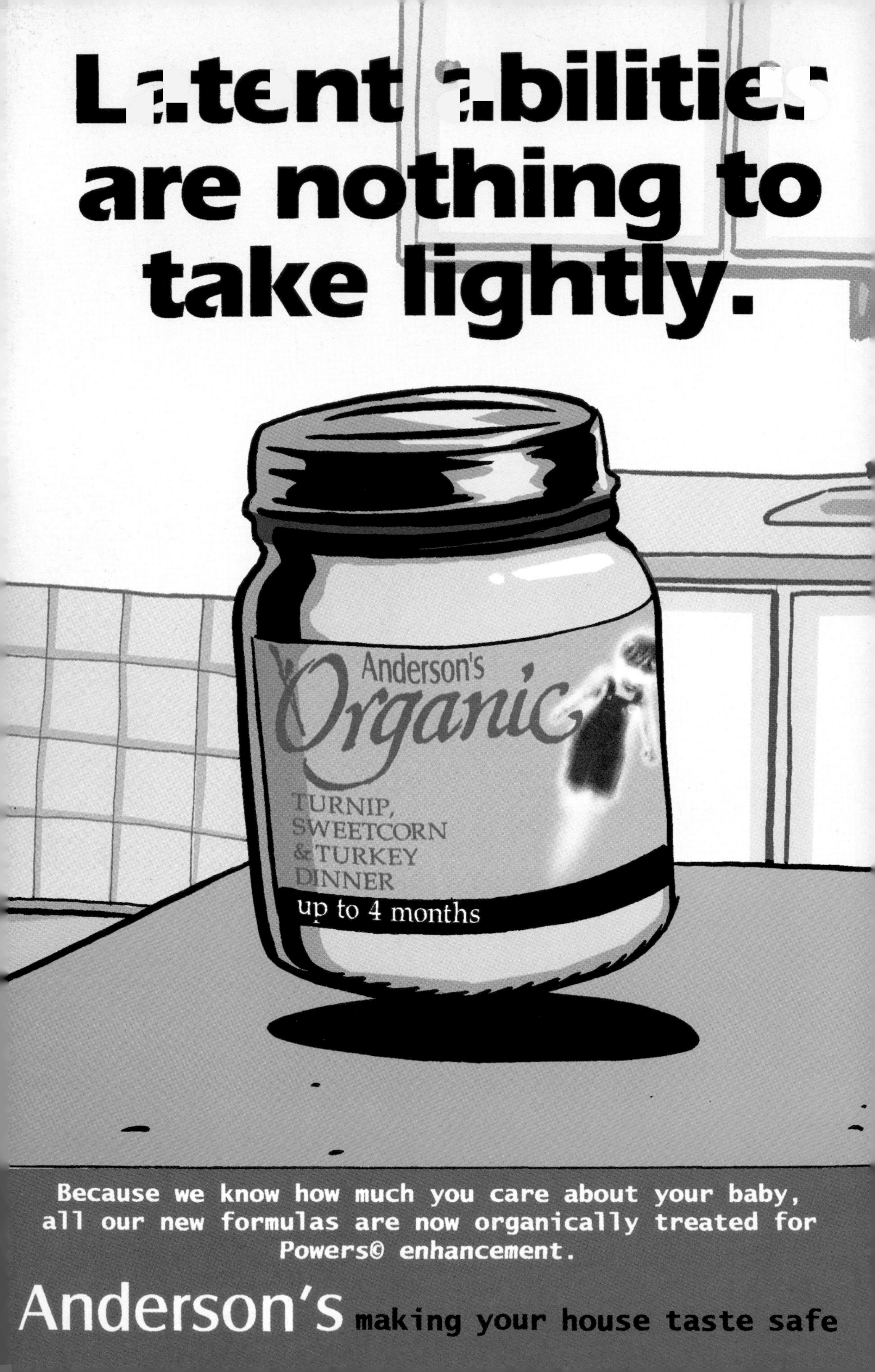
Latent abilities are nothing to take lightly.
Anderson's
Organic
TURNIP, SWEETCORN & TURKEY DINNER
up to 4 months
Because we know how much you care about your baby, all our new formulas are now organically treated for Powers© enhancement.
Anderson's making your house taste safe

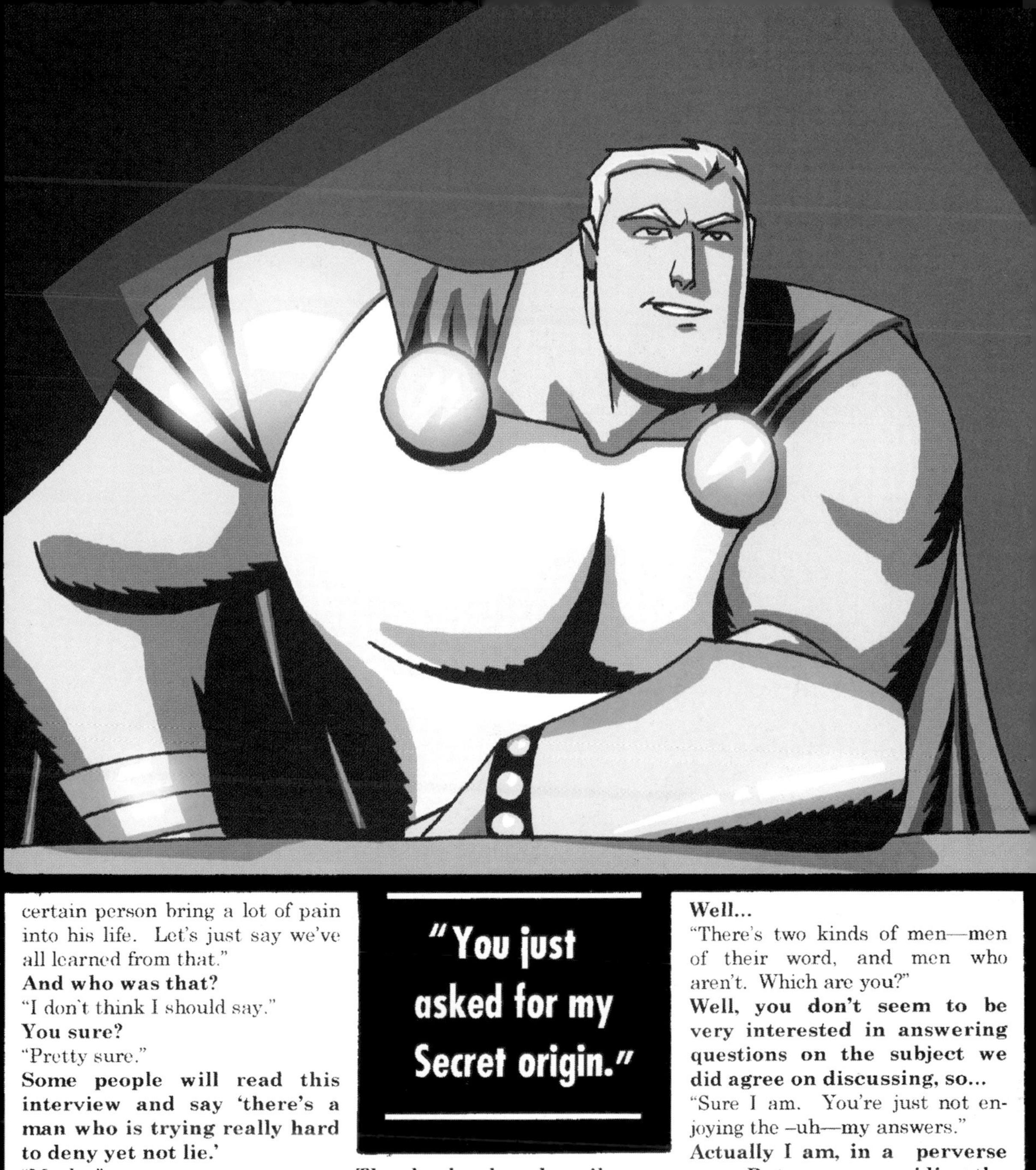

certain person bring a lot of pain into his life. Let's just say we've all learned from that."
And who was that?
"I don't think I should say."
You sure?
"Pretty sure."
Some people will read this interview and say 'there's a man who is trying really hard to deny yet not lie.'
"Maybe."
'There is a guy who is lying by not telling the truth.'
"And, there are those who will say that this interviewer has this chance to sit down with someone with my unique perspective on the world and the only questions he is asking are sex questions."
Maybe. Did you attend the funeral of Retro Girl?
"No."
Why?
"I didn't know where it was."
You knew her.
"Yes. Great girl. One of the best."
In the book by Julia...
"Here we go—"

"You just asked for my Secret origin."

The book also describes an affair between characters that strongly resemble you and Retro Girl.
"Come on, the girl is dead."
Yes. Did you have a relationship with her?
"Yes."
Like described in the book?
"I didn't read the book, so."
What kind of relationship did you have?
(Smiles) "A better one than you and I have."
You know what I mean.
"A deaf man knows what you mean. This—uh—isn't what we agreed the interview would be about."
Well...
"There's two kinds of men—men of their word, and men who aren't. Which are you?"
Well, you don't seem to be very interested in answering questions on the subject we did agree on discussing, so...
"Sure I am. You're just not enjoying the –uh—my answers."
Actually I am, in a perverse way. But you are avoiding the questions that you are being asked.
"Define avoiding."
See?
"I was joking."
Hmmm...I wonder if you were.
"Now you sound like my therapist."
Ho, you have a therapist?
"Ha! You're good."
Not going to answer?
(Olympia does not answer, but does it with a smile.)
Were you saddened by the death of Retro Girl?
"What kind of question is that? Of course."
I didn't mean anything

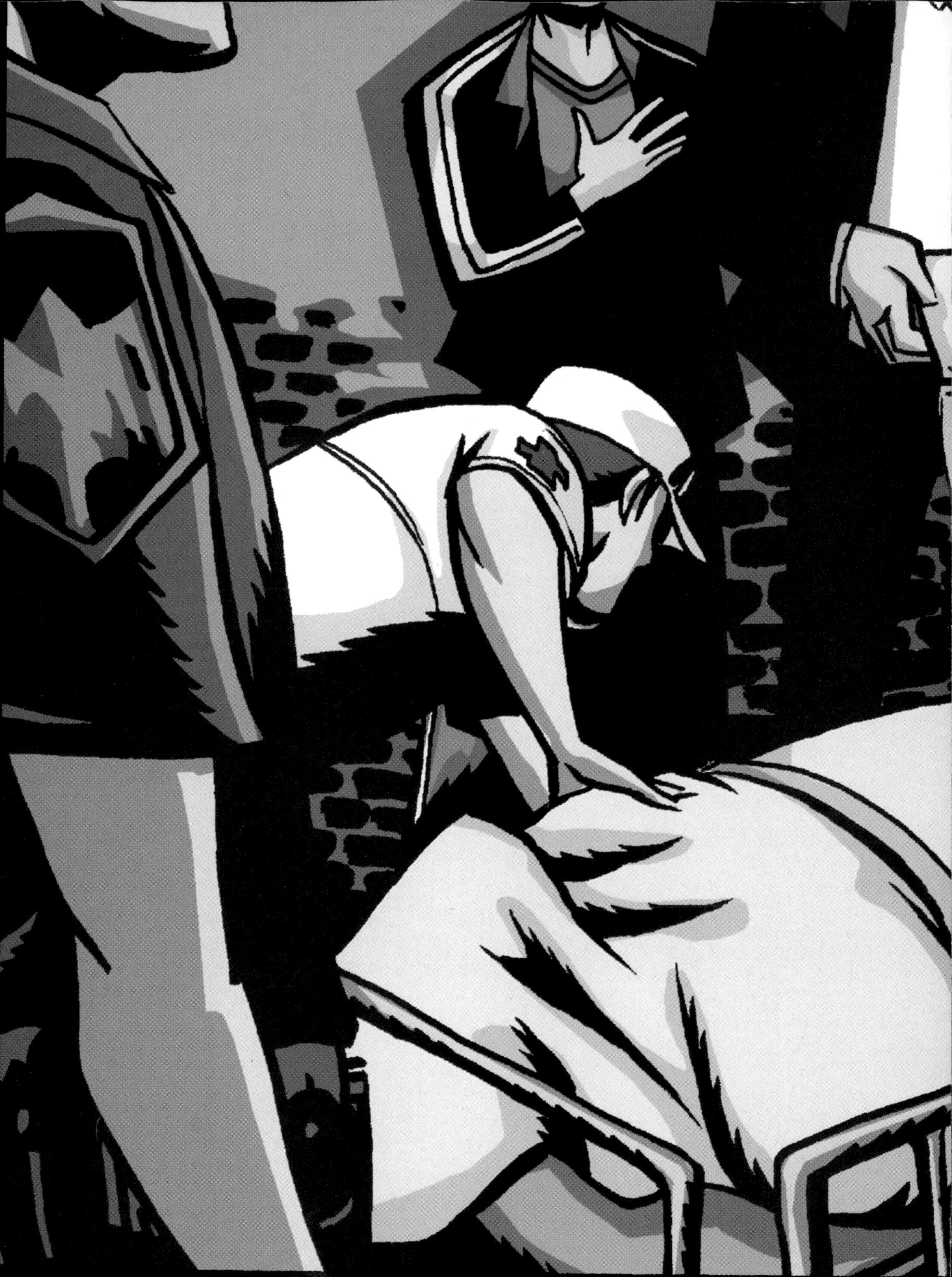

by it. It's just a direct question.
"Lord..."
I thought if I asked you how you felt when you learned of it, that would be more vague and not to your liking.
"Uh-huh. Well, for your information, the whole thing was devastating to me. The death, the whole thing with Triphammer. There were no winners in that terrible story. If you notice, I wasn't around for a while after that. It took a lot out for me to put on my uniform after that..."
Why?
"Just questioning why we do what we do. Is it worth it? Do we make a difference?
And?
"And I think we do. I think we do in a big way. And though that dark chapter in our city's history will always be there, I just—"(He is visibly shaken by the subject.)
Do you want to continue?
(Pauses) "Uh--not really. Tell you what? You and your magazine can run whatever you want. I don't care. I have no regrets about my life or how I conduct myself. My relationships are my own. My friends know who they

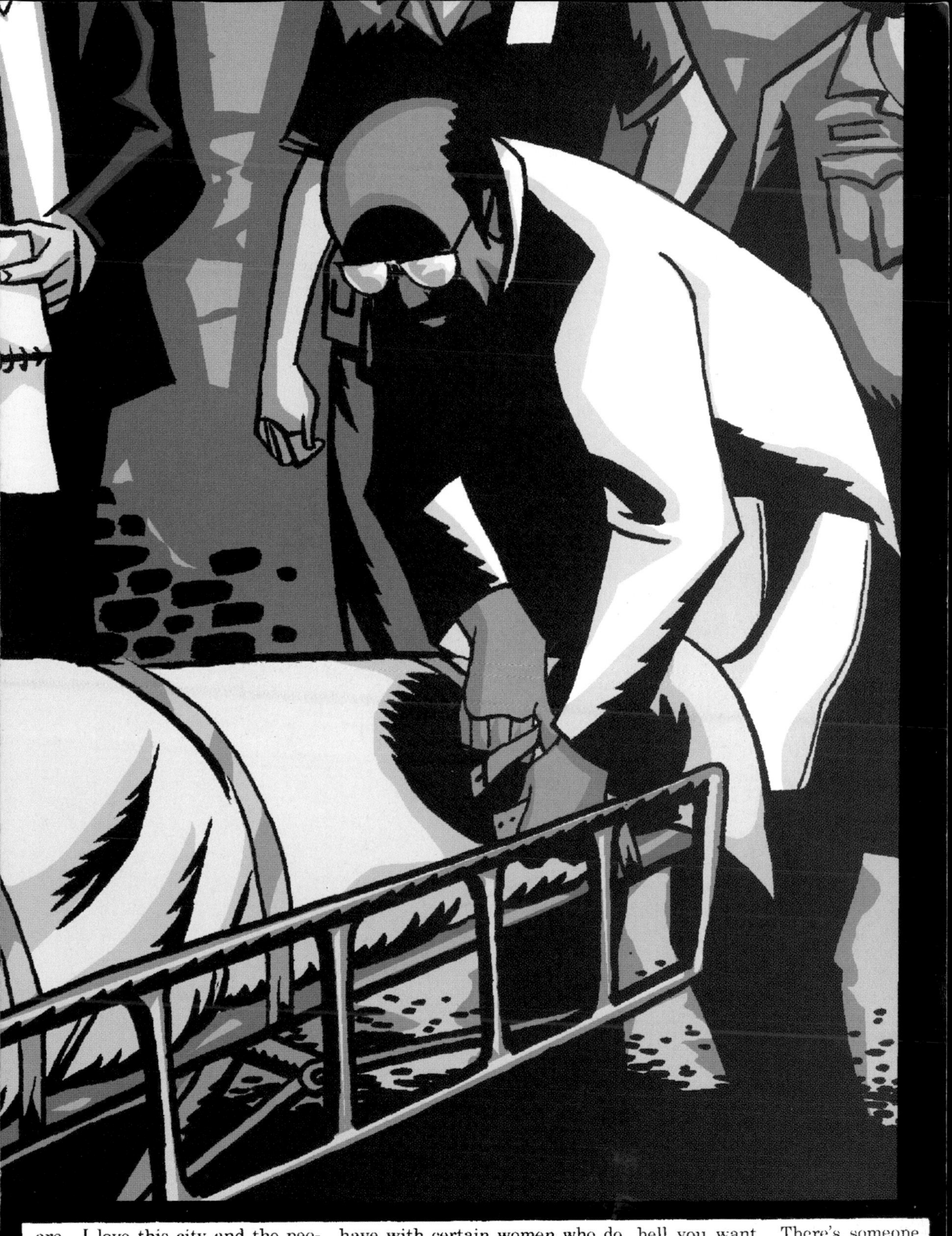

are. I love this city and the people in it, and the love I get back from them is the greatest gift I could ever hope for. The women in my life are all...

The thing is—you couldn't possibly understand the needs of people like myself. Our appetites, our desires. You couldn't possibly understand the special relationships someone like myself could have with certain women who do understand just what we're about. Women who just want to show their appreciation to us for our dedication and hard work. And even if you could understand it---what difference would it make? Would it make me a worse person? Would it take back any of the sacrifices I've made, or...?

"Just—just print whatever the hell you want. There's someone out there who needs me right now."

(Olympia flies away.)

INTERVIEW: MIKE SANGIACOMO
PHOTOS: AVON ARCHIVES

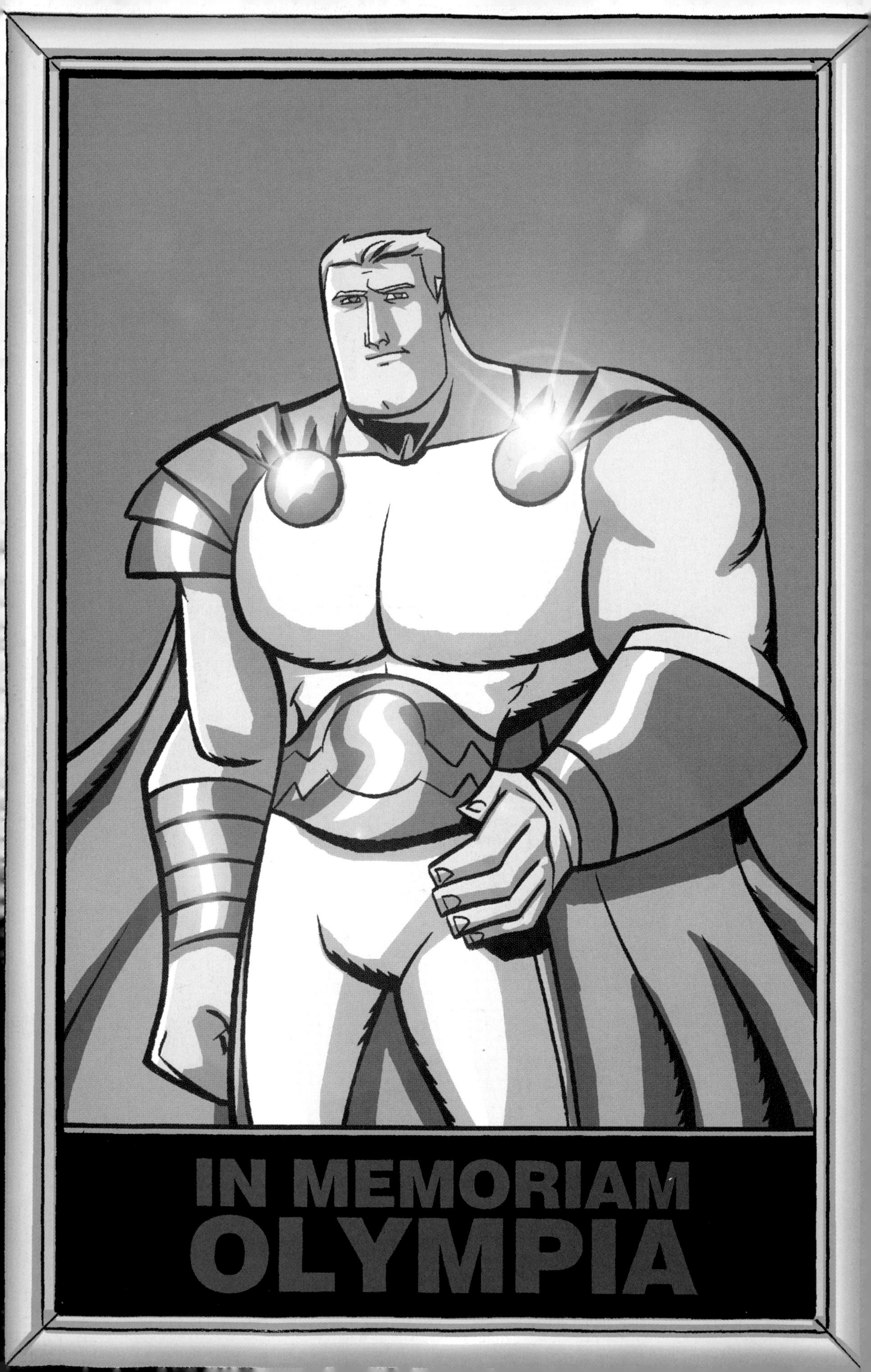
IN MEMORIAM
OLYMPIA

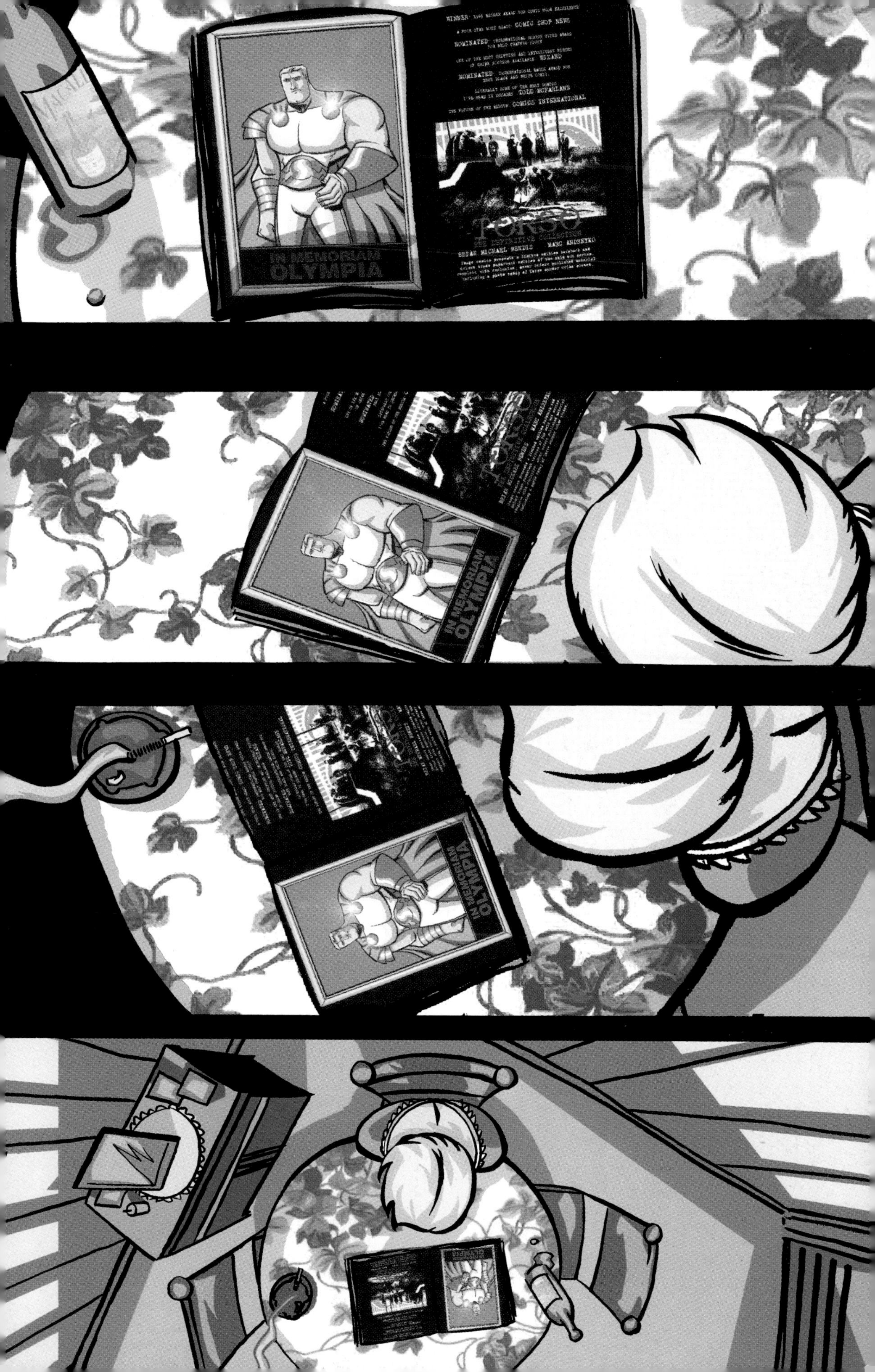
IN MEMORIAM
OLYMPIA
WINNER
COMIC SHOP NEWS
NOMINATED
WIZARD
NOMINATED
TODD MCFARLANE
COMICS INTERNATIONAL
TORSO
MICHAEL BENDIS
MARC ANDREYKO

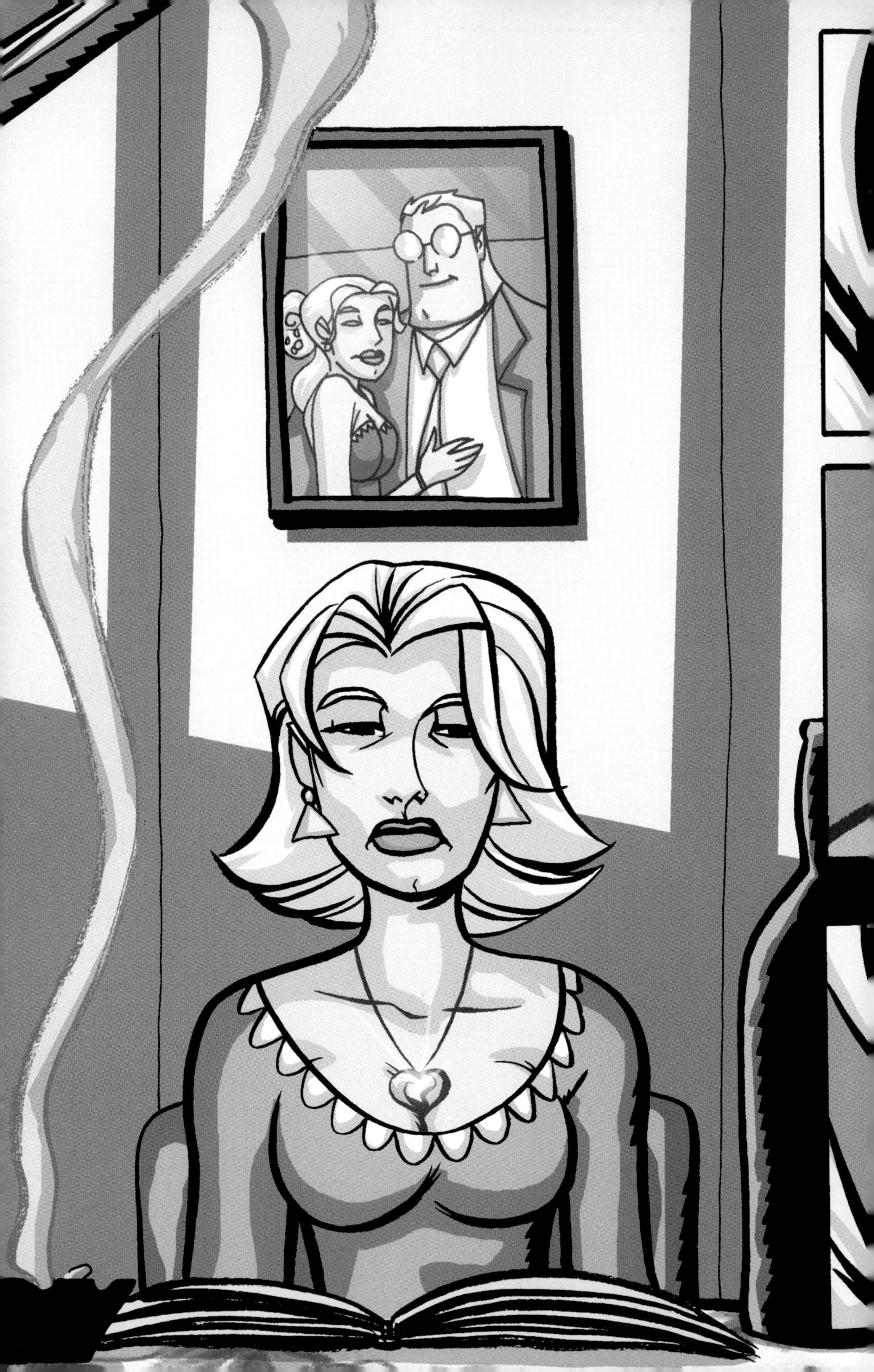

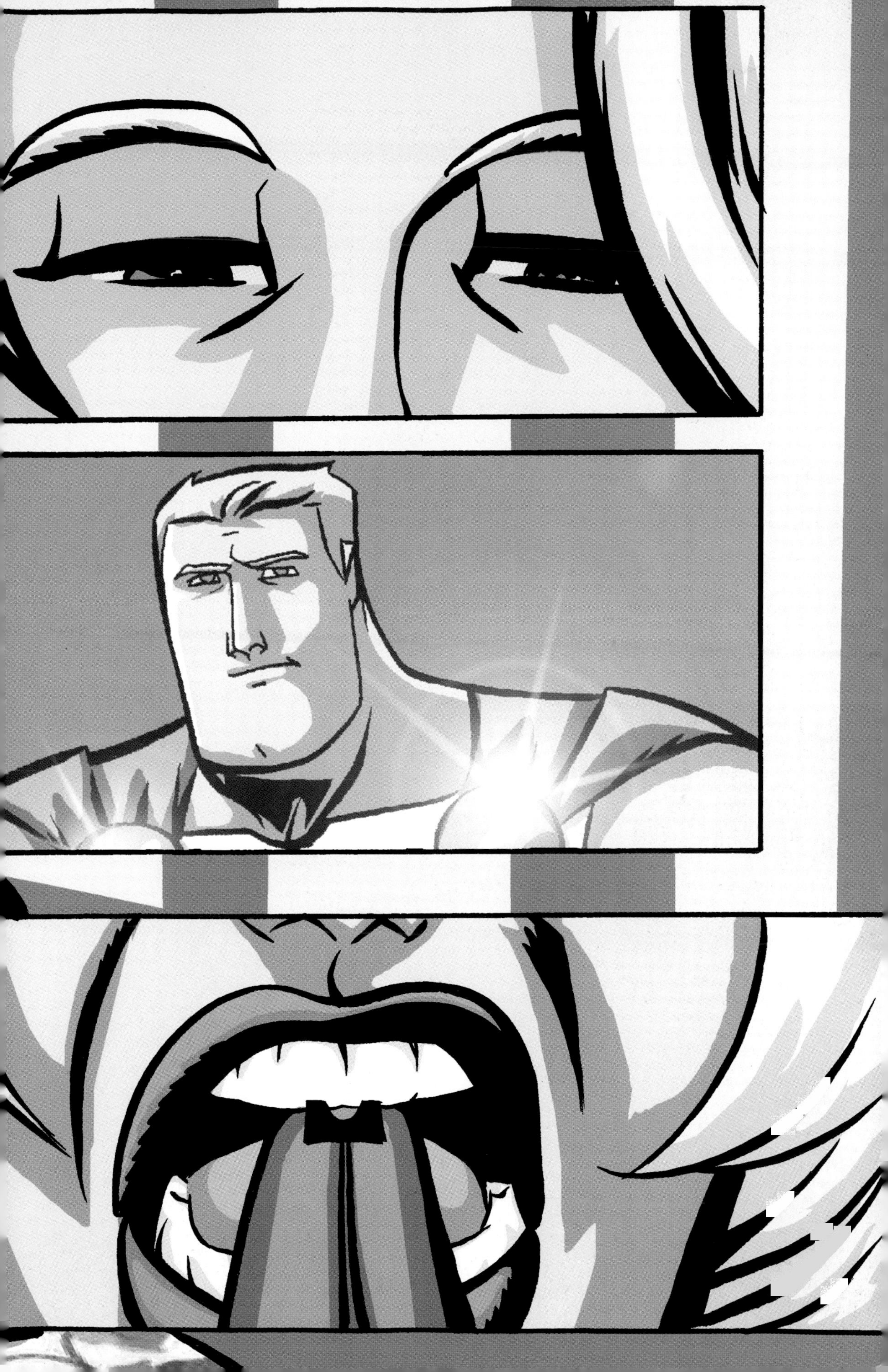

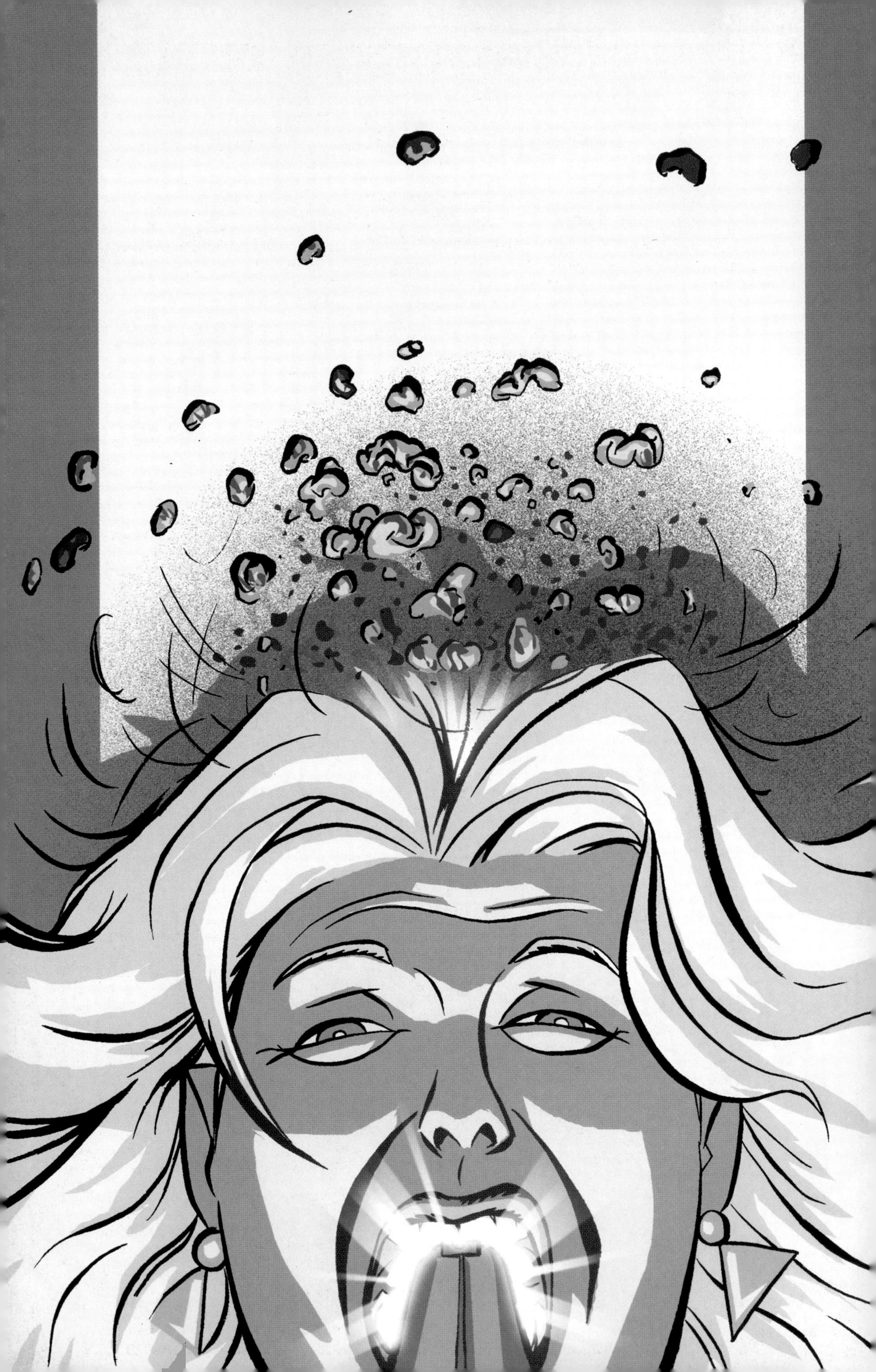

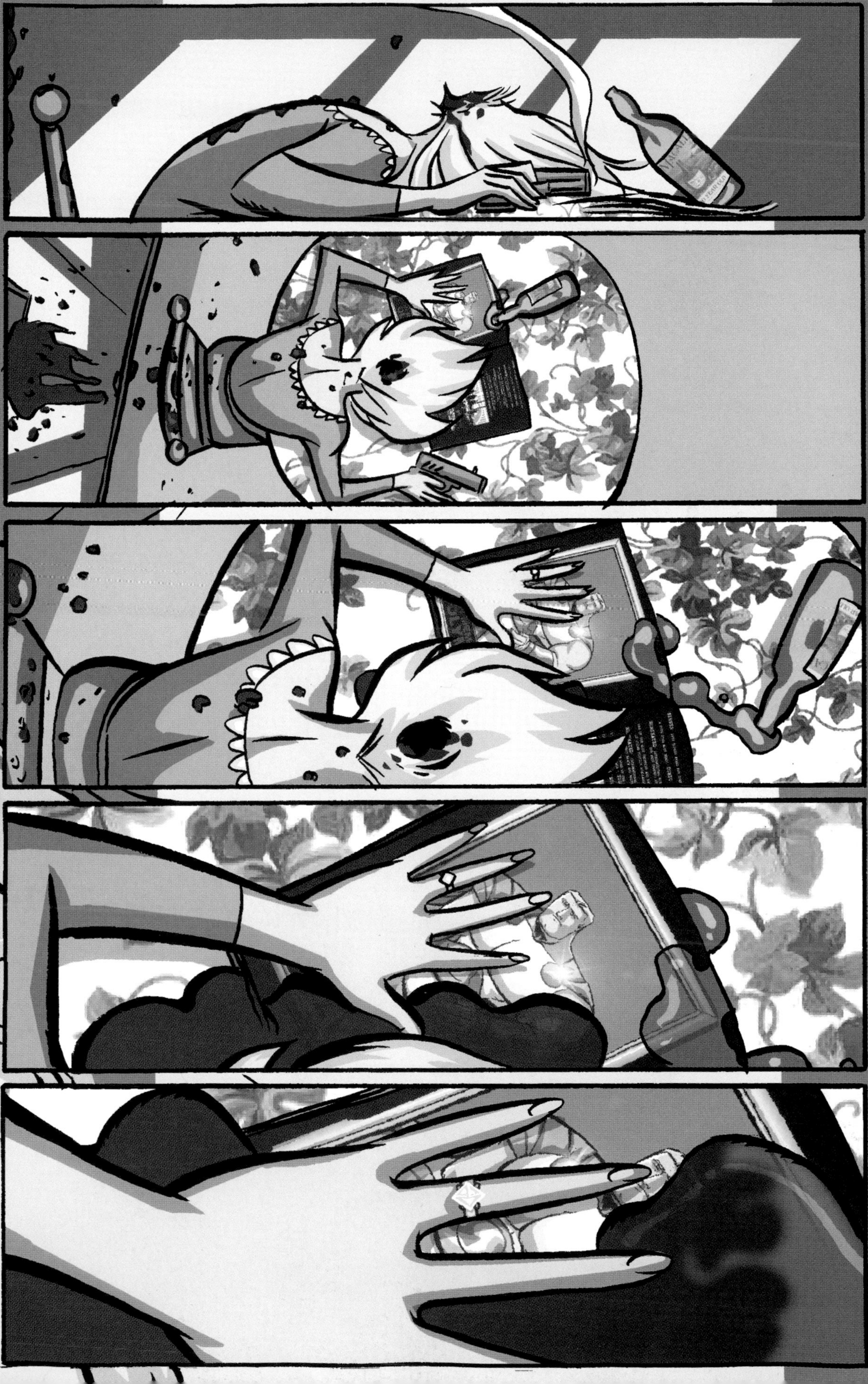

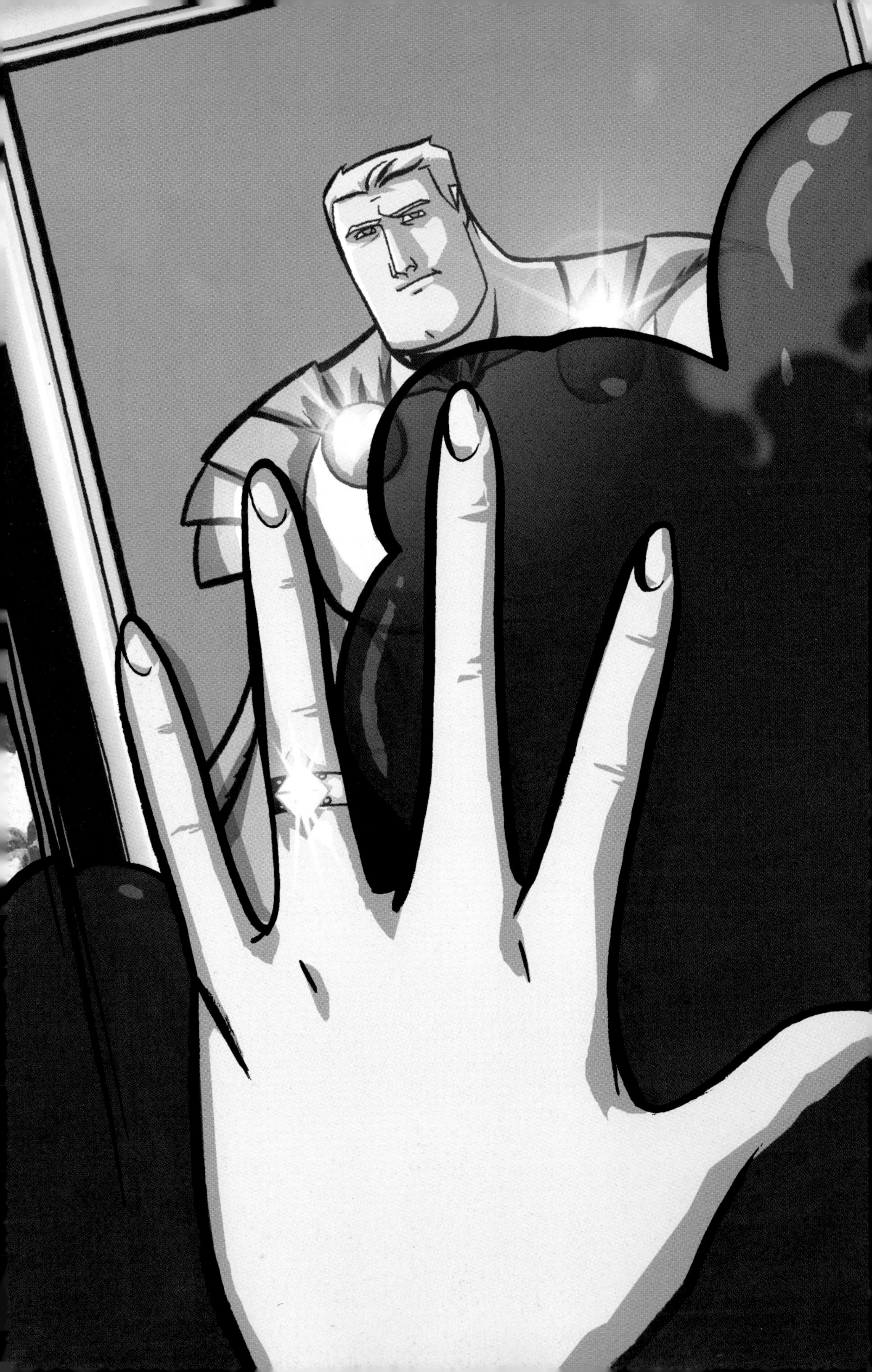

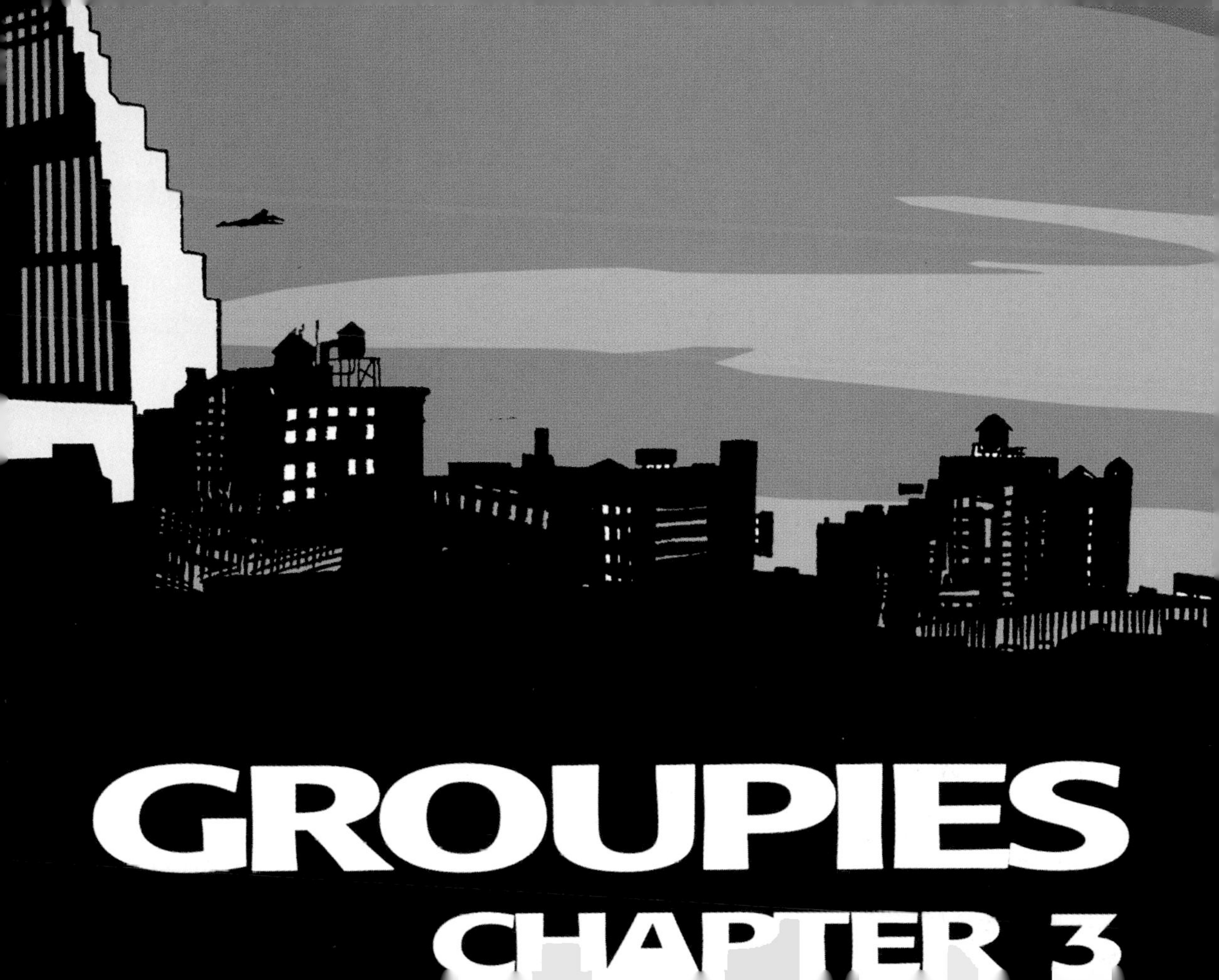

GROUPIES
CHAPTER 3

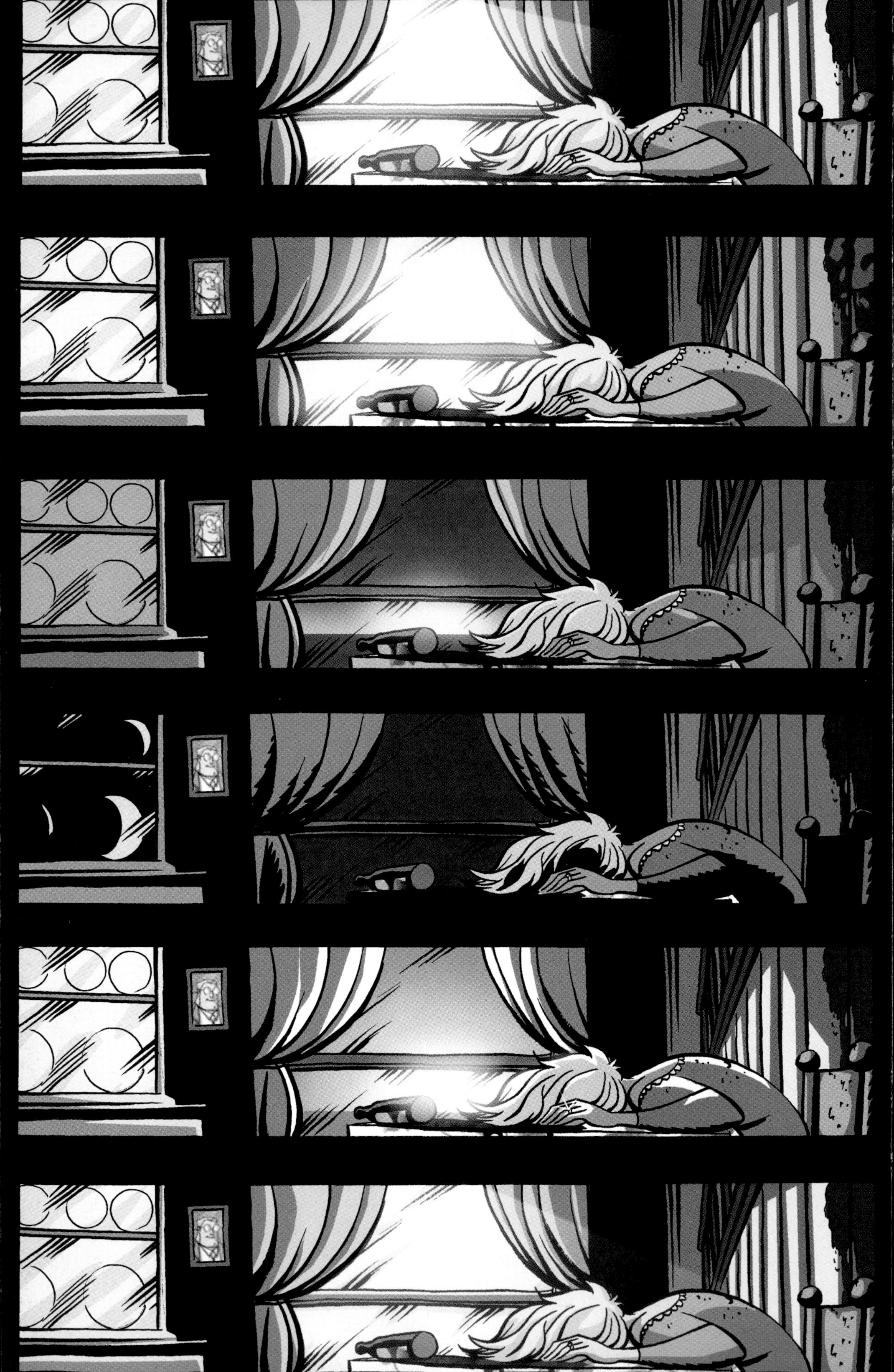

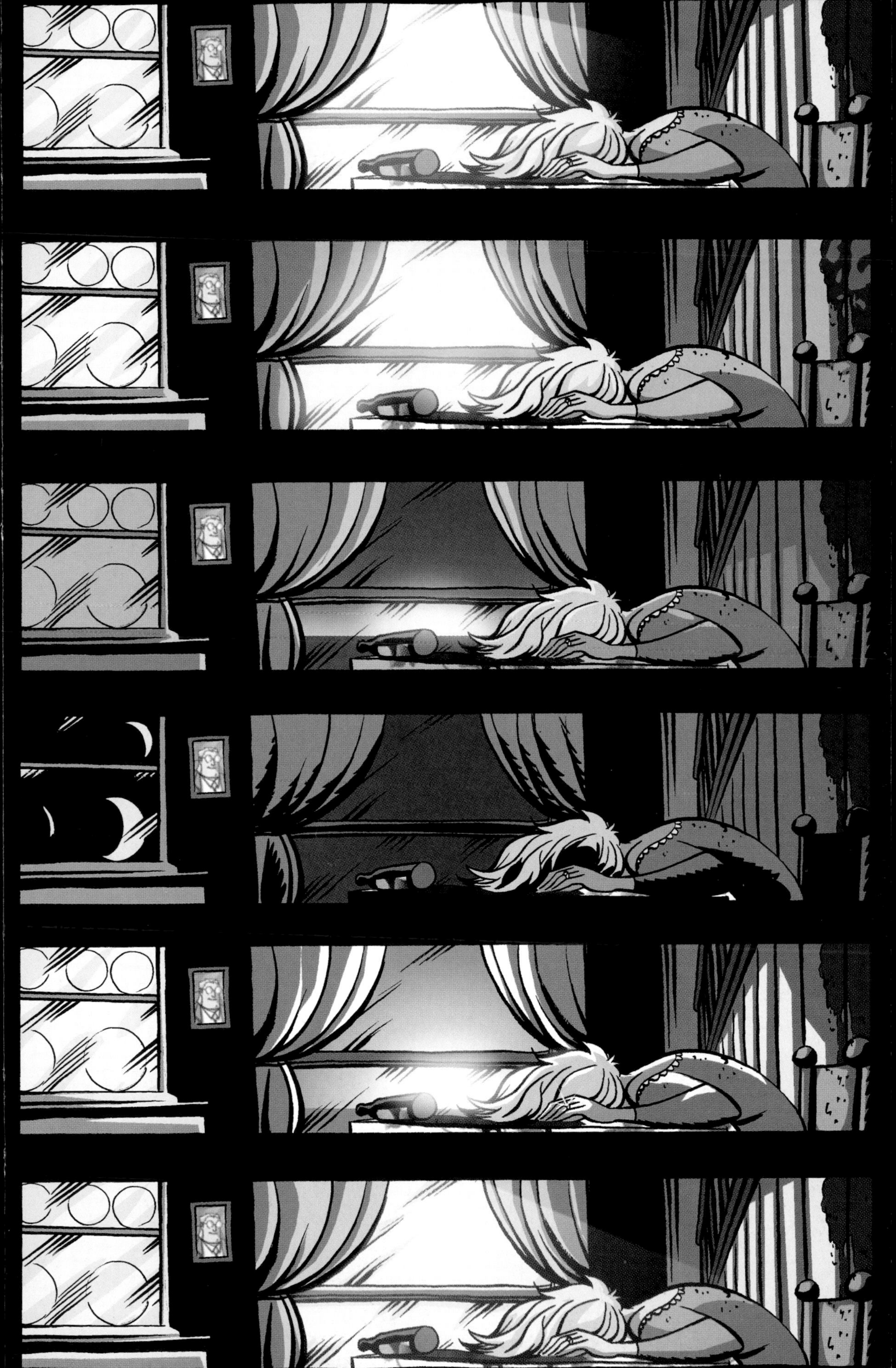

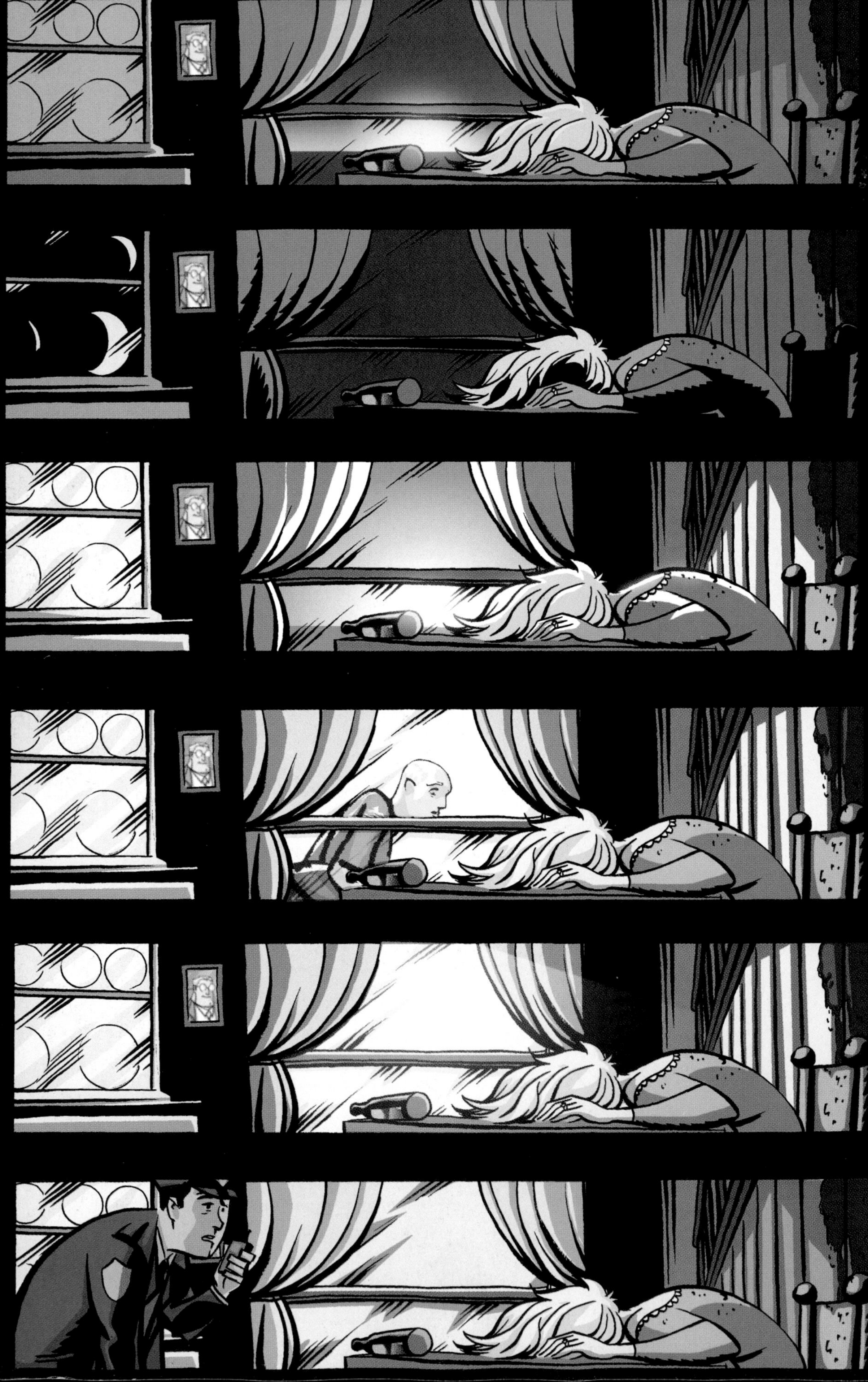

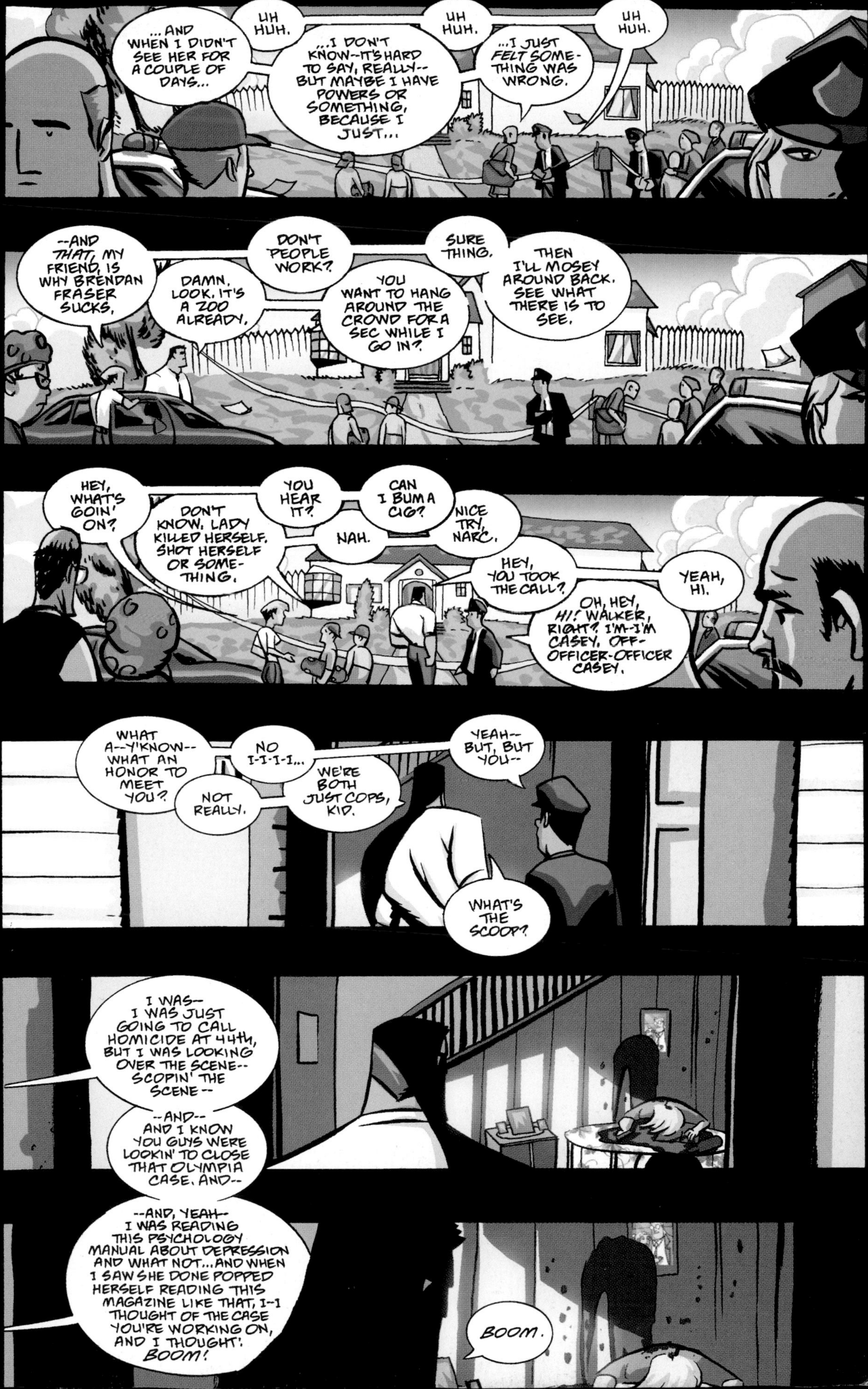
...AND WHEN I DIDN'T SEE HER FOR A COUPLE OF DAYS...
UH HUH.
...I DON'T KNOW--IT'S HARD TO SAY, REALLY--BUT MAYBE I HAVE POWERS OR SOMETHING, BECAUSE I JUST...
UH HUH.
...I JUST FELT SOMETHING WAS WRONG.
UH HUH.
--AND THAT, MY FRIEND, IS WHY BRENDAN FRASER SUCKS.
DON'T PEOPLE WORK?
DAMN, LOOK, IT'S A ZOO ALREADY.
YOU WANT TO HANG AROUND THE CROWD FOR A SEC WHILE I GO IN?
SURE THING.
THEN I'LL MOSEY AROUND BACK, SEE WHAT THERE IS TO SEE.
HEY, WHAT'S GOIN' ON?
DON'T KNOW. LADY KILLED HERSELF. SHOT HERSELF OR SOMETHING.
YOU HEAR IT?
NAH.
CAN I BUM A CIG?
NICE TRY, NARC.
HEY, YOU TOOK THE CALL?
YEAH, HI.
OH, HEY, HI! WALKER, RIGHT? I'M-I'M CASEY. OFF-OFFICER-OFFICER CASEY.
WHAT A--Y'KNOW--WHAT AN HONOR TO MEET YOU?
NO I-I-I-I...
NOT REALLY.
WE'RE BOTH JUST COPS, KID.
YEAH--BUT, BUT YOU--
WHAT'S THE SCOOP?
I WAS--I WAS JUST GOING TO CALL HOMICIDE AT 44th, BUT I WAS LOOKING OVER THE SCENE--SCOPIN' THE SCENE--
--AND--AND I KNOW YOU GUYS WERE LOOKIN' TO CLOSE THAT OLYMPIA CASE, AND--
--AND, YEAH--I WAS READING THIS PSYCHOLOGY MANUAL ABOUT DEPRESSION AND WHAT NOT...AND WHEN I SAW SHE DONE POPPED HERSELF READING THIS MAGAZINE LIKE THAT, I--I THOUGHT OF THE CASE YOU'RE WORKING ON, AND I THOUGHT: BOOM!
BOOM.

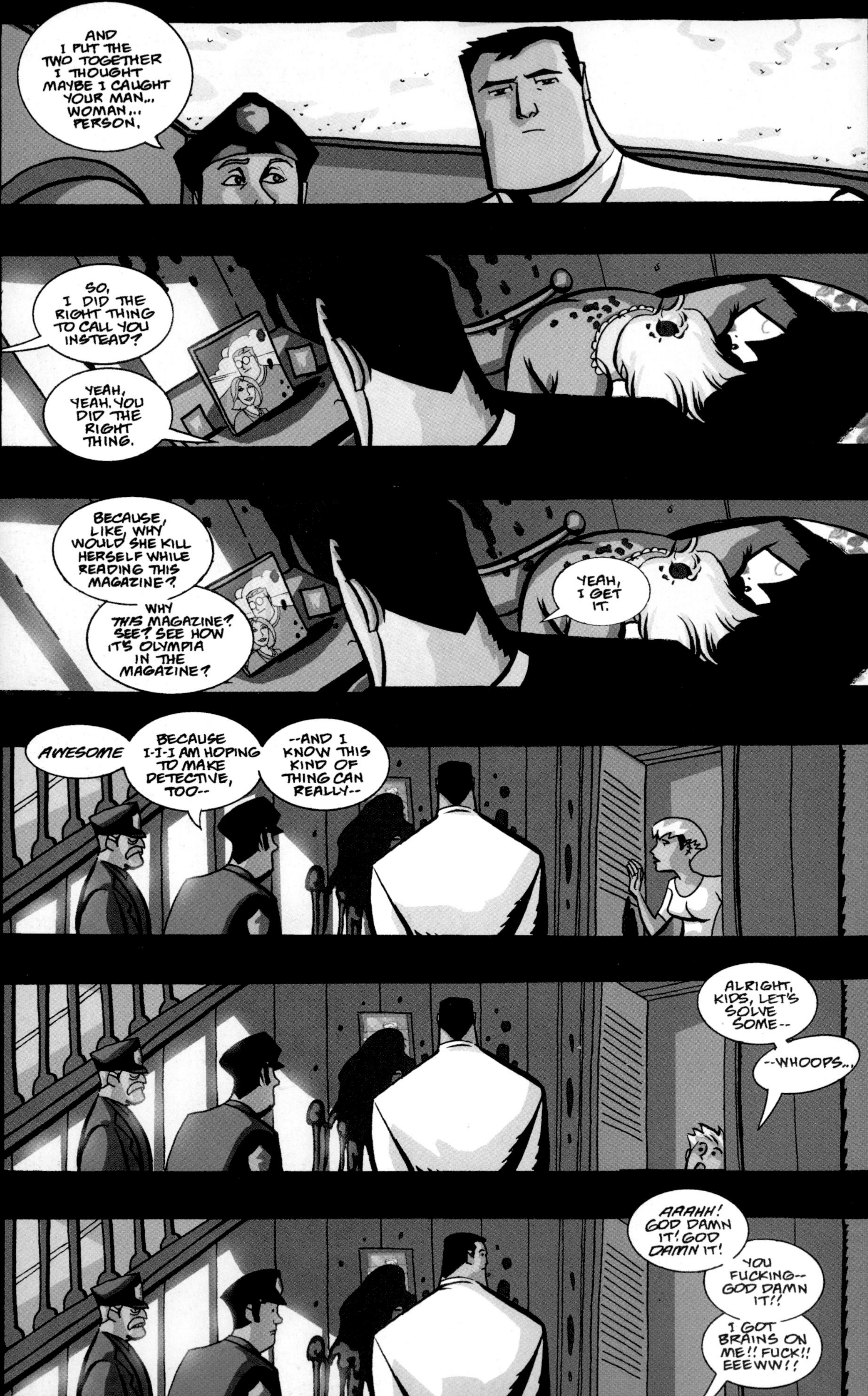

AND I PUT THE TWO TOGETHER I THOUGHT MAYBE I CAUGHT YOUR MAN... WOMAN... PERSON.
SO, I DID THE RIGHT THING TO CALL YOU INSTEAD?
YEAH, YEAH. YOU DID THE RIGHT THING.
BECAUSE, LIKE, WHY WOULD SHE KILL HERSELF WHILE READING THIS MAGAZINE?
WHY *THIS* MAGAZINE? SEE? SEE HOW IT'S OLYMPIA IN THE MAGAZINE?
YEAH, I GET IT.
AWESOME
BECAUSE I-I-I AM HOPING TO MAKE DETECTIVE, TOO--
--AND I KNOW THIS KIND OF THING CAN REALLY--
ALRIGHT, KIDS, LET'S SOLVE SOME--
--WHOOPS...
AAAHH! GOD DAMN IT! GOD *DAMN* IT!
YOU FUCKING-- GOD DAMN IT!!
I GOT BRAINS ON ME!! FUCK!! EEEWW!!

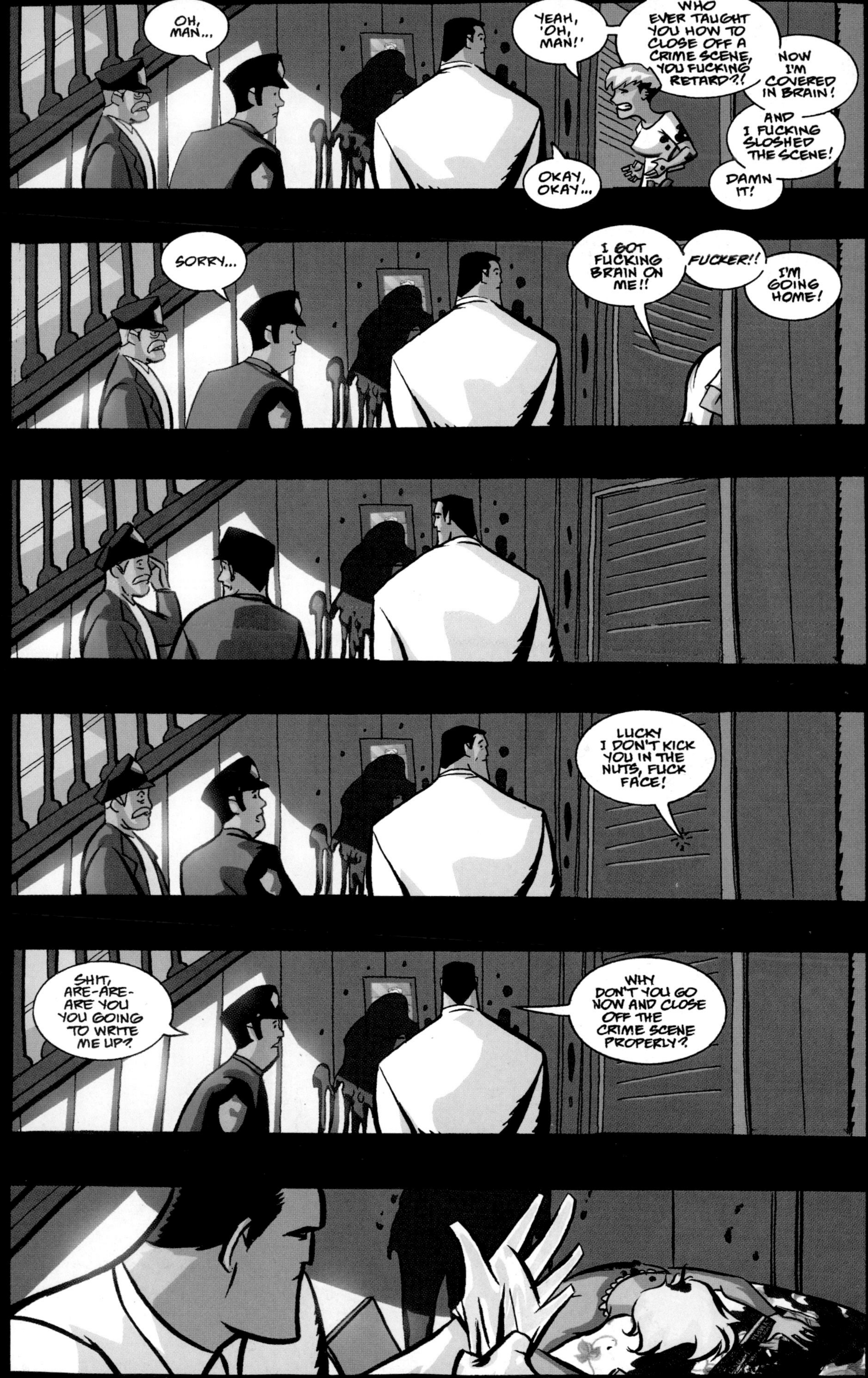
OH, MAN...
YEAH, 'OH, MAN!'
WHO EVER TAUGHT YOU HOW TO CLOSE OFF A CRIME SCENE, YOU FUCKING RETARD?!
NOW I'M COVERED IN BRAIN!
AND I FUCKING SLOSHED THE SCENE!
DAMN IT!
OKAY, OKAY...
SORRY...
I GOT FUCKING BRAIN ON ME!!
FUCKER!!
I'M GOING HOME!
LUCKY I DON'T KICK YOU IN THE NUTS, FUCK FACE!
SHIT, ARE-ARE-ARE YOU GOING TO WRITE ME UP?
WHY DON'T YOU GO NOW AND CLOSE OFF THE CRIME SCENE PROPERLY?

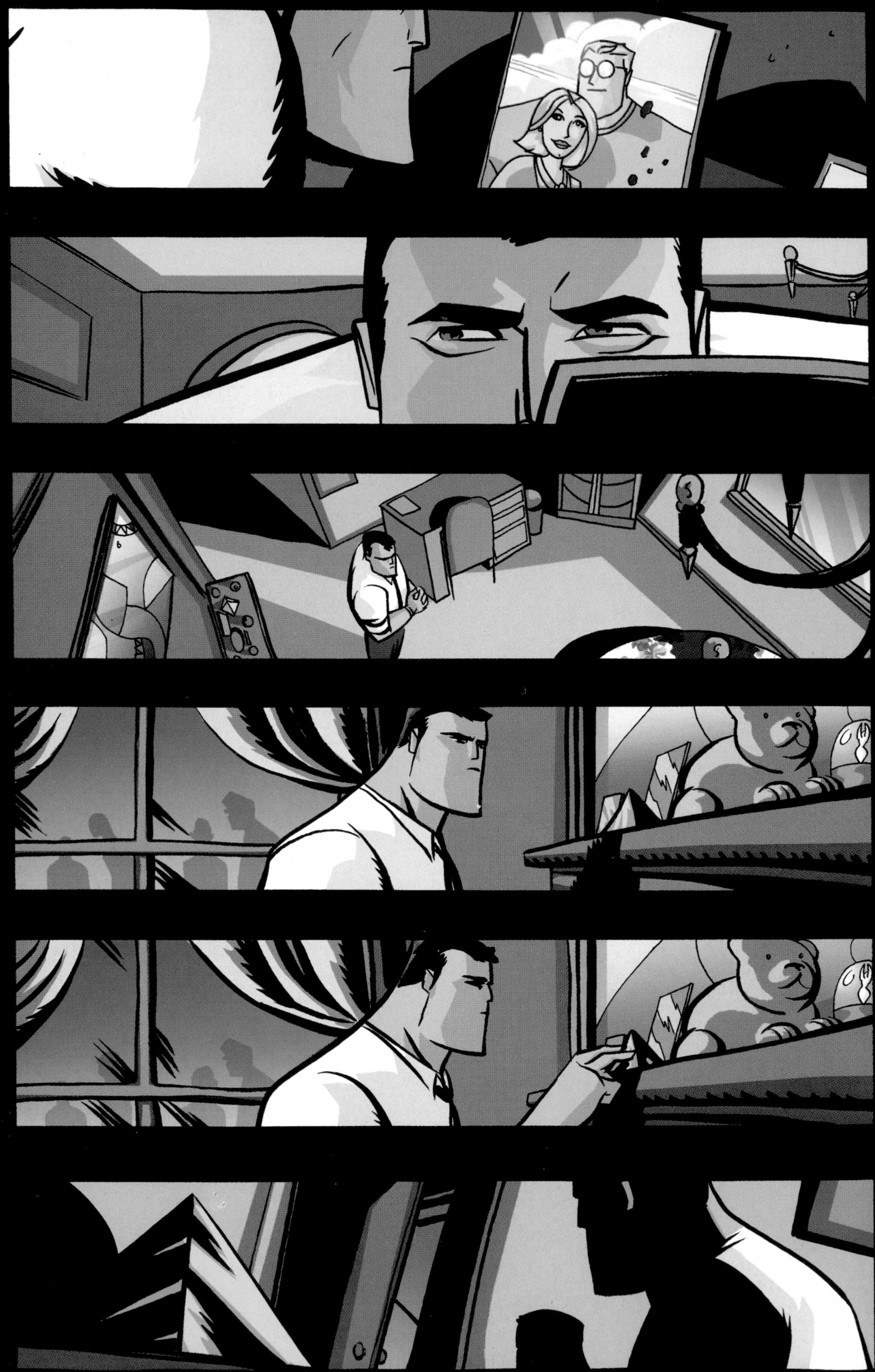

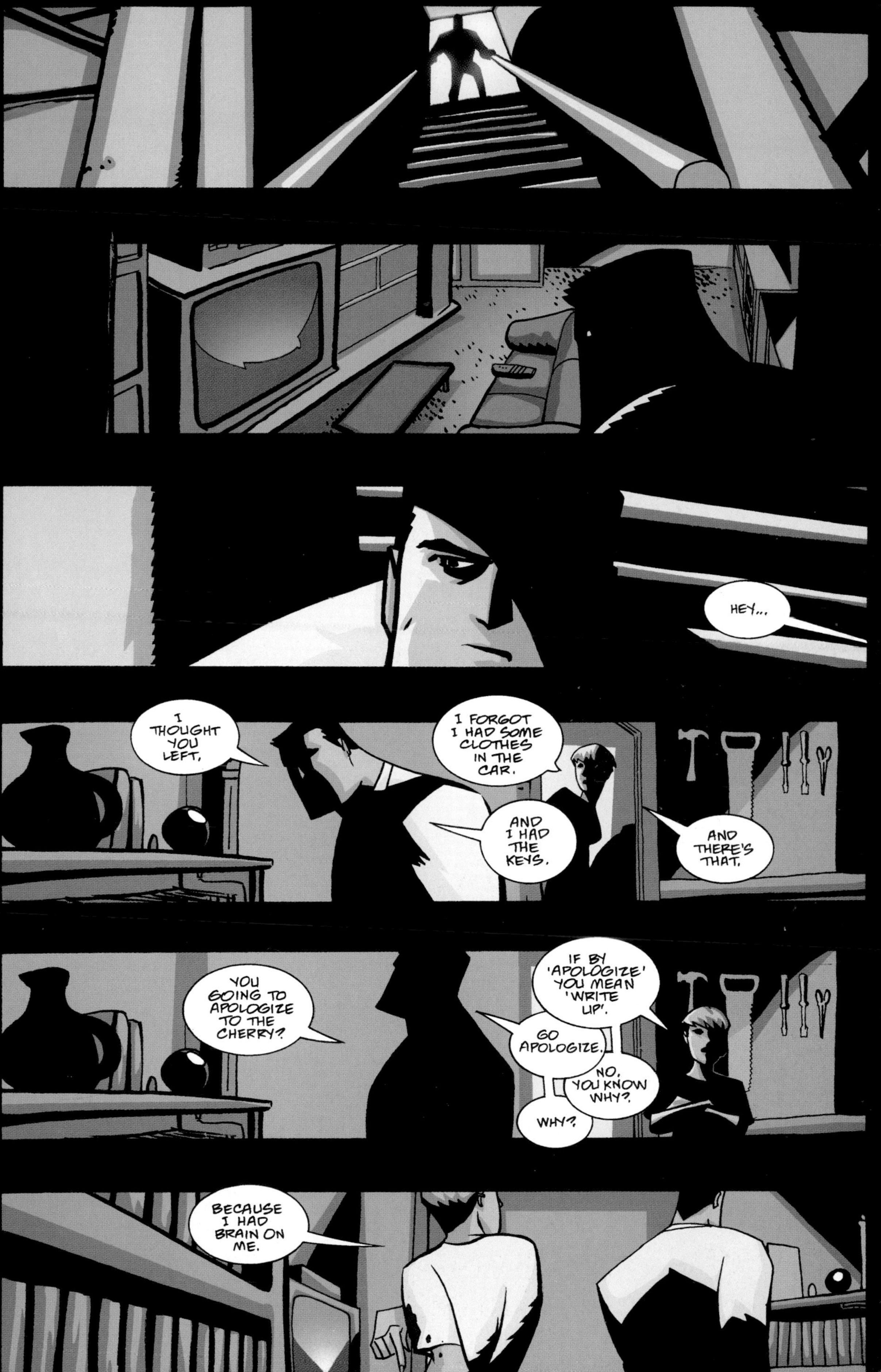
HEY...
I THOUGHT YOU LEFT.
I FORGOT I HAD SOME CLOTHES IN THE CAR.
AND I HAD THE KEYS.
AND THERE'S THAT.
YOU GOING TO APOLOGIZE TO THE CHERRY?
IF BY 'APOLOGIZE' YOU MEAN 'WRITE UP'.
GO APOLOGIZE.
NO. YOU KNOW WHY?
WHY?
BECAUSE I HAD BRAIN ON ME.

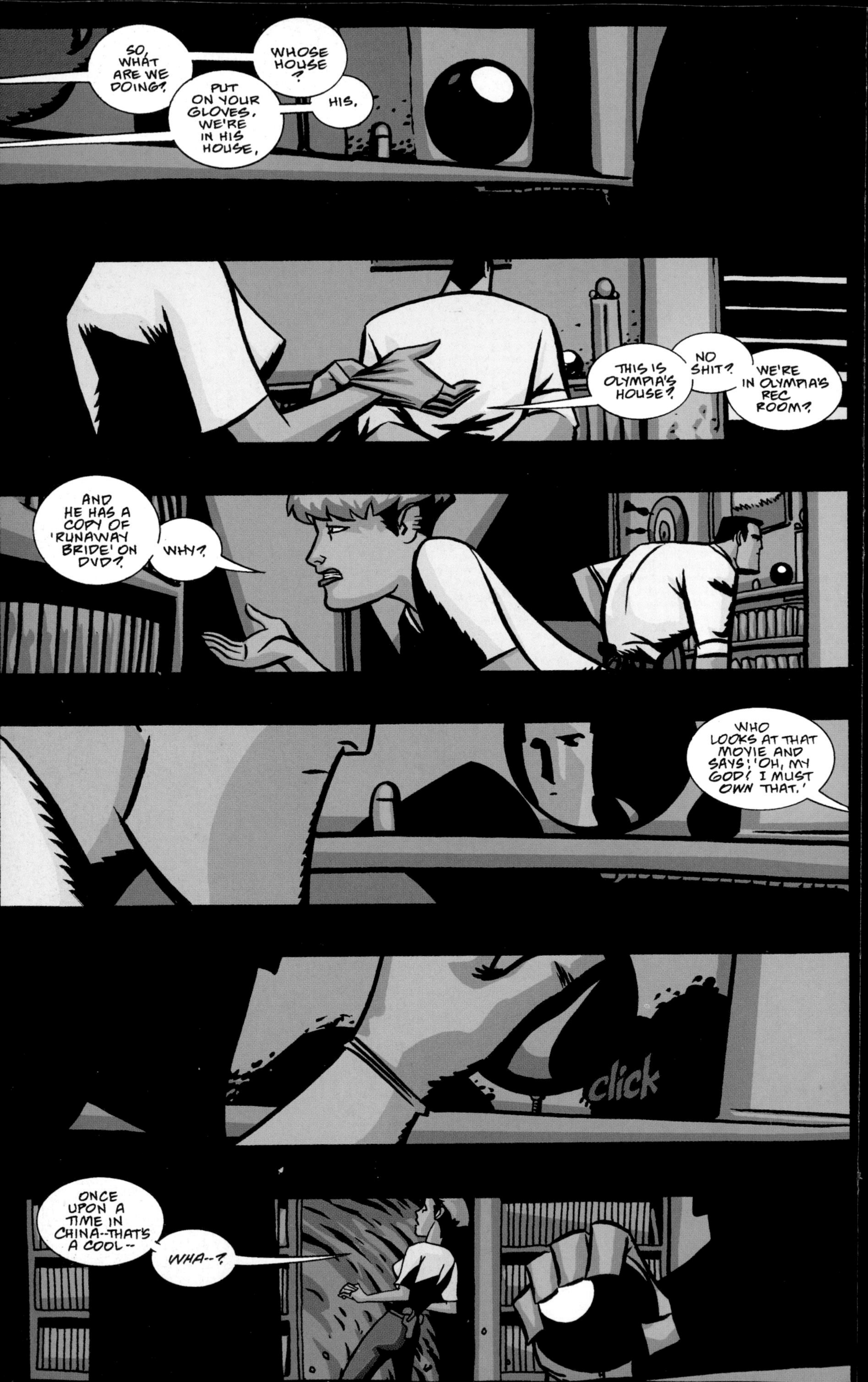
SO, WHAT ARE WE DOING?
WHOSE HOUSE?
PUT ON YOUR GLOVES. WE'RE IN HIS HOUSE.
HIS.
THIS IS OLYMPIA'S HOUSE?
NO SHIT?
WE'RE IN OLYMPIA'S REC ROOM?
AND HE HAS A COPY OF 'RUNAWAY BRIDE' ON DVD?
WHY?
WHO LOOKS AT THAT MOVIE AND SAYS: 'OH, MY GOD! I MUST OWN THAT.'
click
ONCE UPON A TIME IN CHINA--THAT'S A COOL--
WHA--?

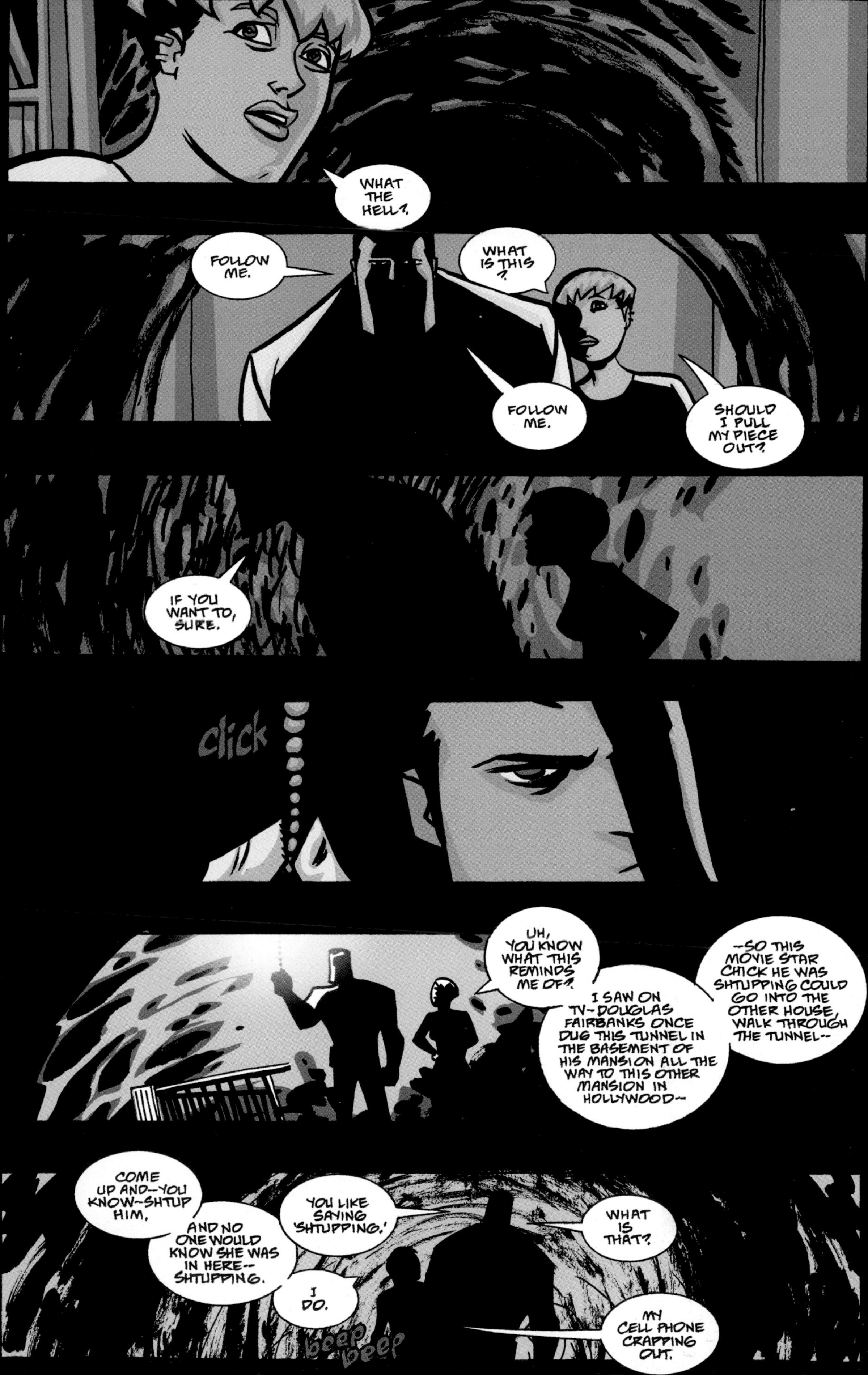
WHAT THE HELL?
FOLLOW ME.
WHAT IS THIS?
FOLLOW ME.
SHOULD I PULL MY PIECE OUT?
IF YOU WANT TO, SURE.
click
UH, YOU KNOW WHAT THIS REMINDS ME OF?
I SAW ON TV-- DOUGLAS FAIRBANKS ONCE DUG THIS TUNNEL IN THE BASEMENT OF HIS MANSION ALL THE WAY TO THIS OTHER MANSION IN HOLLYWOOD--
--SO THIS MOVIE STAR CHICK HE WAS SHTUPPING COULD GO INTO THE OTHER HOUSE, WALK THROUGH THE TUNNEL--
COME UP AND--YOU KNOW--SHTUP HIM,
AND NO ONE WOULD KNOW SHE WAS IN HERE-- SHTUPPING.
YOU LIKE SAYING 'SHTUPPING.'
I DO.
WHAT IS THAT?
beep beep
MY CELL PHONE CRAPPING OUT.

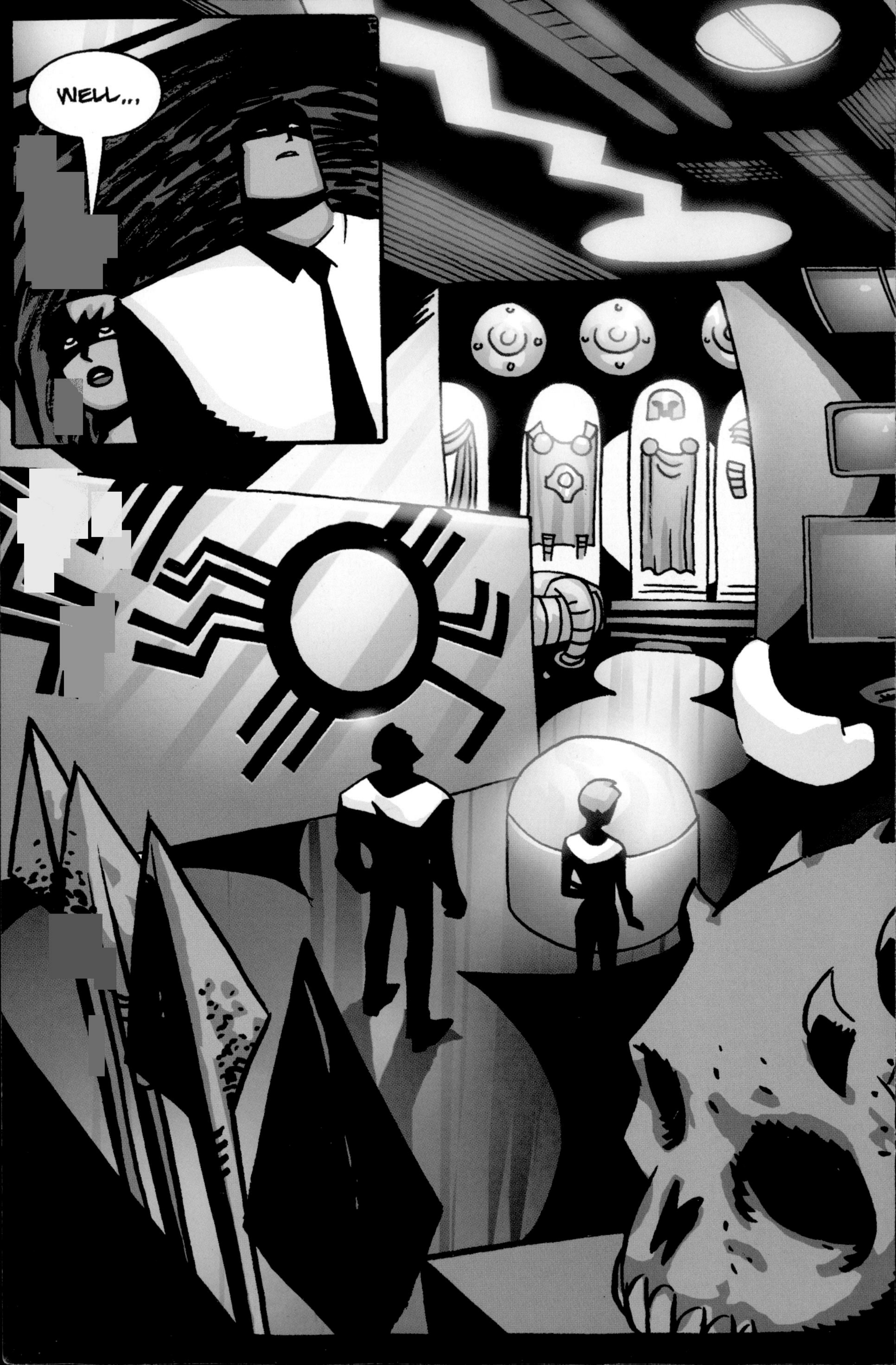
WELL...

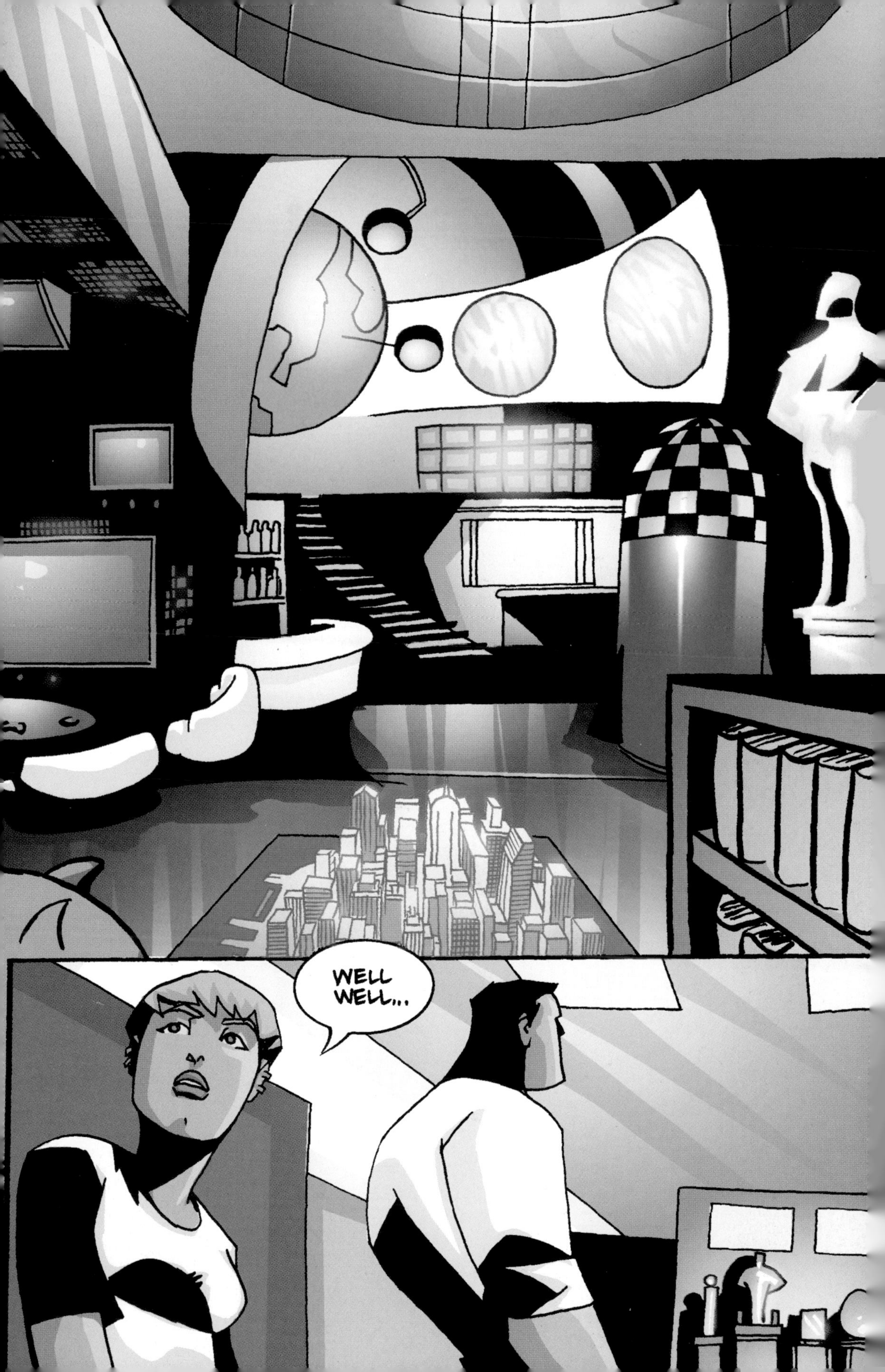
WELL WELL...

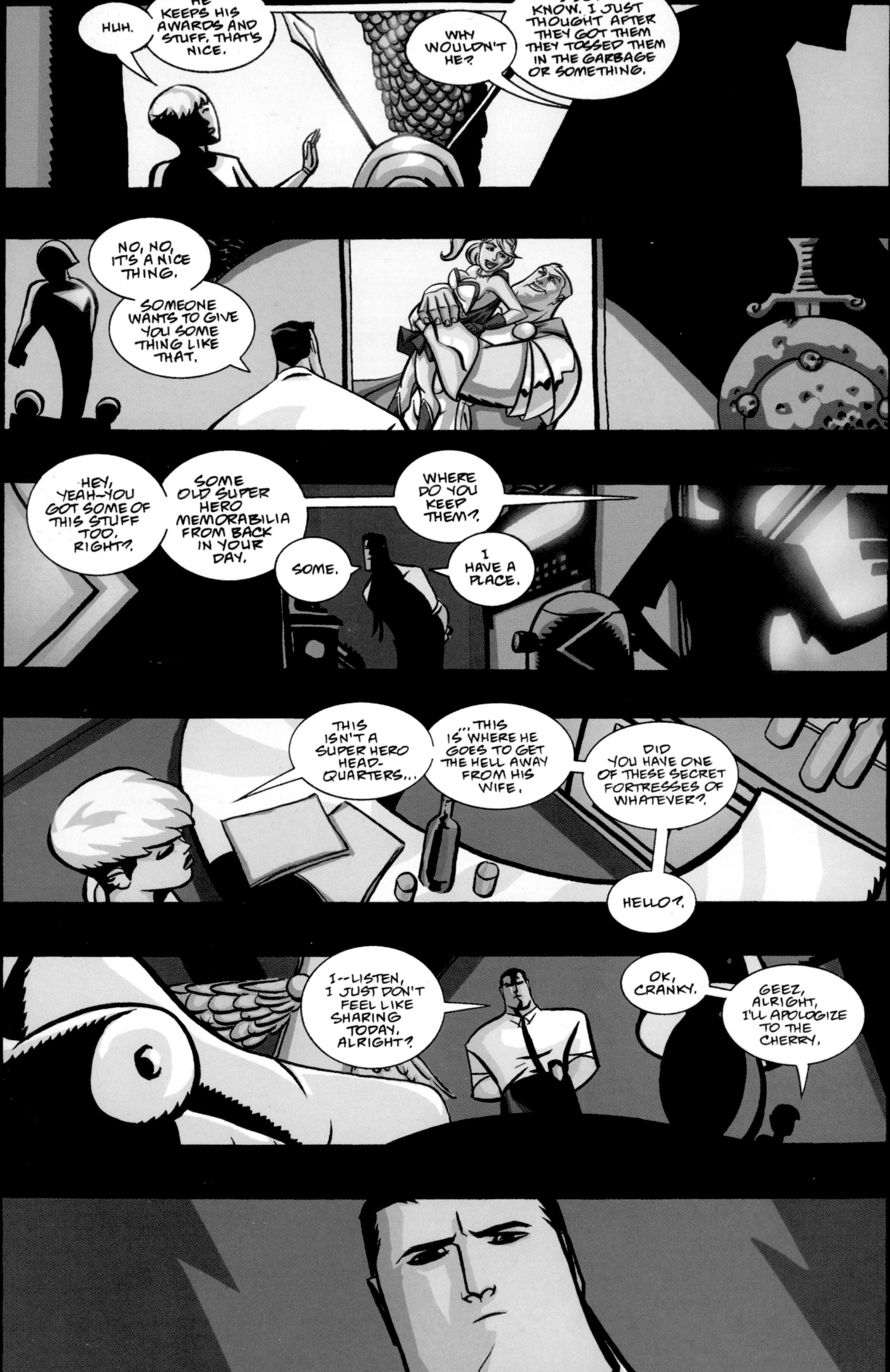
HUH.
HE KEEPS HIS AWARDS AND STUFF. THAT'S NICE.
WHY WOULDN'T HE?
I DON'T KNOW. I JUST THOUGHT AFTER THEY GOT THEM THEY TOSSED THEM IN THE GARBAGE OR SOMETHING.
NO, NO, IT'S A NICE THING.
SOMEONE WANTS TO GIVE YOU SOME THING LIKE THAT.
HEY, YEAH--YOU GOT SOME OF THIS STUFF TOO, RIGHT?
SOME OLD SUPER HERO MEMORABILIA FROM BACK IN YOUR DAY.
SOME.
WHERE DO YOU KEEP THEM?
I HAVE A PLACE.
THIS ISN'T A SUPER HERO HEAD-QUARTERS...
...THIS IS WHERE HE GOES TO GET THE HELL AWAY FROM HIS WIFE.
DID YOU HAVE ONE OF THESE SECRET FORTRESSES OF WHATEVER?
HELLO?
I--LISTEN, I JUST DON'T FEEL LIKE SHARING TODAY, ALRIGHT?
OK, CRANKY.
GEEZ, ALRIGHT, I'LL APOLOGIZE TO THE CHERRY.

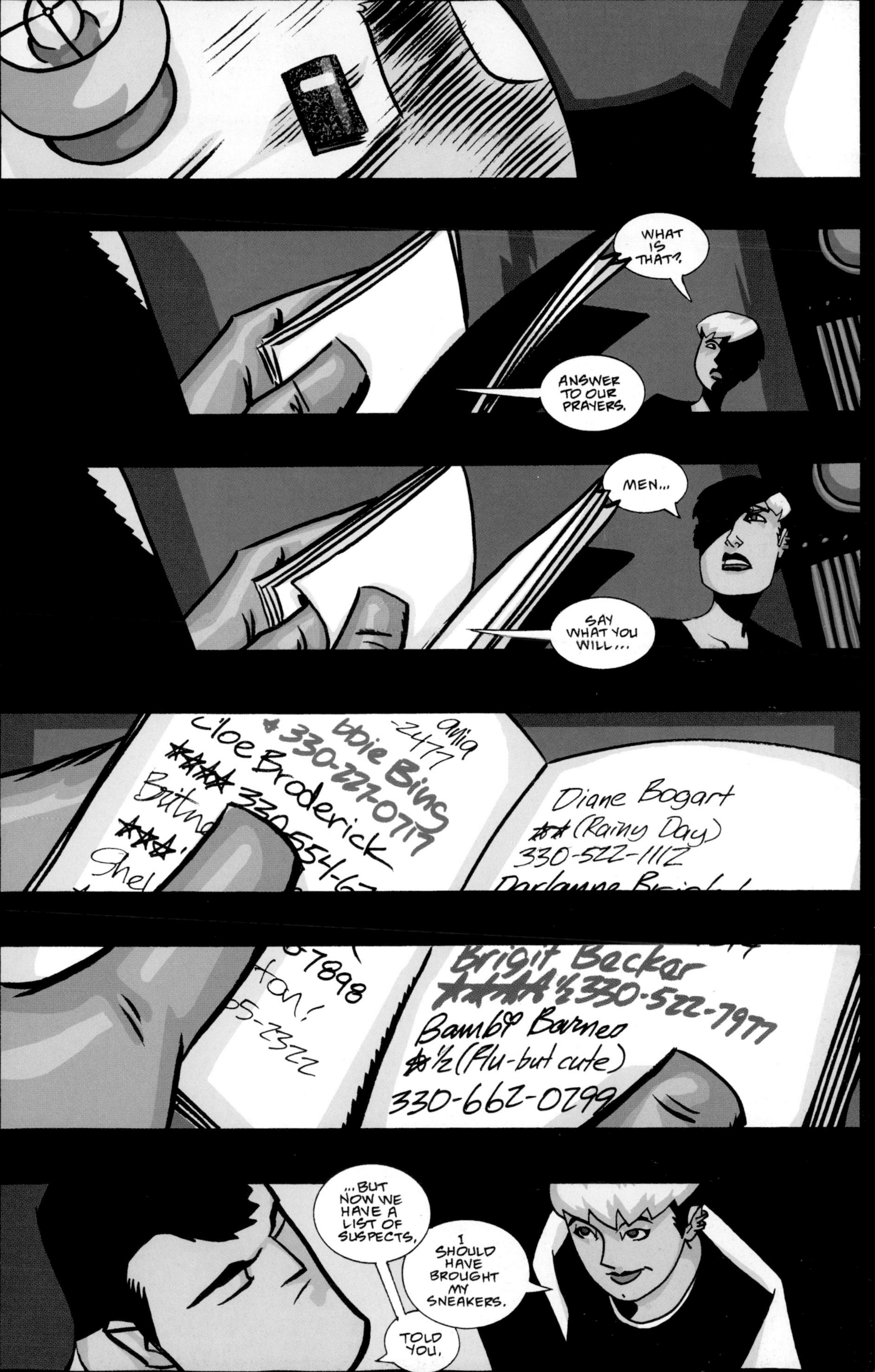
WHAT IS THAT?
ANSWER TO OUR PRAYERS.
MEN...
SAY WHAT YOU WILL...
Cloe Broderick
Diane Bogart
(Rainy Day)
330-522-1112
Brigit Becker
330-522-7977
Bambi Barnes
(Flu-but cute)
330-662-0299
...BUT NOW WE HAVE A LIST OF SUSPECTS.
TOLD YOU.
I SHOULD HAVE BROUGHT MY SNEAKERS.

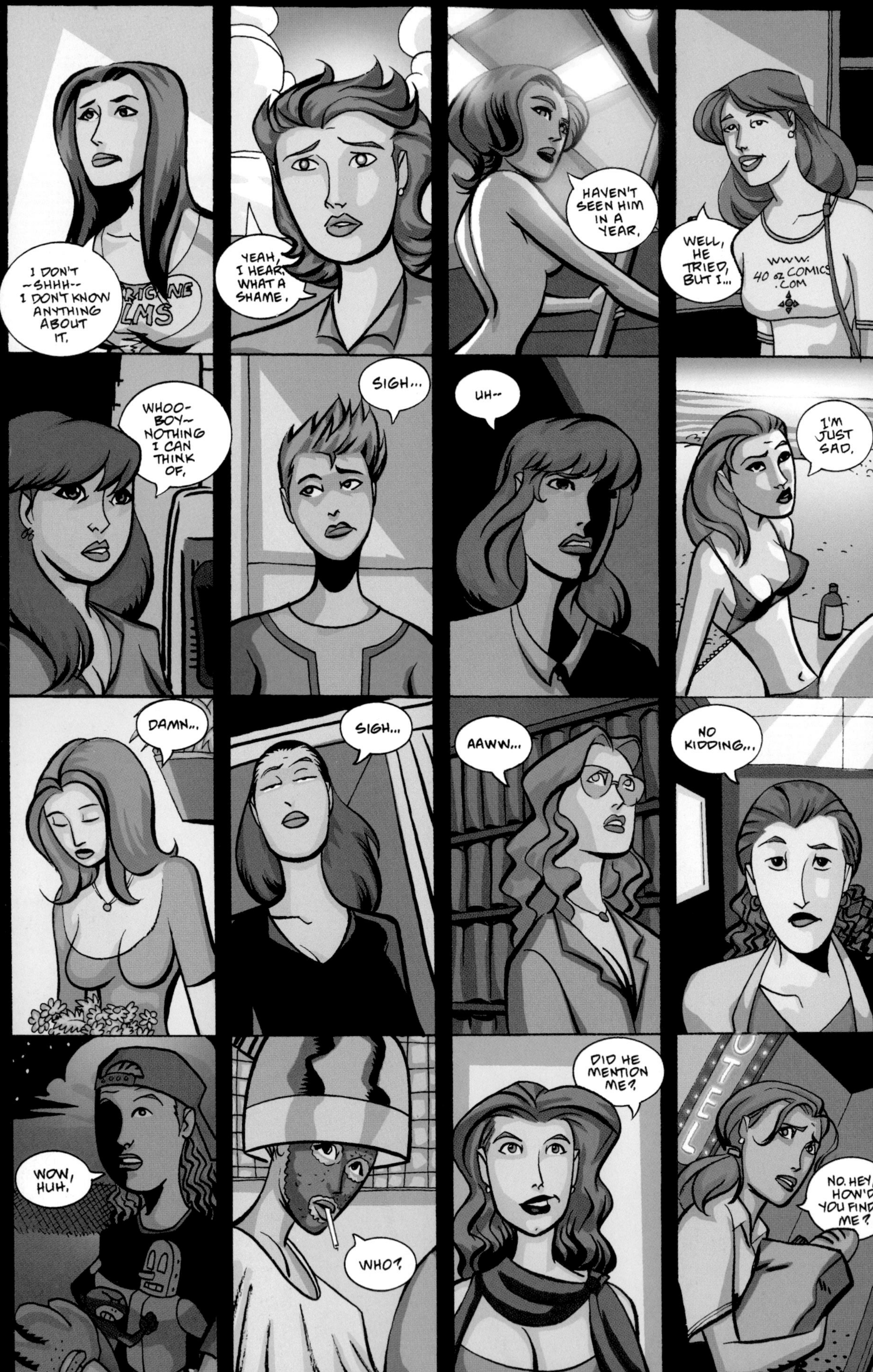
I DON'T --SHHH-- I DON'T KNOW ANYTHING ABOUT IT.
YEAH, I HEAR. WHAT A SHAME.
HAVEN'T SEEN HIM IN A YEAR.
WELL, HE TRIED, BUT I...
WWW. 40 oz COMICS .COM
WHOO-BOY-- NOTHING I CAN THINK OF.
SIGH...
UH--
I'M JUST SAD.
DAMN...
SIGH...
AAWW...
NO KIDDING...
WOW, HUH.
WHO?
DID HE MENTION ME?
NO. HEY, HOW'D YOU FIND ME?

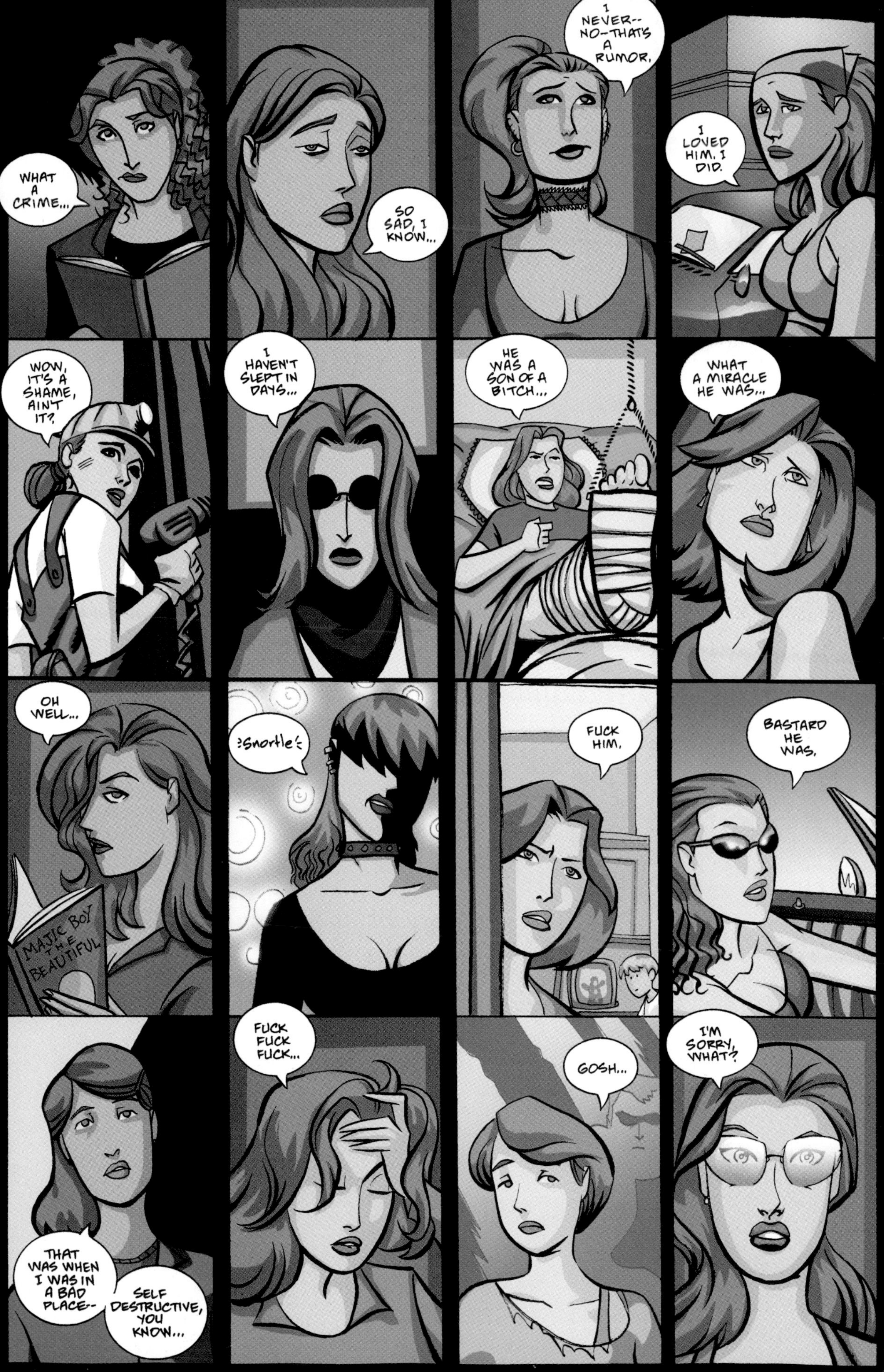
WHAT A CRIME...
SO SAD, I KNOW...
I NEVER-- NO--THAT'S A RUMOR,
I LOVED HIM. I DID.
WOW, IT'S A SHAME, AIN'T IT?
I HAVEN'T SLEPT IN DAYS...
HE WAS A SON OF A BITCH...
WHAT A MIRACLE HE WAS...
OH WELL...
MAJIC BOY THE BEAUTIFUL
Snortle
FUCK HIM.
BASTARD HE WAS.
THAT WAS WHEN I WAS IN A BAD PLACE--
SELF DESTRUCTIVE, YOU KNOW...
FUCK FUCK FUCK...
GOSH...
I'M SORRY, WHAT?

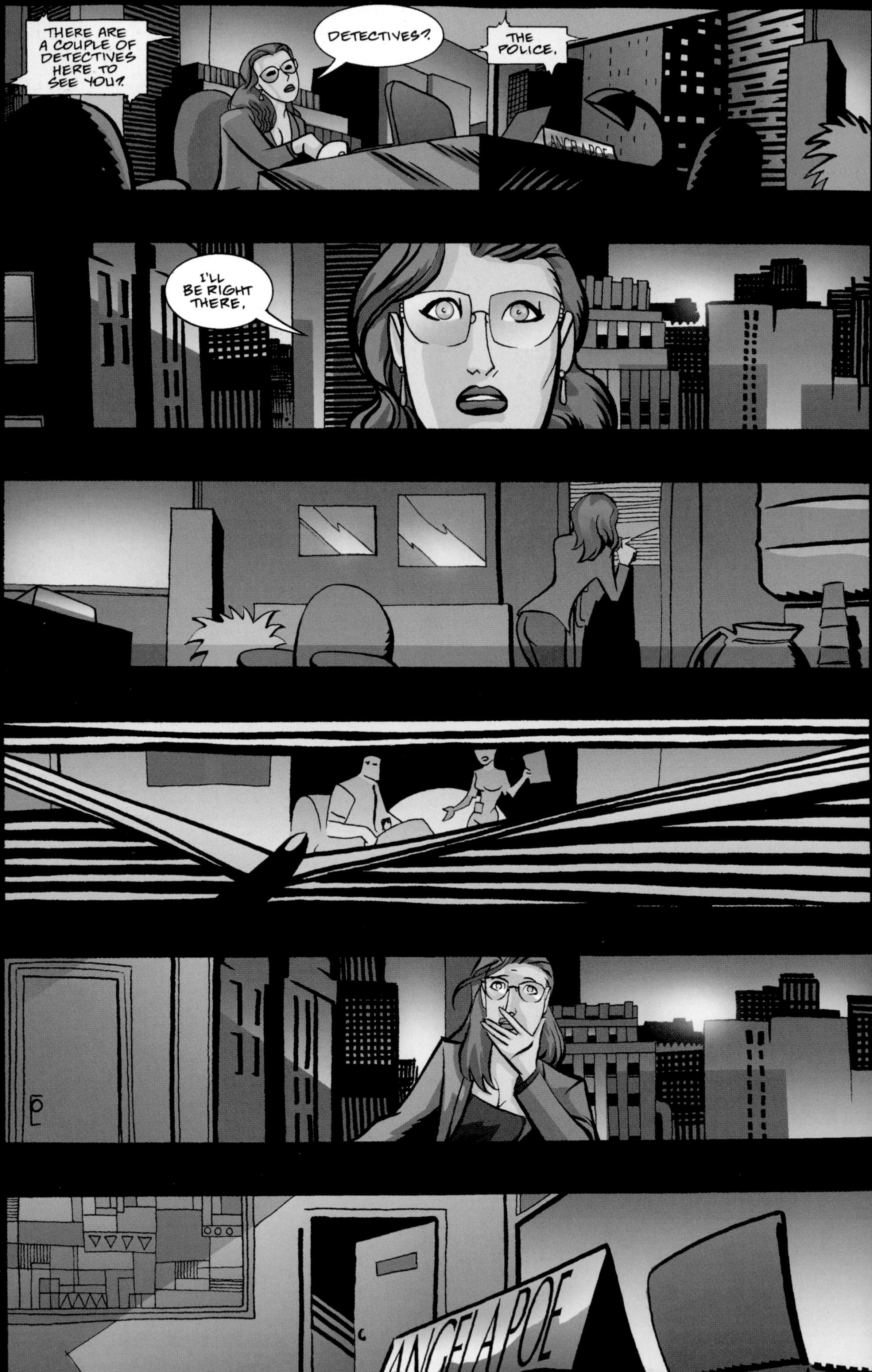
THERE ARE A COUPLE OF DETECTIVES HERE TO SEE YOU?
DETECTIVES?
THE POLICE.
I'LL BE RIGHT THERE.
ANGELA POE

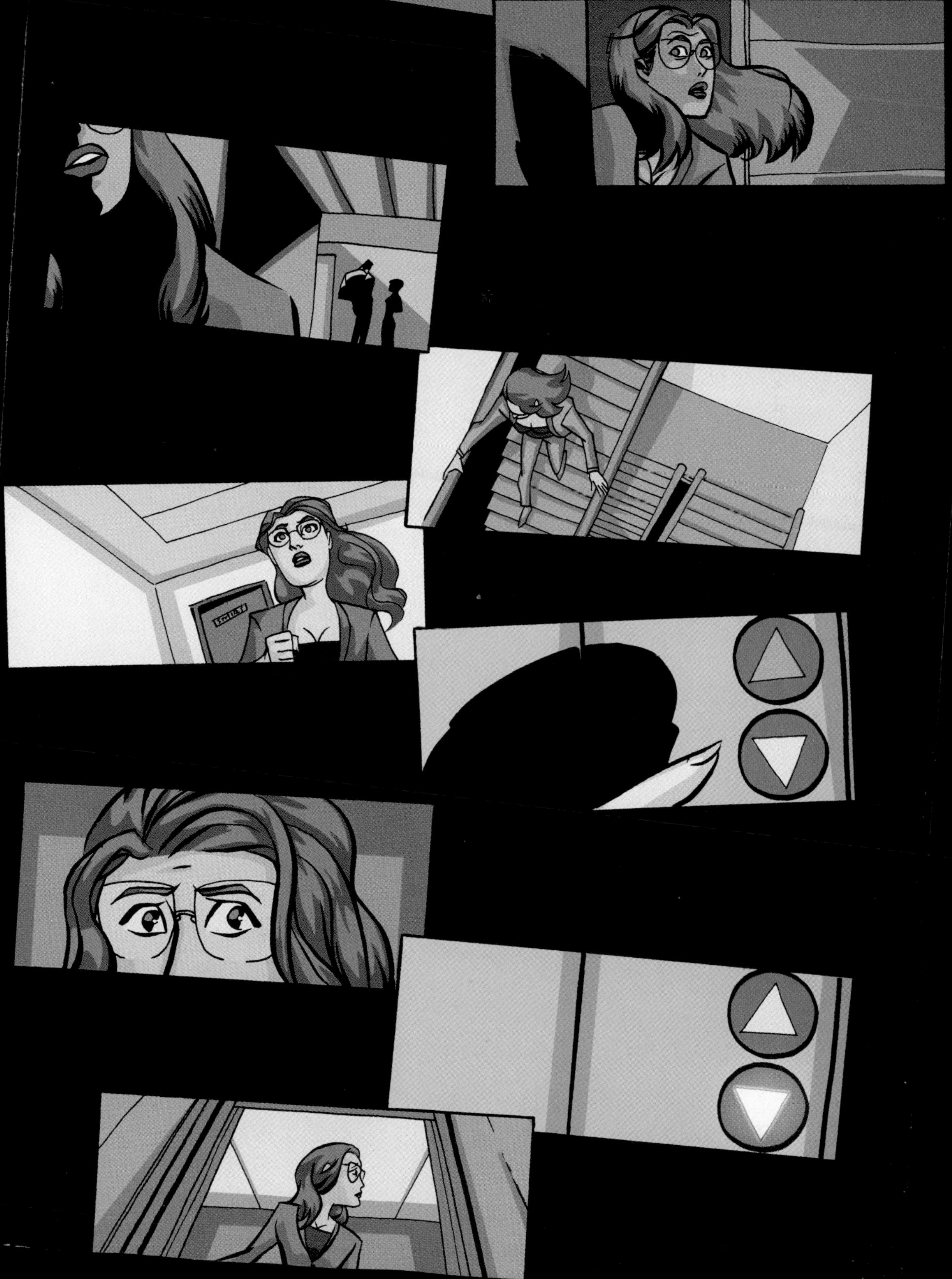

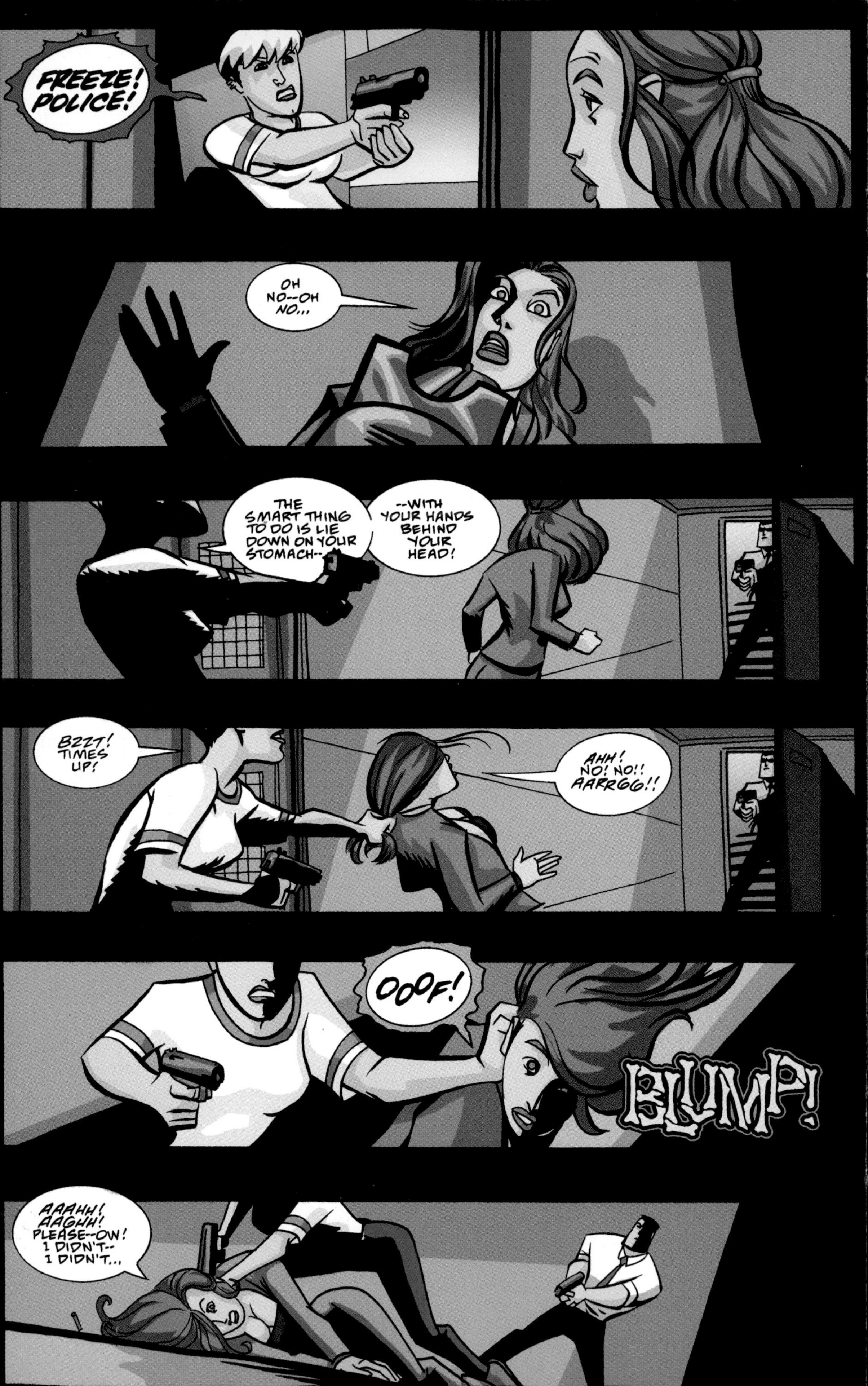
FREEZE! POLICE!
OH NO--OH NO...
THE SMART THING TO DO IS LIE DOWN ON YOUR STOMACH--
--WITH YOUR HANDS BEHIND YOUR HEAD!
BZZT! TIMES UP!
AHH! NO! NO!! AARRGG!!
OOOF!
BUMP!
AAAHH! AAGHH! PLEASE--OW! I DIDN'T-- I DIDN'T...

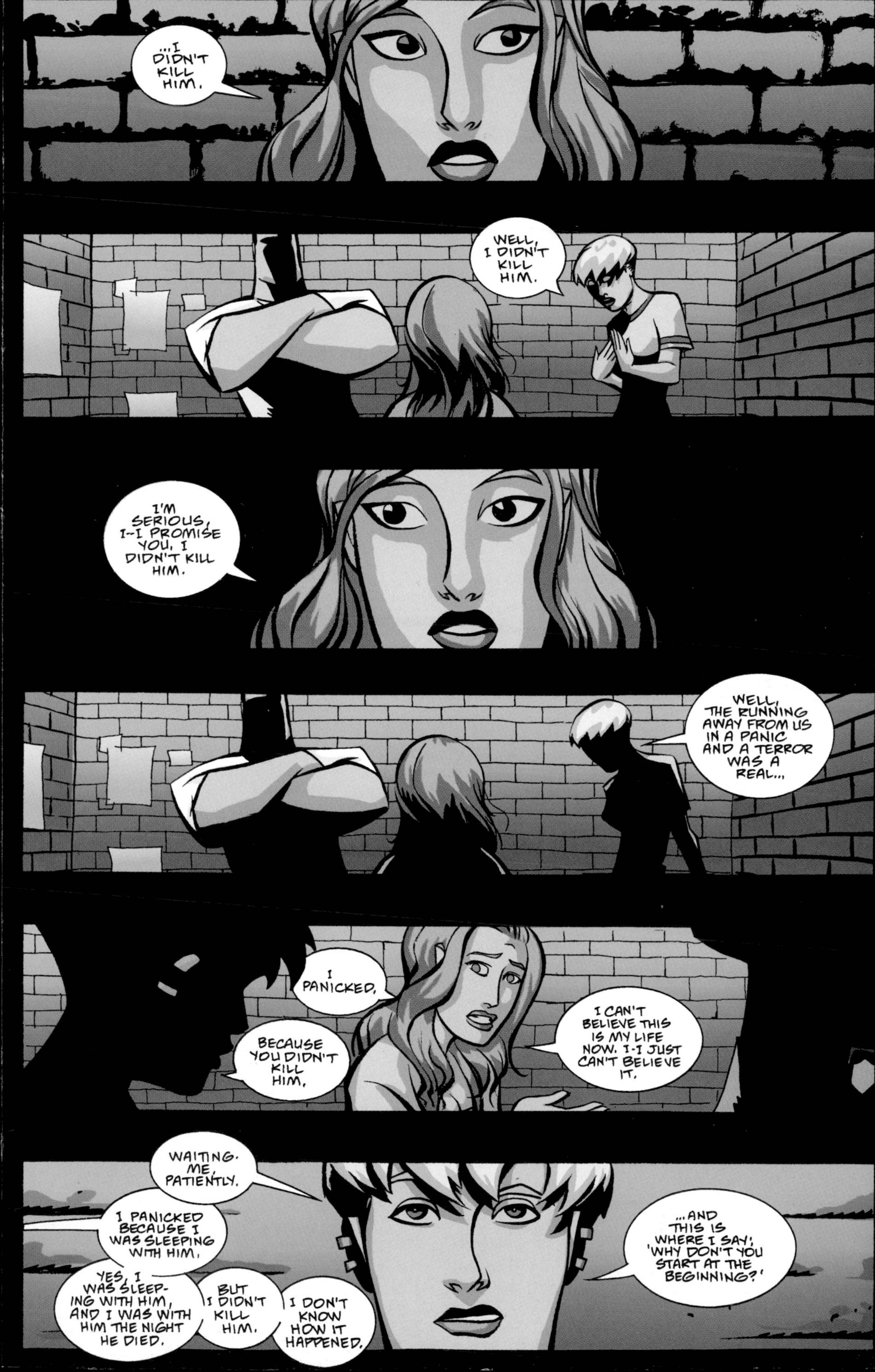
...I DIDN'T KILL HIM.
WELL, I DIDN'T KILL HIM.
I'M SERIOUS, I--I PROMISE YOU, I DIDN'T KILL HIM.
WELL, THE RUNNING AWAY FROM US IN A PANIC AND A TERROR WAS A REAL...
I PANICKED.
BECAUSE YOU DIDN'T KILL HIM.
I CAN'T BELIEVE THIS IS MY LIFE NOW. I-I JUST CAN'T BELIEVE IT.
WAITING. ME, PATIENTLY.
I PANICKED BECAUSE I WAS SLEEPING WITH HIM.
YES, I WAS SLEEPING WITH HIM, AND I WAS WITH HIM THE NIGHT HE DIED.
BUT I DIDN'T KILL HIM.
I DON'T KNOW HOW IT HAPPENED.
...AND THIS IS WHERE I SAY: 'WHY DON'T YOU START AT THE BEGINNING?'

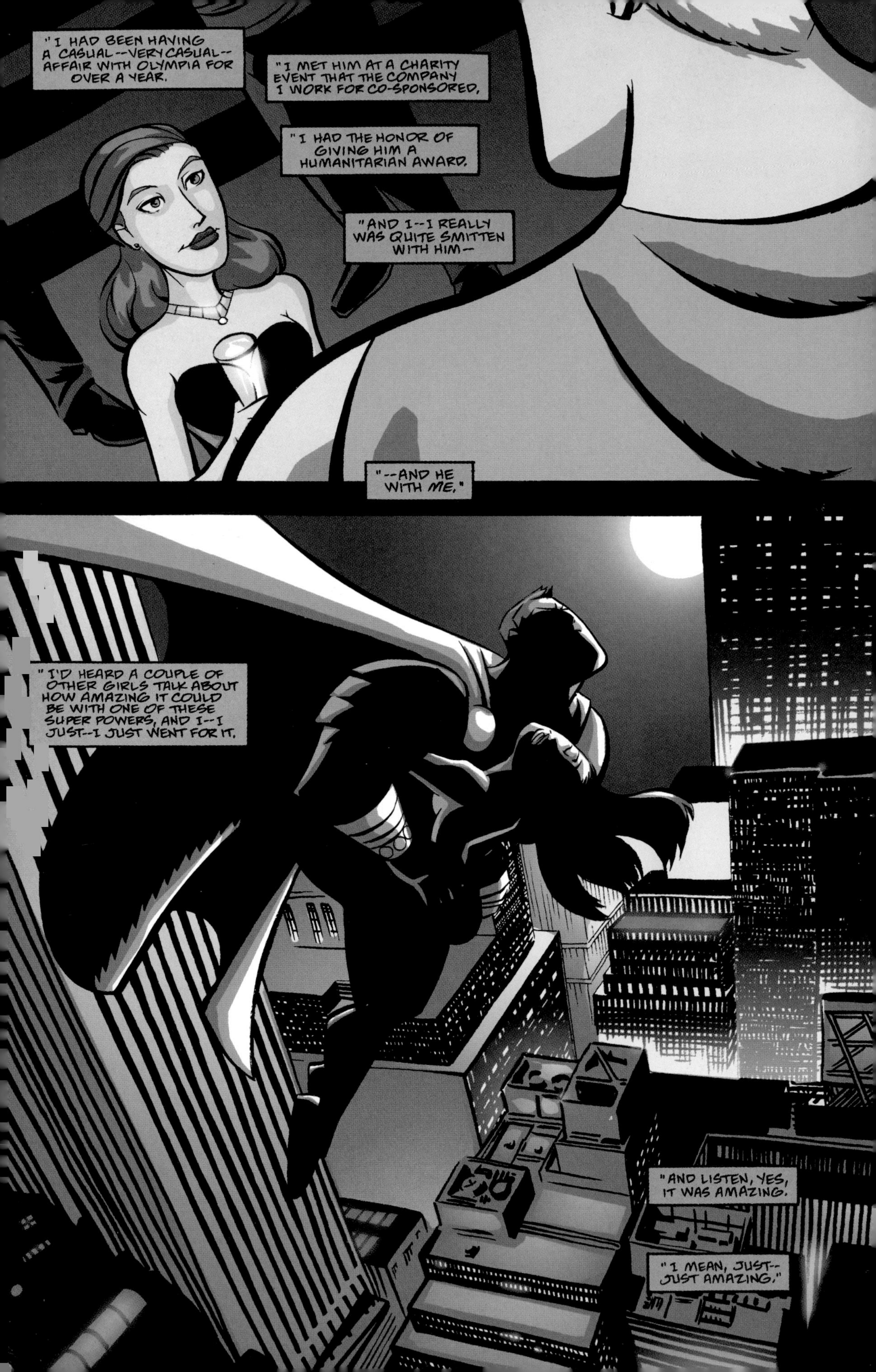
"I HAD BEEN HAVING A CASUAL--VERY CASUAL--AFFAIR WITH OLYMPIA FOR OVER A YEAR.
"I MET HIM AT A CHARITY EVENT THAT THE COMPANY I WORK FOR CO-SPONSORED.
"I HAD THE HONOR OF GIVING HIM A HUMANITARIAN AWARD.
"AND I--I REALLY WAS QUITE SMITTEN WITH HIM--
"--AND HE WITH ME."
"I'D HEARD A COUPLE OF OTHER GIRLS TALK ABOUT HOW AMAZING IT COULD BE WITH ONE OF THESE SUPER POWERS, AND I--I JUST--I JUST WENT FOR IT.
"AND LISTEN, YES, IT WAS AMAZING.
"I MEAN, JUST--JUST AMAZING."

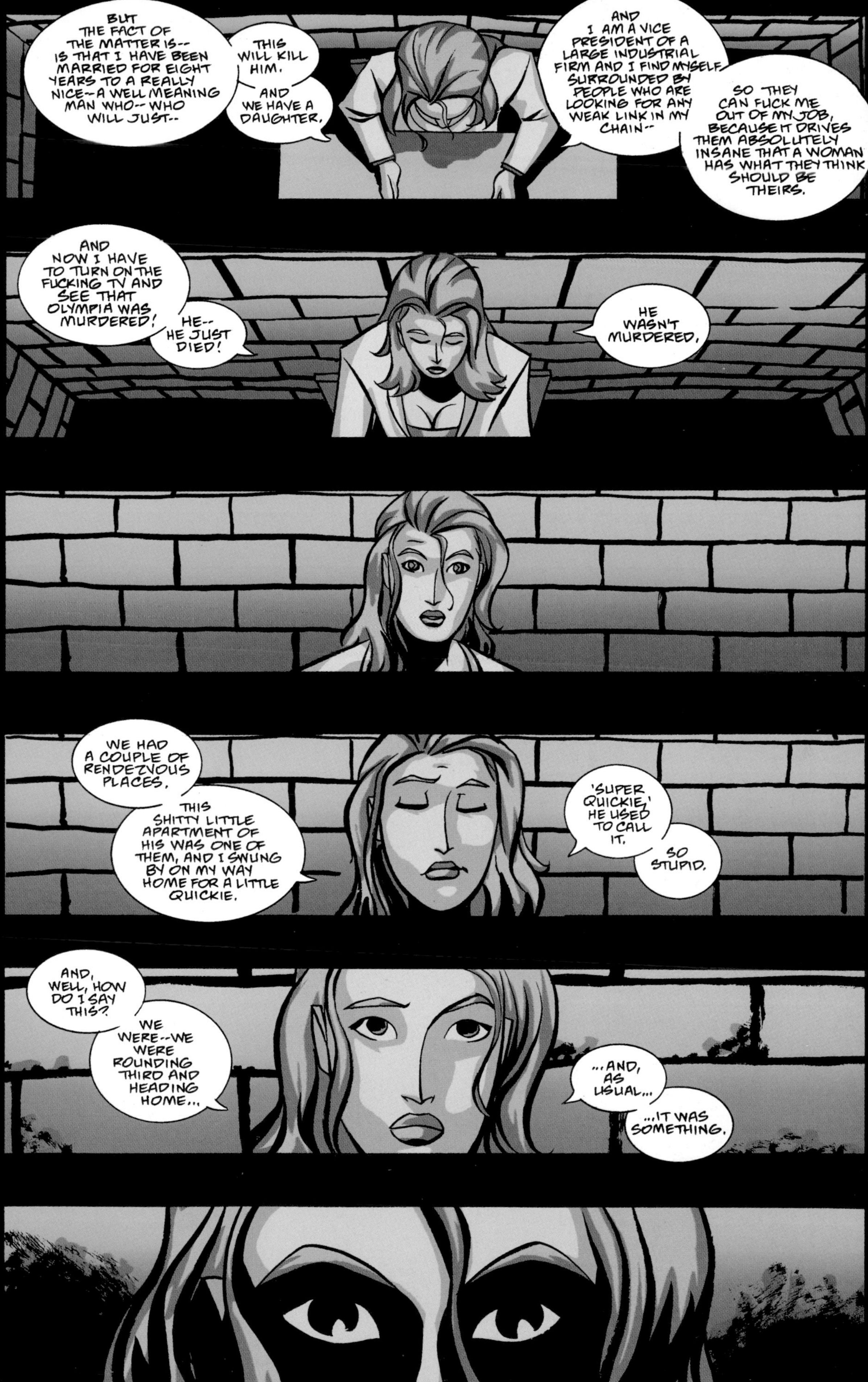
BUT THE FACT OF THE MATTER IS-- IS THAT I HAVE BEEN MARRIED FOR EIGHT YEARS TO A REALLY NICE--A WELL MEANING MAN WHO--WHO WILL JUST--
THIS WILL KILL HIM.
AND WE HAVE A DAUGHTER.
AND I AM A VICE PRESIDENT OF A LARGE INDUSTRIAL FIRM AND I FIND MYSELF SURROUNDED BY PEOPLE WHO ARE LOOKING FOR ANY WEAK LINK IN MY CHAIN--
SO THEY CAN FUCK ME OUT OF MY JOB, BECAUSE IT DRIVES THEM ABSOLUTELY INSANE THAT A WOMAN HAS WHAT THEY THINK SHOULD BE THEIRS.
AND NOW I HAVE TO TURN ON THE FUCKING TV AND SEE THAT OLYMPIA WAS MURDERED!
HE-- HE JUST DIED!
HE WASN'T MURDERED.
WE HAD A COUPLE OF RENDEZVOUS PLACES.
THIS SHITTY LITTLE APARTMENT OF HIS WAS ONE OF THEM, AND I SWUNG BY ON MY WAY HOME FOR A LITTLE QUICKIE.
'SUPER QUICKIE,' HE USED TO CALL IT.
SO STUPID.
AND, WELL, HOW DO I SAY THIS?
WE WERE--WE WERE ROUNDING THIRD AND HEADING HOME...
...AND, AS USUAL...
...IT WAS SOMETHING.

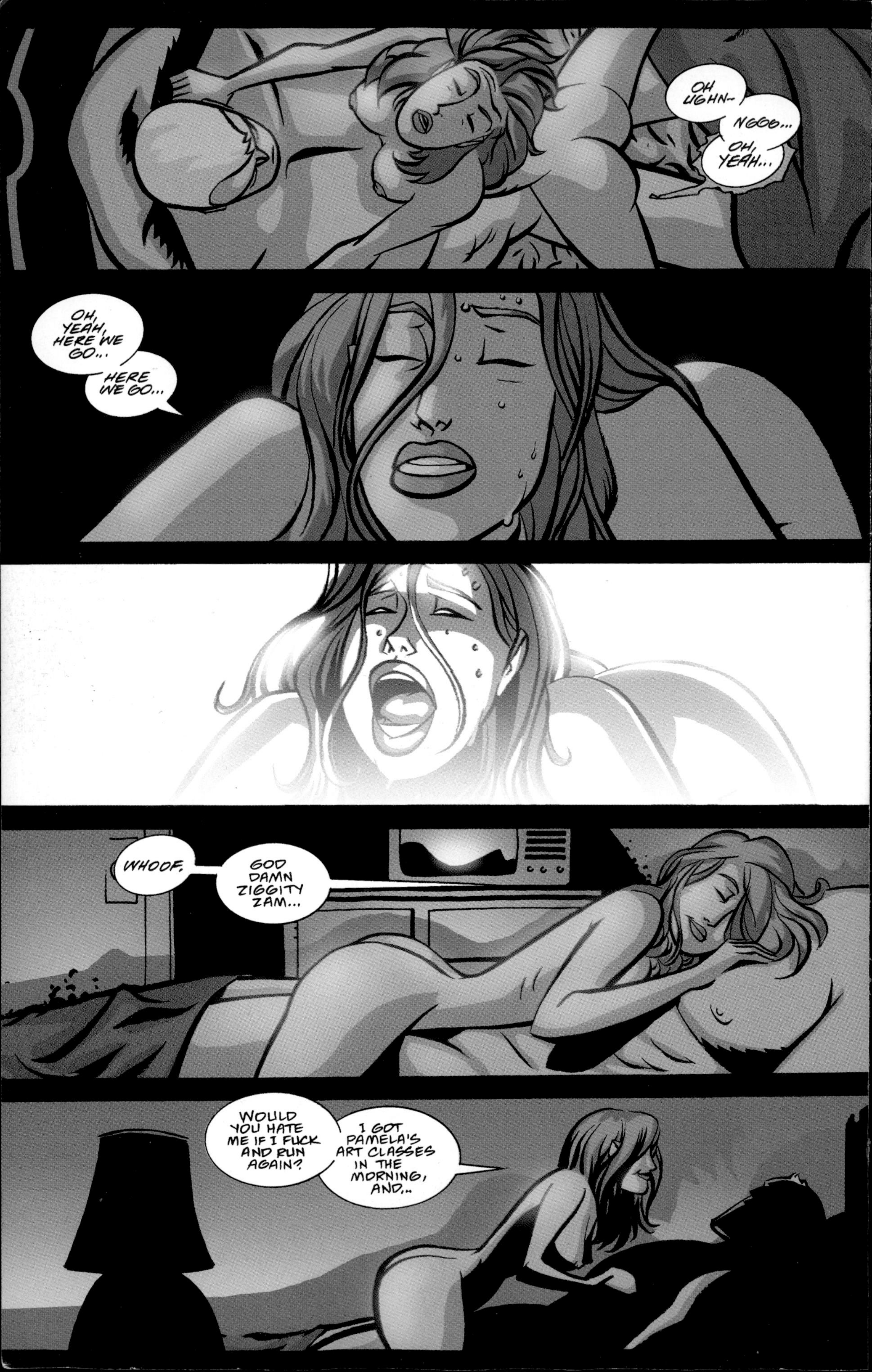
OH UGHN--
NGGG...
OH, YEAH...
OH, YEAH, HERE WE GO...
HERE WE GO...
WHOOF.
GOD DAMN ZIGGITY ZAM...
WOULD YOU HATE ME IF I FUCK AND RUN AGAIN?
I GOT PAMELA'S ART CLASSES IN THE MORNING, AND..

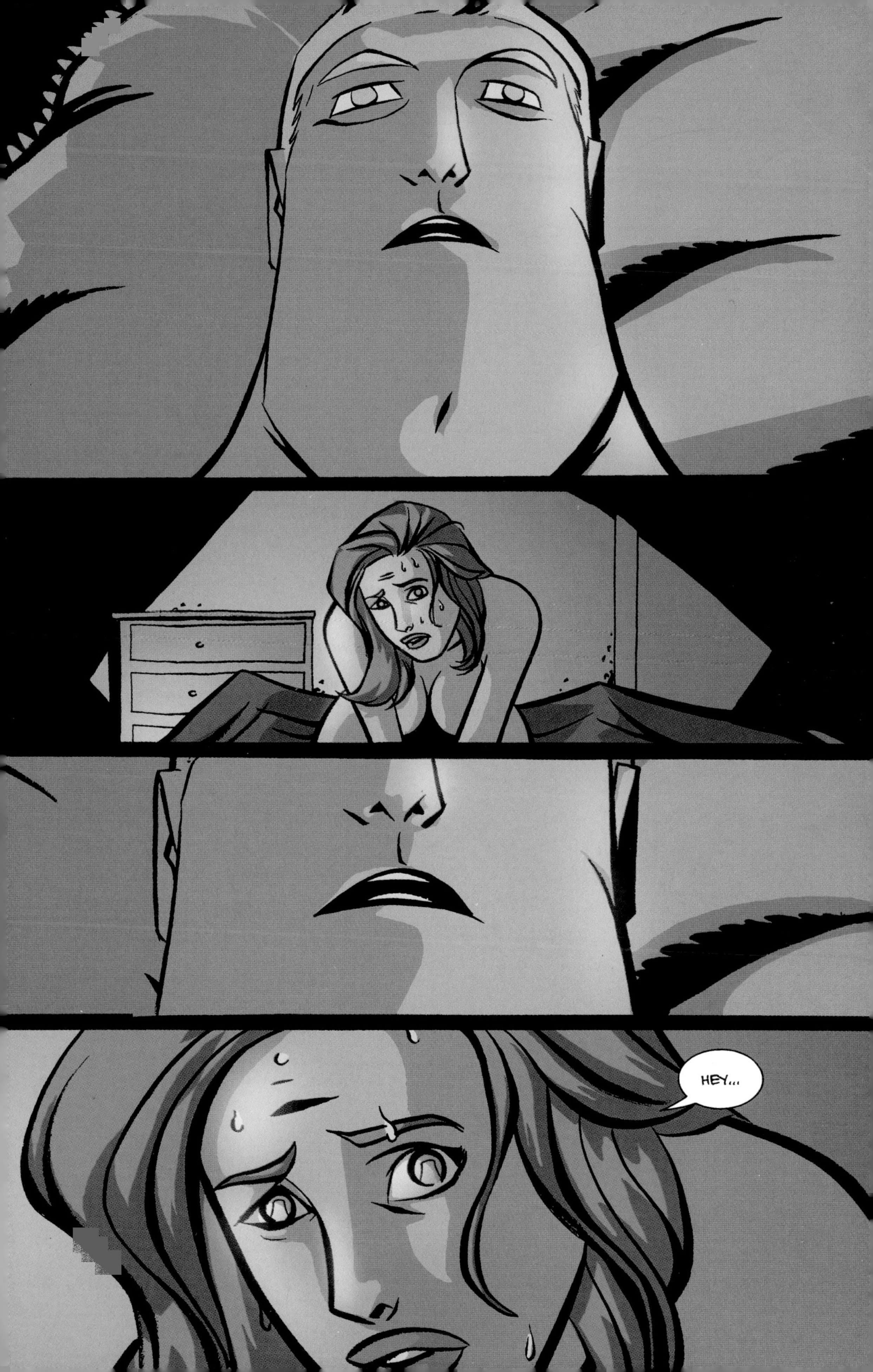
HEY...

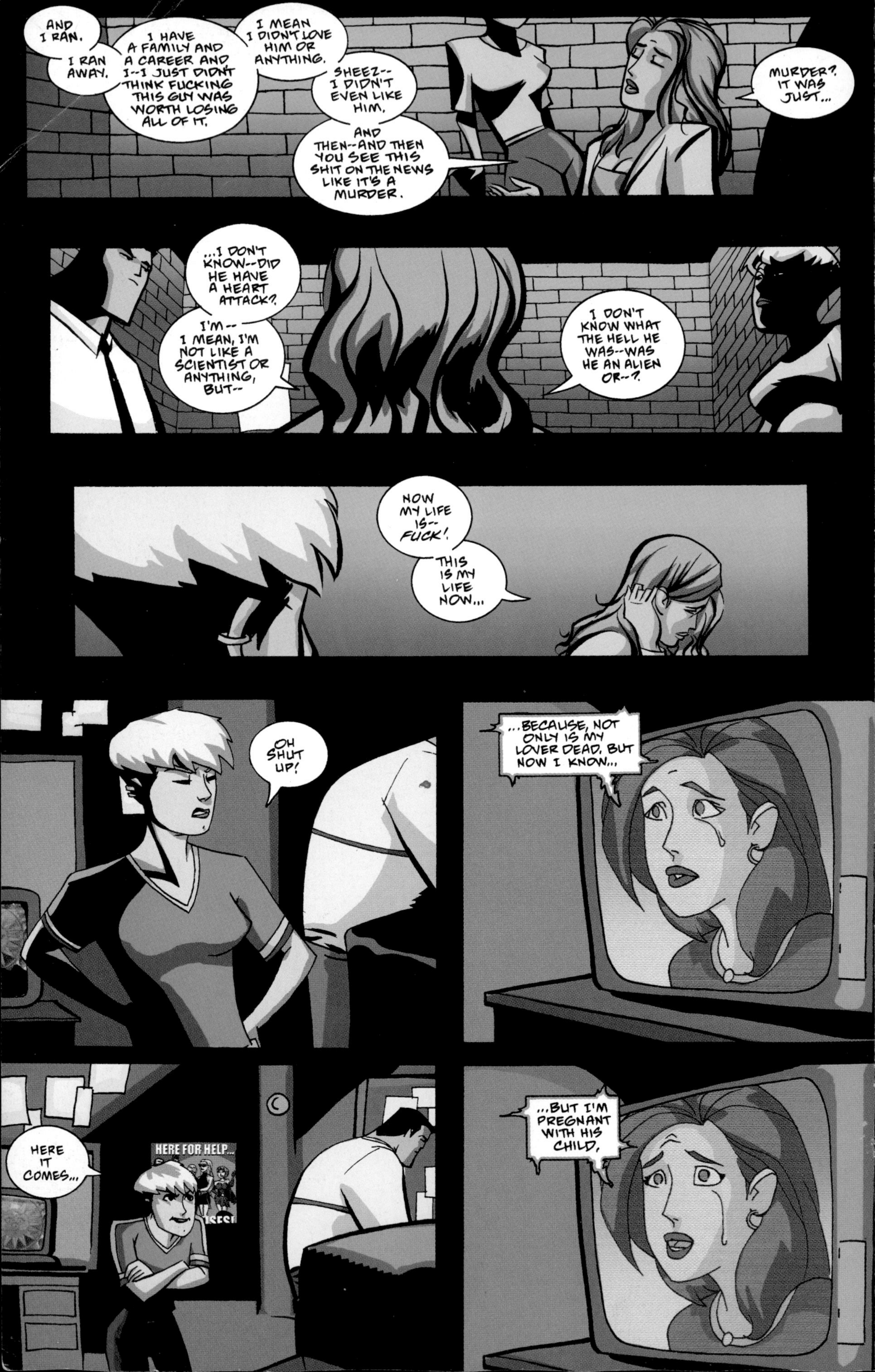
AND I RAN.
I RAN AWAY.
I HAVE A FAMILY AND A CAREER AND I--I JUST DIDN'T THINK FUCKING THIS GUY WAS WORTH LOSING ALL OF IT.
I MEAN I DIDN'T LOVE HIM OR ANYTHING.
SHEEZ-- I DIDN'T EVEN LIKE HIM.
AND THEN--AND THEN YOU SEE THIS SHIT ON THE NEWS LIKE IT'S A MURDER.
MURDER? IT WAS JUST...
...I DON'T KNOW--DID HE HAVE A HEART ATTACK?
I'M-- I MEAN, I'M NOT LIKE A SCIENTIST OR ANYTHING, BUT--
I DON'T KNOW WHAT THE HELL HE WAS--WAS HE AN ALIEN OR--?
NOW MY LIFE IS-- FUCK!
THIS IS MY LIFE NOW...
OH SHUT UP!
...BECAUSE, NOT ONLY IS MY LOVER DEAD, BUT NOW I KNOW...
HERE IT COMES...
HERE FOR HELP...
...BUT I'M PREGNANT WITH HIS CHILD.

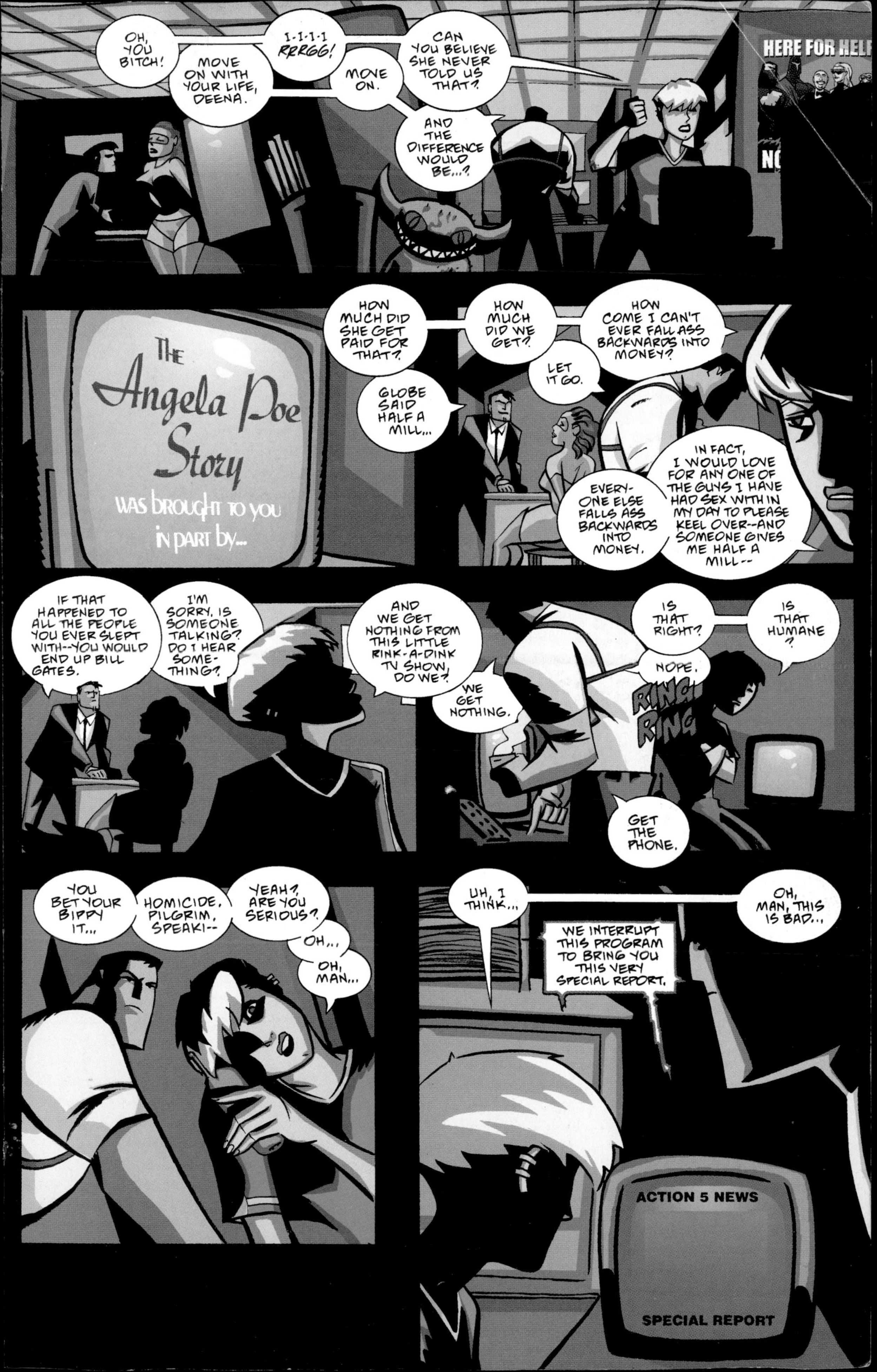
OH, YOU BITCH!
MOVE ON WITH YOUR LIFE, DEENA.
I-I-I-I RRRGG!
MOVE ON.
CAN YOU BELIEVE SHE NEVER TOLD US THAT?
AND THE DIFFERENCE WOULD BE...?
HERE FOR HEL
The Angela Poe Story was brought to you in part by...
HOW MUCH DID SHE GET PAID FOR THAT?
GLOBE SAID HALF A MILL...
HOW MUCH DID WE GET?
LET IT GO.
HOW COME I CAN'T EVER FALL ASS BACKWARDS INTO MONEY?
EVERY-ONE ELSE FALLS ASS BACKWARDS INTO MONEY.
IN FACT, I WOULD LOVE FOR ANY ONE OF THE GUYS I HAVE HAD SEX WITH IN MY DAY TO PLEASE KEEL OVER--AND SOMEONE GIVES ME HALF A MILL--
IF THAT HAPPENED TO ALL THE PEOPLE YOU EVER SLEPT WITH--YOU WOULD END UP BILL GATES.
I'M SORRY, IS SOMEONE TALKING? DO I HEAR SOME-THING?
AND WE GET NOTHING FROM THIS LITTLE RINK-A-DINK TV SHOW, DO WE?
WE GET NOTHING.
IS THAT RIGHT?
IS THAT HUMANE?
NOPE.
RING RING
GET THE PHONE.
YOU BET YOUR BIPPY IT...
HOMICIDE, PILGRIM, SPEAKI--
YEAH? ARE YOU SERIOUS?
OH...
OH, MAN...
UH, I THINK...
OH, MAN, THIS IS BAD...
WE INTERRUPT THIS PROGRAM TO BRING YOU THIS VERY SPECIAL REPORT.
ACTION 5 NEWS
SPECIAL REPORT

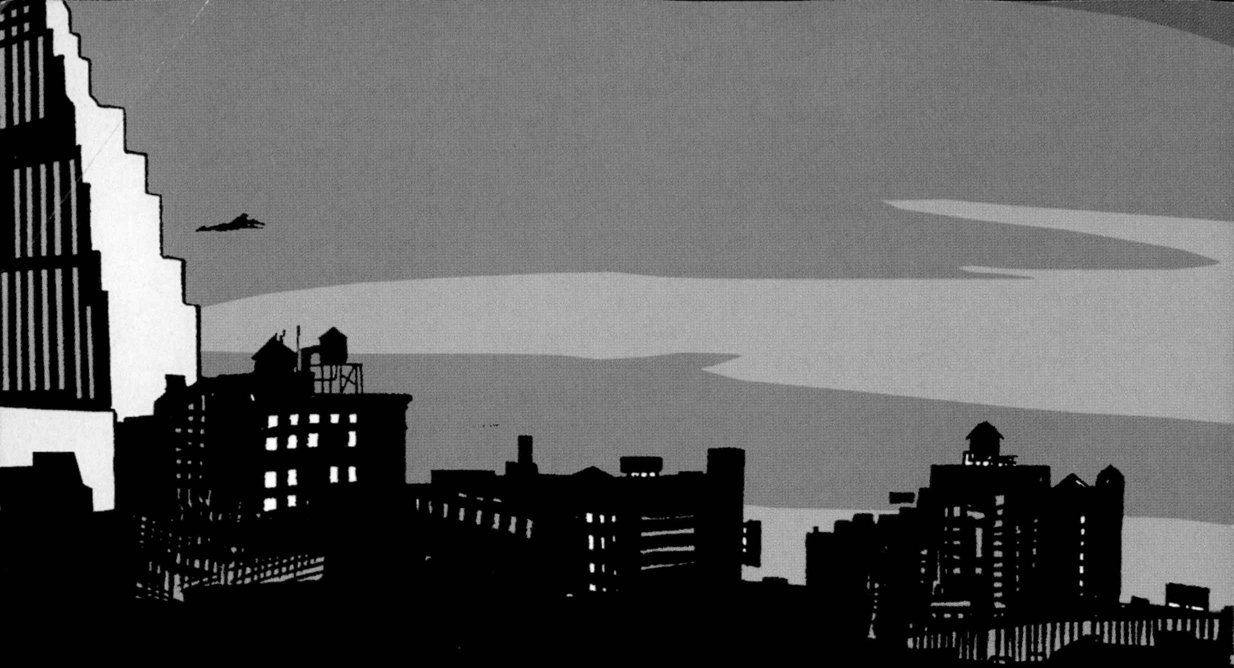

RIDE ALONG

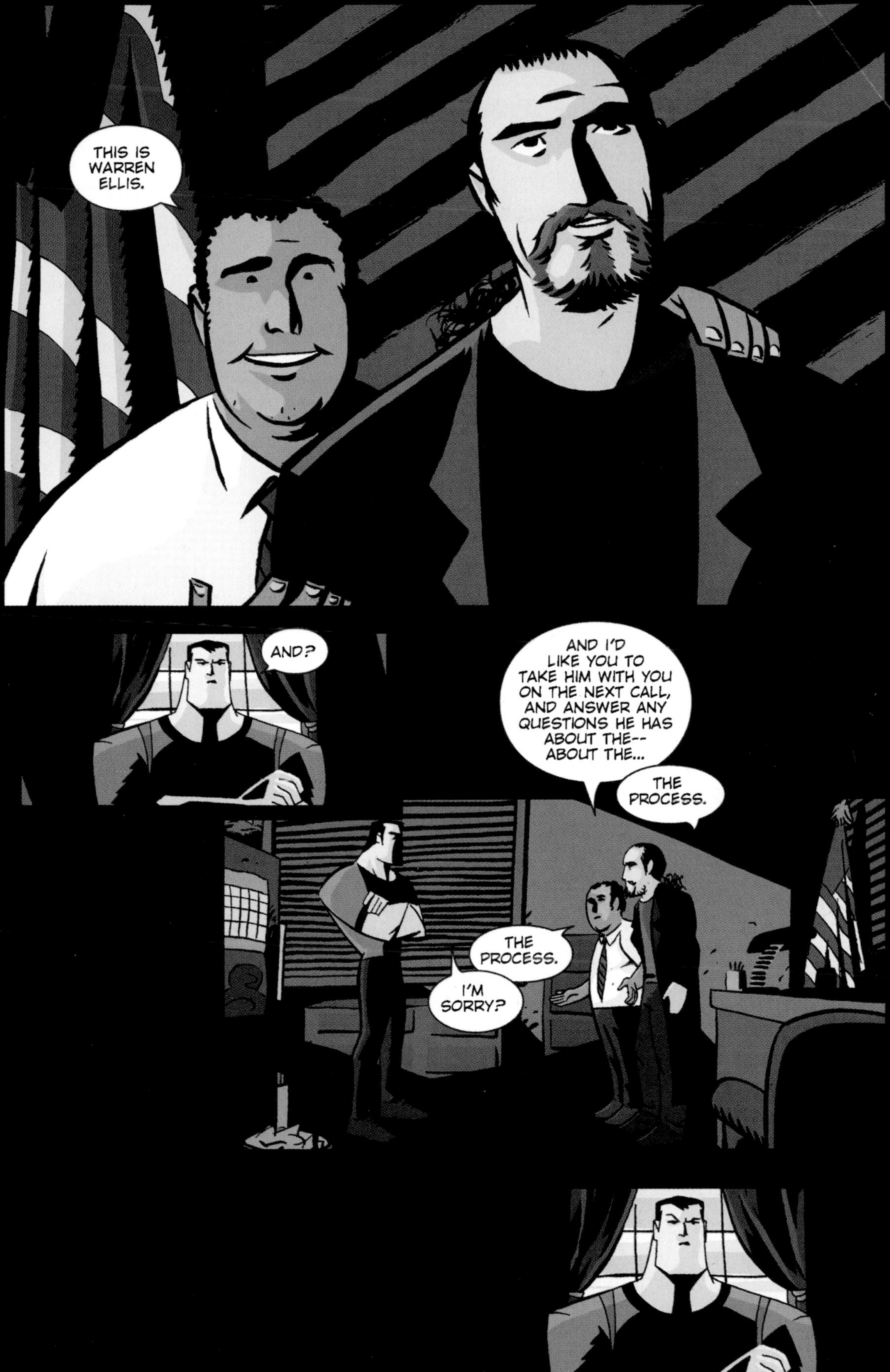
THIS IS WARREN ELLIS.
AND?
AND I'D LIKE YOU TO TAKE HIM WITH YOU ON THE NEXT CALL, AND ANSWER ANY QUESTIONS HE HAS ABOUT THE-- ABOUT THE...
THE PROCESS.
THE PROCESS.
I'M SORRY?

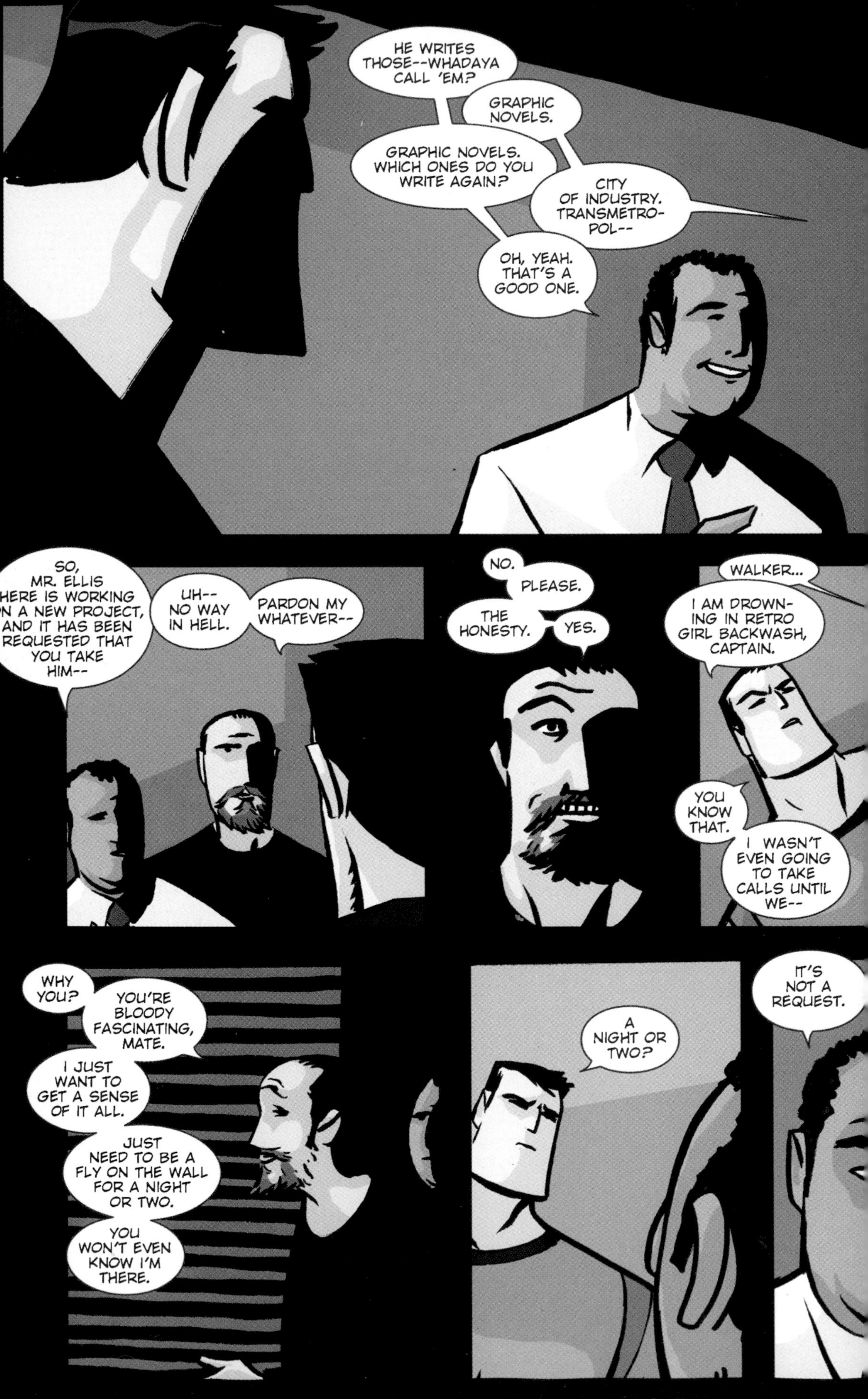
HE WRITES THOSE--WHADAYA CALL 'EM?
GRAPHIC NOVELS.
GRAPHIC NOVELS. WHICH ONES DO YOU WRITE AGAIN?
CITY OF INDUSTRY. TRANSMETRO-POL--
OH, YEAH. THAT'S A GOOD ONE.
SO, MR. ELLIS HERE IS WORKING ON A NEW PROJECT, AND IT HAS BEEN REQUESTED THAT YOU TAKE HIM--
UH-- NO WAY IN HELL.
PARDON MY WHATEVER--
NO.
PLEASE.
THE HONESTY.
YES.
WALKER...
I AM DROWNING IN RETRO GIRL BACKWASH, CAPTAIN.
YOU KNOW THAT.
I WASN'T EVEN GOING TO TAKE CALLS UNTIL WE--
WHY YOU?
YOU'RE BLOODY FASCINATING, MATE.
I JUST WANT TO GET A SENSE OF IT ALL.
JUST NEED TO BE A FLY ON THE WALL FOR A NIGHT OR TWO.
YOU WON'T EVEN KNOW I'M THERE.
A NIGHT OR TWO?
IT'S NOT A REQUEST.

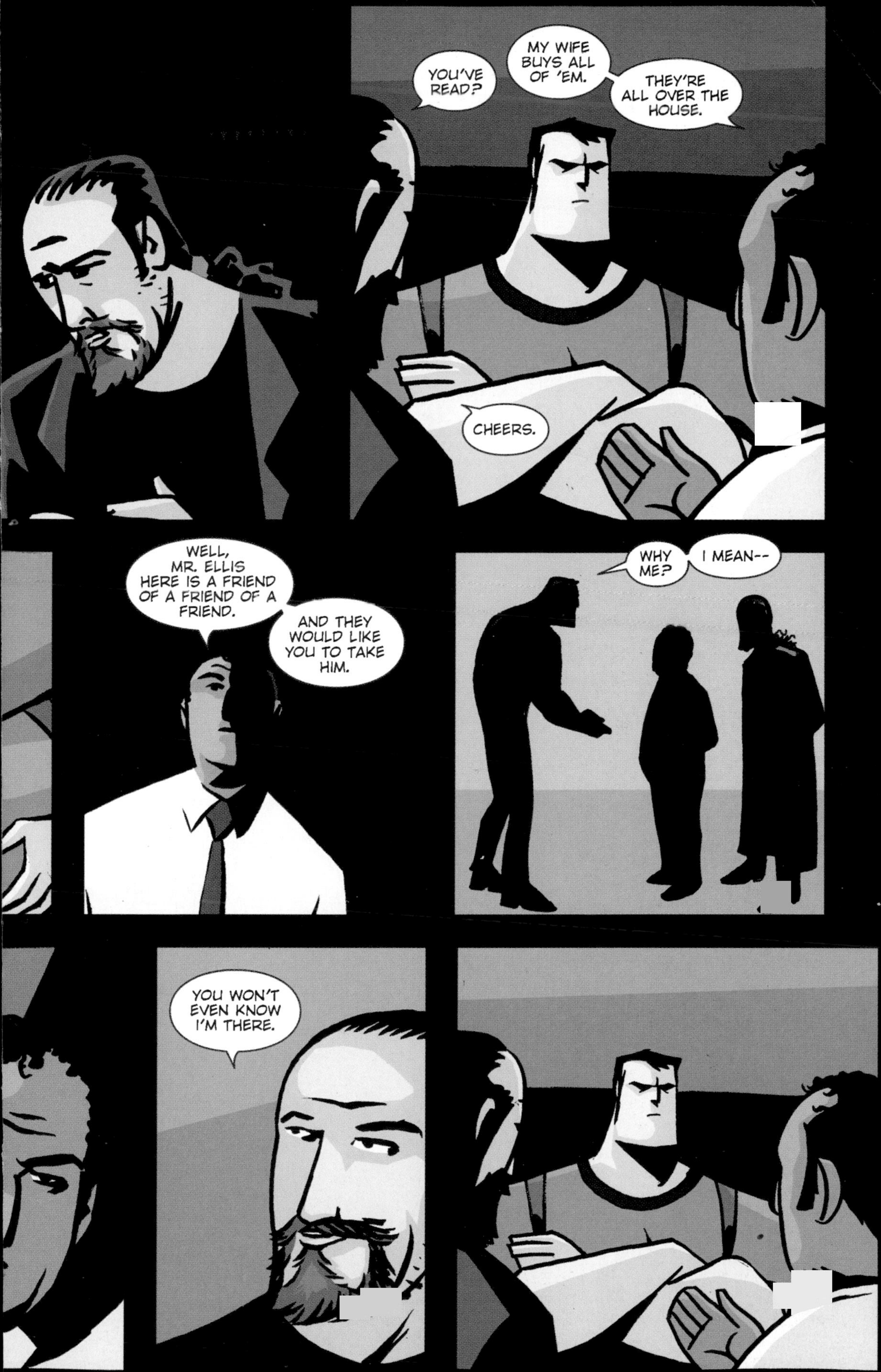
YOU'VE READ?
MY WIFE BUYS ALL OF 'EM.
THEY'RE ALL OVER THE HOUSE.
CHEERS.
WELL, MR. ELLIS HERE IS A FRIEND OF A FRIEND OF A FRIEND.
AND THEY WOULD LIKE YOU TO TAKE HIM.
WHY ME?
I MEAN--
YOU WON'T EVEN KNOW I'M THERE.

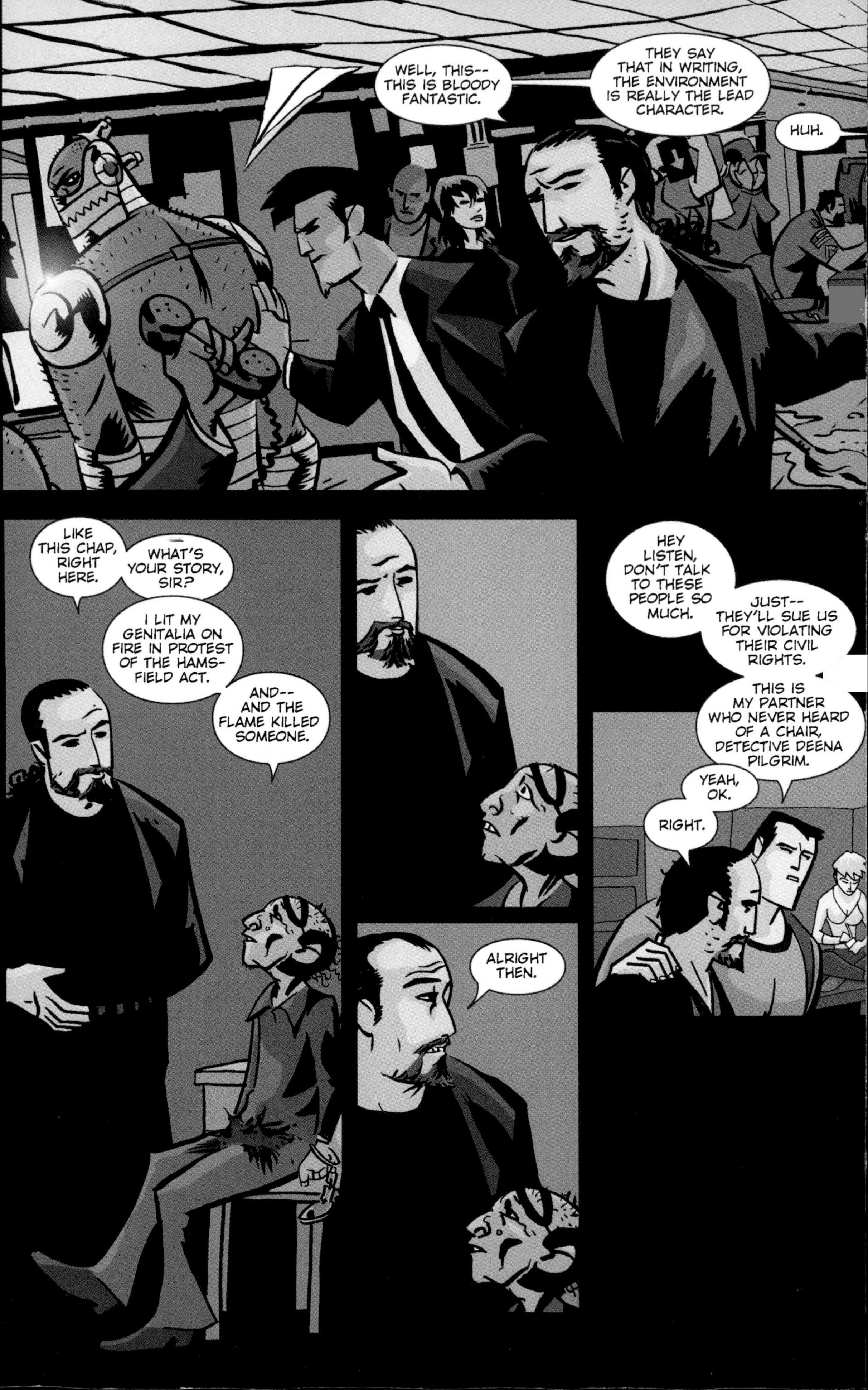
WELL, THIS--
THIS IS BLOODY FANTASTIC.
THEY SAY THAT IN WRITING, THE ENVIRONMENT IS REALLY THE LEAD CHARACTER.
HUH.
LIKE THIS CHAP, RIGHT HERE.
WHAT'S YOUR STORY, SIR?
I LIT MY GENITALIA ON FIRE IN PROTEST OF THE HAMS-FIELD ACT.
AND--
AND THE FLAME KILLED SOMEONE.
ALRIGHT THEN.
HEY LISTEN, DON'T TALK TO THESE PEOPLE SO MUCH.
JUST--
THEY'LL SUE US FOR VIOLATING THEIR CIVIL RIGHTS.
THIS IS MY PARTNER WHO NEVER HEARD OF A CHAIR, DETECTIVE DEENA PILGRIM.
YEAH, OK.
RIGHT.

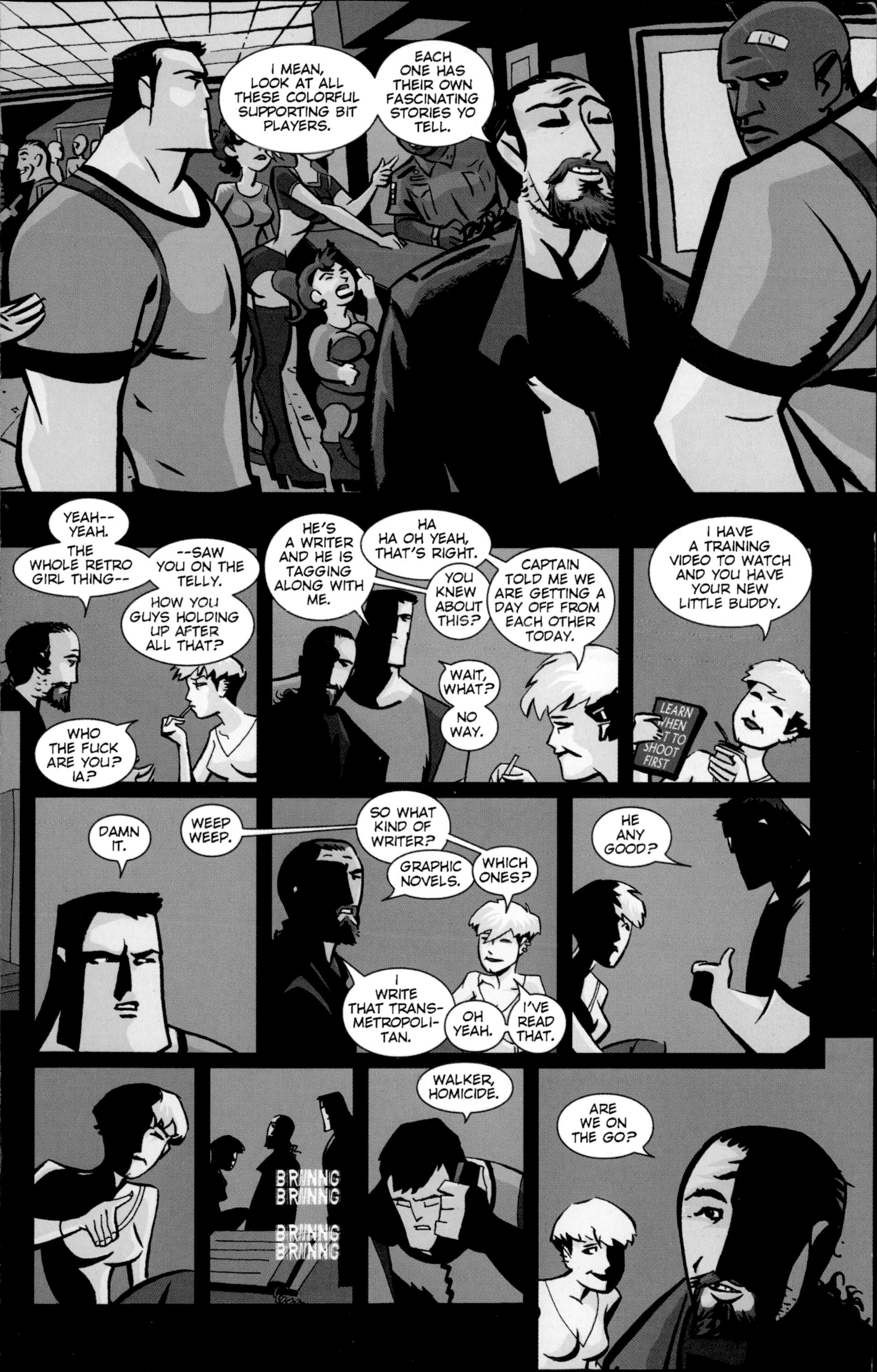

I MEAN, LOOK AT ALL THESE COLORFUL SUPPORTING BIT PLAYERS.
EACH ONE HAS THEIR OWN FASCINATING STORIES YO TELL.
YEAH-- YEAH.
THE WHOLE RETRO GIRL THING--
--SAW YOU ON THE TELLY.
HOW YOU GUYS HOLDING UP AFTER ALL THAT?
WHO THE FUCK ARE YOU? IA?
HE'S A WRITER AND HE IS TAGGING ALONG WITH ME.
HA HA OH YEAH, THAT'S RIGHT.
YOU KNEW ABOUT THIS?
CAPTAIN TOLD ME WE ARE GETTING A DAY OFF FROM EACH OTHER TODAY.
WAIT, WHAT?
NO WAY.
I HAVE A TRAINING VIDEO TO WATCH AND YOU HAVE YOUR NEW LITTLE BUDDY.
LEARN WHEN NOT TO SHOOT FIRST
DAMN IT.
WEEP WEEP.
SO WHAT KIND OF WRITER?
GRAPHIC NOVELS.
WHICH ONES?
I WRITE THAT TRANS-METROPOLI-TAN.
OH YEAH.
I'VE READ THAT.
HE ANY GOOD?
BRIINNG BRIINNG
BRIINNG BRIINNG
WALKER, HOMICIDE.
ARE WE ON THE GO?

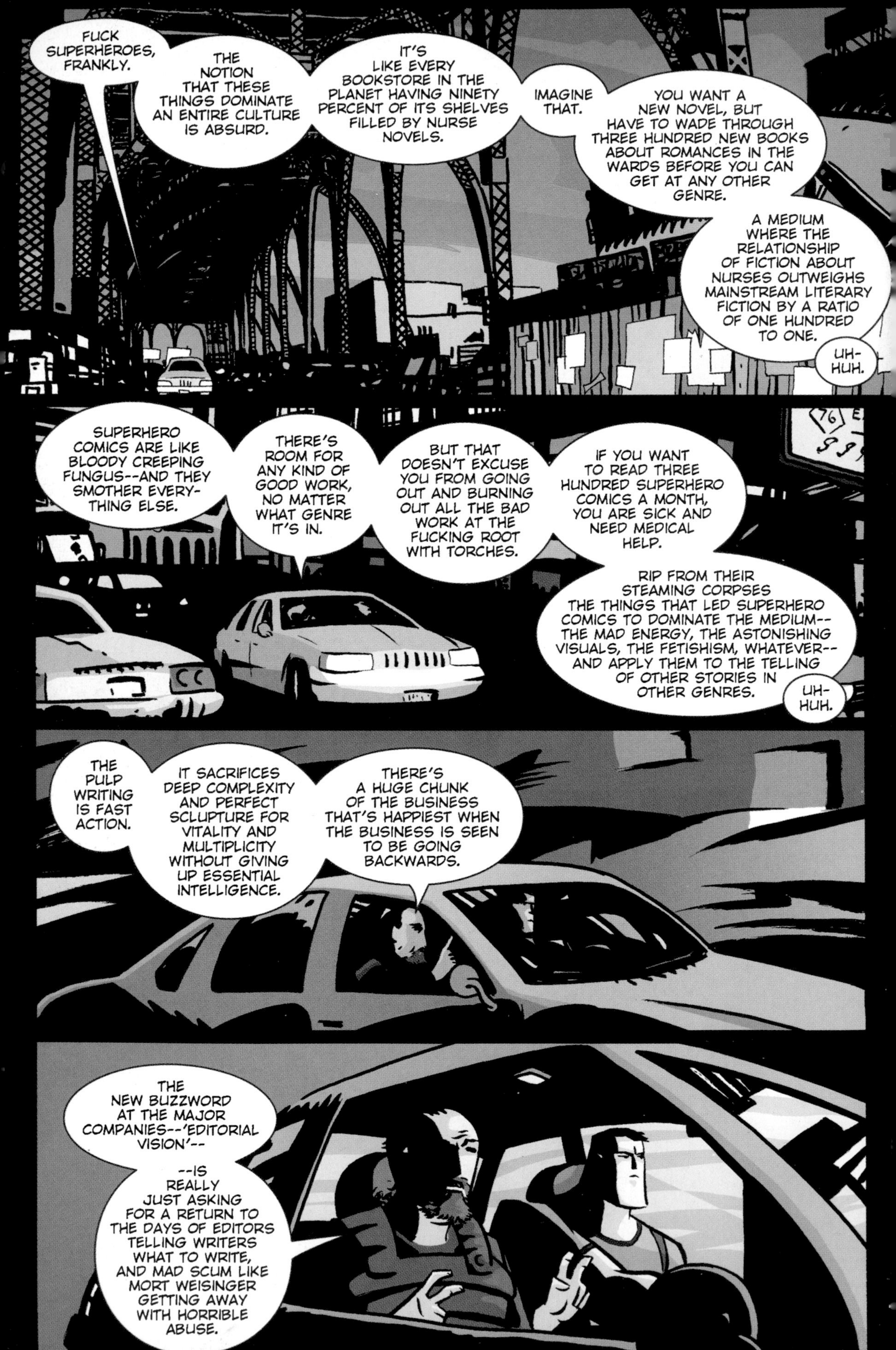
FUCK SUPERHEROES, FRANKLY.
THE NOTION THAT THESE THINGS DOMINATE AN ENTIRE CULTURE IS ABSURD.
IT'S LIKE EVERY BOOKSTORE IN THE PLANET HAVING NINETY PERCENT OF ITS SHELVES FILLED BY NURSE NOVELS.
IMAGINE THAT.
YOU WANT A NEW NOVEL, BUT HAVE TO WADE THROUGH THREE HUNDRED NEW BOOKS ABOUT ROMANCES IN THE WARDS BEFORE YOU CAN GET AT ANY OTHER GENRE.
A MEDIUM WHERE THE RELATIONSHIP OF FICTION ABOUT NURSES OUTWEIGHS MAINSTREAM LITERARY FICTION BY A RATIO OF ONE HUNDRED TO ONE.
UH-HUH.
SUPERHERO COMICS ARE LIKE BLOODY CREEPING FUNGUS--AND THEY SMOTHER EVERY-THING ELSE.
THERE'S ROOM FOR ANY KIND OF GOOD WORK, NO MATTER WHAT GENRE IT'S IN.
BUT THAT DOESN'T EXCUSE YOU FROM GOING OUT AND BURNING OUT ALL THE BAD WORK AT THE FUCKING ROOT WITH TORCHES.
IF YOU WANT TO READ THREE HUNDRED SUPERHERO COMICS A MONTH, YOU ARE SICK AND NEED MEDICAL HELP.
RIP FROM THEIR STEAMING CORPSES THE THINGS THAT LED SUPERHERO COMICS TO DOMINATE THE MEDIUM--THE MAD ENERGY, THE ASTONISHING VISUALS, THE FETISHISM, WHATEVER--AND APPLY THEM TO THE TELLING OF OTHER STORIES IN OTHER GENRES.
UH-HUH.
THE PULP WRITING IS FAST ACTION.
IT SACRIFICES DEEP COMPLEXITY AND PERFECT SCLUPTURE FOR VITALITY AND MULTIPLICITY WITHOUT GIVING UP ESSENTIAL INTELLIGENCE.
THERE'S A HUGE CHUNK OF THE BUSINESS THAT'S HAPPIEST WHEN THE BUSINESS IS SEEN TO BE GOING BACKWARDS.
THE NEW BUZZWORD AT THE MAJOR COMPANIES--'EDITORIAL VISION'--
--IS REALLY JUST ASKING FOR A RETURN TO THE DAYS OF EDITORS TELLING WRITERS WHAT TO WRITE, AND MAD SCUM LIKE MORT WEISINGER GETTING AWAY WITH HORRIBLE ABUSE.

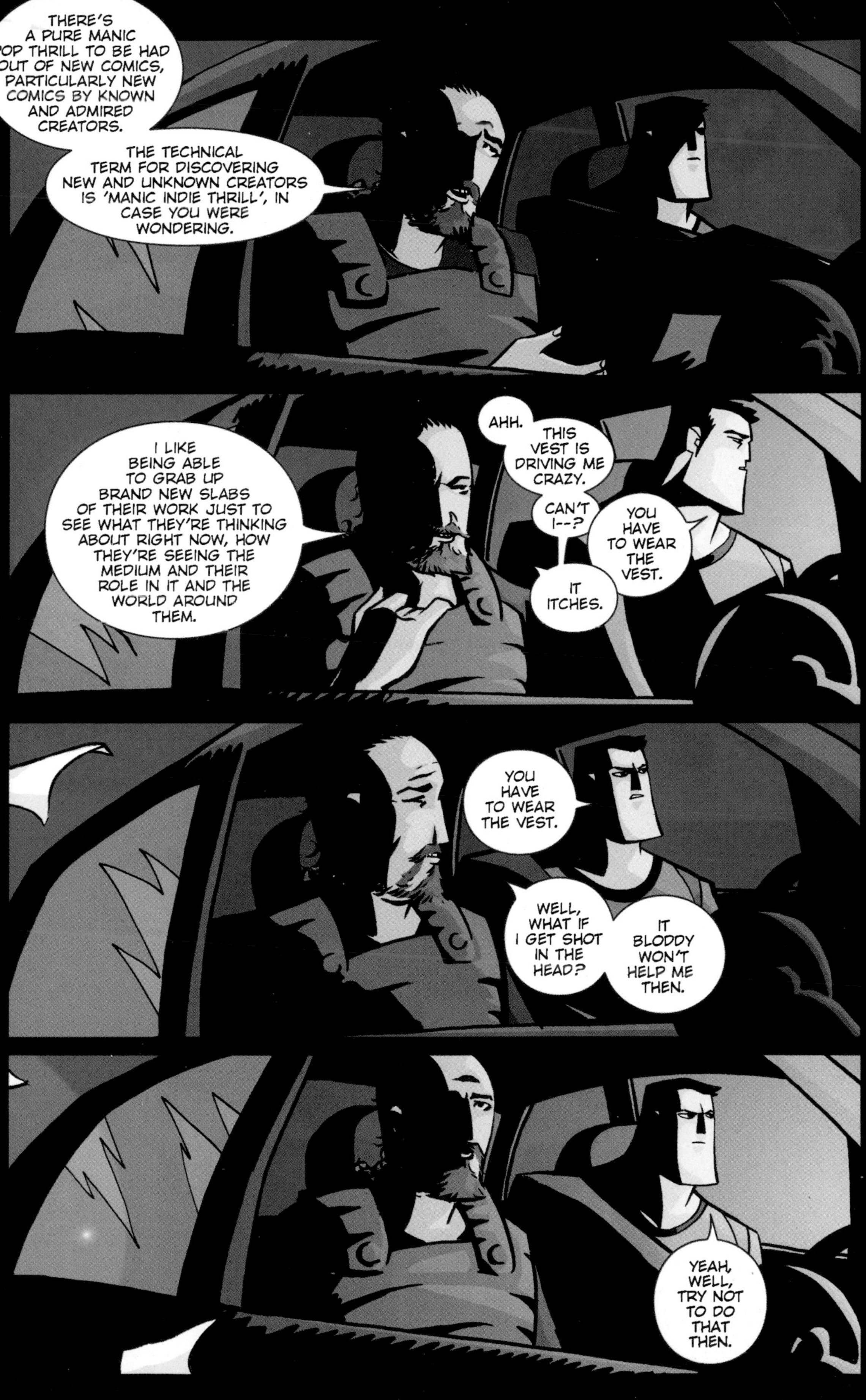
THERE'S A PURE MANIC POP THRILL TO BE HAD OUT OF NEW COMICS, PARTICULARLY NEW COMICS BY KNOWN AND ADMIRED CREATORS.
THE TECHNICAL TERM FOR DISCOVERING NEW AND UNKNOWN CREATORS IS 'MANIC INDIE THRILL', IN CASE YOU WERE WONDERING.
I LIKE BEING ABLE TO GRAB UP BRAND NEW SLABS OF THEIR WORK JUST TO SEE WHAT THEY'RE THINKING ABOUT RIGHT NOW, HOW THEY'RE SEEING THE MEDIUM AND THEIR ROLE IN IT AND THE WORLD AROUND THEM.
AHH.
THIS VEST IS DRIVING ME CRAZY.
CAN'T I--?
YOU HAVE TO WEAR THE VEST.
IT ITCHES.
YOU HAVE TO WEAR THE VEST.
WELL, WHAT IF I GET SHOT IN THE HEAD?
IT BLODDY WON'T HELP ME THEN.
YEAH, WELL, TRY NOT TO DO THAT THEN.

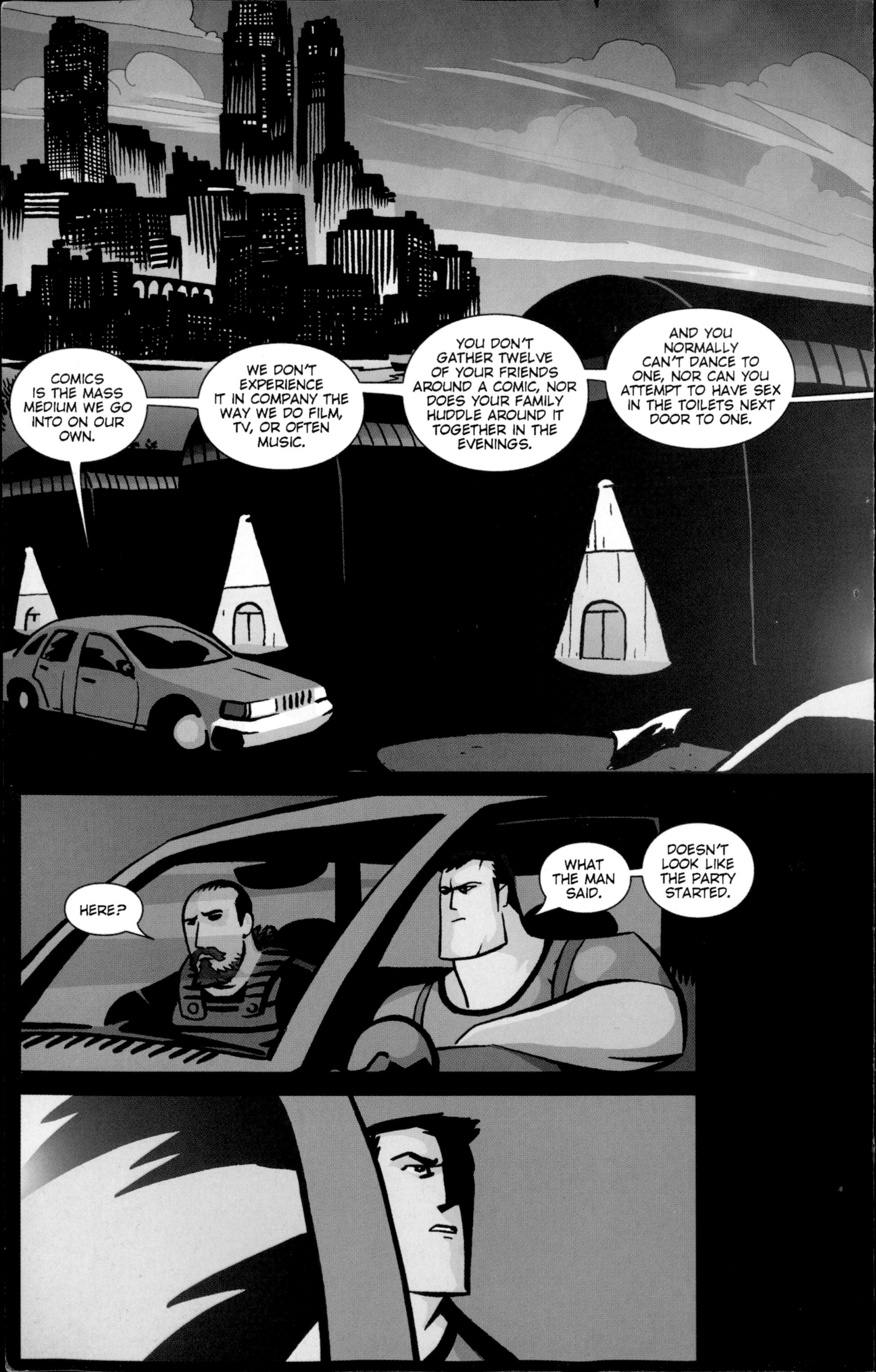
COMICS IS THE MASS MEDIUM WE GO INTO ON OUR OWN.
WE DON'T EXPERIENCE IT IN COMPANY THE WAY WE DO FILM, TV, OR OFTEN MUSIC.
YOU DON'T GATHER TWELVE OF YOUR FRIENDS AROUND A COMIC, NOR DOES YOUR FAMILY HUDDLE AROUND IT TOGETHER IN THE EVENINGS.
AND YOU NORMALLY CAN'T DANCE TO ONE, NOR CAN YOU ATTEMPT TO HAVE SEX IN THE TOILETS NEXT DOOR TO ONE.
HERE?
WHAT THE MAN SAID.
DOESN'T LOOK LIKE THE PARTY STARTED.

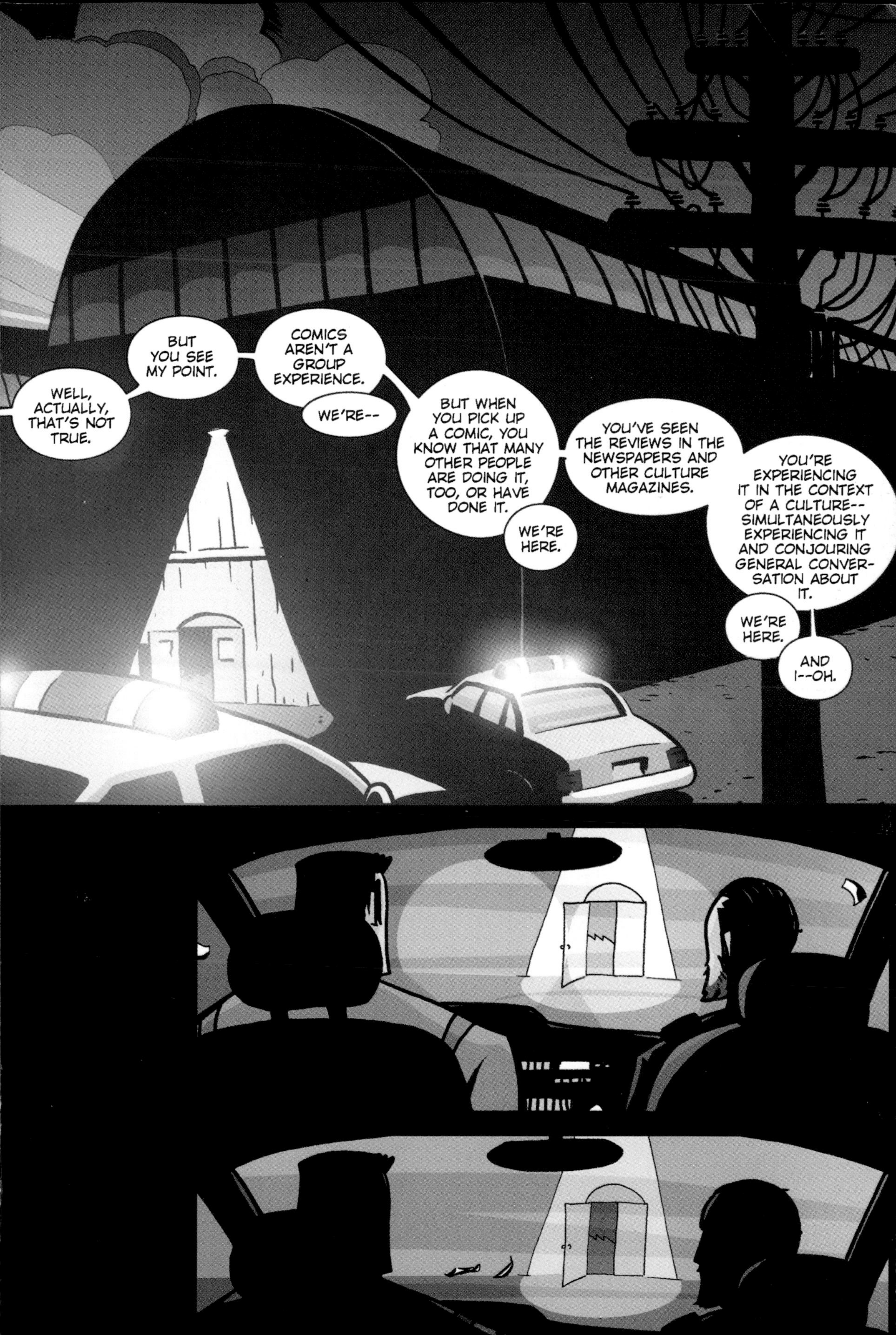
WELL, ACTUALLY, THAT'S NOT TRUE.
BUT YOU SEE MY POINT.
COMICS AREN'T A GROUP EXPERIENCE.
WE'RE--
BUT WHEN YOU PICK UP A COMIC, YOU KNOW THAT MANY OTHER PEOPLE ARE DOING IT, TOO, OR HAVE DONE IT.
YOU'VE SEEN THE REVIEWS IN THE NEWSPAPERS AND OTHER CULTURE MAGAZINES.
WE'RE HERE.
YOU'RE EXPERIENCING IT IN THE CONTEXT OF A CULTURE--SIMULTANEOUSLY EXPERIENCING IT AND CONJOURING GENERAL CONVERSATION ABOUT IT.
WE'RE HERE.
AND I--OH.

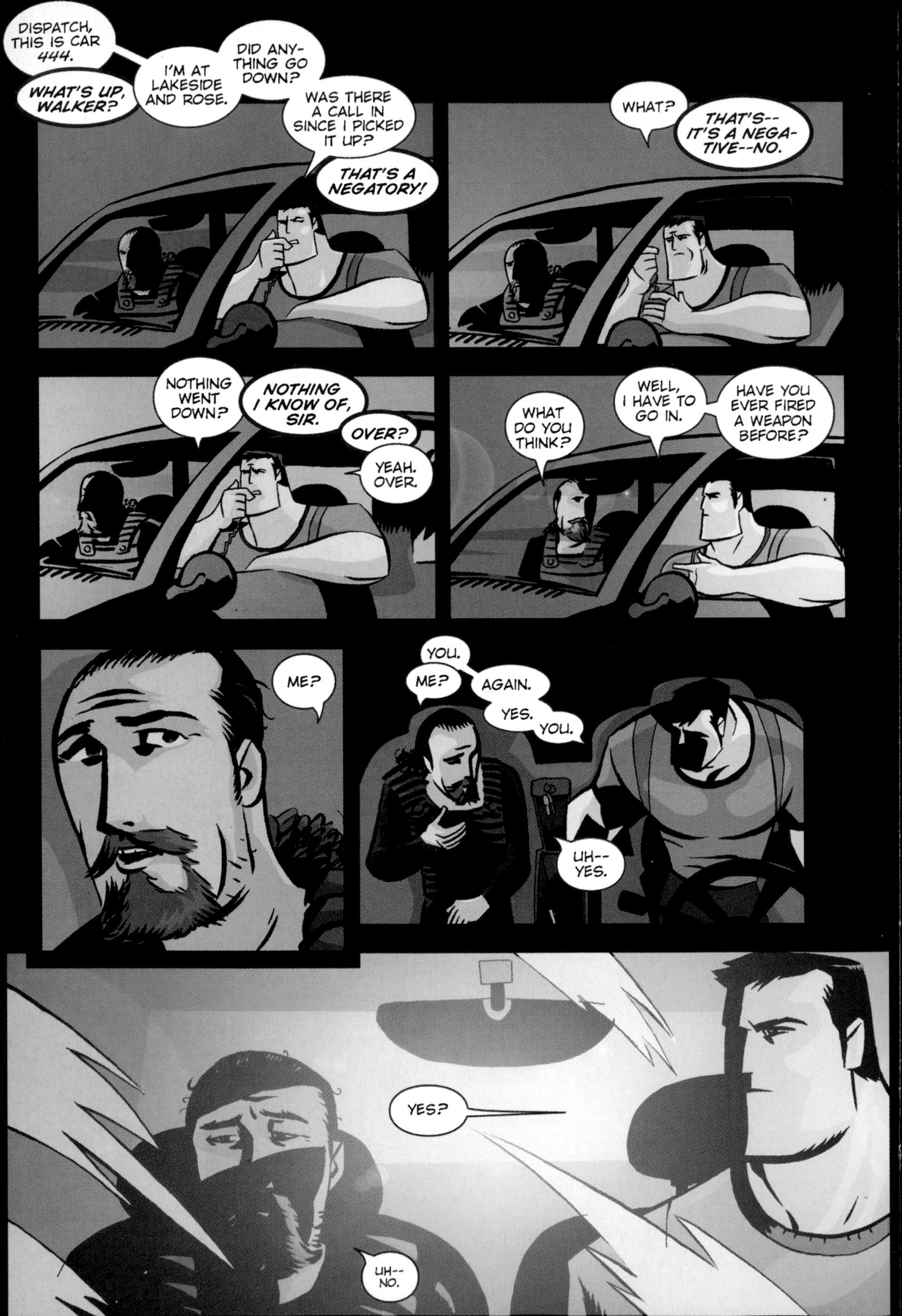
DISPATCH, THIS IS CAR 444.
WHAT'S UP, WALKER?
I'M AT LAKESIDE AND ROSE.
DID ANYTHING GO DOWN?
WAS THERE A CALL IN SINCE I PICKED IT UP?
THAT'S A NEGATORY!
WHAT?
THAT'S-- IT'S A NEGATIVE--NO.
NOTHING WENT DOWN?
NOTHING I KNOW OF, SIR.
OVER?
YEAH. OVER.
WHAT DO YOU THINK?
WELL, I HAVE TO GO IN.
HAVE YOU EVER FIRED A WEAPON BEFORE?
ME?
YOU.
ME?
AGAIN.
YES.
YOU.
UH-- YES.
YES?
UH-- NO.

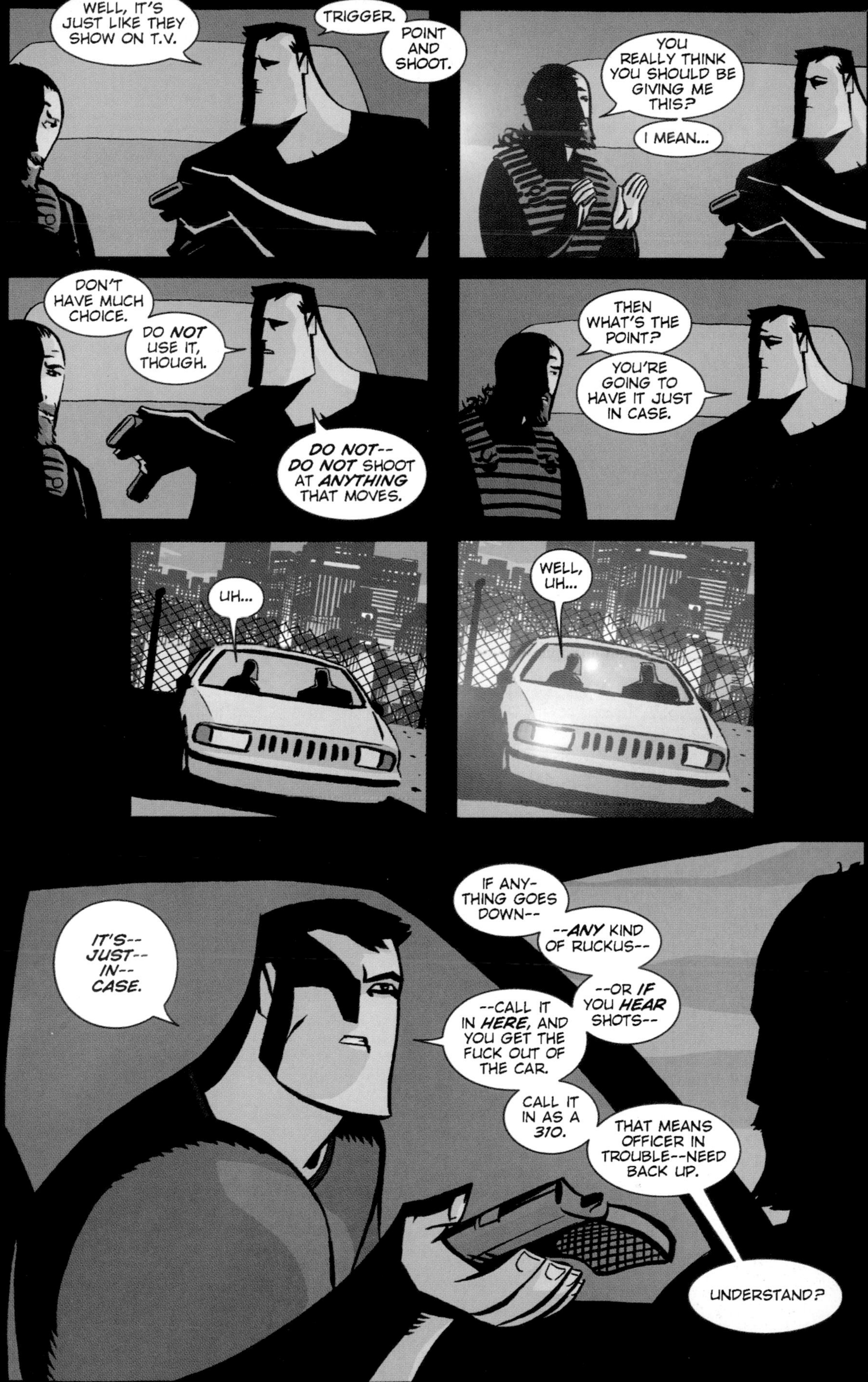

WELL, IT'S JUST LIKE THEY SHOW ON T.V.
TRIGGER.
POINT AND SHOOT.
YOU REALLY THINK YOU SHOULD BE GIVING ME THIS?
I MEAN...
DON'T HAVE MUCH CHOICE.
DO *NOT* USE IT, THOUGH.
DO NOT-- DO NOT SHOOT AT *ANYTHING* THAT MOVES.
THEN WHAT'S THE POINT?
YOU'RE GOING TO HAVE IT JUST IN CASE.
UH...
WELL, UH...
IT'S-- JUST-- IN-- CASE.
IF ANY-THING GOES DOWN--
--*ANY* KIND OF RUCKUS--
--OR *IF* YOU *HEAR* SHOTS--
--CALL IT IN *HERE,* AND YOU GET THE FUCK OUT OF THE CAR.
CALL IT IN AS A *310.*
THAT MEANS OFFICER IN TROUBLE--NEED BACK UP.
UNDERSTAND?

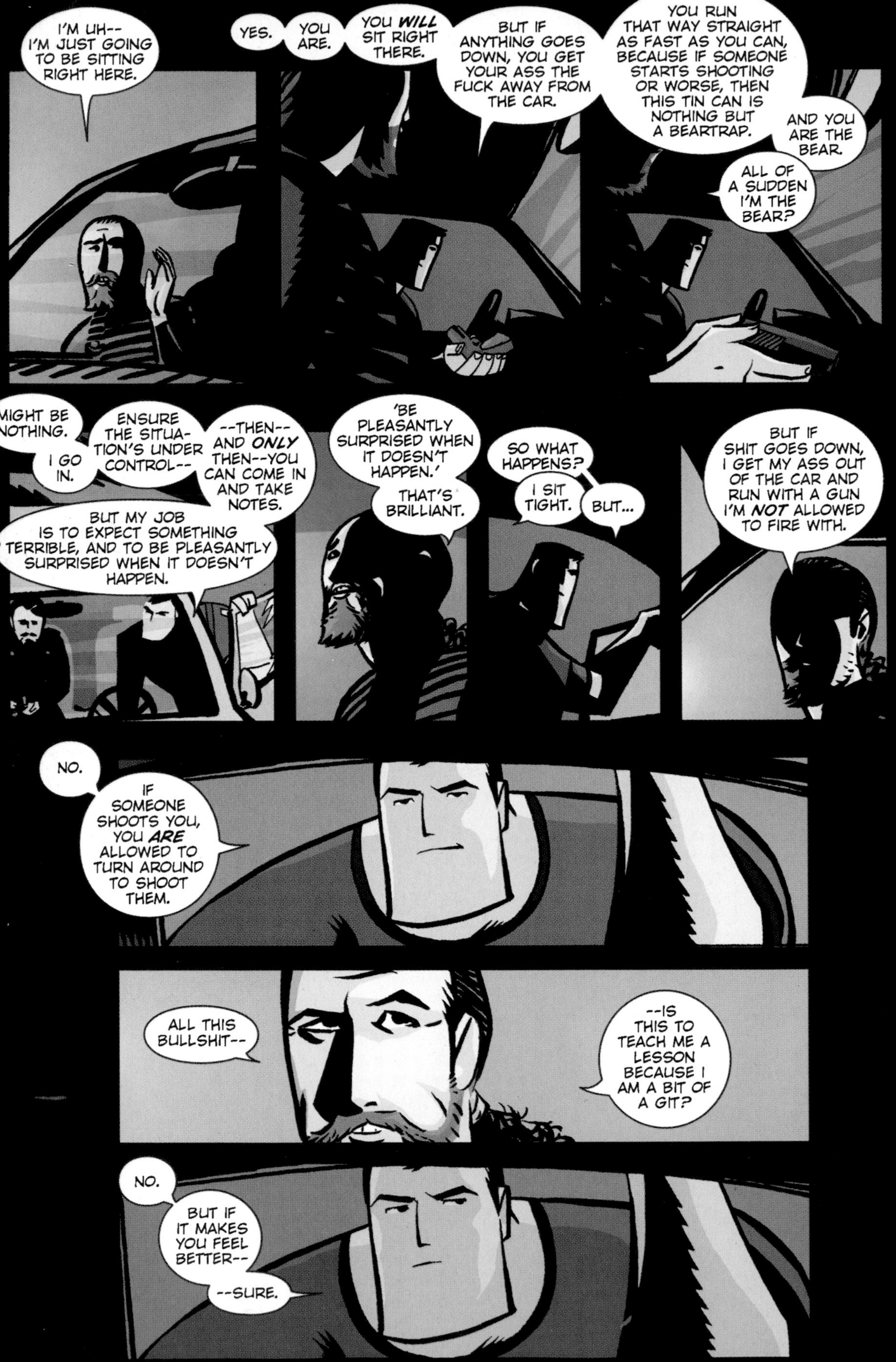
I'M UH-- I'M JUST GOING TO BE SITTING RIGHT HERE.
YES.
YOU ARE.
YOU *WILL* SIT RIGHT THERE.
BUT IF ANYTHING GOES DOWN, YOU GET YOUR ASS THE FUCK AWAY FROM THE CAR.
YOU RUN THAT WAY STRAIGHT AS FAST AS YOU CAN, BECAUSE IF SOMEONE STARTS SHOOTING OR WORSE, THEN THIS TIN CAN IS NOTHING BUT A BEARTRAP.
AND YOU ARE THE BEAR.
ALL OF A SUDDEN I'M THE BEAR?
MIGHT BE NOTHING.
I GO IN.
ENSURE THE SITUATION'S UNDER CONTROL--
--THEN-- AND *ONLY* THEN--YOU CAN COME IN AND TAKE NOTES.
BUT MY JOB IS TO EXPECT SOMETHING TERRIBLE, AND TO BE PLEASANTLY SURPRISED WHEN IT DOESN'T HAPPEN.
'BE PLEASANTLY SURPRISED WHEN IT DOESN'T HAPPEN.'
THAT'S BRILLIANT.
SO WHAT HAPPENS?
I SIT TIGHT.
BUT...
BUT IF SHIT GOES DOWN, I GET MY ASS OUT OF THE CAR AND RUN WITH A GUN I'M *NOT* ALLOWED TO FIRE WITH.
NO.
IF SOMEONE SHOOTS YOU, YOU *ARE* ALLOWED TO TURN AROUND TO SHOOT THEM.
ALL THIS BULLSHIT--
--IS THIS TO TEACH ME A LESSON BECAUSE I AM A BIT OF A GIT?
NO.
BUT IF IT MAKES YOU FEEL BETTER--
--SURE.

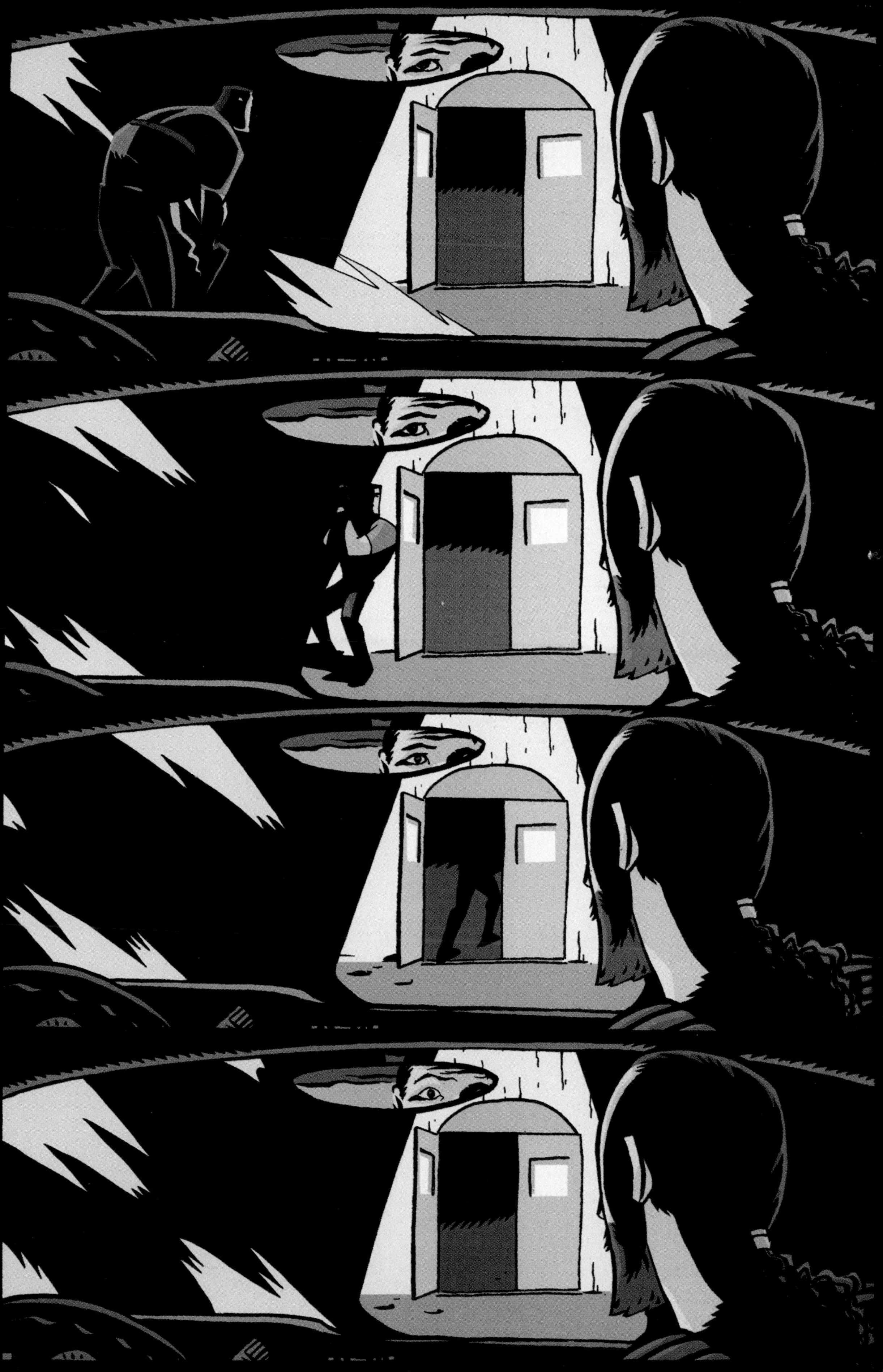

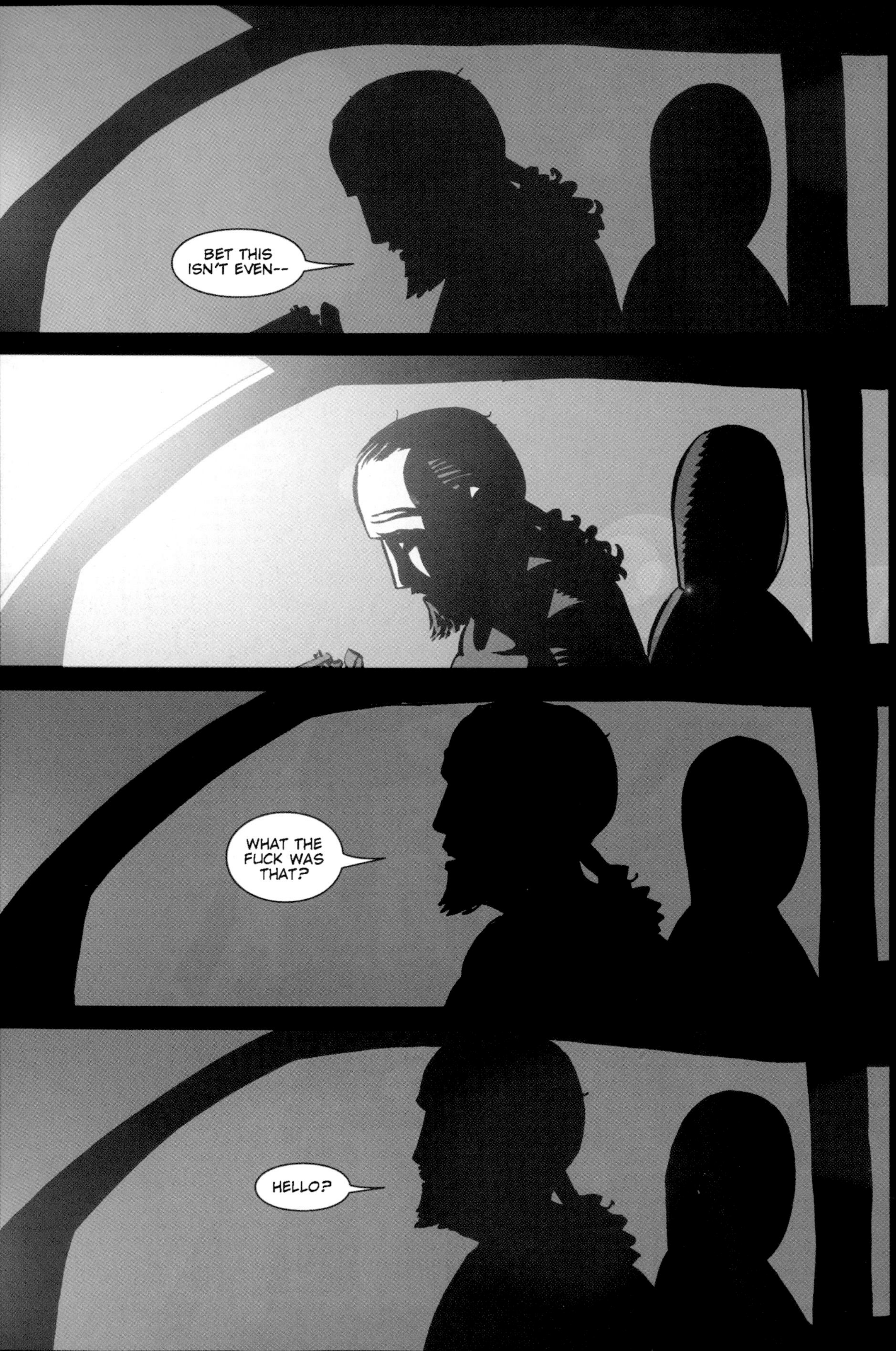
BET THIS ISN'T EVEN--
WHAT THE FUCK WAS THAT?
HELLO?

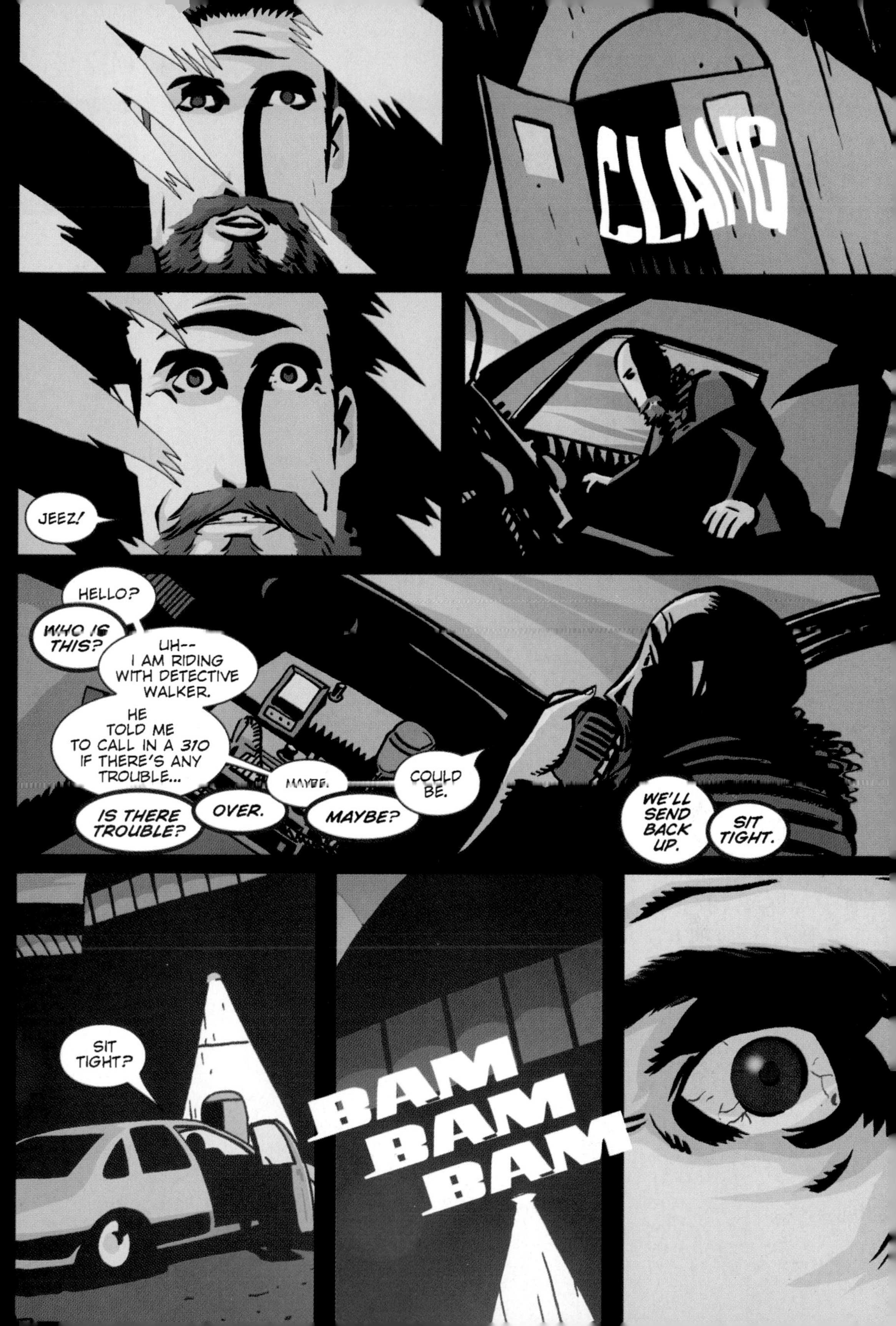

CLANG
JEEZ!
HELLO?
WHO IS THIS?
UH-- I AM RIDING WITH DETECTIVE WALKER.
HE TOLD ME TO CALL IN A 310 IF THERE'S ANY TROUBLE...
IS THERE TROUBLE?
OVER.
MAYBE?
MAYBE.
COULD BE.
WE'LL SEND BACK UP.
SIT TIGHT.
SIT TIGHT?
BAM
BAM
BAM

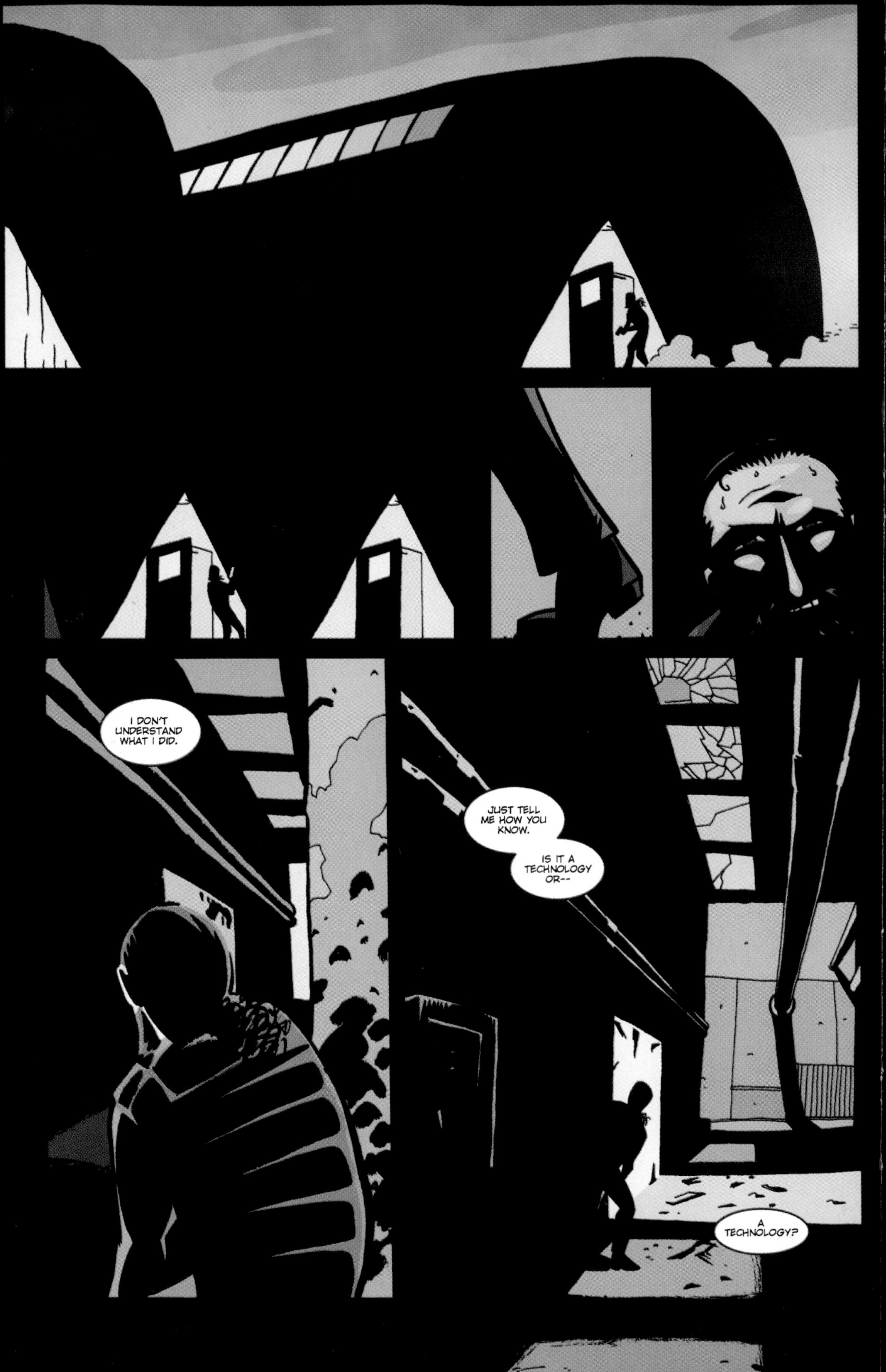
I DON'T UNDERSTAND WHAT I DID.
JUST TELL ME HOW YOU KNOW.
IS IT A TECHNOLOGY OR--
A TECHNOLOGY?

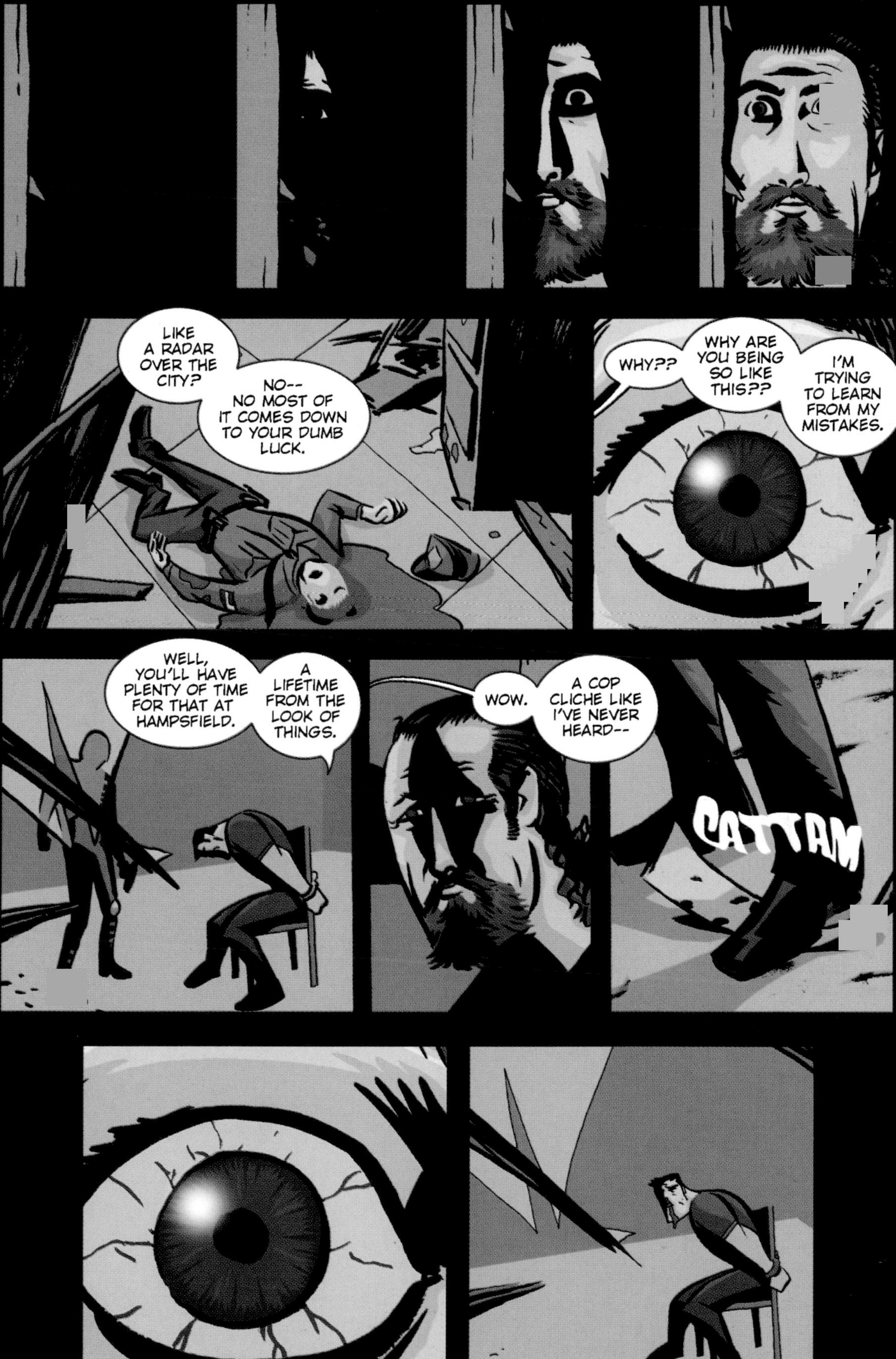
LIKE A RADAR OVER THE CITY?
NO-- NO MOST OF IT COMES DOWN TO YOUR DUMB LUCK.
WHY??
WHY ARE YOU BEING SO LIKE THIS??
I'M TRYING TO LEARN FROM MY MISTAKES.
WELL, YOU'LL HAVE PLENTY OF TIME FOR THAT AT HAMPSFIELD.
A LIFETIME FROM THE LOOK OF THINGS.
WOW.
A COP CLICHE LIKE I'VE NEVER HEARD--
CATTAM

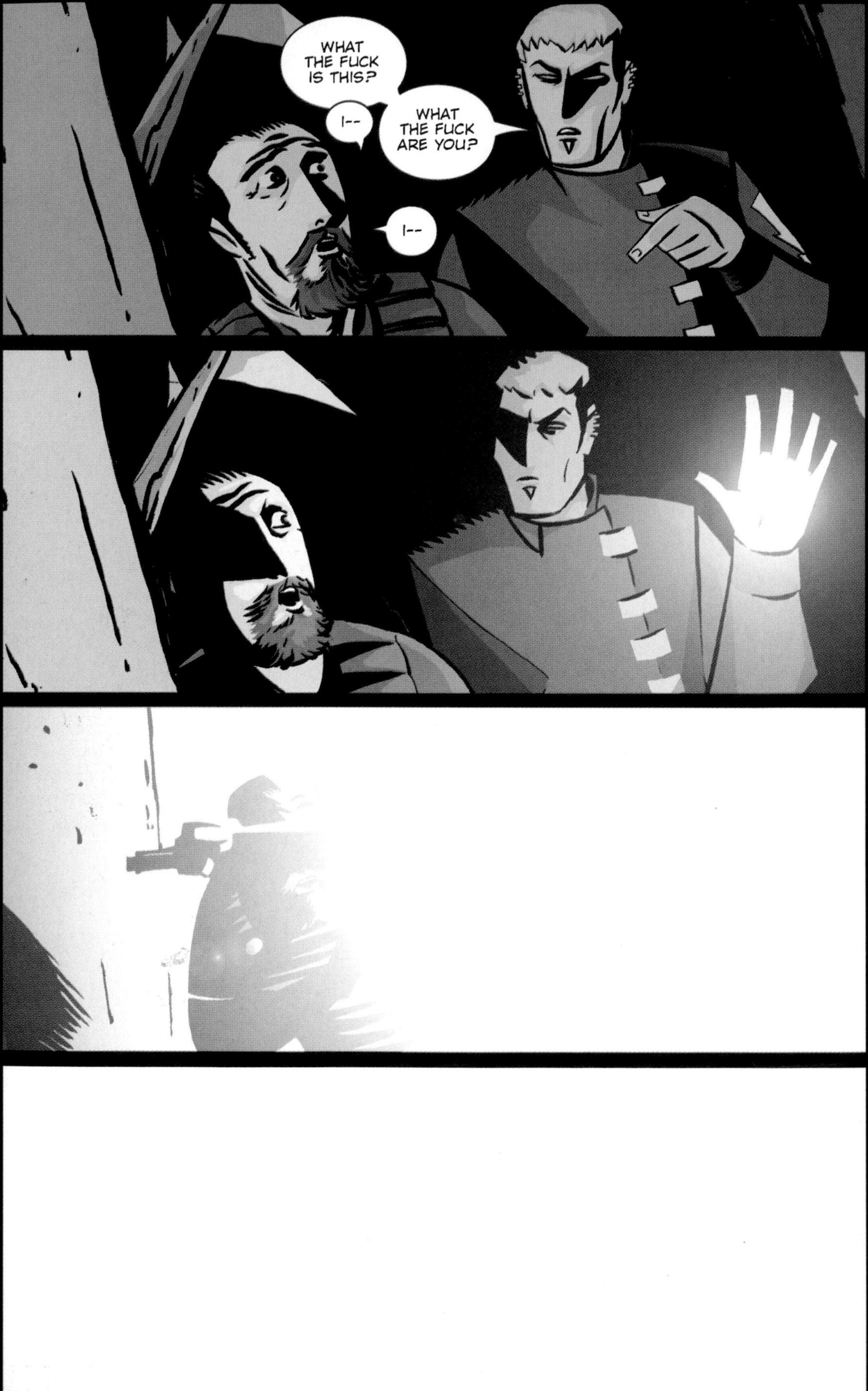
WHAT THE FUCK IS THIS?
I--
WHAT THE FUCK ARE YOU?
I--

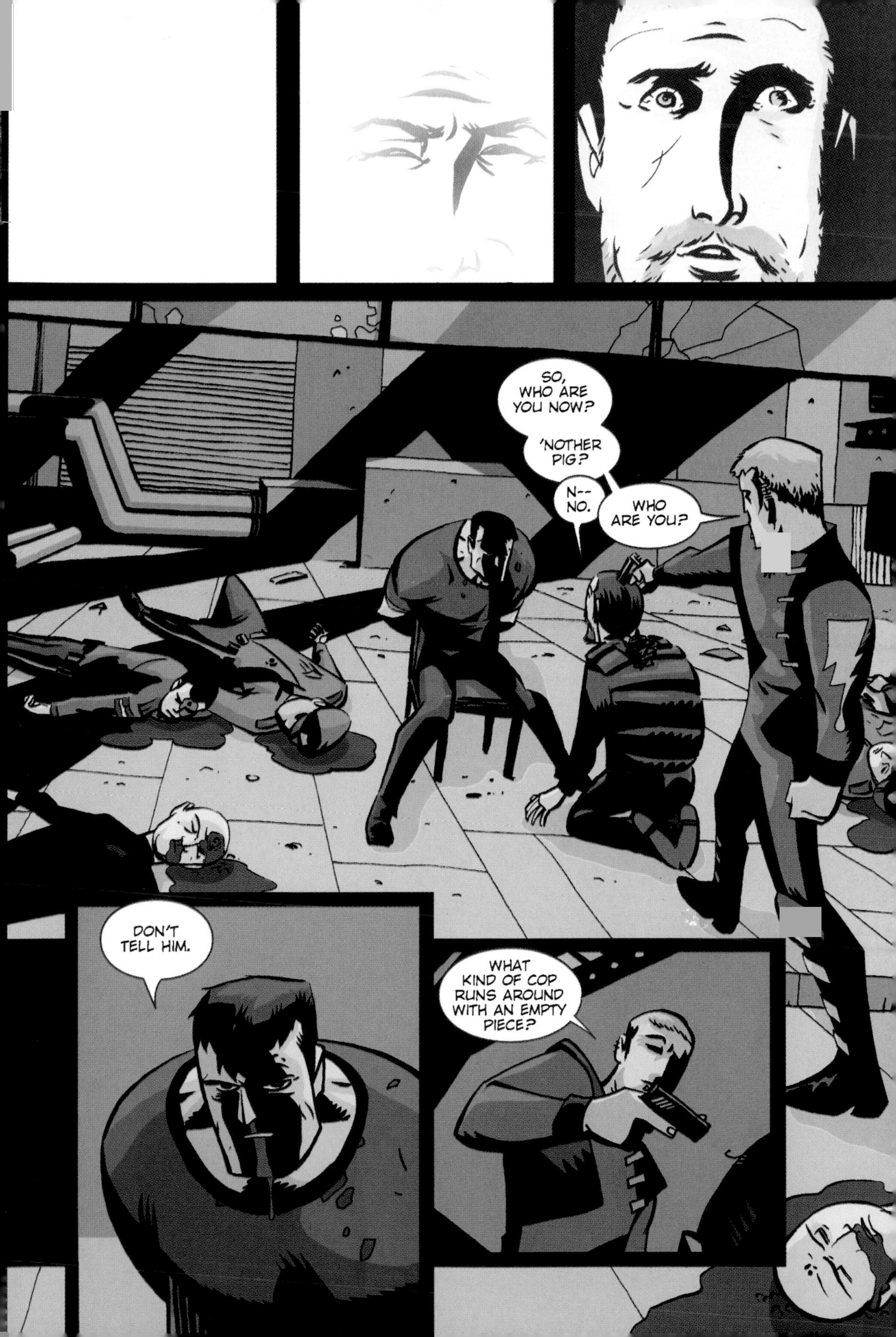
SO, WHO ARE YOU NOW?
'NOTHER PIG?
N-- NO.
WHO ARE YOU?
DON'T TELL HIM.
WHAT KIND OF COP RUNS AROUND WITH AN EMPTY PIECE?

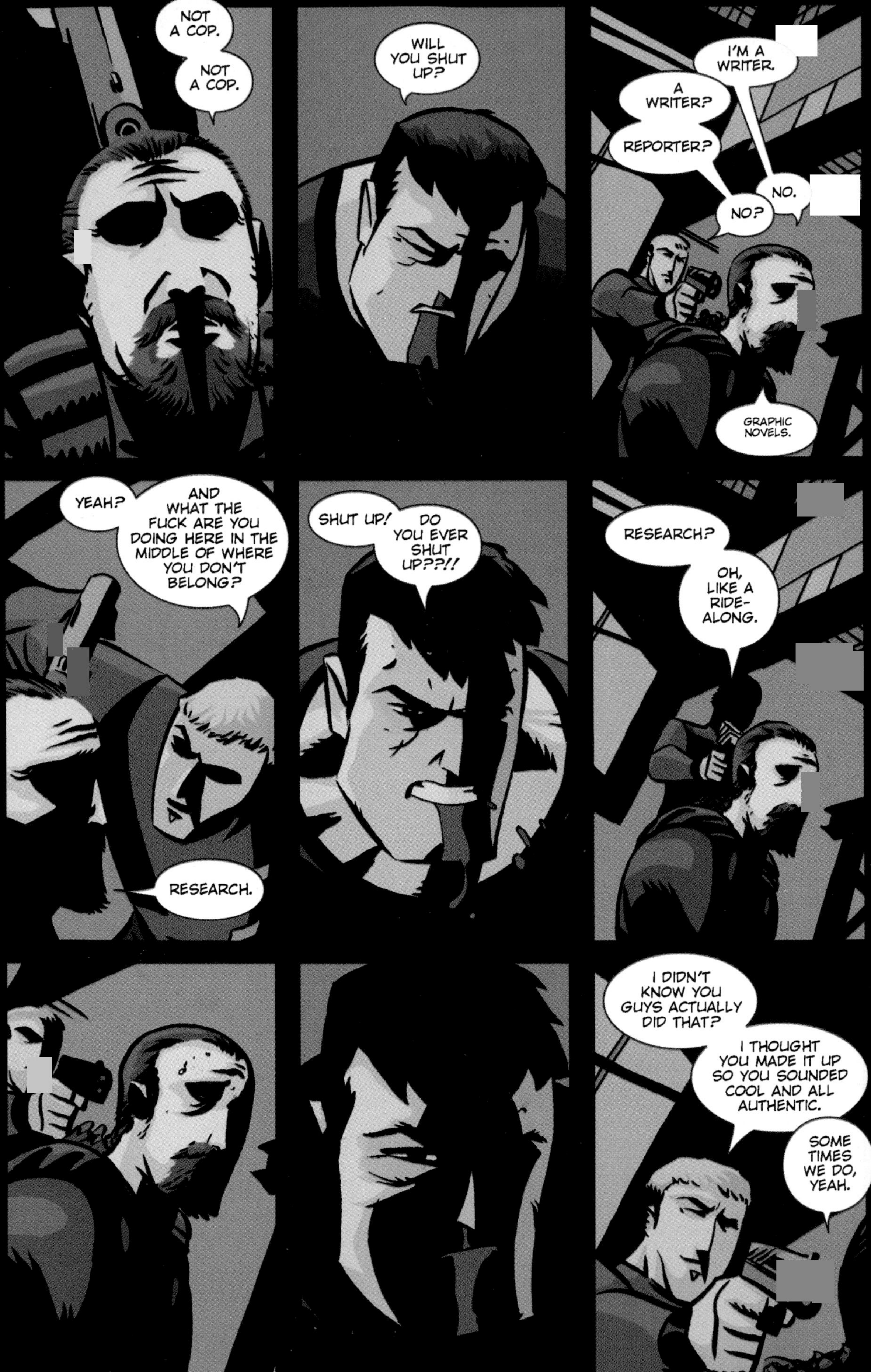
NOT A COP.
NOT A COP.
WILL YOU SHUT UP?
I'M A WRITER.
A WRITER?
REPORTER?
NO.
NO?
GRAPHIC NOVELS.
YEAH?
AND WHAT THE FUCK ARE YOU DOING HERE IN THE MIDDLE OF WHERE YOU DON'T BELONG?
RESEARCH.
SHUT UP!
DO YOU EVER SHUT UP??!!
RESEARCH?
OH, LIKE A RIDE-ALONG.
I DIDN'T KNOW YOU GUYS ACTUALLY DID THAT?
I THOUGHT YOU MADE IT UP SO YOU SOUNDED COOL AND ALL AUTHENTIC.
SOME TIMES WE DO, YEAH.

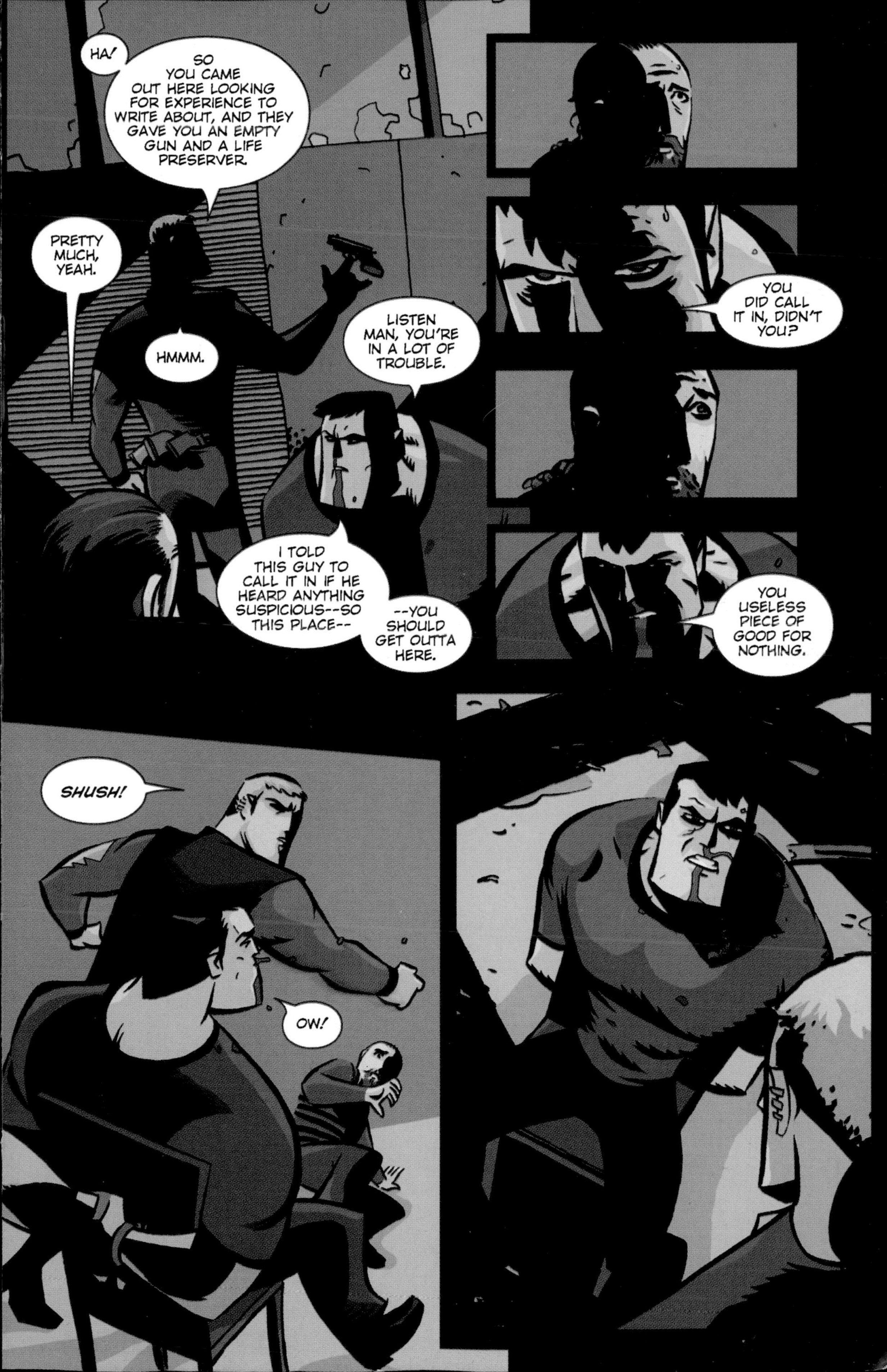
HA!
SO YOU CAME OUT HERE LOOKING FOR EXPERIENCE TO WRITE ABOUT, AND THEY GAVE YOU AN EMPTY GUN AND A LIFE PRESERVER.
PRETTY MUCH, YEAH.
HMMM.
LISTEN MAN, YOU'RE IN A LOT OF TROUBLE.
I TOLD THIS GUY TO CALL IT IN IF HE HEARD ANYTHING SUSPICIOUS--SO THIS PLACE--
--YOU SHOULD GET OUTTA HERE.
YOU DID CALL IT IN, DIDN'T YOU?
YOU USELESS PIECE OF GOOD FOR NOTHING.
SHUSH!
OW!

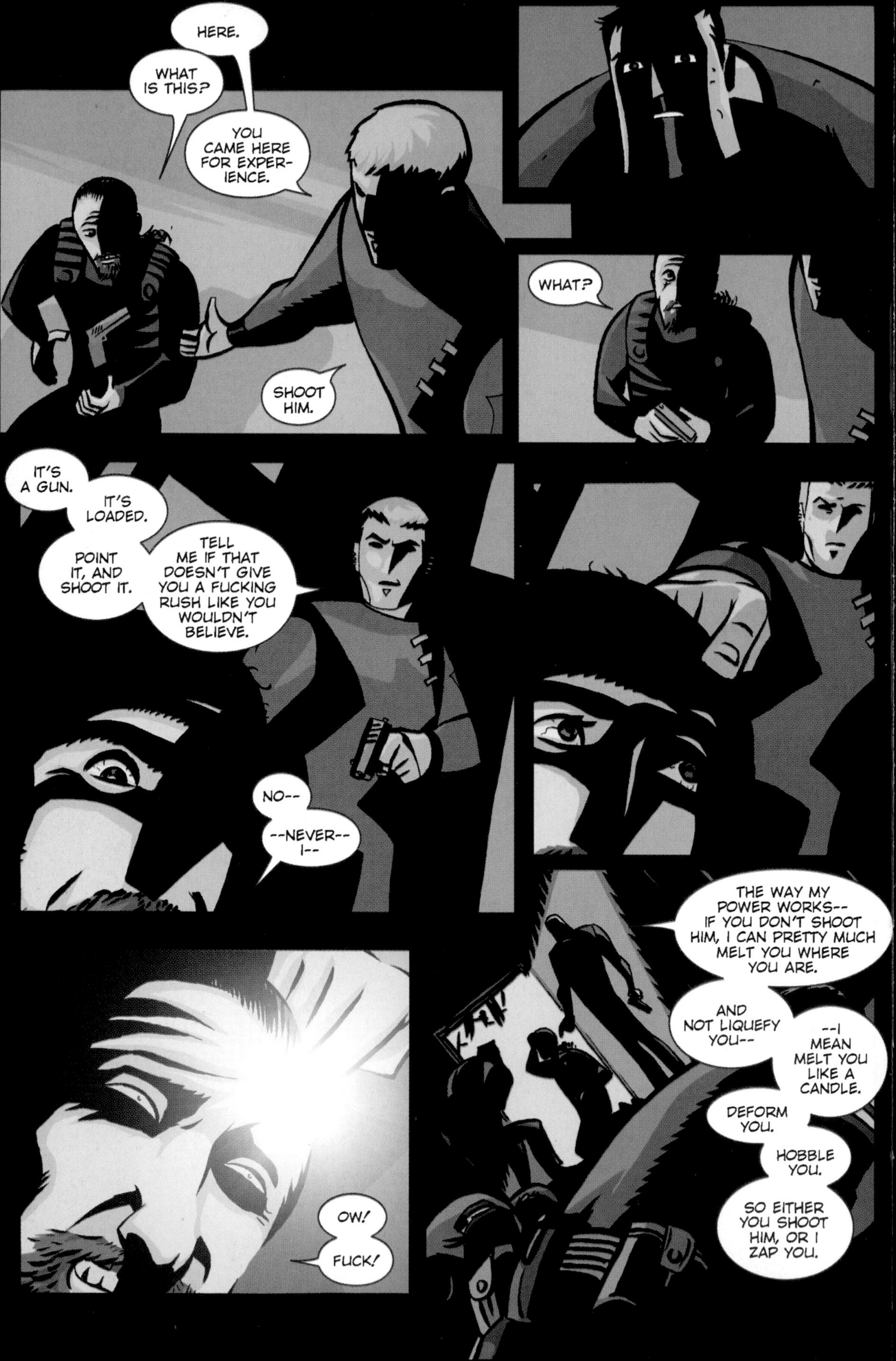
HERE.
WHAT IS THIS?
YOU CAME HERE FOR EXPER-IENCE.
SHOOT HIM.
WHAT?
IT'S A GUN.
IT'S LOADED.
POINT IT, AND SHOOT IT.
TELL ME IF THAT DOESN'T GIVE YOU A FUCKING RUSH LIKE YOU WOULDN'T BELIEVE.
NO--
--NEVER--
I--
OW!
FUCK!
THE WAY MY POWER WORKS-- IF YOU DON'T SHOOT HIM, I CAN PRETTY MUCH MELT YOU WHERE YOU ARE.
AND NOT LIQUEFY YOU--
--I MEAN MELT YOU LIKE A CANDLE.
DEFORM YOU.
HOBBLE YOU.
SO EITHER YOU SHOOT HIM, OR I ZAP YOU.

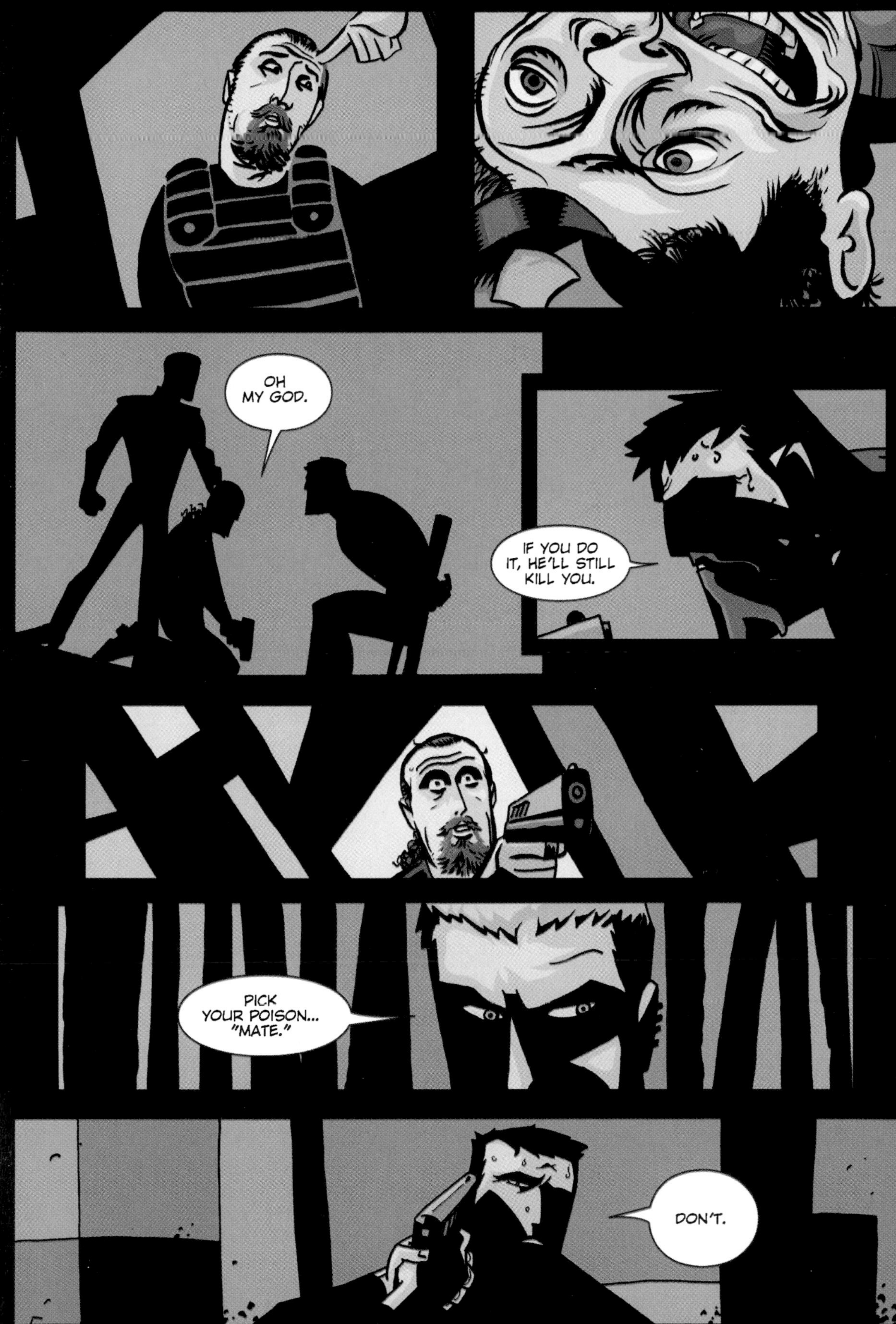
OH
MY GOD.
IF YOU DO
IT, HE'LL STILL
KILL YOU.
PICK
YOUR POISON...
"MATE."
DON'T.

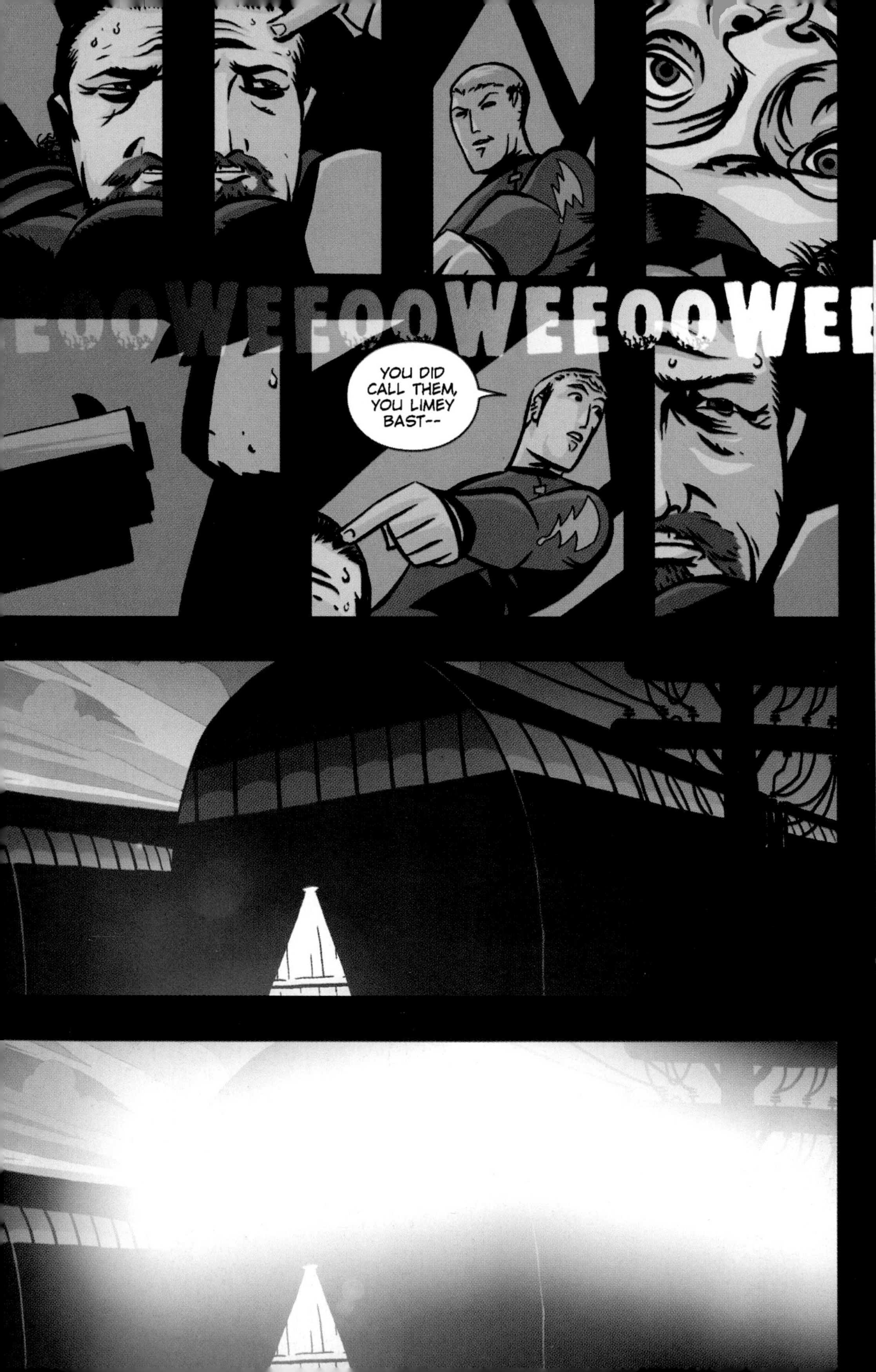
EOOWEEOOWEEOOWEE
YOU DID CALL THEM, YOU LIMEY BAST--

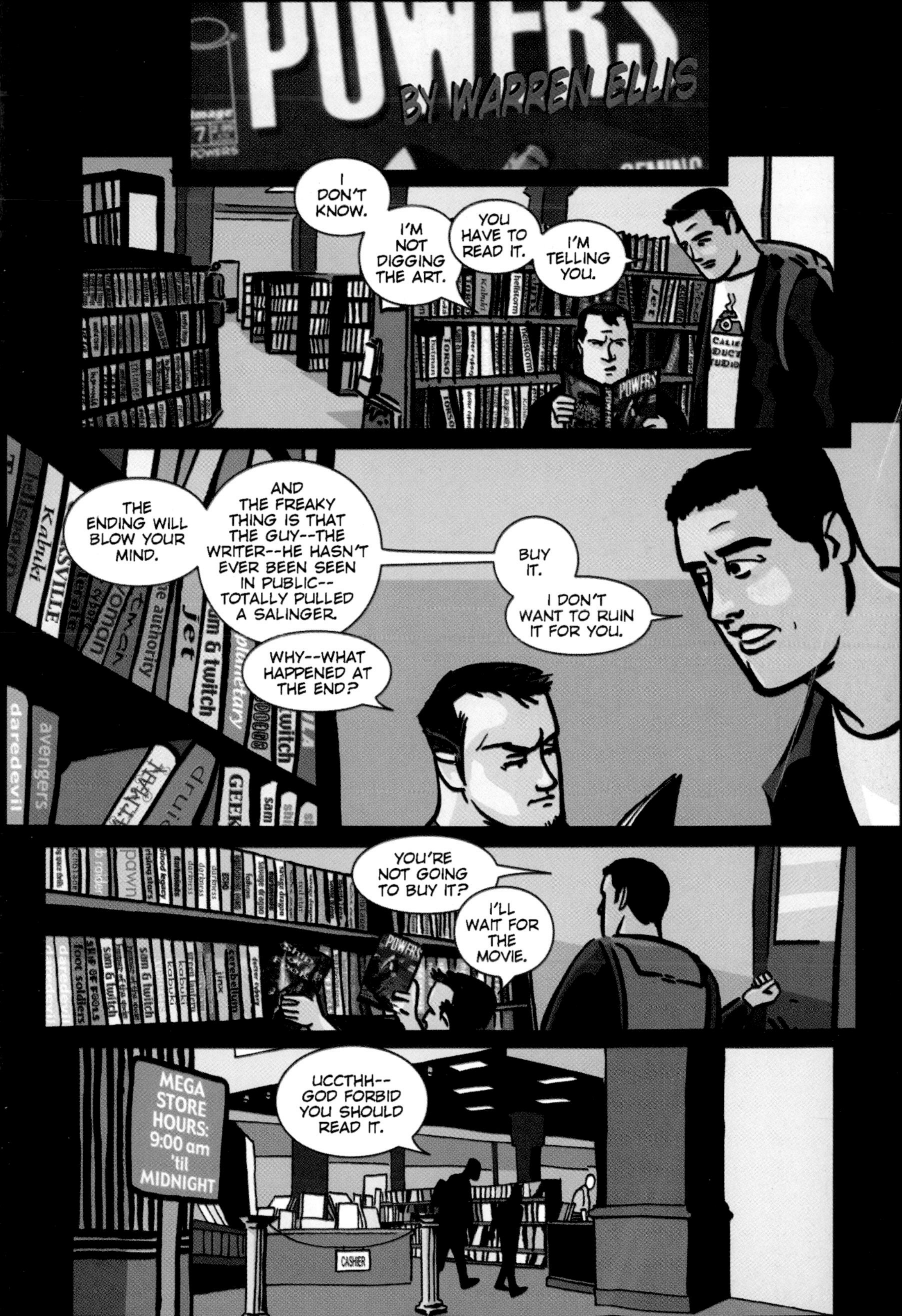
POWERS
BY WARREN ELLIS
I DON'T KNOW.
I'M NOT DIGGING THE ART.
YOU HAVE TO READ IT.
I'M TELLING YOU.
THE ENDING WILL BLOW YOUR MIND.
AND THE FREAKY THING IS THAT THE GUY--THE WRITER--HE HASN'T EVER BEEN SEEN IN PUBLIC--TOTALLY PULLED A SALINGER.
BUY IT.
I DON'T WANT TO RUIN IT FOR YOU.
WHY--WHAT HAPPENED AT THE END?
YOU'RE NOT GOING TO BUY IT?
I'LL WAIT FOR THE MOVIE.
MEGA STORE HOURS: 9:00 am 'til MIDNIGHT
UCCTHH--GOD FORBID YOU SHOULD READ IT.
CASHIER

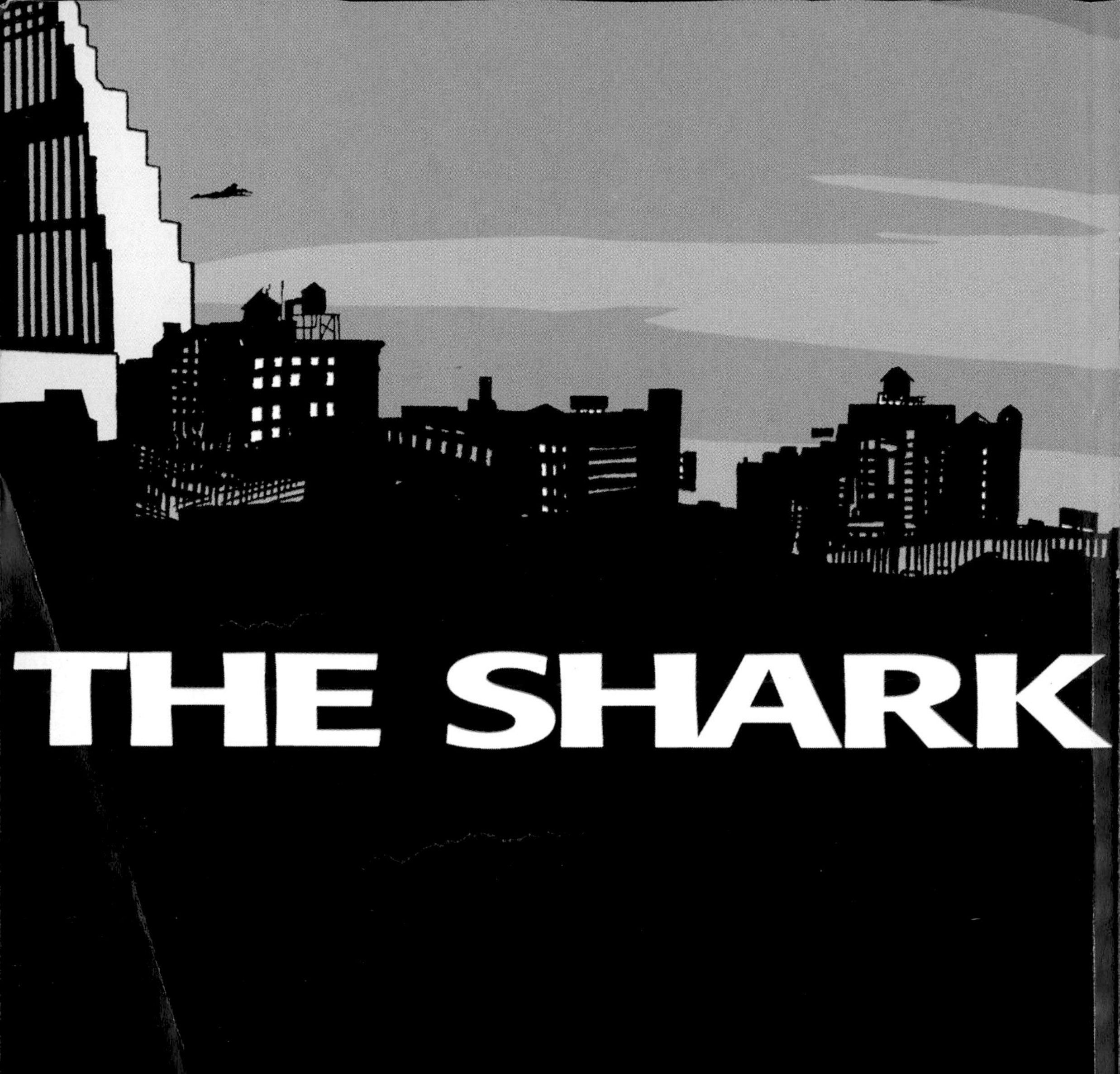
THE SHARK

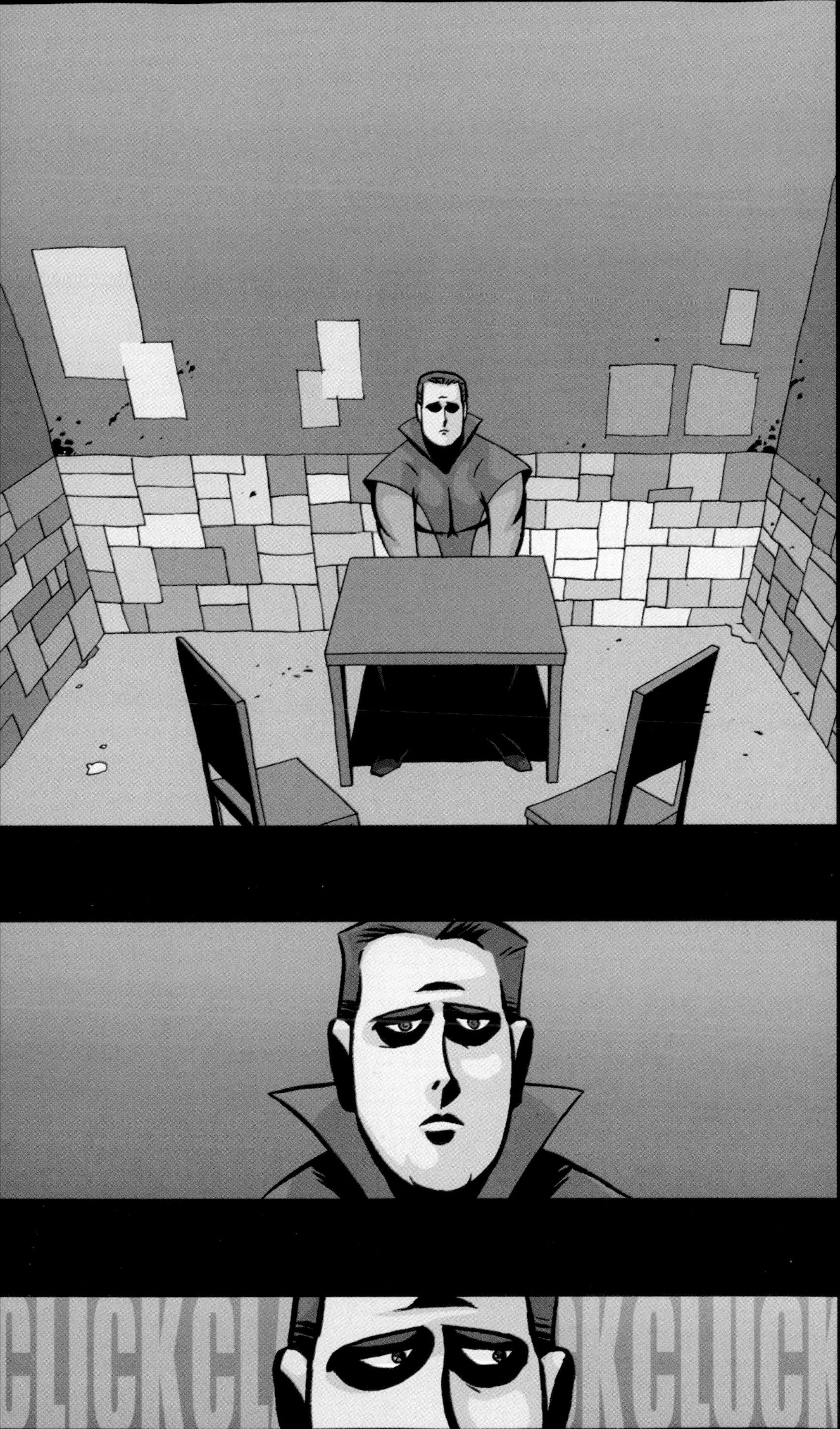
CLICKCL
KCLUCK

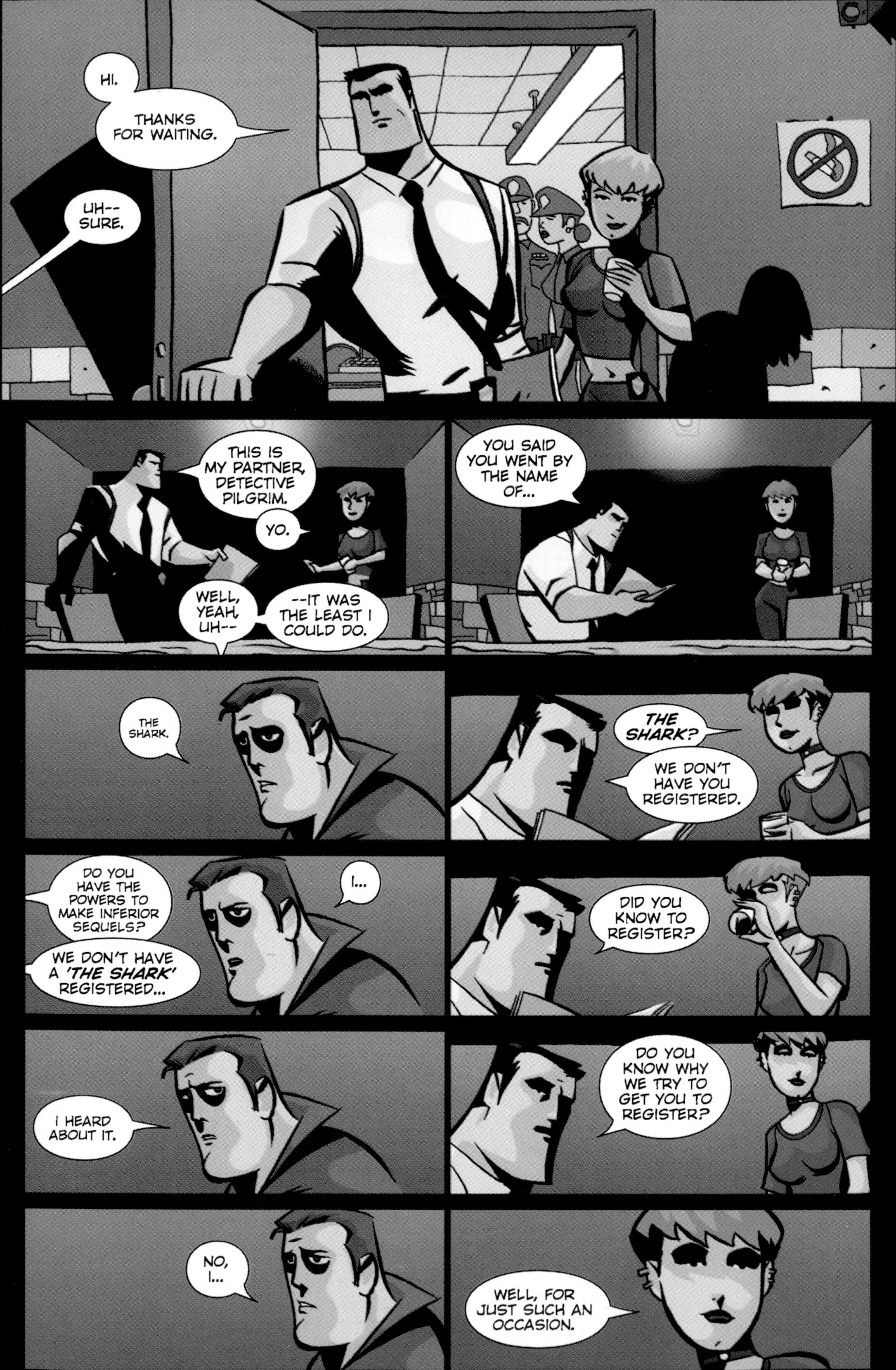
HI.
THANKS FOR WAITING.
UH-- SURE.
THIS IS MY PARTNER, DETECTIVE PILGRIM.
YO.
WELL, YEAH, UH--
--IT WAS THE LEAST I COULD DO.
YOU SAID YOU WENT BY THE NAME OF...
THE SHARK.
THE SHARK?
WE DON'T HAVE YOU REGISTERED.
DO YOU HAVE THE POWERS TO MAKE INFERIOR SEQUELS?
I...
WE DON'T HAVE A 'THE SHARK' REGISTERED...
DID YOU KNOW TO REGISTER?
I HEARD ABOUT IT.
DO YOU KNOW WHY WE TRY TO GET YOU TO REGISTER?
NO, I...
WELL, FOR JUST SUCH AN OCCASION.

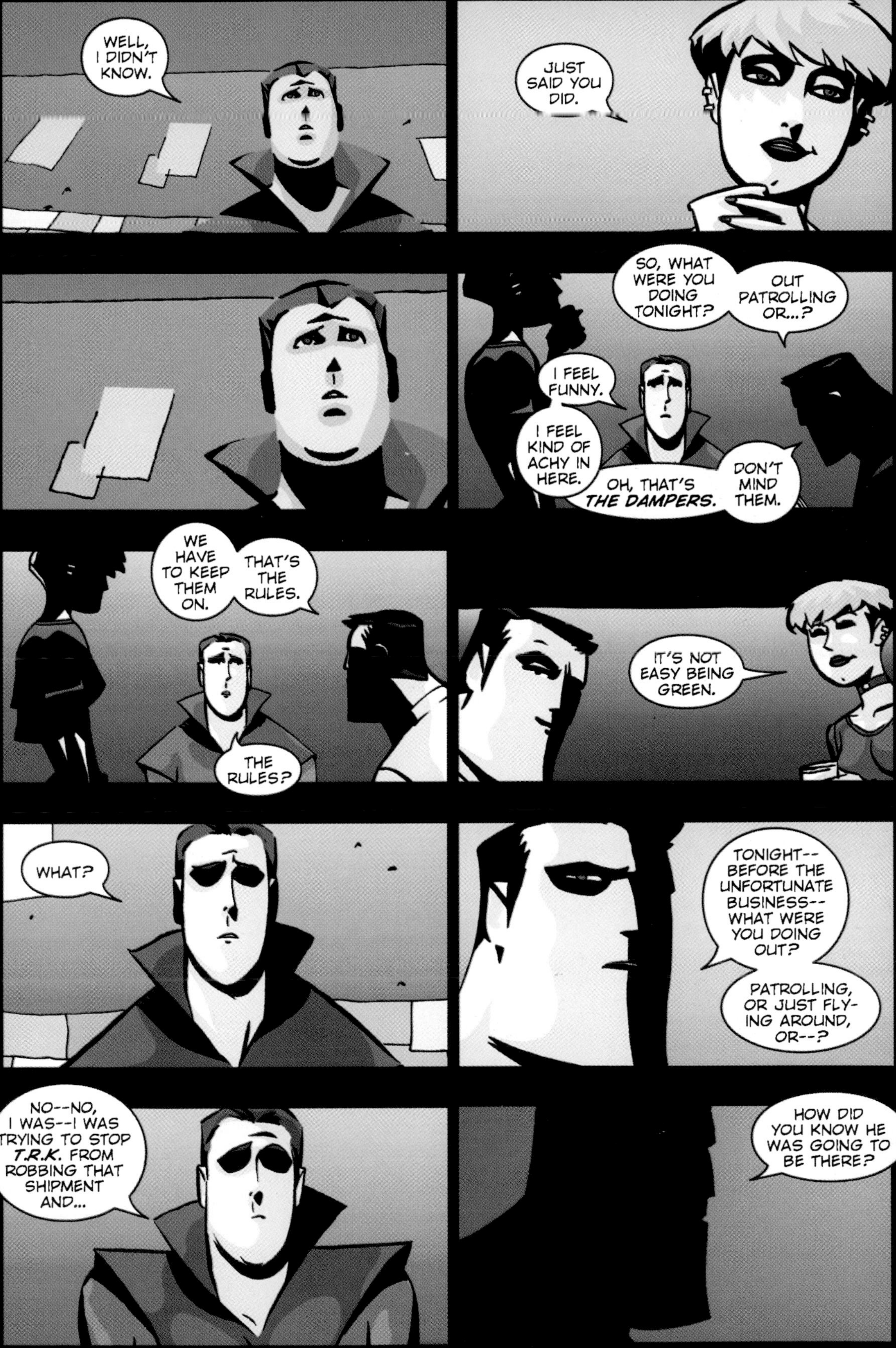
WELL, I DIDN'T KNOW.
JUST SAID YOU DID.
SO, WHAT WERE YOU DOING TONIGHT?
OUT PATROLLING OR...?
I FEEL FUNNY.
I FEEL KIND OF ACHY IN HERE.
OH, THAT'S *THE DAMPERS.*
DON'T MIND THEM.
WE HAVE TO KEEP THEM ON.
THAT'S THE RULES.
THE RULES?
IT'S NOT EASY BEING GREEN.
WHAT?
TONIGHT--BEFORE THE UNFORTUNATE BUSINESS--WHAT WERE YOU DOING OUT?
PATROLLING, OR JUST FLYING AROUND, OR--?
NO--NO, I WAS--I WAS TRYING TO STOP *T.R.K.* FROM ROBBING THAT SHIPMENT AND...
HOW DID YOU KNOW HE WAS GOING TO BE THERE?

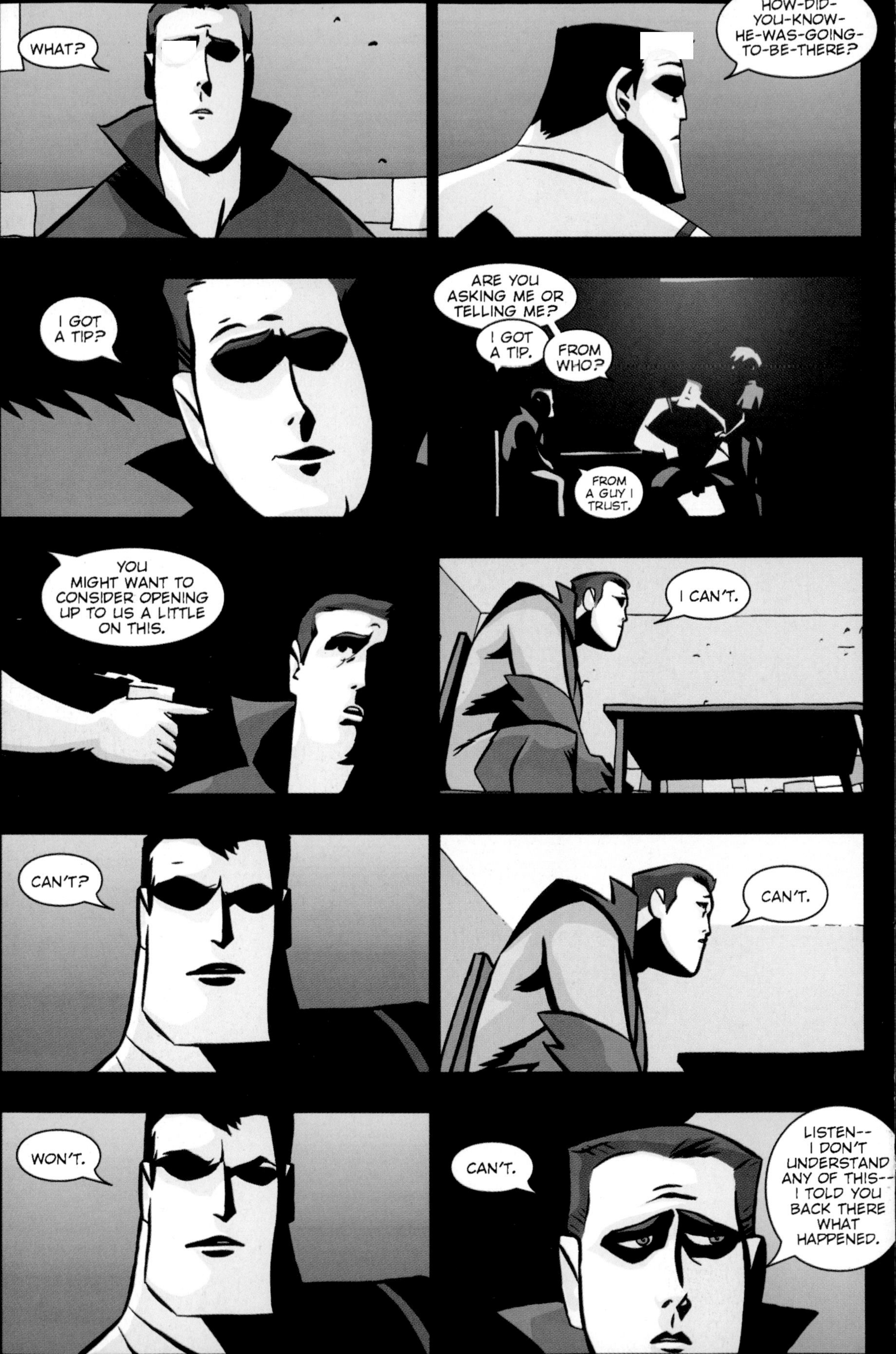
WHAT?
HOW-DID-YOU-KNOW-HE-WAS-GOING-TO-BE-THERE?
I GOT A TIP?
ARE YOU ASKING ME OR TELLING ME?
I GOT A TIP.
FROM WHO?
FROM A GUY I TRUST.
YOU MIGHT WANT TO CONSIDER OPENING UP TO US A LITTLE ON THIS.
I CAN'T.
CAN'T?
CAN'T.
WON'T.
CAN'T.
LISTEN-- I DON'T UNDERSTAND ANY OF THIS-- I TOLD YOU BACK THERE WHAT HAPPENED.

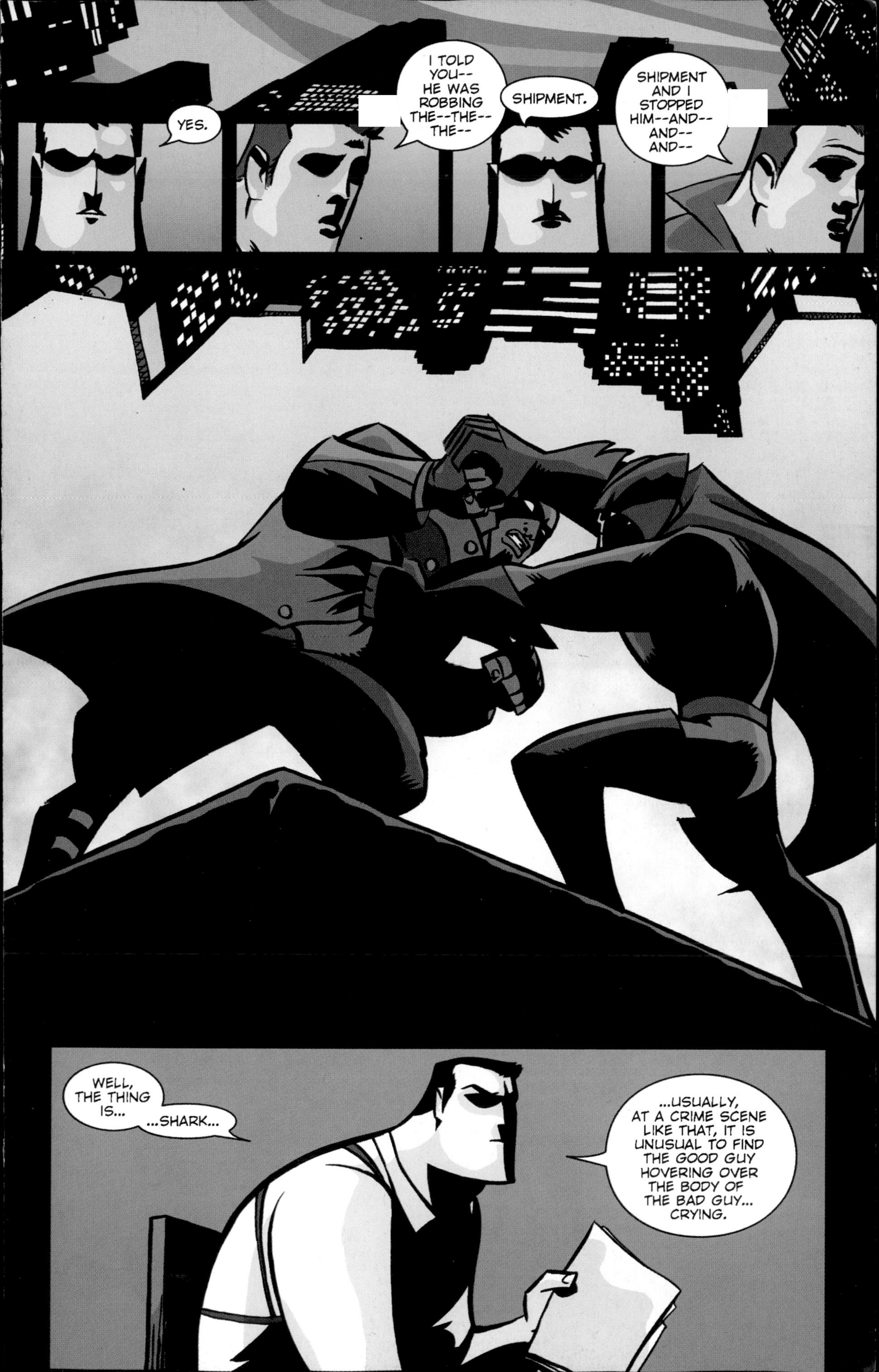
YES.
I TOLD YOU-- HE WAS ROBBING THE--THE-- THE--
SHIPMENT.
SHIPMENT AND I STOPPED HIM--AND-- AND-- AND--
WELL, THE THING IS...
...SHARK...
...USUALLY, AT A CRIME SCENE LIKE THAT, IT IS UNUSUAL TO FIND THE GOOD GUY HOVERING OVER THE BODY OF THE BAD GUY... CRYING.

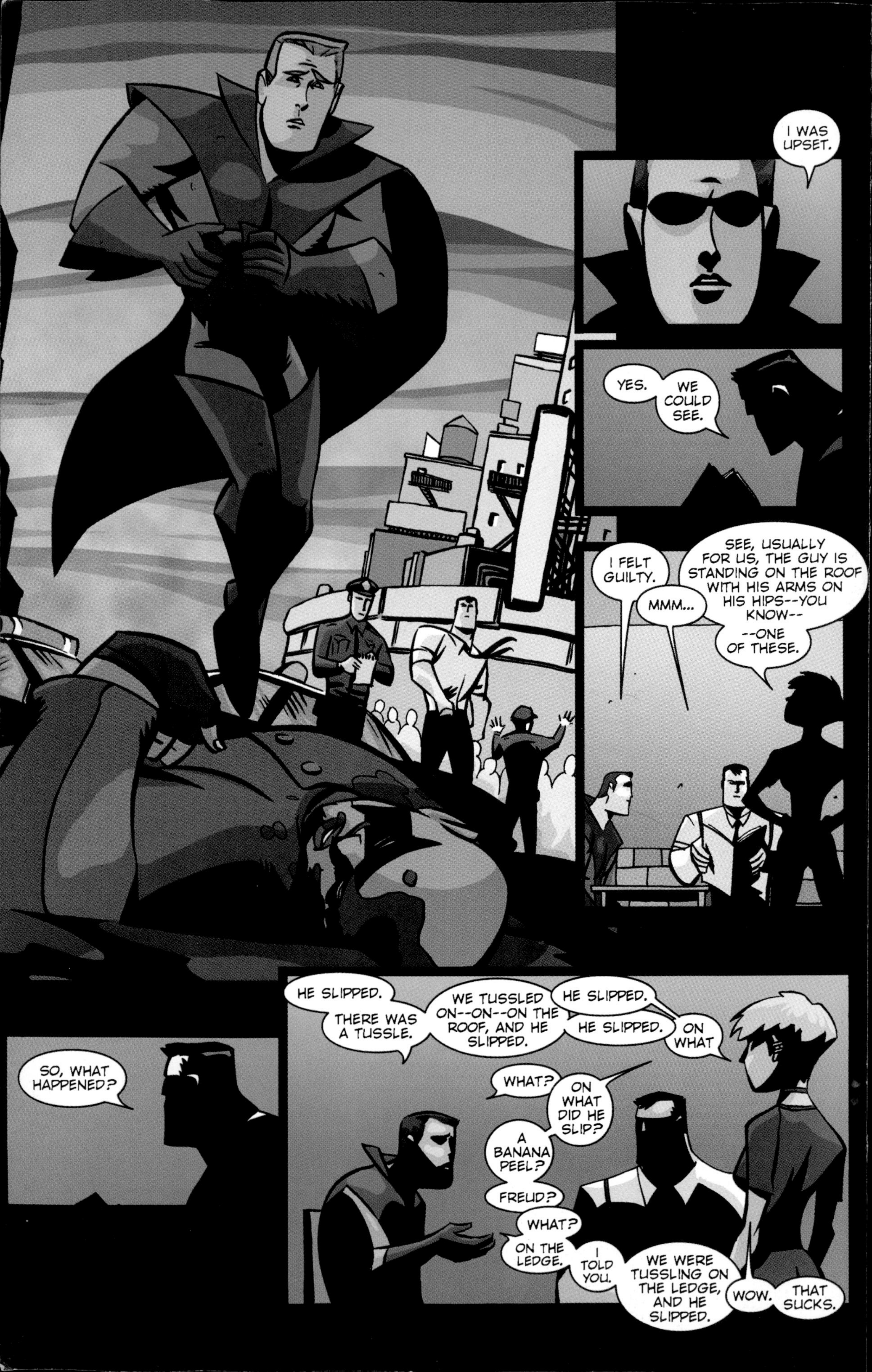

I WAS UPSET.
YES.
WE COULD SEE.
I FELT GUILTY.
MMM...
SEE, USUALLY FOR US, THE GUY IS STANDING ON THE ROOF WITH HIS ARMS ON HIS HIPS--YOU KNOW--
--ONE OF THESE.
SO, WHAT HAPPENED?
HE SLIPPED.
THERE WAS A TUSSLE.
WE TUSSLED ON--ON--ON THE ROOF, AND HE SLIPPED.
HE SLIPPED.
HE SLIPPED.
ON WHAT
WHAT?
ON WHAT DID HE SLIP?
A BANANA PEEL?
FREUD?
WHAT?
ON THE LEDGE.
I TOLD YOU.
WE WERE TUSSLING ON THE LEDGE, AND HE SLIPPED.
WOW.
THAT SUCKS.

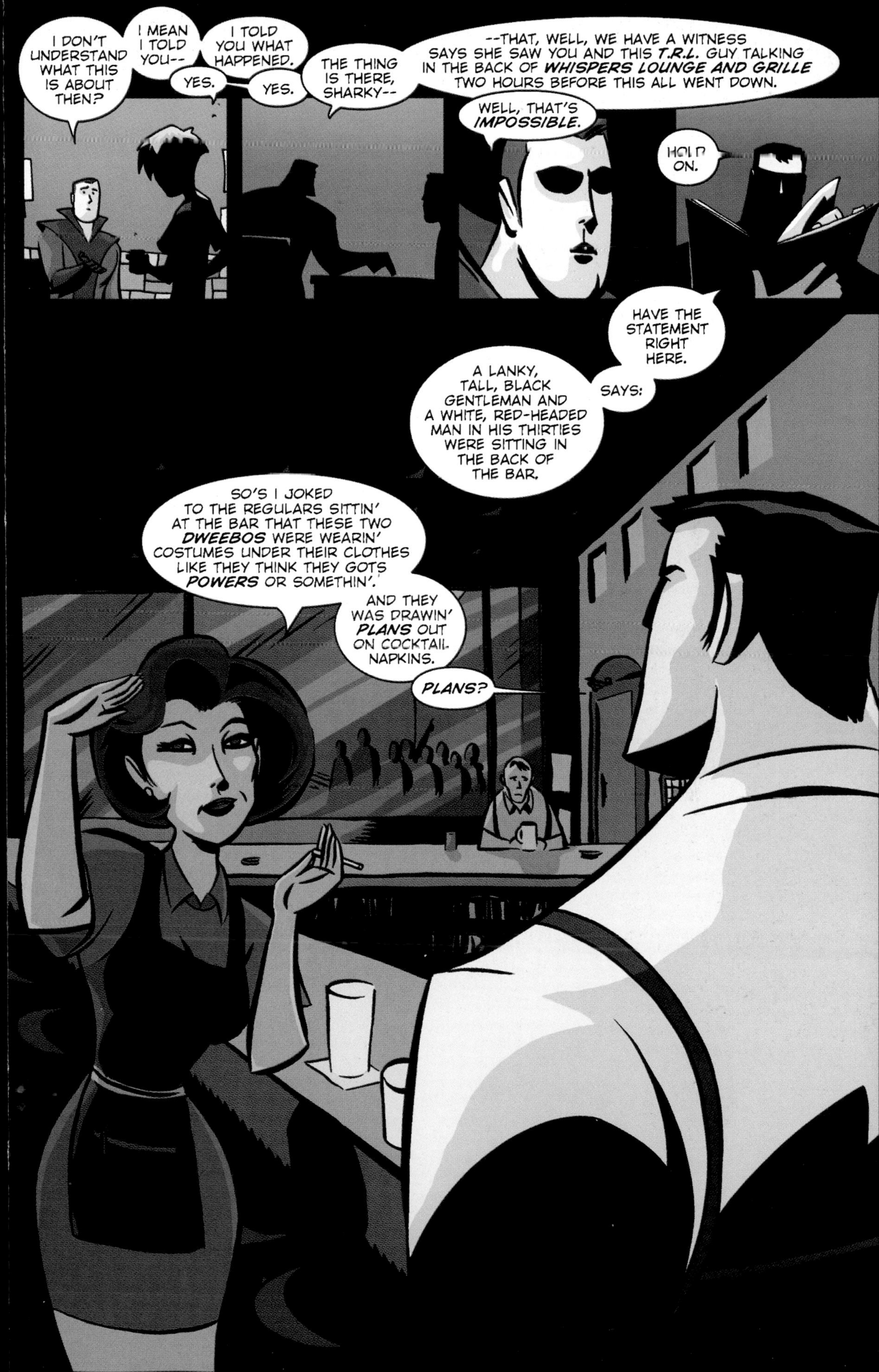
I DON'T UNDERSTAND WHAT THIS IS ABOUT THEN?
I MEAN I TOLD YOU--
I TOLD YOU WHAT HAPPENED.
YES.
YES.
THE THING IS THERE, SHARKY--
--THAT, WELL, WE HAVE A WITNESS SAYS SHE SAW YOU AND THIS T.R.L. GUY TALKING IN THE BACK OF WHISPERS LOUNGE AND GRILLE TWO HOURS BEFORE THIS ALL WENT DOWN.
WELL, THAT'S IMPOSSIBLE.
HOLD ON.
HAVE THE STATEMENT RIGHT HERE.
SAYS:
A LANKY, TALL, BLACK GENTLEMAN AND A WHITE, RED-HEADED MAN IN HIS THIRTIES WERE SITTING IN THE BACK OF THE BAR.
SO'S I JOKED TO THE REGULARS SITTIN' AT THE BAR THAT THESE TWO DWEEBOS WERE WEARIN' COSTUMES UNDER THEIR CLOTHES LIKE THEY THINK THEY GOTS POWERS OR SOMETHIN'.
AND THEY WAS DRAWIN' PLANS OUT ON COCKTAIL NAPKINS.
PLANS?

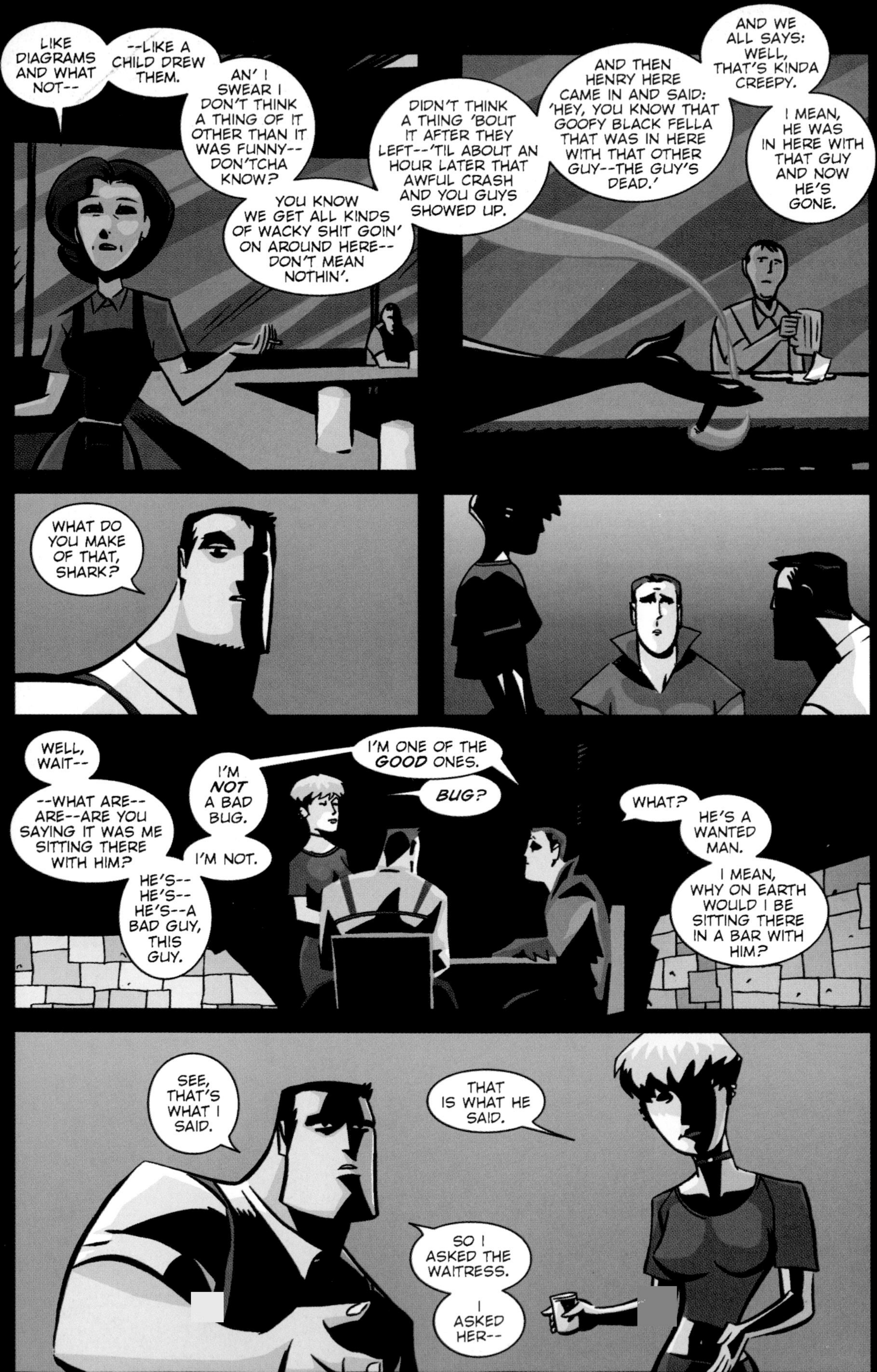
LIKE DIAGRAMS AND WHAT NOT--
--LIKE A CHILD DREW THEM.
AN' I SWEAR I DON'T THINK A THING OF IT OTHER THAN IT WAS FUNNY--DON'TCHA KNOW?
YOU KNOW WE GET ALL KINDS OF WACKY SHIT GOIN' ON AROUND HERE--DON'T MEAN NOTHIN'.
DIDN'T THINK A THING 'BOUT IT AFTER THEY LEFT--'TIL ABOUT AN HOUR LATER THAT AWFUL CRASH AND YOU GUYS SHOWED UP.
AND THEN HENRY HERE CAME IN AND SAID: 'HEY, YOU KNOW THAT GOOFY BLACK FELLA THAT WAS IN HERE WITH THAT OTHER GUY--THE GUY'S DEAD.'
AND WE ALL SAYS: WELL, THAT'S KINDA CREEPY.
I MEAN, HE WAS IN HERE WITH THAT GUY AND NOW HE'S GONE.
WHAT DO YOU MAKE OF THAT, SHARK?
WELL, WAIT--
--WHAT ARE--ARE--ARE YOU SAYING IT WAS ME SITTING THERE WITH HIM?
HE'S--HE'S--HE'S--A BAD GUY, THIS GUY.
I'M NOT A BAD BUG.
I'M NOT.
I'M ONE OF THE GOOD ONES.
BUG?
WHAT?
HE'S A WANTED MAN.
I MEAN, WHY ON EARTH WOULD I BE SITTING THERE IN A BAR WITH HIM?
SEE, THAT'S WHAT I SAID.
THAT IS WHAT HE SAID.
SO I ASKED THE WAITRESS.
I ASKED HER--

MA'AM, DO YOU THINK YOU COULD *DESCRIBE* THE OTHER GENTLEMAN THAT WAS HERE?
THE *CAUCASIAN* FELLOW?
I GUESS.
GOOD. LET'S...
HE PAID WITH A CREDIT CARD.
DOES THAT HELP YOU?
I HAVE THE RECEIPT IN THE REGISTER...

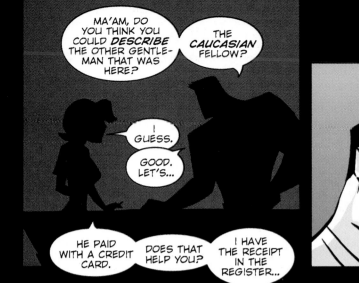

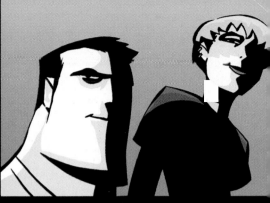

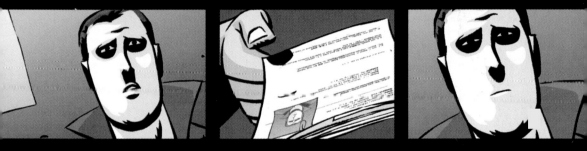

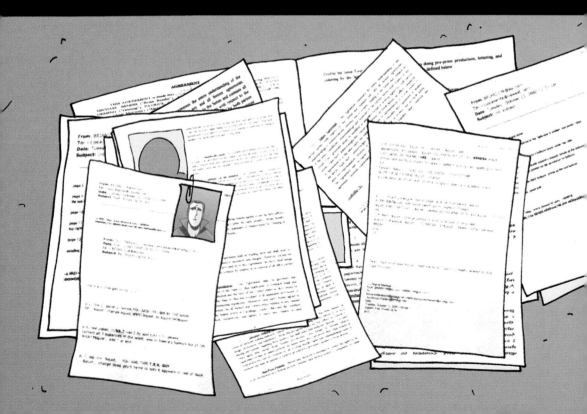

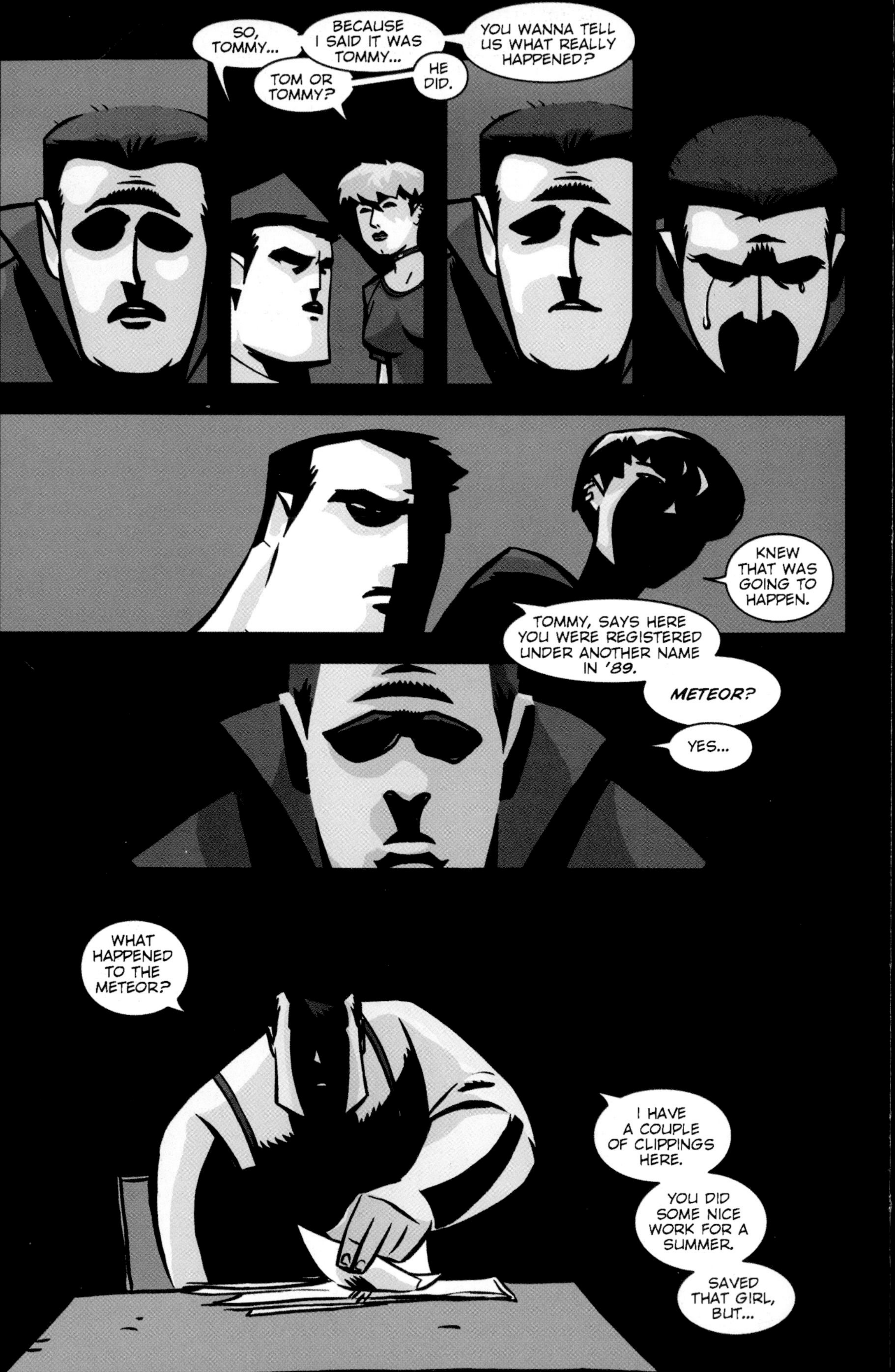
SO, TOMMY...
BECAUSE I SAID IT WAS TOMMY...
TOM OR TOMMY?
HE DID.
YOU WANNA TELL US WHAT REALLY HAPPENED?
KNEW THAT WAS GOING TO HAPPEN.
TOMMY, SAYS HERE YOU WERE REGISTERED UNDER ANOTHER NAME IN '89.
METEOR?
YES...
WHAT HAPPENED TO THE METEOR?
I HAVE A COUPLE OF CLIPPINGS HERE.
YOU DID SOME NICE WORK FOR A SUMMER.
SAVED THAT GIRL, BUT...

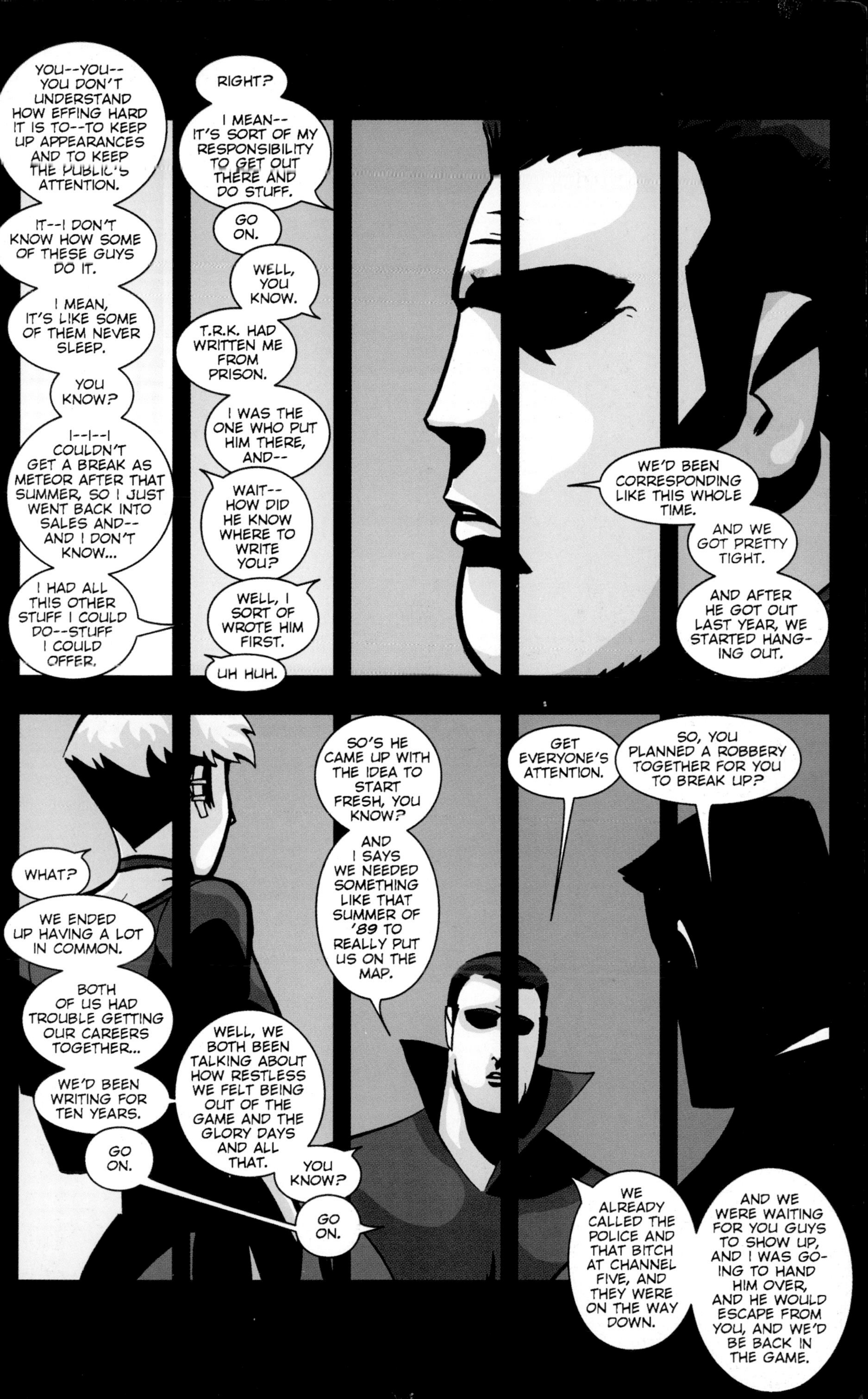

YOU--YOU--YOU DON'T UNDERSTAND HOW EFFING HARD IT IS TO--TO KEEP UP APPEARANCES AND TO KEEP THE PUBLIC'S ATTENTION.
IT--I DON'T KNOW HOW SOME OF THESE GUYS DO IT.
I MEAN, IT'S LIKE SOME OF THEM NEVER SLEEP.
YOU KNOW?
I--I--I COULDN'T GET A BREAK AS METEOR AFTER THAT SUMMER, SO I JUST WENT BACK INTO SALES AND--AND I DON'T KNOW...
I HAD ALL THIS OTHER STUFF I COULD DO--STUFF I COULD OFFER.
RIGHT?
I MEAN--IT'S SORT OF MY RESPONSIBILITY TO GET OUT THERE AND DO STUFF.
GO ON.
WELL, YOU KNOW.
T.R.K. HAD WRITTEN ME FROM PRISON.
I WAS THE ONE WHO PUT HIM THERE, AND--
WAIT--HOW DID HE KNOW WHERE TO WRITE YOU?
WELL, I SORT OF WROTE HIM FIRST.
UH HUH.
WE'D BEEN CORRESPONDING LIKE THIS WHOLE TIME.
AND WE GOT PRETTY TIGHT.
AND AFTER HE GOT OUT LAST YEAR, WE STARTED HANGING OUT.
WHAT?
WE ENDED UP HAVING A LOT IN COMMON.
BOTH OF US HAD TROUBLE GETTING OUR CAREERS TOGETHER...
WE'D BEEN WRITING FOR TEN YEARS.
GO ON.
WELL, WE BOTH BEEN TALKING ABOUT HOW RESTLESS WE FELT BEING OUT OF THE GAME AND THE GLORY DAYS AND ALL THAT.
YOU KNOW?
GO ON.
SO'S HE CAME UP WITH THE IDEA TO START FRESH, YOU KNOW?
AND I SAYS WE NEEDED SOMETHING LIKE THAT SUMMER OF '89 TO REALLY PUT US ON THE MAP.
GET EVERYONE'S ATTENTION.
SO, YOU PLANNED A ROBBERY TOGETHER FOR YOU TO BREAK UP?
WE ALREADY CALLED THE POLICE AND THAT BITCH AT CHANNEL FIVE, AND THEY WERE ON THE WAY DOWN.
AND WE WERE WAITING FOR YOU GUYS TO SHOW UP, AND I WAS GOING TO HAND HIM OVER, AND HE WOULD ESCAPE FROM YOU, AND WE'D BE BACK IN THE GAME.

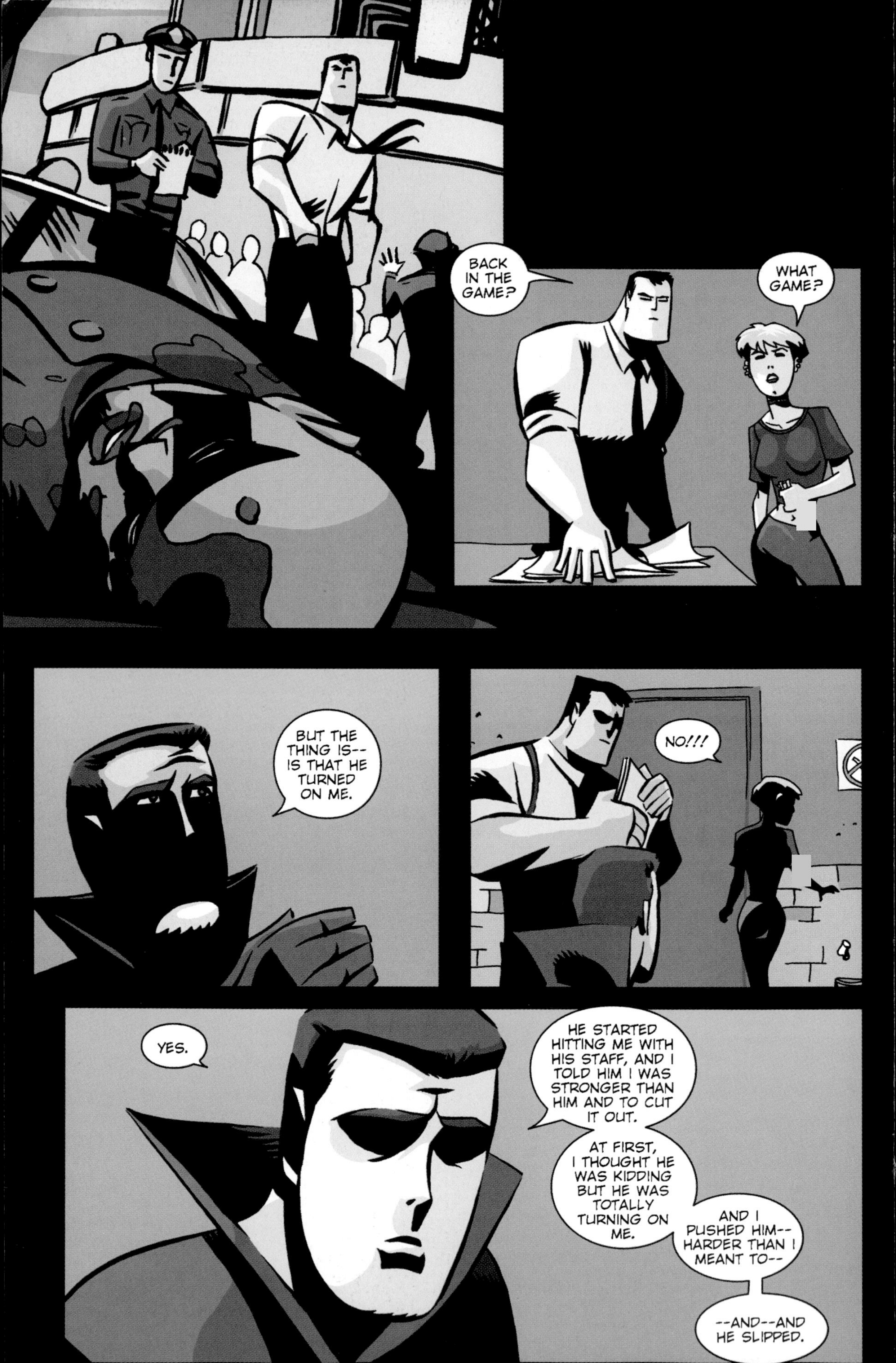

BACK IN THE GAME?
WHAT GAME?
BUT THE THING IS-- IS THAT HE TURNED ON ME.
NO!!!
YES.
HE STARTED HITTING ME WITH HIS STAFF, AND I TOLD HIM I WAS STRONGER THAN HIM AND TO CUT IT OUT.
AT FIRST, I THOUGHT HE WAS KIDDING BUT HE WAS TOTALLY TURNING ON ME.
AND I PUSHED HIM-- HARDER THAN I MEANT TO--
--AND--AND HE SLIPPED.

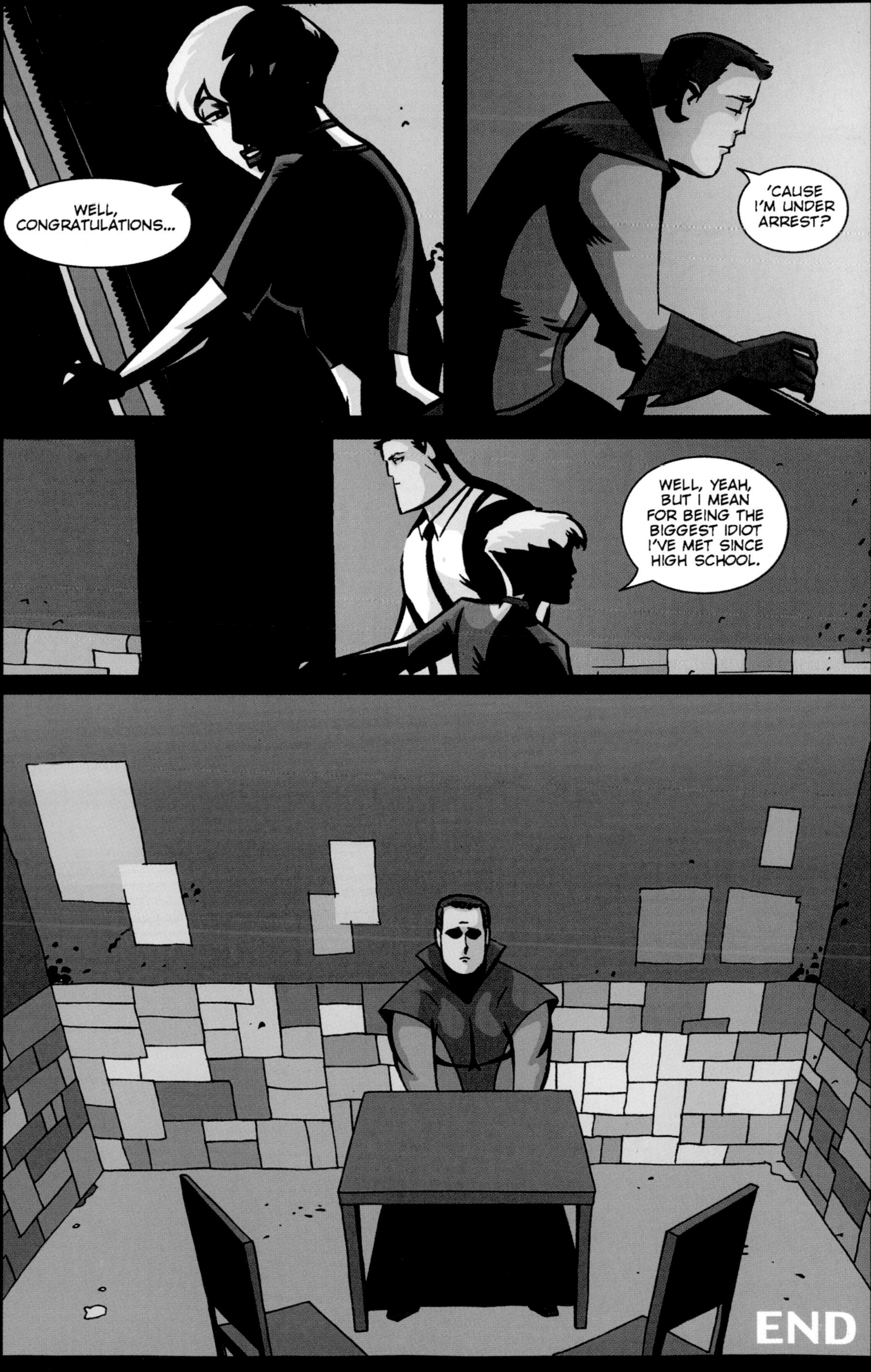
WELL, CONGRATULATIONS...
'CAUSE I'M UNDER ARREST?
WELL, YEAH, BUT I MEAN FOR BEING THE BIGGEST IDIOT I'VE MET SINCE HIGH SCHOOL.
END

PARTIAL TRANSCRIPT FROM COURT DOCKET 55673-2433

THE PEOPLE VS. GRIFFIN MILLS.

APPEARANCES:

For Plaintiff:

Attorney CLIVE BARROW

For Defendant:

NICHOLAS CORIC District Attorney

JULIET PECK Assistant District Attorney

CSR# 45564

OFFICIAL REPORTER ROBERT STRICT

DATED October 25, 2001 COURTROOM 4

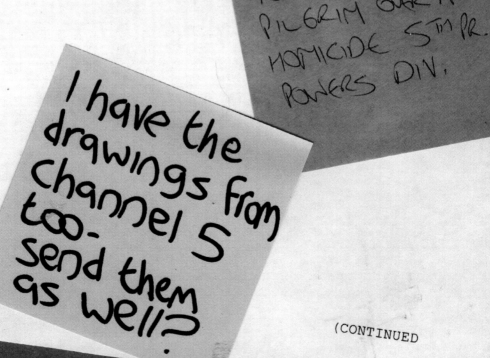

CC: THIS PUPPY OVER TO A DET. DEENA PILGRIM OVER AT HOMICIDE STH PR. POWERS DIV.

I have the drawings from channel 5 too - send them as well?

(CONTINUED

CONTINUED:

COURT RESUMES. 10:11 am October 22, 2001

                    DEFENSE ATTORNEY CLIVE BARROW
          THE DEFENSE WOULD LIKE TO CALL TO THE
          STAND... MR. THOMAS MILLS.

DEFENDANT THOMAS MILLS TAKES THE STAND. THE BAILIFF
APPROACHES.

                    BAILIFF
          DO YOU SWEAR TO TELL THE TRUTH, THE WHOLE
          TRUTH, AND NOTHING BUT THE TRUTH, SO HELP
          YOU GOD?

                    TOMMY MILLS
          YES. YES, I DO.

                    BAILIFF
          YOU MAY SIT.

DEFENSE ATTORNEY CLIVE BARROW APPROACHES.

                    DEFENSE ATTORNEY CLIVE BARROW
          THOMAS...

                    TOMMY MILLS
          TOMMY IS OK?

                    DEFENSE ATTORNEY CLIVE BARROW
          TOMMY, TELL THE COURT HOW YOU CAME TO
          HAVE POWERS?

                    TOMMY MILLS
          WELL, IN COLLEGE I WAS WORKING A- A
          SUMMER CONSTRUCTION JOB. JUST MANUAL
          STUFF. WE WERE MAKING ROOM FOR THIS RIG-
          DIGGING. CLEARING AN AREA OUT FOR IT. AND
          ONE OF THE GUYS HIT ONE OF THE
          UNDERGROUND PIPES- OR WE THOUGHT IT WAS A
          PIPE, BUT IT WAS ACTUALLY THIS METAL
          CANISTER OF SOME KIND. AND WHEN THE GUY-
          SCOTTY- WHEN HE HIT IT WITH HIS SHOVEL-
          THIS GAS CAME SEEPING OUT. IT WAS FULL OF
          THIS BLUEISH GAS. AND EVERYONE AROUND ME.
          WE- WE ALL STARTED CHOKING. I FAINTED. I
          NEVER DID THAT BEFORE, BUT I FAINTED. I
          WAS HOLDING MY EYES. AND WHEN I WOKE UP
          IN THE HOSPITAL, THEY TOLD ME THAT
          EVERYONE ELSE AT THE SITE HAD DIED.
          EVERYONE EXCEPT FOR ME.

                    DEFENSE ATTORNEY CLIVE BARROW
          A BLUE-ISH GAS.

                                        (CONTINUED

                    TOMMY MILLS
          YES.

                    DEFENSE ATTORNEY CLIVE BARROW
          DID YOU EVER FIND OUT WHAT THE GAS WAS?

                    TOMMY MILLS
          NO, NO BUT I ASKED AROUND. I ASKED THE
          CONSTRUCTION COMPANY I WORKED FOR BUT
          THEY SAID THEY DIDN'T KNOW. SOMEONE TOLD
          ME SOMETHING ABOUT THE F.B.I. BEING
          INVOLVED, BUT I DON'T REALLY KNOW
          ANYTHING BEYOND THAT.

                    PROSECUTOR CORIC
          OBJECTION.

                    JUDGE ROLLINS
          SUSTAINED.

                    DEFENSE ATTORNEY CLIVE BARROW
          HOW MANY PEOPLE DIED IN THE ACCIDENT,
          TOMMY?

                    TOMMY MILLS
          UH- TEN. TEN.

                    DEFENSE ATTORNEY CLIVE BARROW
          AND YOU WERE THE SOLE SURVIVOR?

                    TOMMY MILLS
          WELL, SOME OTHER GUYS RAN AWAY BEFORE THE
          GAS REACHED THEM, BUT I WAS THE ONLY ONE
          IN THE IMMEDIATE AREA. YEAH, IT WAS
          REALLY SAD.

                    DEFENSE ATTORNEY CLIVE BARROW
          THE SOLE SURVIVOR.

                    TOMMY MILLS
          I DON'T KNOW WHY? BUT YEAH, I GUESS.

                    DEFENSE ATTORNEY CLIVE BARROW
          AND WHEN YOU RECOVERED YOU FOUND THAT YOU
          HAD POWERS.

                    TOMMY MILLS
          YES, SIR.

                    DEFENSE ATTORNEY CLIVE BARROW
          WHAT POWERS DO YOU HAVE, TOMMY?

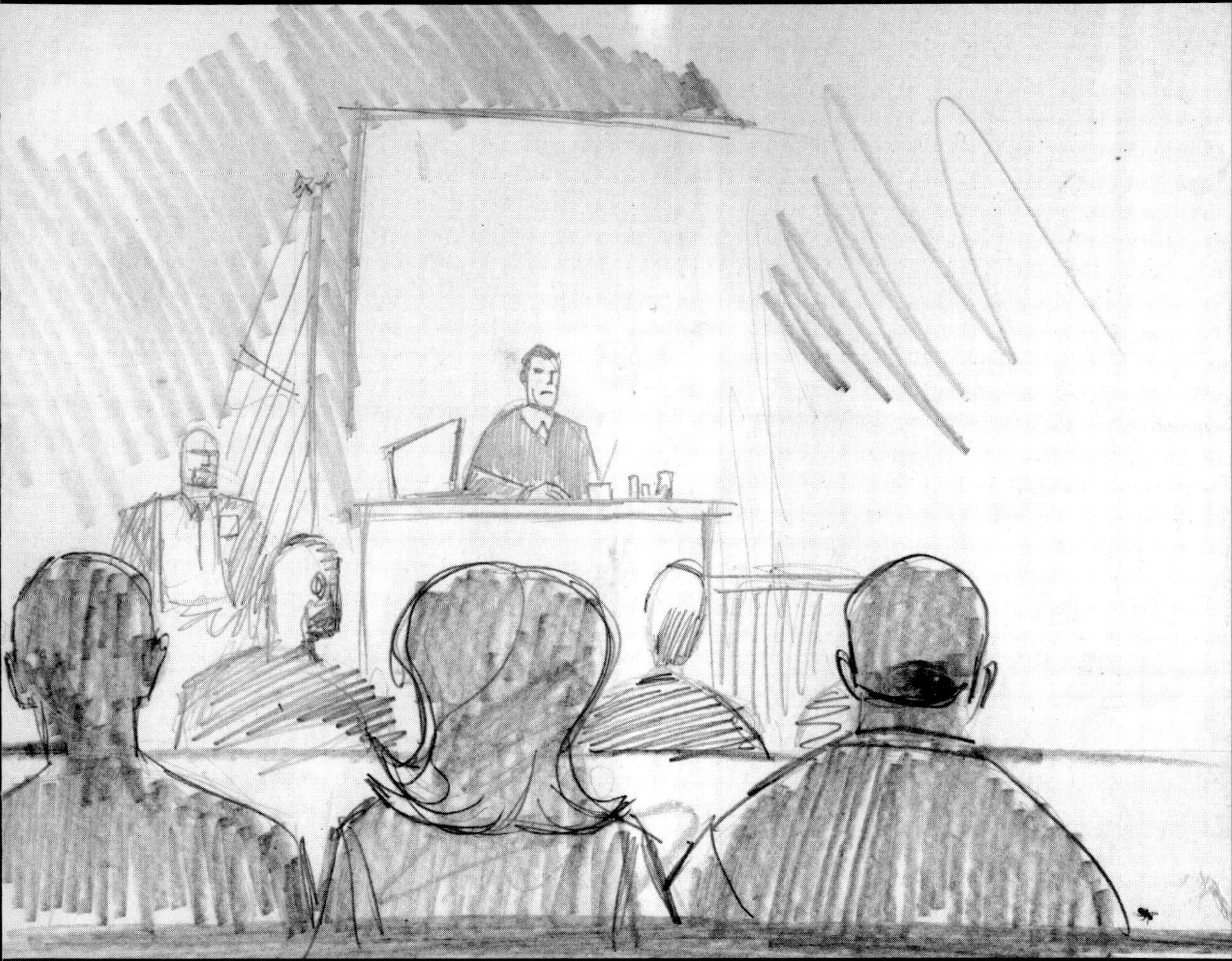

COURTROOM DRAWINGS COURTESY OEMING STUDIOS

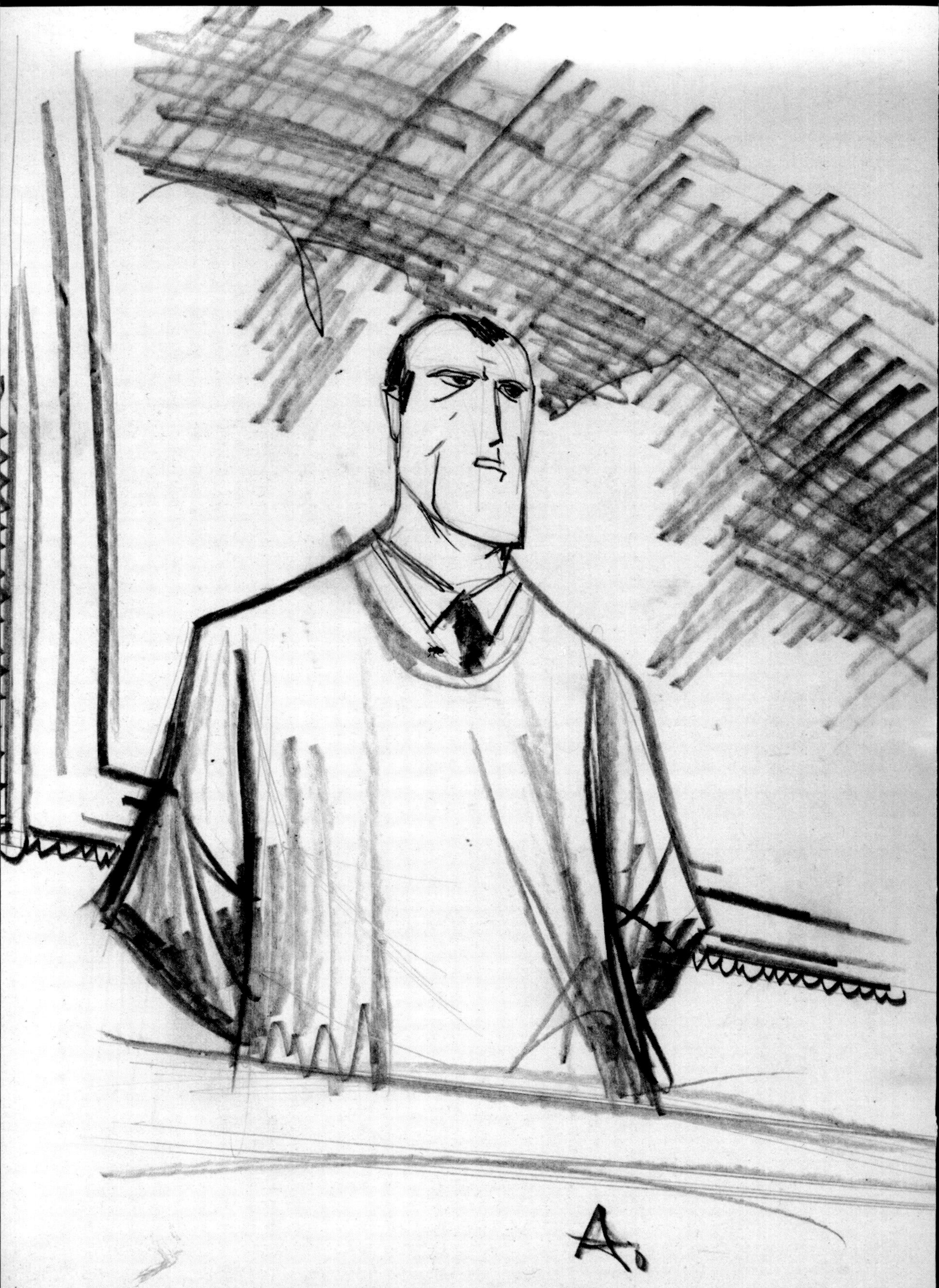

> TOMMY MILLS
> I HAVE - WELL, I'M PRETTY STRONG AND I
> CAN JUMP REALLY HIGH. CAN'T FLY, JUST
> JUMP. AND I'M PRETTY FAST NOW, AND MY
> SKIN IS- IT DOESN'T BREAK THAT EASILY.
> AND MY EYE SIGHT. ALL MY SENSES REALLY-
> THEY'RE REALLY STRONG. I REGISTERED IN AT
> LEVEL FIVE.

> DEFENSE ATTORNEY CLIVE BARROW
> AND WHEN YOU FOUND YOU HAD THESE POWERS,
> WHAT DID YOU DO?

> TOMMY MILLS
> I- WELL, IT WAS KIND OF FATE REALLY,
> BECAUSE THAT SAME WEEK I HAPPENED TO WALK
> INTO A CONVENIENT STORE THAN WAS BEING
> HELD UP AND I - I WAS ABLE TO STOP THE
> BURGLARY. NO ONE WAS HURT. IT- IT WAS A
> GOOD FEELING.

> DEFENSE ATTORNEY CLIVE BARROW
> WOW.

> TOMMY MILLS
> AND I REALIZED THAT I- I HAD A CALLING-
> THAT I WAS REALLY LUCKY.

> DEFENSE ATTORNEY CLIVE BARROW
> INDEED.

> TOMMY MILLS
> SO, I REGISTERED MY COSTUME, GAVE MYSELF
> A NAME.

> DEFENSE ATTORNEY CLIVE BARROW
> 'METEOR?'

> TOMMY MILLS
> METEOR.

> DEFENSE ATTORNEY CLIVE BARROW
> WHY METEOR?

> TOMMY MILLS
> THOUGHT IT SOUNDED PRETTY COOL.

COURTROOM SNICKERS. JUDGE HITS THE GAVEL.

> JUDGE ROLLINS
> ORDER.

                    TOMMY MILLS
          WELL, I-I-I DID.

                    DEFENSE ATTORNEY CLIVE BARROW
          YOU HAD A PRETTY STRONG START WITH YOUR
          NEW CAREER. A COUPLE OF COLORFUL DISPLAYS
          OF HEROISM.

                    TOMMY MILLS
          YES, SIR.

                    DEFENSE ATTORNEY CLIVE BARROW
          YOU SAVED THAT GIRL IN THE PARK.

                    TOMMY MILLS
          YES, SIR.

                    DEFENSE ATTORNEY CLIVE BARROW
          POWERS MAGAZINE FEATURED YOU IN THEIR 'ON
          THE RISE' SIDE BAR

                    TOMMY MILLS
          YES, SIR.

                    DEFENSE ATTORNEY CLIVE BARROW
          BUT YOU KIND OF FELL OUT OF THE SPOTLIGHT
          AFTER THAT...

                    TOMMY MILLS
          YES, SIR.

                    DEFENSE ATTORNEY CLIVE BARROW
          WHAT HAPPENED? WHERE'D YOU GO?

                    TOMMY MILLS
          WELL, I WAS STILL PRETTY NEW AT ALL OF
          IT, AND I DIDN'T UNDERSTAND, REALLY, HOW
          THE MEDIA WORKED. SO WHEN I WAS ASKED BY
          THIS MAGAZINE SOMETHING ABOUT A POWERED
          PERSONS RESPONSIBILITY IN OUR SOCIETY AND
          IF IT WAS GOOD FOR THE CITY- WELL, I HAD
          MY QUOTE TAKEN OUT OF CONTEXT AND-

                    DEFENSE ATTORNEY CLIVE BARROW
          WHAT DID YOU SAY?

                    TOMMY MILLS
          I SAID THAT I THOUGHT IT WAS GOOD FOR THE
          CITY TO HAVE PEOPLE WHO WERE WILLING TO
          BE WHERE THE COPS WEREN'T ABLE TO BE OR
          COULDN'T BE. BUT IN THE ARTICLE IT
          SOUNDED WRONG.
                         (MORE)

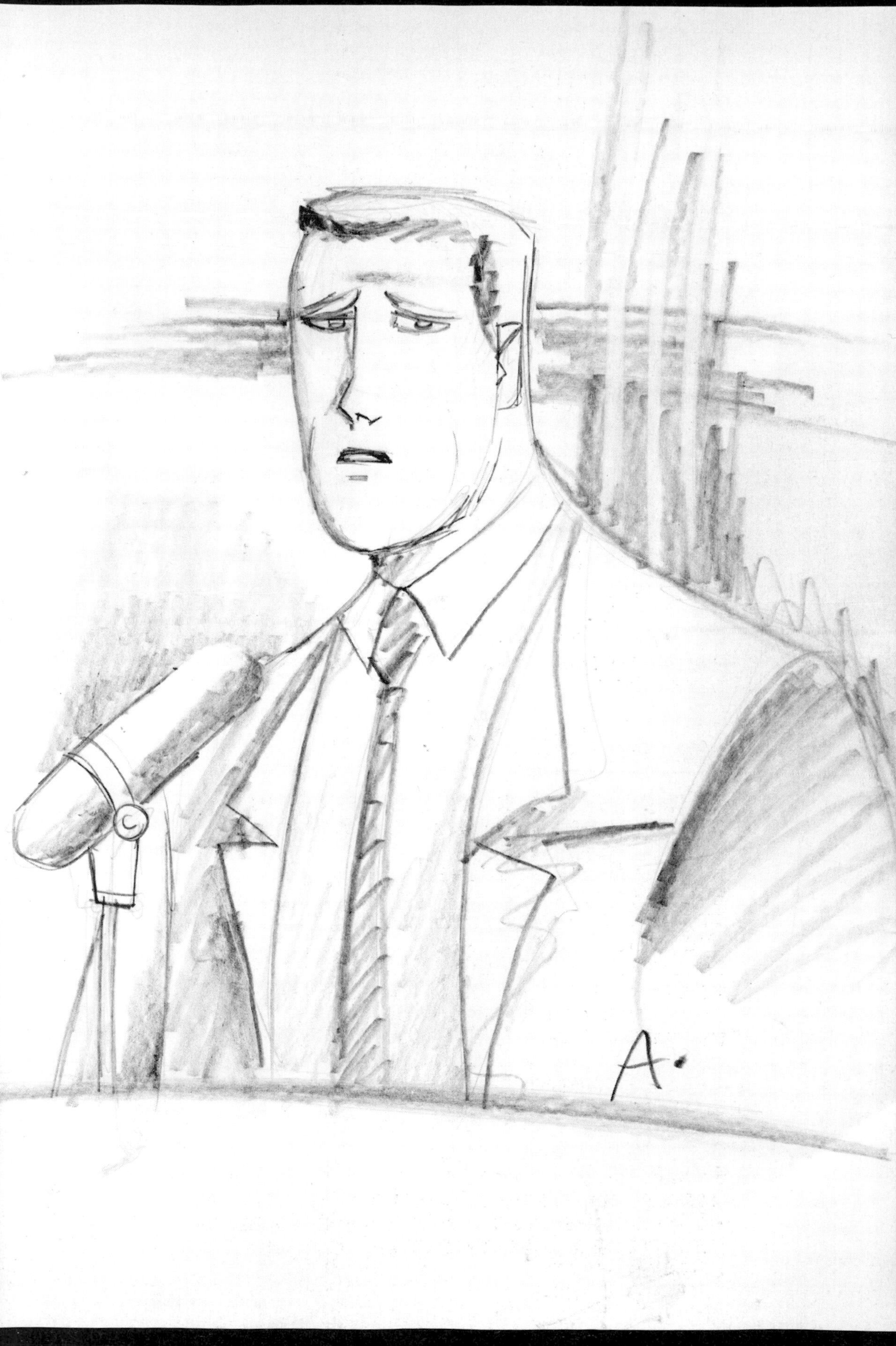
A.

CONTINUED: (5)

> TOMMY MILLS (CONT'D)
> IT SOUNDED IN THE ARTICLE AS IF I THOUGHT
> SUPER POWERED PEOPLE WERE DOING THE COPS
> JOB FOR THEM. THE TONE OF THE PIECE, IT-
> IT WASN'T WHAT I WAS TOLD IT WAS GOING TO
> BE.

> DEFENSE ATTORNEY CLIVE BARROW
> AND WHERE DID THIS ARTICLE RUN?

> TOMMY MILLS
> IN AIR MAGAZINE.

> DEFENSE ATTORNEY CLIVE BARROW
> YOU THINK THE COMMENTS WERE TAKEN OUT OF
> CONTEXT?

> TOMMY MILLS
> OH, DEFINITELY. I WASN'T SLAMMING THE
> COPS. I ADMIRE THE COPS. I- I WAS TRYING
> TO SAY SOMETHING POSITIVE. I THOUGHT IT
> WAS NICE THAT WE HAVE THE COPS PLUS WE
> ALSO HAVE PEOPLE WHO ARE WILLING TO DRESS
> UP AND SYMBOLIZE SOMETHING AND BE
> PROACTIVE IN THE COMMUNITY.

> DEFENSE ATTORNEY CLIVE BARROW
> 'PROACTIVE IN THE COMMUNITY.' WELL SAID.

> TOMMY MILLS
> THANKS, WELL, THIS- THIS ARTICLE WAS LIKE
> A DEATH RATTLE FOR MY CAREER AS A SUPER
> HERO. ALL THE COPS PUT ME ON THEIR SHIT
> LIST OR SOMETHING. EXCUSE MY LANGUAGE. I-
> I COULDN'T CATCH A BREAK AFTER THE
> ARTICLE. IT WAS WEIRD.

> DEFENSE ATTORNEY CLIVE BARROW
> HOW SO?

> TOMMY MILLS
> THE COPS- THE POLICE WOULD IGNORE ME WHEN
> THEY SHOWED UP. WHICH IS FINE, I GUESS. I
> MEAN, THEY CERTAINLY DON'T OWE ME
> ANYTHING. OR- YEAH- OR THEY WOULD TAKE
> THE GUY I CAUGHT FOR THEM AND BOOK HIM
> WITHOUT GIVING ME ANY CREDIT IN THE
> REPORT. AND IN SOME INSTANCES THEY WOULD
> JUST LET THE GUY GO. JUST LET HIM GO
> RIGHT IN FRONT OF ME.

> PROSECUTOR CORIC
> OBJECTION. MOVE TO STRIKE.

(CONTINUED

                    JUDGE ROLLINS
SUSTAINED. COUNSELLOR? ROUND IT HOME.

               DEFENSE ATTORNEY CLIVE BARROW
SO YOU FELT YOUR ACTIONS WERE...?

                    TOMMY MILLS
I WAS TRYING TO BE HELPFUL. I WAS TRYING
TO BE PART OF THE COMMUNITY- BUT ITS HARD
WHEN THE COMMUNITY IS GIVING YOU THE COLD
SHOULDER. WHEN THE LAW ENFORCEMENT
OFFICIALS WERE-

                    PROSECUTOR CORIC
OBJECTION.

                    JUDGE ROLLINS
SUSTAINED. MOVE FORWARD ON THIS.

                    TOMMY MILLS
WELL, IT- IT WAS MADE VERY CLEAR AFTER
THAT ARTICLE THAT THERE WAS LITTLE OR NO
NEED FOR 'METEOR.' I KNOW WHEN I'M NOT
WANTED.

               DEFENSE ATTORNEY CLIVE BARROW
WHAT DID YOU DO?

                    TOMMY MILLS
I TOOK THE HINT AND I - I WENT BACK TO MY
NORMAL LIFE. CIVILIAN LIFE.

               DEFENSE ATTORNEY CLIVE BARROW
TELL ME HOW YOU MET REGINALD COPPER WHO
WE NOW KNOW PUBLICLY AS T.R.K.

                    TOMMY MILLS
BEFORE I RETIRED, HE TRIED TO ROB THE
NOZAMACK JEWELRY STORE.

               DEFENSE ATTORNEY CLIVE BARROW
THE ONE DOWNTOWN?

                    TOMMY MILLS
YES. AND I GOT TO HIM BEFORE HE DID ANY
REAL DAMAGE OR GOT AWAY.

               DEFENSE ATTORNEY CLIVE BARROW
AND HE WENT TO JAIL BECAUSE OF THIS.
BECAUSE OF YOU'RE TIMELY EFFORTS.

                    TOMMY MILLS
YES.

                    DEFENSE ATTORNEY CLIVE BARROW
AND YOU WERE IN CONTACT WITH HIM AFTER
THAT?

                    TOMMY MILLS
YES, WE CORRESPONDED.

                    DEFENSE ATTORNEY CLIVE BARROW
BY MAIL.

                    TOMMY MILLS
YES. HE TOLD ME IT WAS PART OF A PROGRAM
IN THE PRISON. A PRISON PROGRAM. THE
PRIEST TOLD HIM TO BREAK DOWN THE WALL
BETWEEN WHERE HE WAS AND HOW HE GOT HERE.

                    DEFENSE ATTORNEY CLIVE BARROW
AND YOU RESPONDED?

                    TOMMY MILLS
YES, IT WAS A HEARTFELT LETTER AND I FELT
WE ACTUALLY HAD A LOT IN COMMON. IT
SEEMED LIKE THE RIGHT THING TO DO.

                    DEFENSE ATTORNEY CLIVE BARROW
AND HE FOUND YOU, HOW?

                    TOMMY MILLS
I ASSUMED HE LOOKED IT UP IN THE BOOK. I-
I REALLY DIDN'T SEE THE REASON FOR A
SECRET IDENTITY.

                    DEFENSE ATTORNEY CLIVE BARROW
WHY NOT?

                    TOMMY MILLS
THEY ALWAYS SEEMED TO ME TO BE KIND OF
LIKE LYING. LYING AND HIDING. JUST DIDN'T
OCCUR TO ME TO DO THAT.

                    DEFENSE ATTORNEY CLIVE BARROW
AND YOU KEPT THIS UP- THIS CORRESPONDENCE
FOR THE ENTIRE NINE YEARS HE WAS IN
PRISON.

                    TOMMY MILLS
YES. ON AND OFF. BUT YES.

                    DEFENSE ATTORNEY CLIVE BARROW
SO, YOU WERE FRIENDS?

                    TOMMY MILLS
I THOUGHT SO, YES.

                    DEFENSE ATTORNEY CLIVE BARROW
AND IN ALL THAT TIME DID HE EVER TELL YOU
THAT HE PLANNED ON ROBBING AGAIN WHEN HE
GOT OUT?

                    TOMMY MILLS
NO, SIR. NO.

                    DEFENSE ATTORNEY CLIVE BARROW
HE DIDN'T?

                    TOMMY MILLS
NO, NO I WOULD HAVE ENDED THE
CORRESPONDENCE IMMEDIATELY IF THAT HAD
HAPPENED.

                    DEFENSE ATTORNEY CLIVE BARROW
DID YOU EVER TALK ABOUT IT IN THE
HYPOTHETICAL?

                    TOMMY MILLS
NO. NEVER. HE ONLY BROUGHT UP HIS PAST IN
THE CONTEXT OF HIS TALKS WITH THE PRIEST.
HE ALWAYS SOUNDED VERY REMORSEFUL.
ALWAYS.

                    DEFENSE ATTORNEY CLIVE BARROW
AND WHEN HE GOT OUT OF JAIL, YOU SAW EACH
OTHER SOCIALLY?

                    TOMMY MILLS
ONLY A COUPLE OF TIMES. HE WAS ONLY OUT A
FEW MONTHS.

                    DEFENSE ATTORNEY CLIVE BARROW
WHAT DID YOU TALK ABOUT WHEN YOU GOT
TOGETHER?

                    TOMMY MILLS
WELL, LOTS OF STUFF. MOVIES, GIRLS. BUT
WE TALKED A LOT ABOUT HOW HARD IT WAS FOR
HIM TO READJUST TO CIVILIAN LIFE.

                    DEFENSE ATTORNEY CLIVE BARROW
AND WAS IT DURING THESE TALKS THAT HE
BROUGHT UP THE IDEA OF ROBBING THE-

                    PROSECUTOR CORIC
OBJECTION. LEADING.

                    JUDGE ROLLINS
SUSTAINED. CONTINUE.

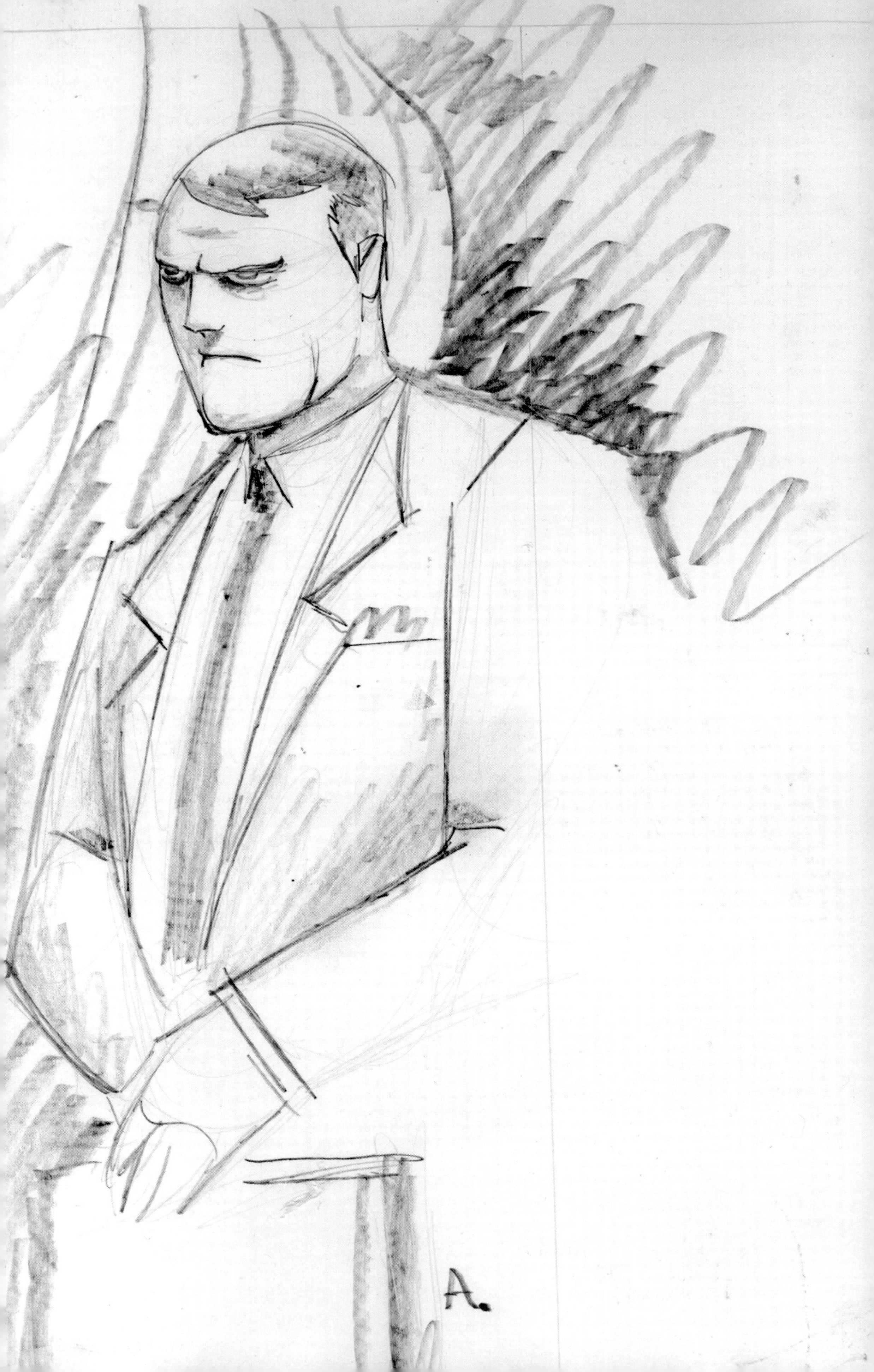
A.

> DEFENSE ATTORNEY CLIVE BARROW
> WHEN WAS THE FIRST TIME REGINALD BROUGHT
> UP THE IDEA OF THE ROBBERY?

> TOMMY MILLS
> THAT DAY. THE DAY HE- HE DIED.

> DEFENSE ATTORNEY CLIVE BARROW
> HOW DID IT COME UP?

> TOMMY MILLS
> HE STARTED TALKING ABOUT HOW RESTLESS HE
> FELT BEING OUT OF 'THE GAME' AND THE
> GLORY DAYS AND ALL THAT. YOU KNOW?

> DEFENSE ATTORNEY CLIVE BARROW
> UH HUH.

> TOMMY MILLS
> HE SAID HE HAD AN IDEA TO START FRESH. HE
> SAID WE- WE NEEDED SOMETHING LIKE THAT
> SUMMER OF '89 TO REALLY PUT US ON THE MAP
> AGAIN. TO GET EVERYONE'S ATTENTION. HE
> SAID HE WAS GOING TO DO THE ROBBERY AND
> THAT I SHOULD TRY TO BREAK IT UP, BUT LET
> HIM GET AWAY JUST IN THE NICK OF TIME. HE
> SAID WE'D BOTH MAKE THE PAPER. I COULDN'T
> BELIEVE WHAT HE WAS SAYING.

> DEFENSE ATTORNEY CLIVE BARROW
> AND WHAT DID YOU SAY?

> TOMMY MILLS
> AT FIRST, I THOUGHT HE WAS JOKING. HE- IT
> WAS SO UNLIKE HIM. IT WAS ONLY AFTER HE
> STARTED TALKING THIS WAY THAT I REALIZED
> THAT HE MIGHT HAVE BEEN DRINKING. HE WAS
> QUITE IRRATIONAL AND VERY UNLIKE HIMSELF-
> EDGY. AND I - AND I FELT BAD FOR HIM
> BECAUSE I KNEW HOW HARD HE HAD TRIED TO
> GET HIS LIFE TOGETHER, BUT AT THE SAME
> TIME- I WAS, WELL, OVERWHELMED WITH A
> FEELING OF DISGUST AND BETRAYAL THAT MY
> FRIEND- THIS PERSON I THOUGHT WAS MY
> FRIEND- WOULD NOW SOMEHOW TRY TO INVOLVE
> ME IN THIS.

> DEFENSE ATTORNEY CLIVE BARROW
> SO, YOU TOLD HIM NO.

> TOMMY MILLS
> I DID, THEN I PAID THE BILL, GOT UP, AND
> I WALKED OUT OF THE DINER.

                    DEFENSE ATTORNEY CLIVE BARROW
BUT YOU CAME BACK.

                    TOMMY MILLS
IT- IT WAS VERY CLEAR THAT I HAD TO STOP
HIM. THAT I HAD TO COME BACK INTO 'THE
GAME' AND STOP HIM.

                    DEFENSE ATTORNEY CLIVE BARROW
WHY DIDN'T YOU CALL THE POLICE?

                    TOMMY MILLS
I DID.

                    DEFENSE ATTORNEY CLIVE BARROW
YOU DID?

                    TOMMY MILLS
I DID. BUT THEY SAID SQUAD CARS WERE
ALREADY ON THE WAY THERE. THEY SAID HE
CALLED IT IN- DARED THEM, TO COME GET
HIM.

                    DEFENSE ATTORNEY CLIVE BARROW
SO WHY DIDN'T YOU JUST STAY HOME?

                    TOMMY MILLS
I COULDN'T- I KNEW WHAT HE COULD DO TO
THE POLICE OFFICERS. I KNEW WHAT HIS
WEAPONRY COULD DO TO THEM IF THEY WEREN'T
PREPARED. AND I COULD GET THERE IN NO
TIME AT ALL. I FELT A RESPONSIBILITY. TEN
YEARS. HE WAS MY FRIEND.

                    DEFENSE ATTORNEY CLIVE BARROW
AND WHEN YOU GOT THERE...

                    TOMMY MILLS
HE SAID HE KNEW I WOULD COME, THAT I
WOULDN'T LET HIM DOWN. I TOLD HIM- I SAID
I WASN'T THERE TO HELP. I WAS THERE TO
STOP HIM BEFORE THINGS GOT OUT OF HAND.
BUT HE STARTED LAUGHING AND SWINGING
WILDLY. HE- HE -HE JUST WENT MANIC ON ME.

                    DEFENSE ATTORNEY CLIVE BARROW
AND THAT'S WHEN HE SLIPPED.

                    TOMMY MILLS
THAT'S WHEN HE SLIPPED.

>   DEFENSE ATTORNEY CLIVE BARROW
>   IN YOUR OPINION, WAS THERE ANYWAY FOR YOU
>   TO SAVE HIM?

>   TOMMY MILLS
>   DON'T YOU THINK I WOULD HAVE IF I COULD?

>   DEFENSE ATTORNEY CLIVE BARROW
>   NO FURTHER QUESTIONS.

PROSECUTOR CORIC APPROACHES.

>   PROSECUTOR CORIC
>   MR. MILLS, YOU TOLD THE DETECTIVES WHO
>   QUESTIONED AND THEN ARRESTED YOU FOR
>   MURDER THAT YOU WERE NOT IN THE DINER
>   THAT NIGHT. YOU HELD TO THAT STORY UNTIL
>   THEY COULD PROVE TO YOU THAT YOU WERE
>   THERE WITH A CREDIT CARD RECEIPT. AND NOW
>   YOU SAY YOU WERE THERE- BUT THAT YOU
>   QUICKLY LEFT AFTER YOU FOUND OUT THE
>   DECEASED HAD A DASTARDLY PLAN.

>   TOMMY MILLS
>   YES.

>   PROSECUTOR CORIC
>   SO AFTER YOUR FRIEND BETRAYED YOUR TRUST
>   AND ADMITTED TO YOU WHAT HIS INTENTIONS
>   WERE- YOU STOPPED AND BOUGHT HIM DINNER?

>   TOMMY MILLS
>   I-

>   PROSECUTOR CORIC
>   YOU DIDN'T JUST WALK RIGHT OUT AND LEAVE
>   IN A HUFF. YOU FELT COMPELLED TO SAY:
>   I'LL GET THIS ONE?

>   TOMMY MILLS
>   I-

>   PROSECUTOR CORIC
>   YES?

>   TOMMY MILLS
>   I JUST DID.

>   PROSECUTOR CORIC
>   MR. MILLS, IN THIS TEN YEARS OF
>   CORRESPONDENCE WITH THE DECEASED DID YOU
>   EVER KEEP ANY OF THE LETTERS?

(CONTINUED

                    TOMMY MILLS
          NO.

                    PROSECUTOR CORIC
          NO?

                    TOMMY MILLS
          NO.

                    PROSECUTOR CORIC
          WHY NOT?

                    TOMMY MILLS
          I'M KIND OF A NEAT FREAK. DON'T LIKE-
          DON'T LIKE A LOT OF CLUTTER.

                    PROSECUTOR CORIC
          WOULD IT SURPRISE YOU TO FIND OUT THAT
          THE DECEASED, IN FACT, DID?

                    TOMMY MILLS
          WHAT?

                    DEFENSE ATTORNEY CLIVE BARROW
          OBJECTION YOUR HONOR!

                    PROSECUTOR CORIC
          YOUR HONOR I WOULD LIKE TO ENTER INTO
          EVIDENCE THIS LOVELY CASE- FULL OF THE
          ACTUAL HANDWRITTEN CORRESPONDENCE BETWEEN
          THE DEFENDANT AND THE DECEASED AND I
          WOULD LIKE TO ENTER IT AS STATES EVIDENCE
          C.

                    DEFENSE ATTORNEY CLIVE BARROW
          OBJECTION!

                    JUDGE ROLLINS
          OVERRULED.

                    TOMMY MILLS
          WHAT IS GOING- ?

                    PROSECUTOR CORIC
          IS THIS YOUR HANDWRITING, SIR?

                    TOMMY MILLS
          I DON'T KNOW.

                    PROSECUTOR CORIC
          DID YOU WRITE THIS?

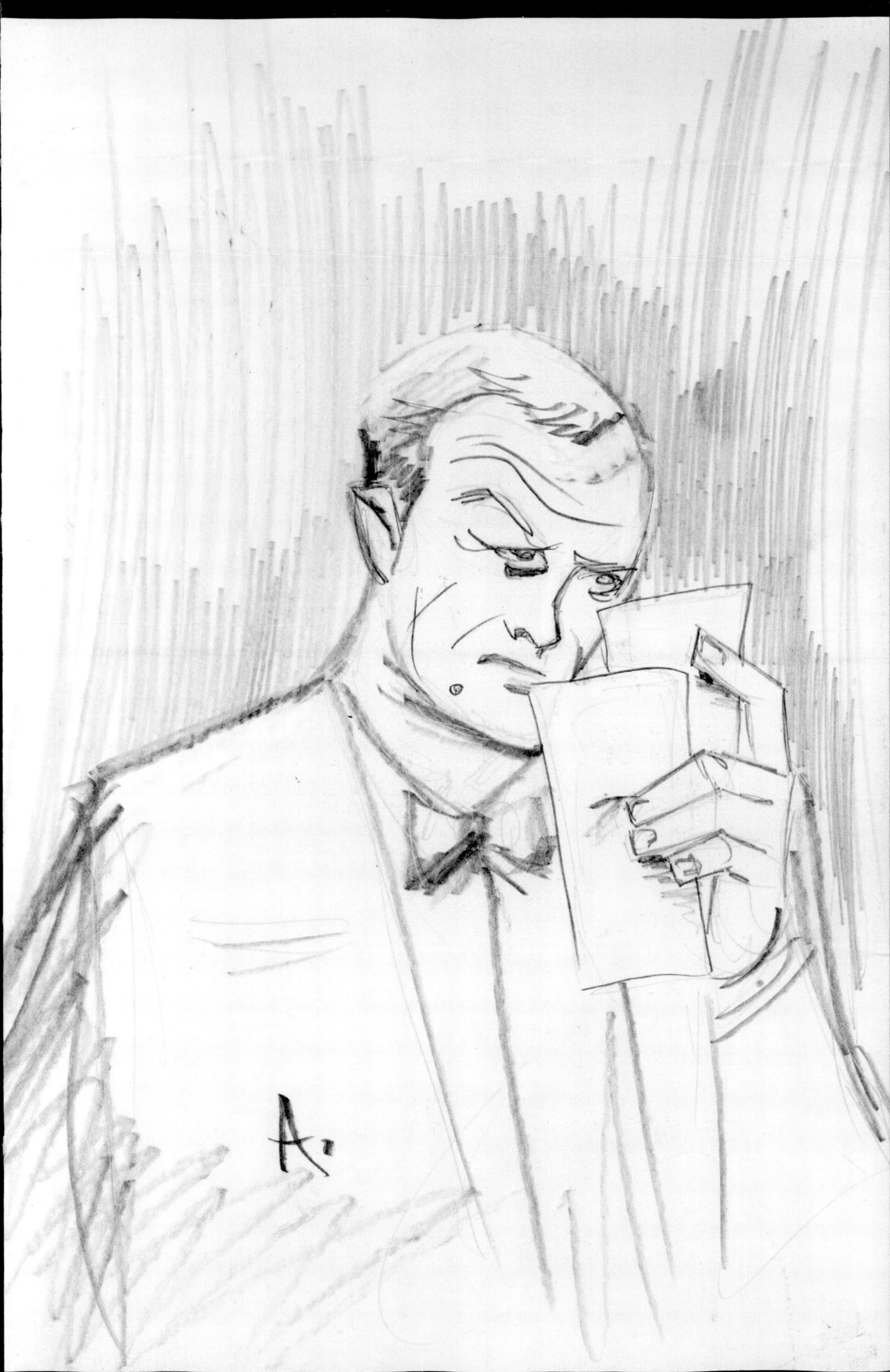
A.

14

CONTINUED: (13)

                    TOMMY MILLS
          I DON'T KNOW.

                    PROSECUTOR CORIC
          YOU DON'T KNOW? WELL, THAT'S OK, WE CAN
          GET A HANDWRITING EXPERT IN HERE IN A FEW
          MINUTES WHO WILL GLADLY TESTIFY THAT IT
          IS, IN FACT, YOUR VERY OWN HANDWRITING.
          WOULD YOU LIKE A CLOSER LOOK?

                    TOMMY MILLS
          NO.

                    PROSECUTOR CORIC
          NO? WOW, IF I WAS ON TRIAL FOR MURDER AND
          THE PROSECUTOR JUST SHOVED A PIECE OF
          PAPER IN MY FACE WHILE I WAS ON THE
          STAND... I WOULD WANT A CLOSER LOOK. BUT
          THAT'S ME. I'M A FREAK.

                    TOMMY MILLS
          IT MIGHT BE MINE.

                    PROSECUTOR CORIC
          'MIGHT BE?'

                    TOMMY MILLS
          ITS HARD TO SAY.

                    PROSECUTOR CORIC
          WELL, READ FOR ME THE HIGHLIGHTED AREA ON
          THIS ONE HERE. SEE IF IT RINGS ANY BELLS
          FOR YOU. THIS ONE IS DATED 2 YEARS AND 3
          MONTHS AGO. READ HERE. YOUR HONOR?

                    JUDGE ROLLINS
          MR. MILLS, PLEASE DO WHAT THE PROSECUTOR
          ASKS.

                    TOMMY MILLS
          'DEAR REG, UCHUM- I- UH- I WAS REALLY
          GLAD YOU WROTE BACK TO ME. I BET YOU WERE
          SHOCKED TO-'

                    PROSECUTOR CORIC
          LOUDER, MR. MILLS.

                    TOMMY MILLS
          'I BET YOU WERE SHOCKED TO HEAR FROM ME,
          OF ALL PEOPLE, OUT OF THE BLUE. I HAD A
          REALLY SHITTY WEEK THIS WEEK.
                    (MORE)

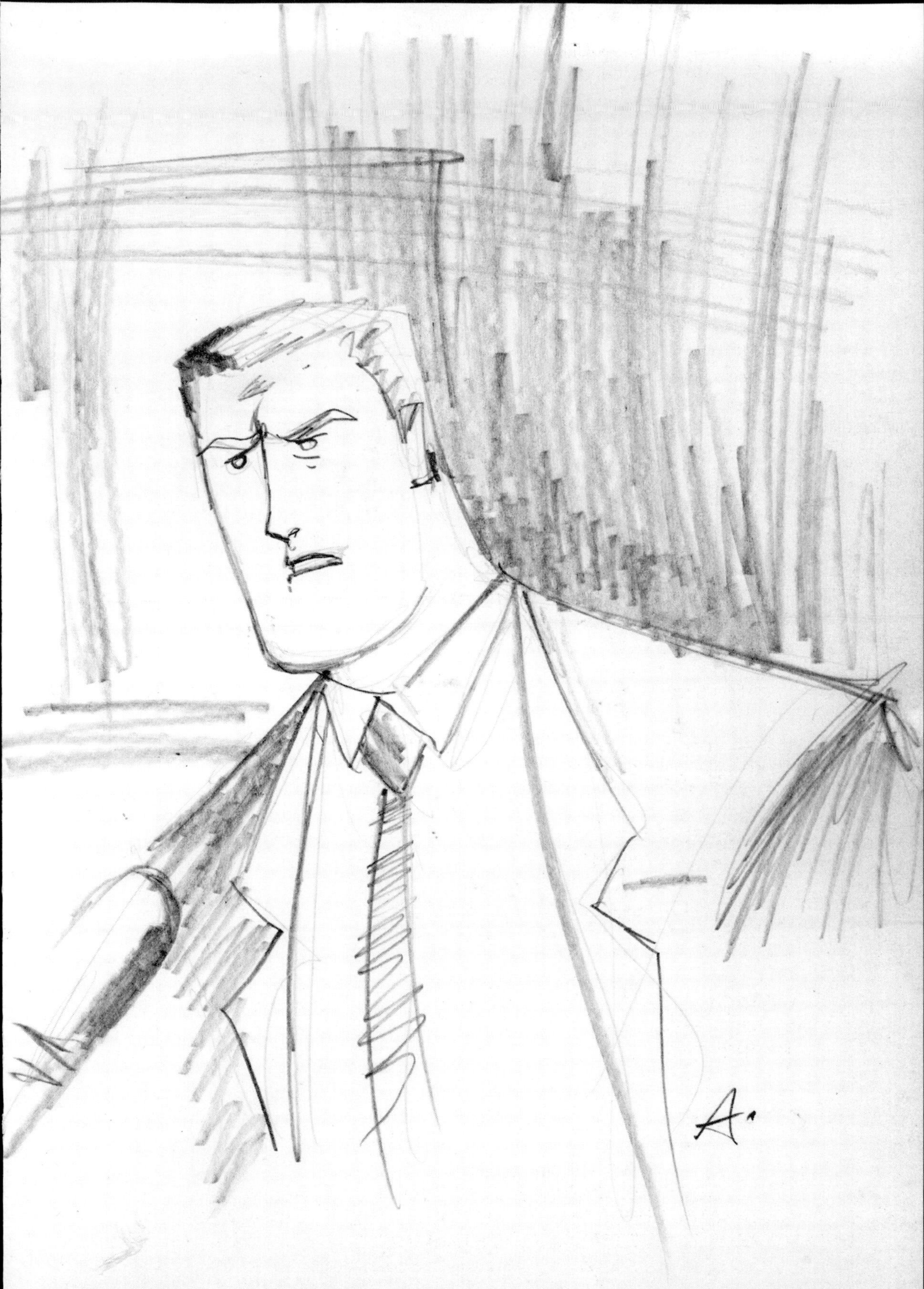

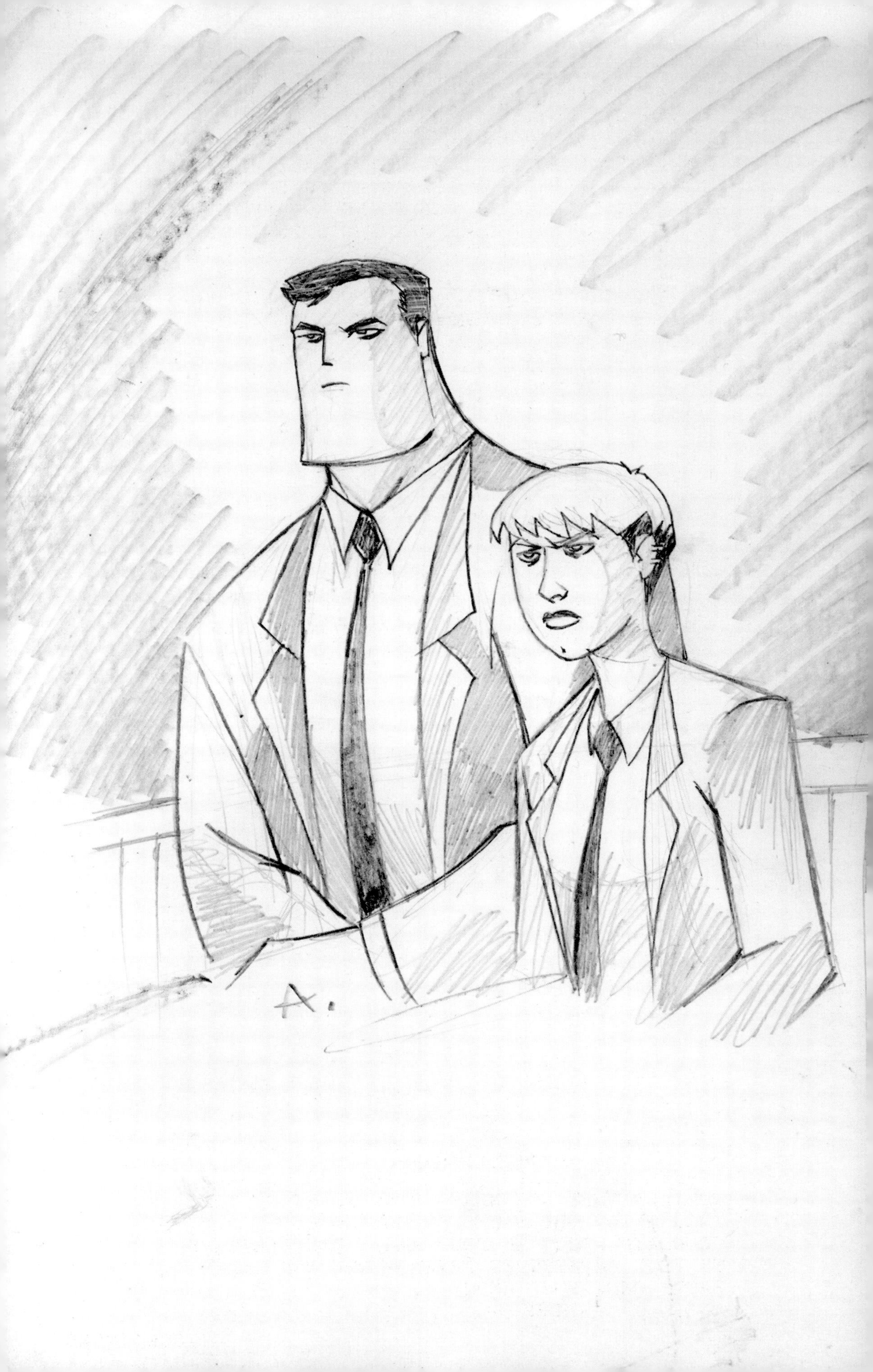

CONTINUED: (14)

                    TOMMY MILLS (CONT'D)
I KIND OF FEEL FUNNY BITCHING ABOUT MY
LIFE CONSIDERING YOUR SITUATION, BUT IT'S
REALLY NOT SO EASY ON THE OUTSIDE WORLD.
I HAVE THIS MENIAL JOB, YET I HAVE ALL
THESE THINGS- THESE POWERS I COULD- UH-
DO. WHEN I THINK OF ALL THOSE UNTALENTED
HACKS WITH ALL THOSE MERCHANDISING DEALS.
AND HERE I AM SITTING IN A CUBICLE HOPING
MY BITCH OF A BOSS DOESN'T BITCH AT ME.
WE GOT FIND A WAY TO... GET BACK IN THE
GAME. I DON'T KNOW ABOUT YOU... BUT I
JUST HAVE TO. ANY IDEAS?'

                    PROSECUTOR CORIC
DID YOU WRITE THAT?

                    TOMMY MILLS
MAYBE.

                    PROSECUTOR CORIC
WELL MR. MILLS, WE WILL HAVE THE
TESTIMONY FROM THE HANDWRITING EXPERT IN
A MINUTE. I HAVE ANOTHER QUESTION: YOU
TOLD THE ARRESTING DETECTIVES THAT THE
DECEASED CONTACTED YOU FROM JAIL FIRST.
THAT HE MADE FIRST CONTACT. WHICH IS IT?

                    TOMMY MILLS
WHAT- WHAT I SAID TODAY-

                    PROSECUTOR CORIC
'WHAT YOU SAID TODAY' WHAT?

                    TOMMY MILLS
WHAT I SAID TODAY- THAT- THAT IS THE
TRUTH.

                    PROSECUTOR CORIC
WILL IT BE THE TRUTH TOMORROW? OR IS WHAT
YOU SAY ONLY TRUE FOR THE DAY...

                    TOMMY MILLS
I...

                    DEFENSE ATTORNEY CLIVE BARROW
OBJECTION!

                    PROSECUTOR CORIC
STRIKE. MR. MILLS, IF, IN FACT, YOU HAD
NO IDEA THAT YOU WERE GOING TO BE GETTING
BACK INTO 'THE GAME' AS YOU SO ELOQUENTLY
COMPLAIN ABOUT IN YOUR MANY, MANY LETTERS
TO YOUR IMPRISONED FRIEND- WHO WAS, IN
FACT, ONCE YOUR ENEMY...
                    (MORE)

                                        (CONTINUED

CONTINUED: (15)

                    PROSECUTOR CORIC (CONT'D)
          HOW IS IT THAT YOU HAD A NEW IDENTITY AND
          COSTUME ALL READY TO GO?

                    TOMMY MILLS
          I DIDN'T SAY-

                    PROSECUTOR CORIC
          WHAT?

                    TOMMY MILLS
          I DIDN'T SAY I DIDN'T WANT TO GET BACK
          INTO 'THE GAME,' I SAID I -

                    PROSECUTOR CORIC
          PLEASE ANSWER THE QUESTION YOU WERE
          ASKED.

                    TOMMY MILLS
          I JUST HAD IT.

                    PROSECUTOR CORIC
          'YOU JUST HAD IT?' WOW. YOU JUST HAD A
          2000 DOLLAR COSTUME MADE. JUST HAPPENED
          TO HAVE IT.

                    TOMMY MILLS
          NO COMMENT.

                    PROSECUTOR CORIC
          NO COMMENT? THIS ISN'T A PRESS
          CONFERENCE. SIR, THIS IS A COURT OF LAW
          AND YOU ARE UNDER OATH.

                    TOMMY MILLS
          I...

                    PROSECUTOR CORIC
          IT'S OK MR. MILLS. I THINK YOU ANSWERED
          THE QUESTION QUITE CLEARLY. I'LL PUT THAT
          ANSWER INTO THE GIANT HOLE IN YOUR STORY
          ALONG WITH THE REST OF THEM.

                    DEFENSE ATTORNEY CLIVE BARROW
          OBJECTION.

                    PROSECUTOR CORIC
          NO FURTHER QUESTIONS.

DEFENSE ATTORNEY CLIVE BARROW APPROACHES.

                    DEFENSE ATTORNEY CLIVE BARROW
          TOMMY, WHEN YOU WERE BEING QUESTIONED BY
          THE POLICE WERE YOU UNDER WHAT THEY CALL:
          A DRAINER?

                    TOMMY MILLS
          YES, OH YEAH- YES.

                    DEFENSE ATTORNEY CLIVE BARROW
          WAS IT HARD FOR YOU TO THINK UNDER THE
          DRAINER?

                    PROSECUTOR CORIC
          OBJECTION.

                    JUDGE ROLLINS
          OVERRULED.

                    DEFENSE ATTORNEY CLIVE BARROW
          DID YOU COMPLAIN TO THE DETECTIVES THAT
          THE DRAINER WAS MAKING IT HARD TO THINK?

                    TOMMY MILLS
          YES, YES I DID. I TOLD THEM THAT I FELT
          ACHY AND NAUSEOUS, BUT THEY IGNORED ME.

                    DEFENSE ATTORNEY CLIVE BARROW
          THEY IGNORED YOU AGAIN. THESE POLICE.

                    PROSECUTOR CORIC
          OBJECTION YOUR HONOR! DRAINERS IN THE
          POLICE INTERROGATION ROOM ARE STANDARD
          ISSUE AND TOTALLY LEGAL. THEY ARE AN
          INTEGRAL PART OF THE OFFICER'S ARSENAL
          AGAINST PERPS WITH A HIGH FLIGHT RISK,
          LIKE MR. MILLS.

                    JUDGE ROLLINS
          SUSTAINED.

                    DEFENSE ATTORNEY CLIVE BARROW
          LET ME ASK YOU, TOMMY, DID YOU FEEL WHILE
          YOU WERE SITTING UNDER THE DRAINER, THAT
          YOU WERE BEING QUESTIONED IN A SITUATION
          IN WHICH YOU COULD CLEARLY, AND TO THE
          BEST OF YOUR ABILITIES, HELP THE
          DETECTIVES IN THEIR QUEST?

                    TOMMY MILLS
          NO. NO, NOT AT ALL.

                    DEFENSE ATTORNEY CLIVE BARROW
          IN YOUR OPINION, IS THIS THE MAGAZINE
          ARTICLE YOU MENTIONED COMING BACK TO
          HAUNT YOU ALL OVER AGAIN?

                    TOMMY MILLS
          THE THOUGHT DID CROSS MY MIND.

CONTINUED: (17)

PROSECUTOR CORIC
OBJECTION!

DEFENSE ATTORNEY CLIVE BARROW
NO FURTHER QUESTIONS YOUR HONOR.

JUDGE ROLLINS
MR. MILLS YOU MAY STEP DOWN. BAILIFF? I
WOULD LIKE TO SEE COUNCIL IN MY CHAMBERS.
WE'RE GOING TO TAKE A RECESS UNTIL
TOMORROW MORNING AT 10 AM. EVERYONE HAVE
A GOOD NIGHT AND WE WILL SEE YOU
TOMORROW.

JUDGE DISMISSES JURY.

PARTIAL TRANSCRIPT FROM COURT DOCKET 55673-2433 THE PEOPLE
VS. THOMAS MILLS.

DATED 10:14 am October 23, 2001

JUDGE ROLLINS (CONT'D)
LADIES AND GENTLEMAN OF THE JURY, IT IS
MY REGRET TO INFORM YOU THAT THIS TRIAL
HAD ENDED. LAST NIGHT IN HIS HOLDING
CELL, THE ACCUSED, TOOK HIS OWN LIFE IN A
VIOLENT MANNER. THIS, OF COURSE, ENDS THE
PROCEEDINGS AND NULLIFIES ANY JUDGEMENT
YOU WERE TO BRING FORTH. I HOPE YOU WILL
ACCEPT MY SINCEREST APOLOGIES FOR THE
WASTE OF TIME THIS HAS BECOME FOR ALL OF
US- BUT I DO DECLARE YOUR DUTIES TO THIS
COURT COMPLETED. CASE DISMISSED.

JURY IS DISMISSED. 10:22 am October 23, 2001

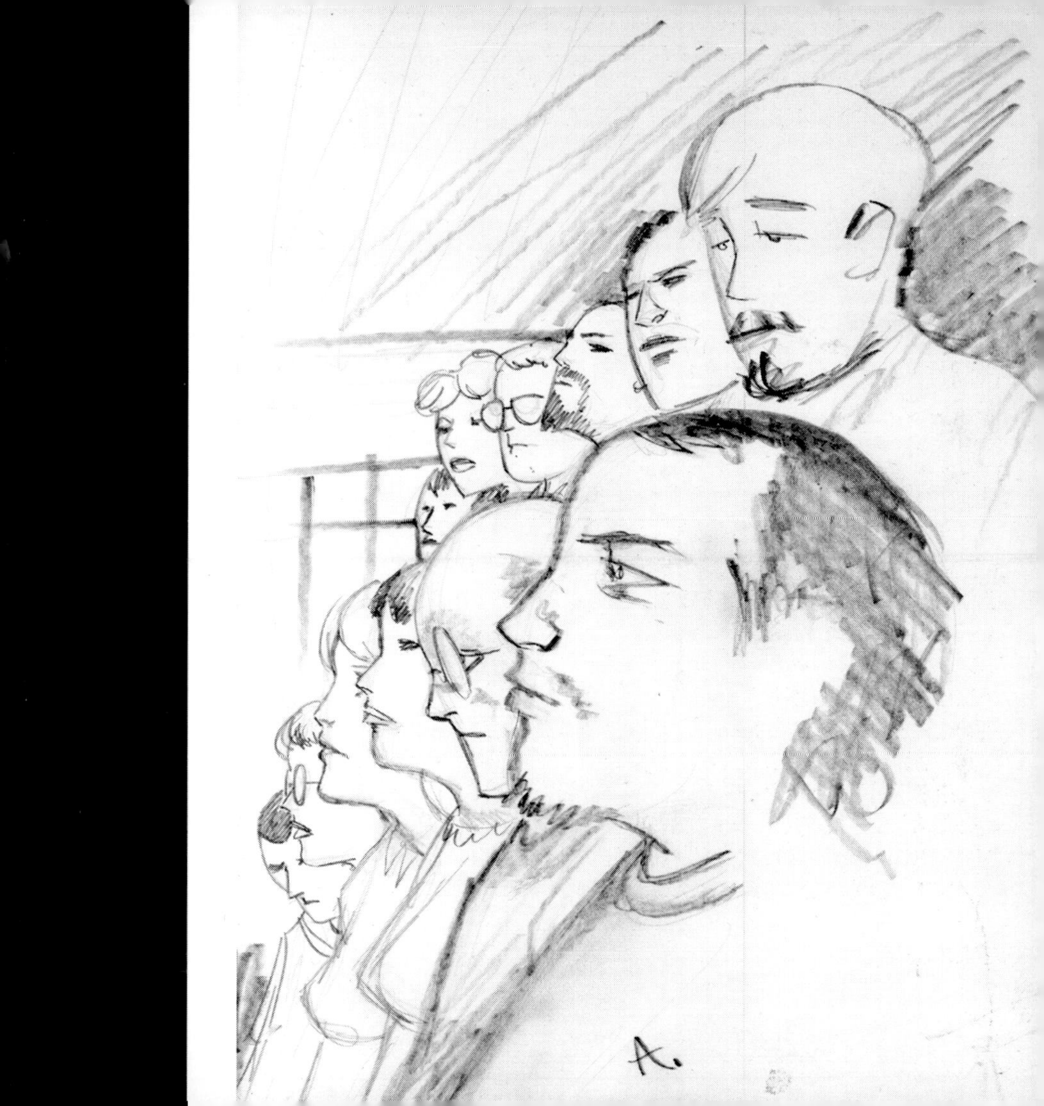
A.

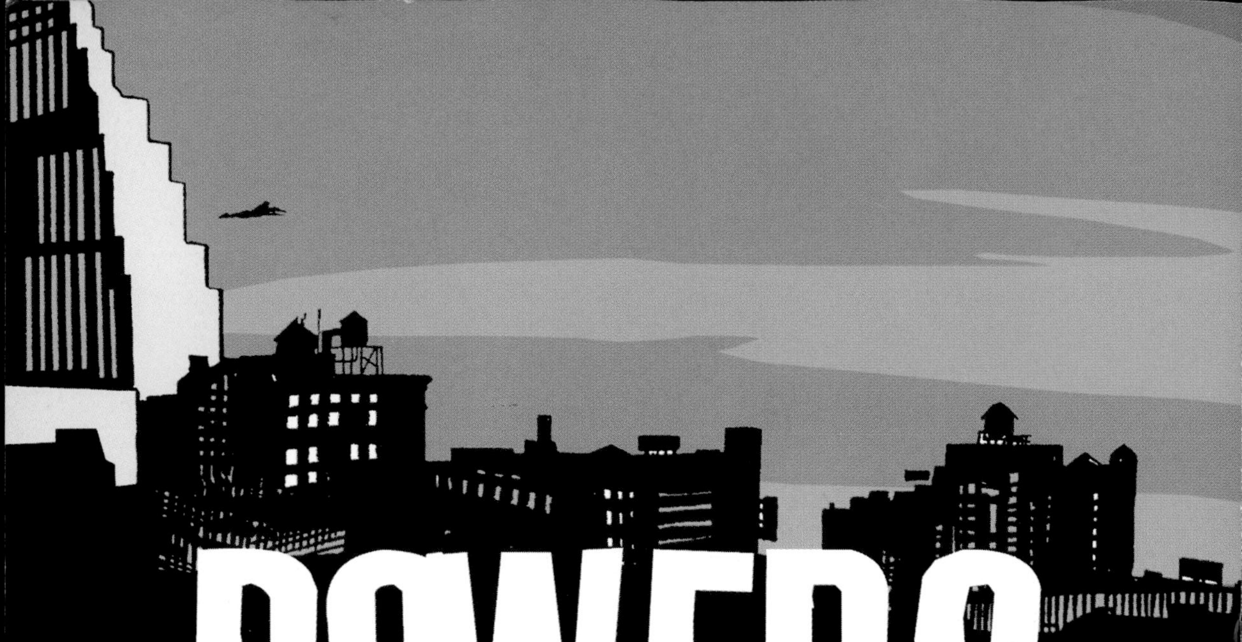

POWERS

COLORING/ACTIVITY BOOK

THE FOLLOWING PAGES ARE FROM AN ACTUAL COLORING/ ACTIVITY BOOK

WHEN YOU VISIT THE POLICE STATION IN POWERS, THIS IS THE COLORING BOOK THEY WOULD GIVE THE KIDS.

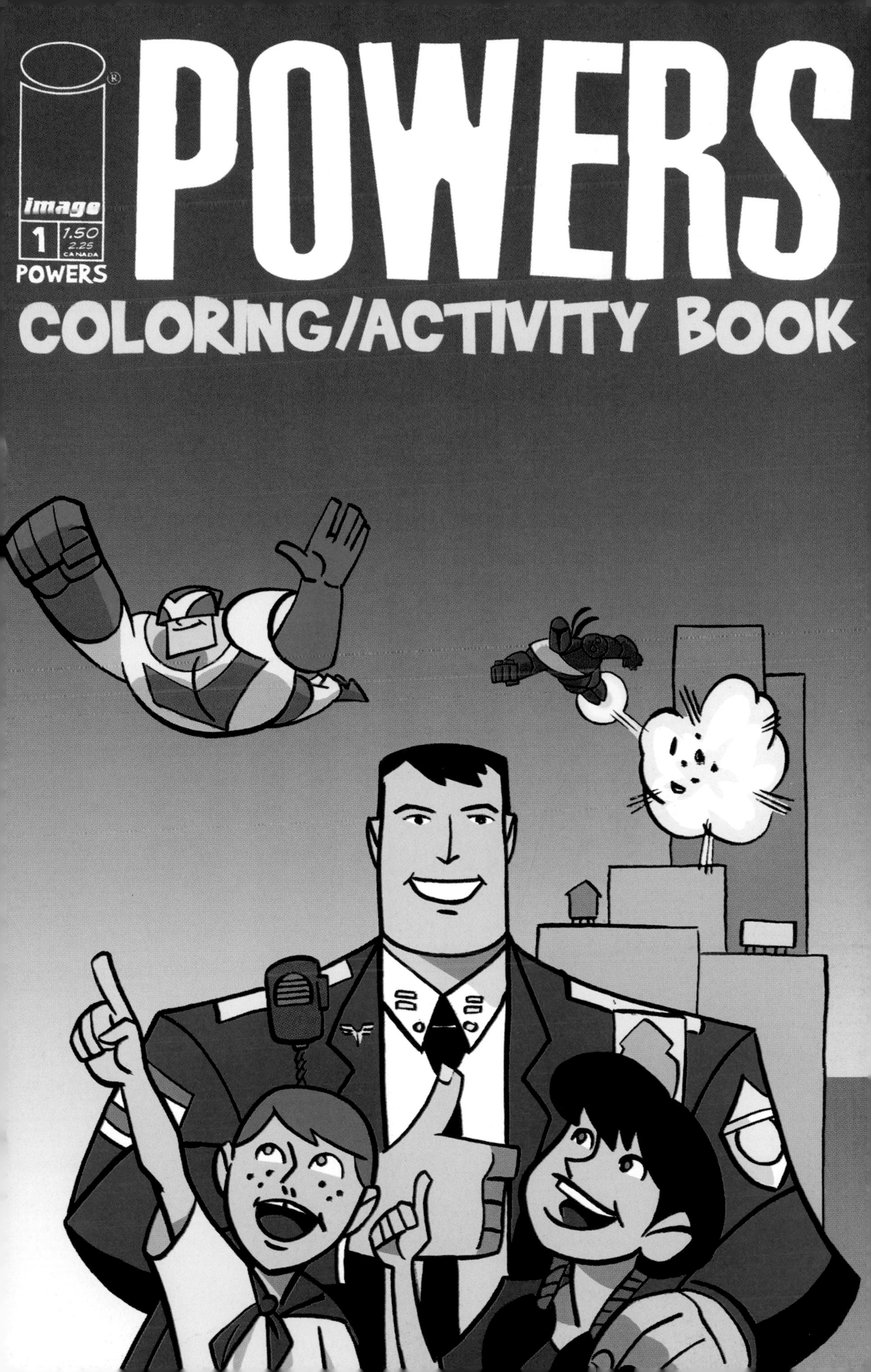
image
1
1.50
2.25 CANADA
POWERS
POWERS
COLORING/ACTIVITY BOOK

SAFETY KID

I, _____ , promise to use caution and safety everywhere I go. I will remind my relatives and friends how important it is to use safety all day long because this world is filled with super-powered maniacs and assorted radioactive menaces hellbent on destroying the Universe. So I will look both ways before I cross the street, always use a safety belt, and never touch anything in my house that has the word 'NULLIFIER' written on it.

_____
WRITE YOUR NAME HERE

_____   _____
DATE   AGE

image ®
COMICS PRESENTS:

JIM VALENTINO	Publisher
BRENT BRAUN	Director of Production
ERIC STEPHENSON	Director of Marketing
TRACI HALE	Controller/Foreign Licensing
BRETT EVANS	Art Director
ALLEN HUI	Web Developer
SEAN O'BRIEN	Inventory Controller
CYNDIE ESPINOZA	Accoutning Assistant

POWERS

CREATED BY
BRIAN MICHAEL BENDIS
AND MICHAEL AVON OEMING
COLOR ART LETTERING AND PRODUCTION BY
PAT GARRAHY

BUSINESS AFFAIRS
ALISA BENDIS

WORD SEARCH
MELISSA APONTE

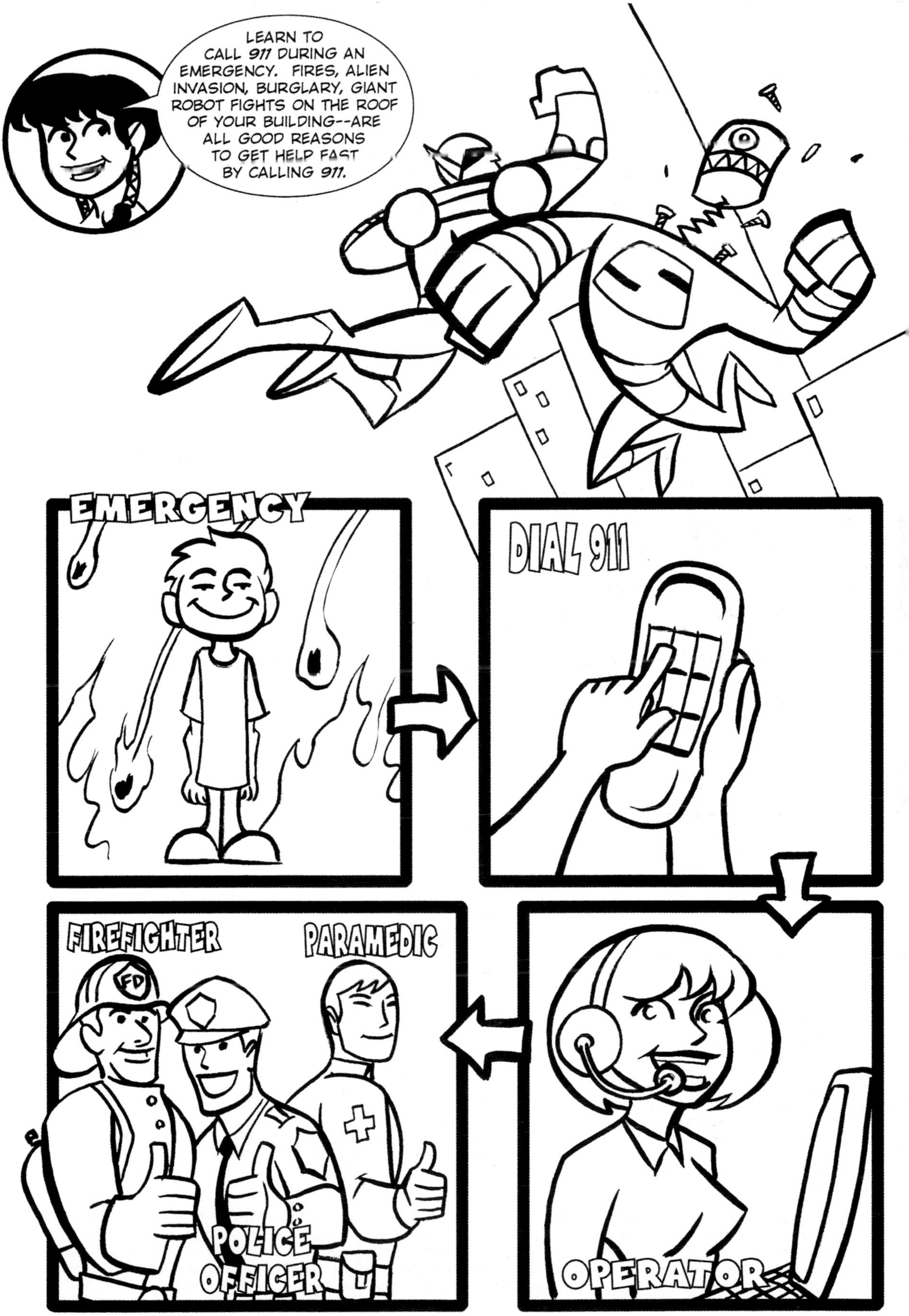
LEARN TO CALL 911 DURING AN EMERGENCY. FIRES, ALIEN INVASION, BURGLARY, GIANT ROBOT FIGHTS ON THE ROOF OF YOUR BUILDING--ARE ALL GOOD REASONS TO GET HELP FAST BY CALLING 911.
EMERGENCY
DIAL 911
OPERATOR
FIREFIGHTER
PARAMEDIC
POLICE OFFICER

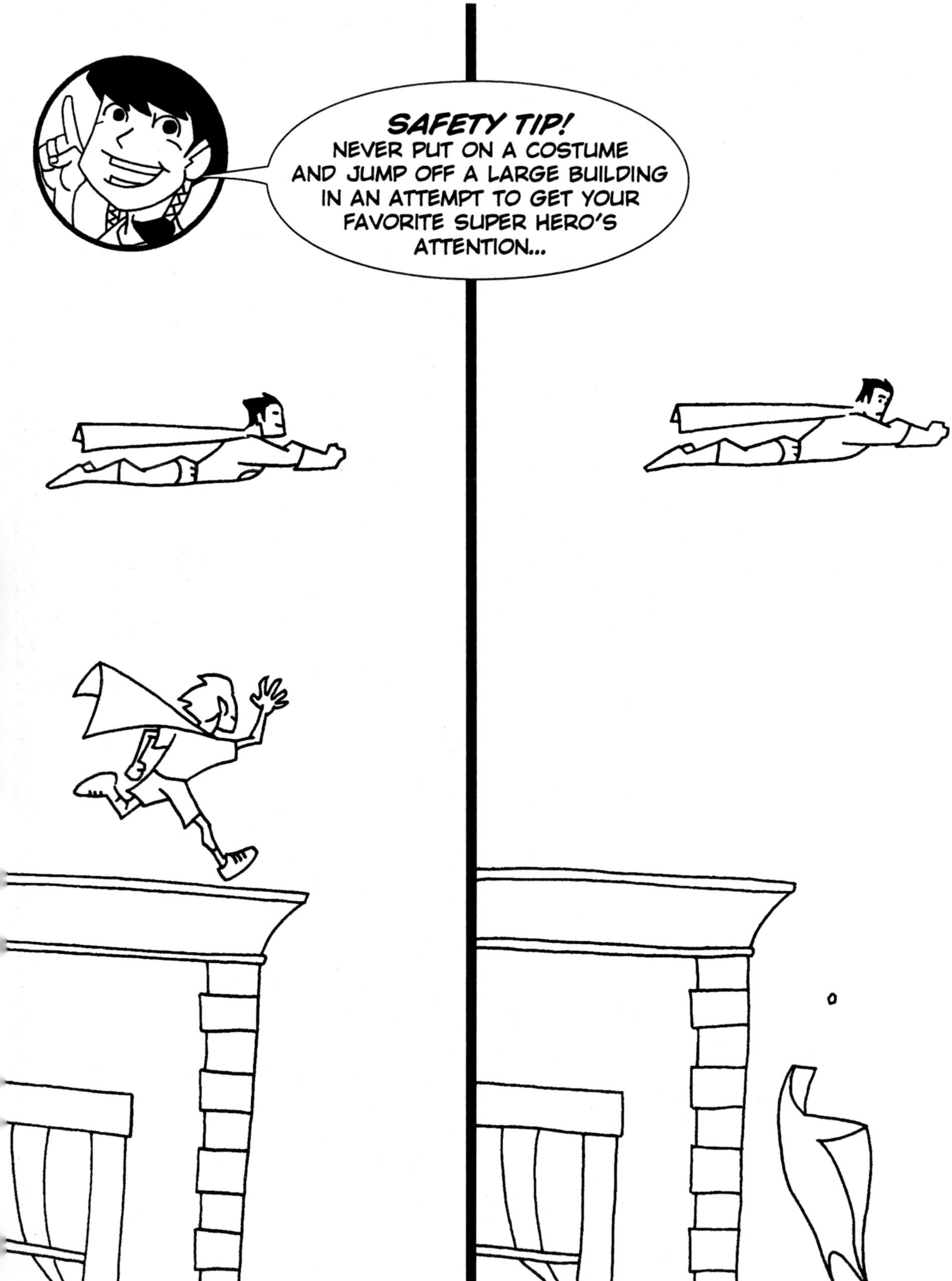
SAFETY TIP!
NEVER PUT ON A COSTUME AND JUMP OFF A LARGE BUILDING IN AN ATTEMPT TO GET YOUR FAVORITE SUPER HERO'S ATTENTION...

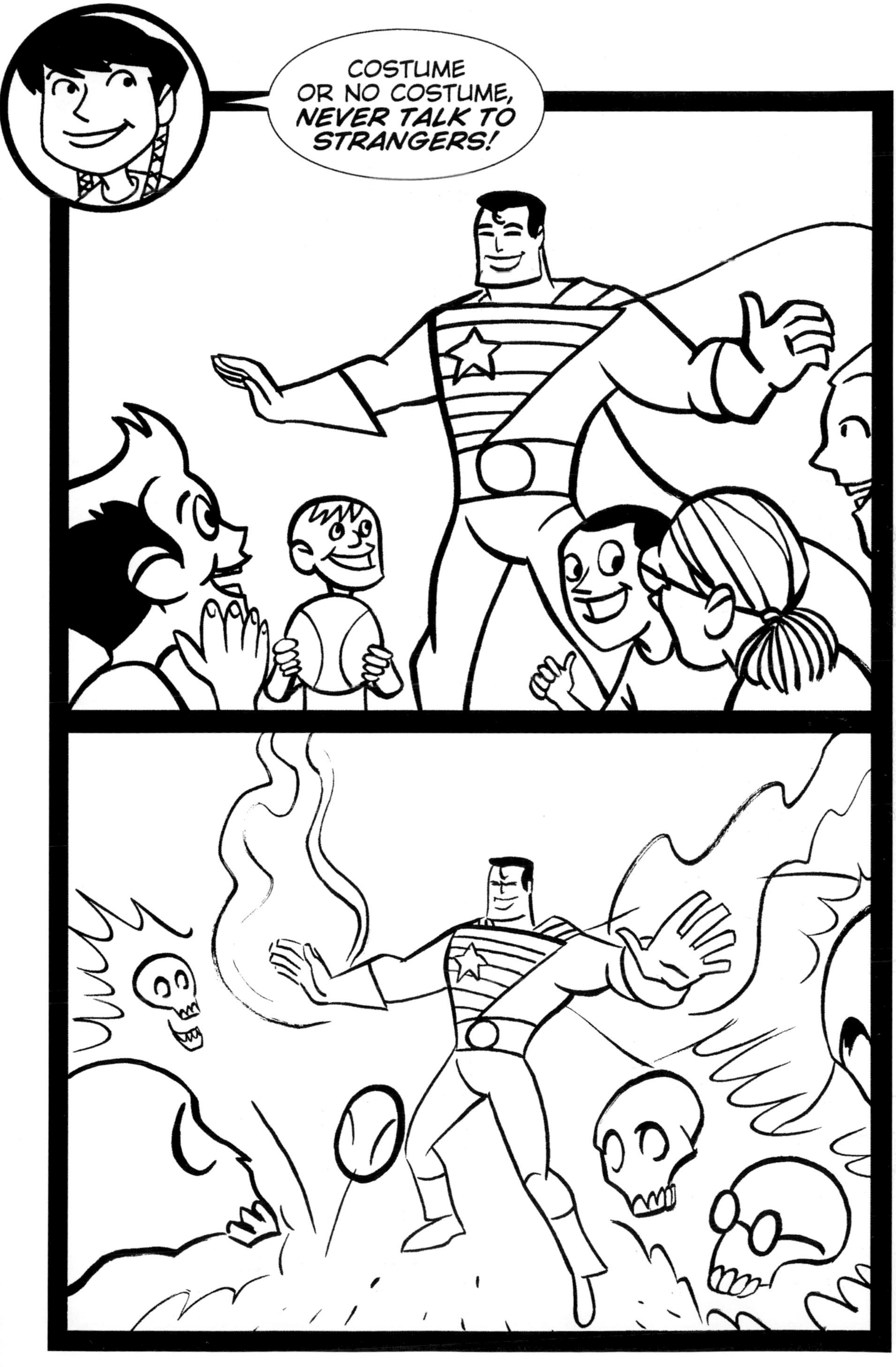
COSTUME OR NO COSTUME, NEVER TALK TO STRANGERS!

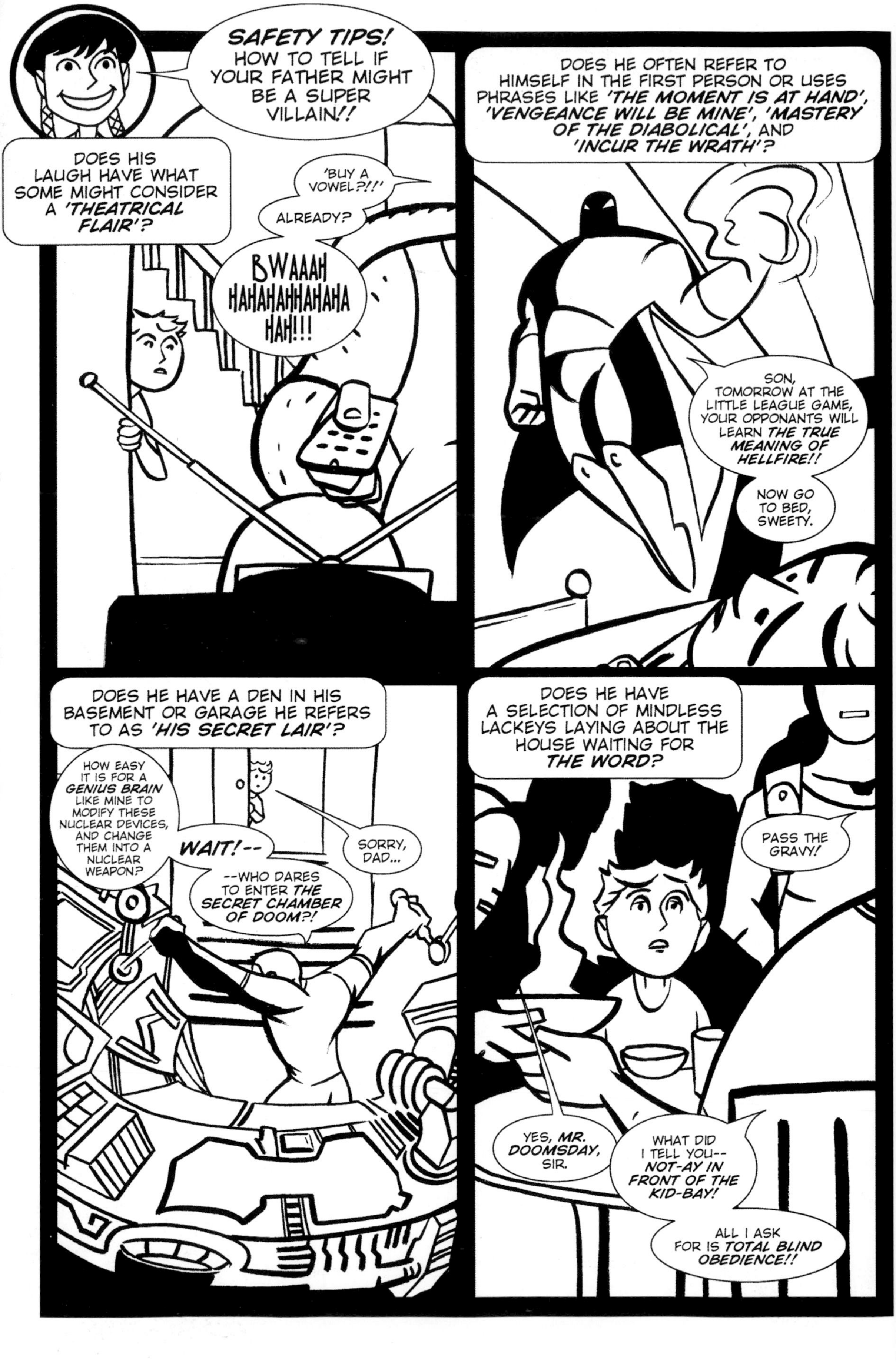
SAFETY TIPS! HOW TO TELL IF YOUR FATHER MIGHT BE A SUPER VILLAIN!!
DOES HIS LAUGH HAVE WHAT SOME MIGHT CONSIDER A 'THEATRICAL FLAIR'?
'BUY A VOWEL?!!'
ALREADY?
BWAAAH HAHAHAHHAHAHA HAH!!!
DOES HE OFTEN REFER TO HIMSELF IN THE FIRST PERSON OR USES PHRASES LIKE 'THE MOMENT IS AT HAND', 'VENGEANCE WILL BE MINE', 'MASTERY OF THE DIABOLICAL', AND 'INCUR THE WRATH'?
SON, TOMORROW AT THE LITTLE LEAGUE GAME, YOUR OPPONANTS WILL LEARN THE TRUE MEANING OF HELLFIRE!!
NOW GO TO BED, SWEETY.
DOES HE HAVE A DEN IN HIS BASEMENT OR GARAGE HE REFERS TO AS 'HIS SECRET LAIR'?
HOW EASY IT IS FOR A GENIUS BRAIN LIKE MINE TO MODIFY THESE NUCLEAR DEVICES, AND CHANGE THEM INTO A NUCLEAR WEAPON?
WAIT!--
--WHO DARES TO ENTER THE SECRET CHAMBER OF DOOM?!
SORRY, DAD...
DOES HE HAVE A SELECTION OF MINDLESS LACKEYS LAYING ABOUT THE HOUSE WAITING FOR THE WORD?
PASS THE GRAVY!
YES, MR. DOOMSDAY, SIR.
WHAT DID I TELL YOU-- NOT-AY IN FRONT OF THE KID-BAY!
ALL I ASK FOR IS TOTAL BLIND OBEDIENCE!!

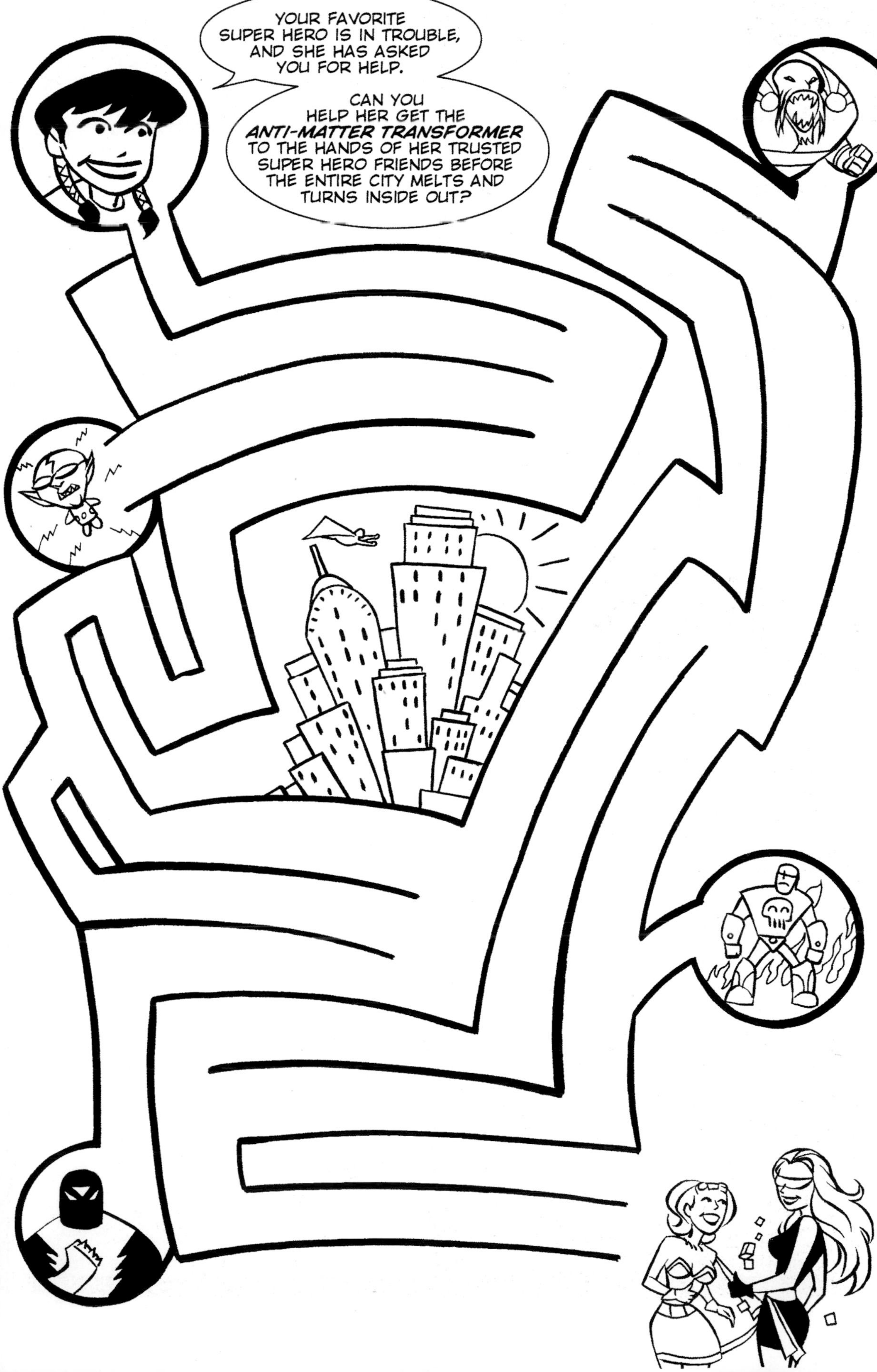
YOUR FAVORITE SUPER HERO IS IN TROUBLE, AND SHE HAS ASKED YOU FOR HELP.
CAN YOU HELP HER GET THE ANTI-MATTER TRANSFORMER TO THE HANDS OF HER TRUSTED SUPER HERO FRIENDS BEFORE THE ENTIRE CITY MELTS AND TURNS INSIDE OUT?

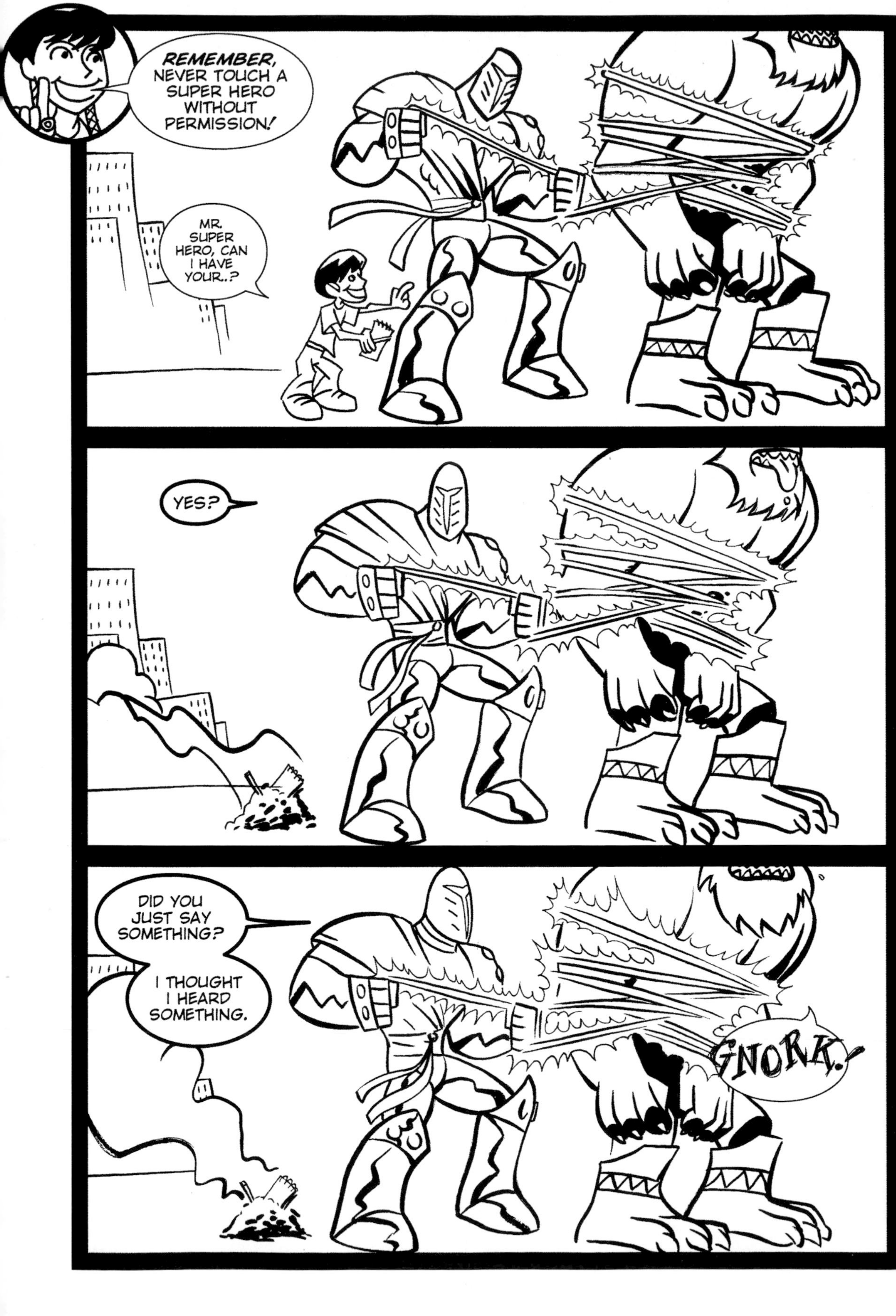
REMEMBER, NEVER TOUCH A SUPER HERO WITHOUT PERMISSION!
MR. SUPER HERO, CAN I HAVE YOUR..?
YES?
DID YOU JUST SAY SOMETHING?
I THOUGHT I HEARD SOMETHING.
GNORK!

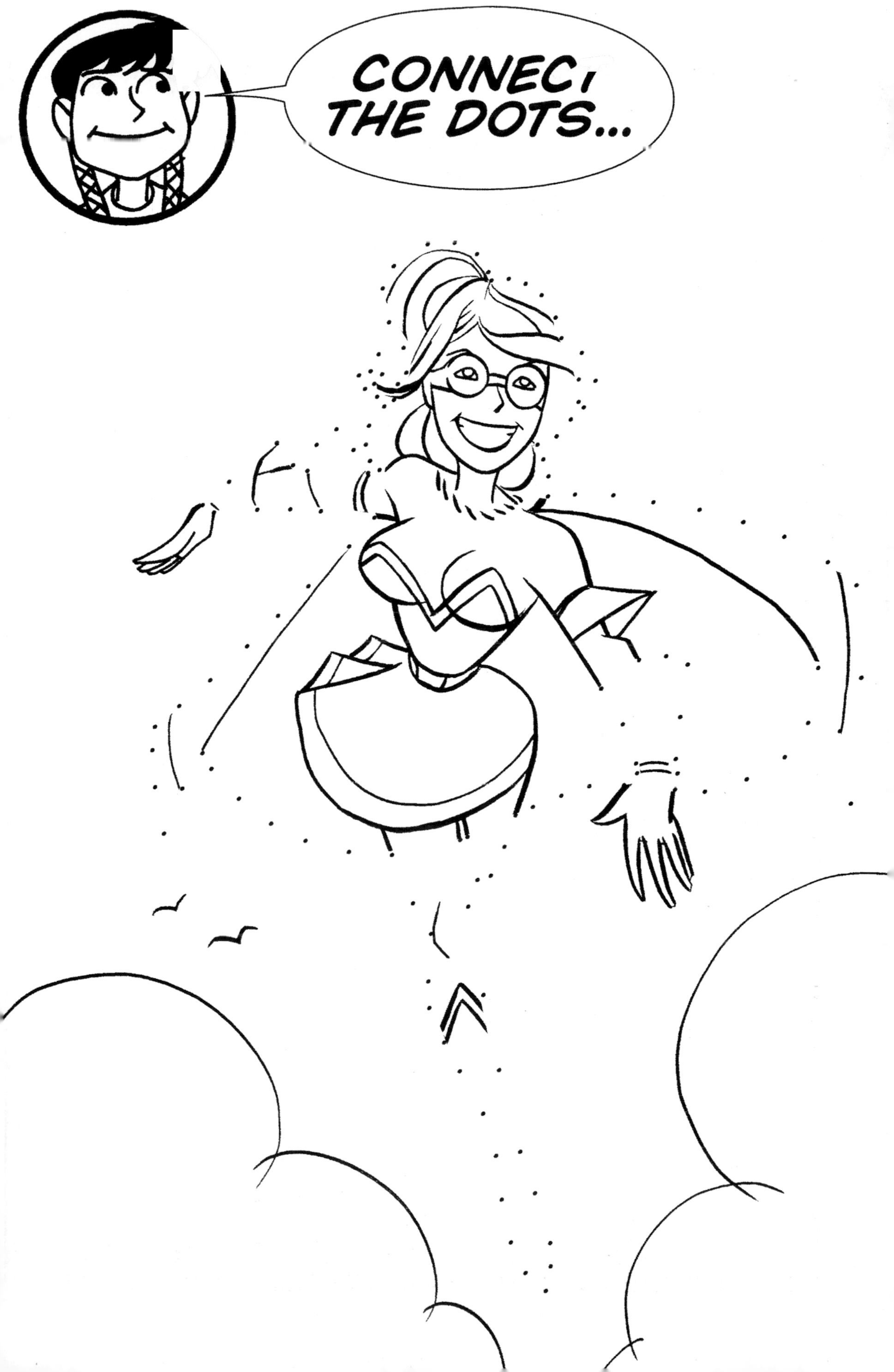
CONNECT
THE DOTS...

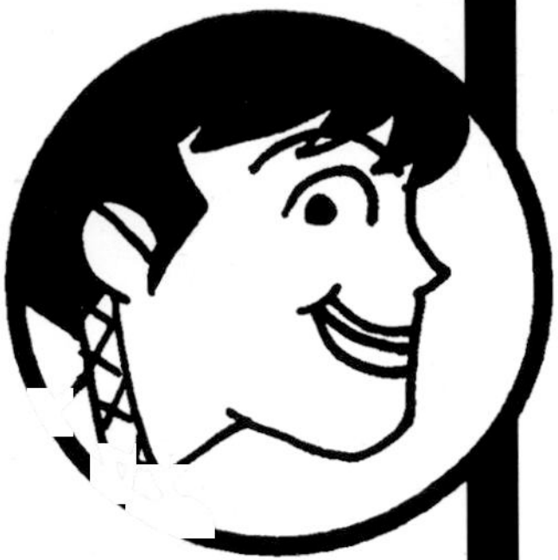

IT'S TIME TO PLAY...

FIND THE SUPER VILLAIN!

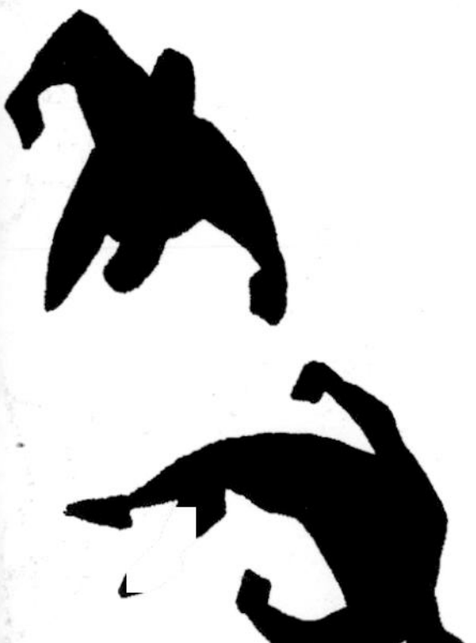

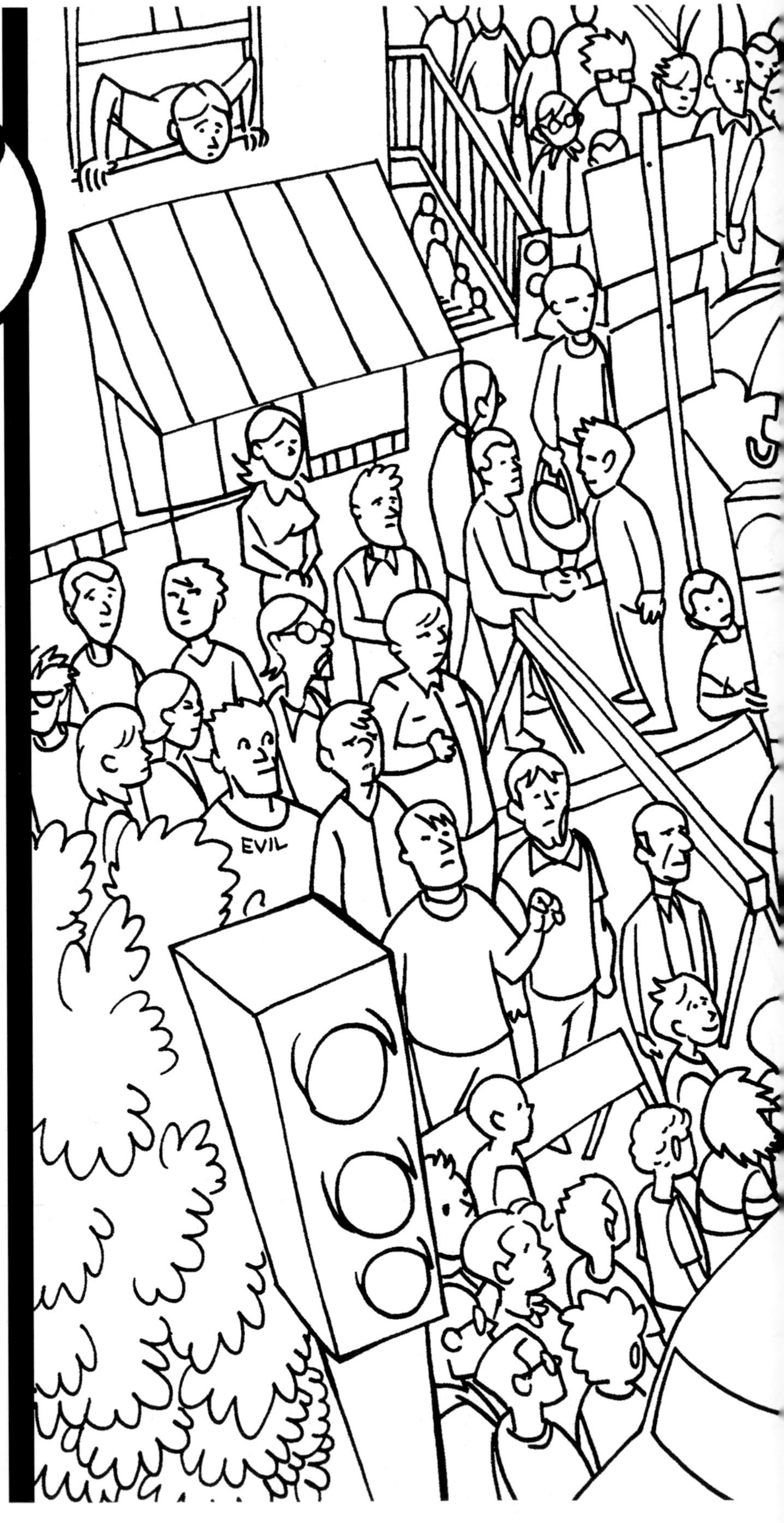

EVIL

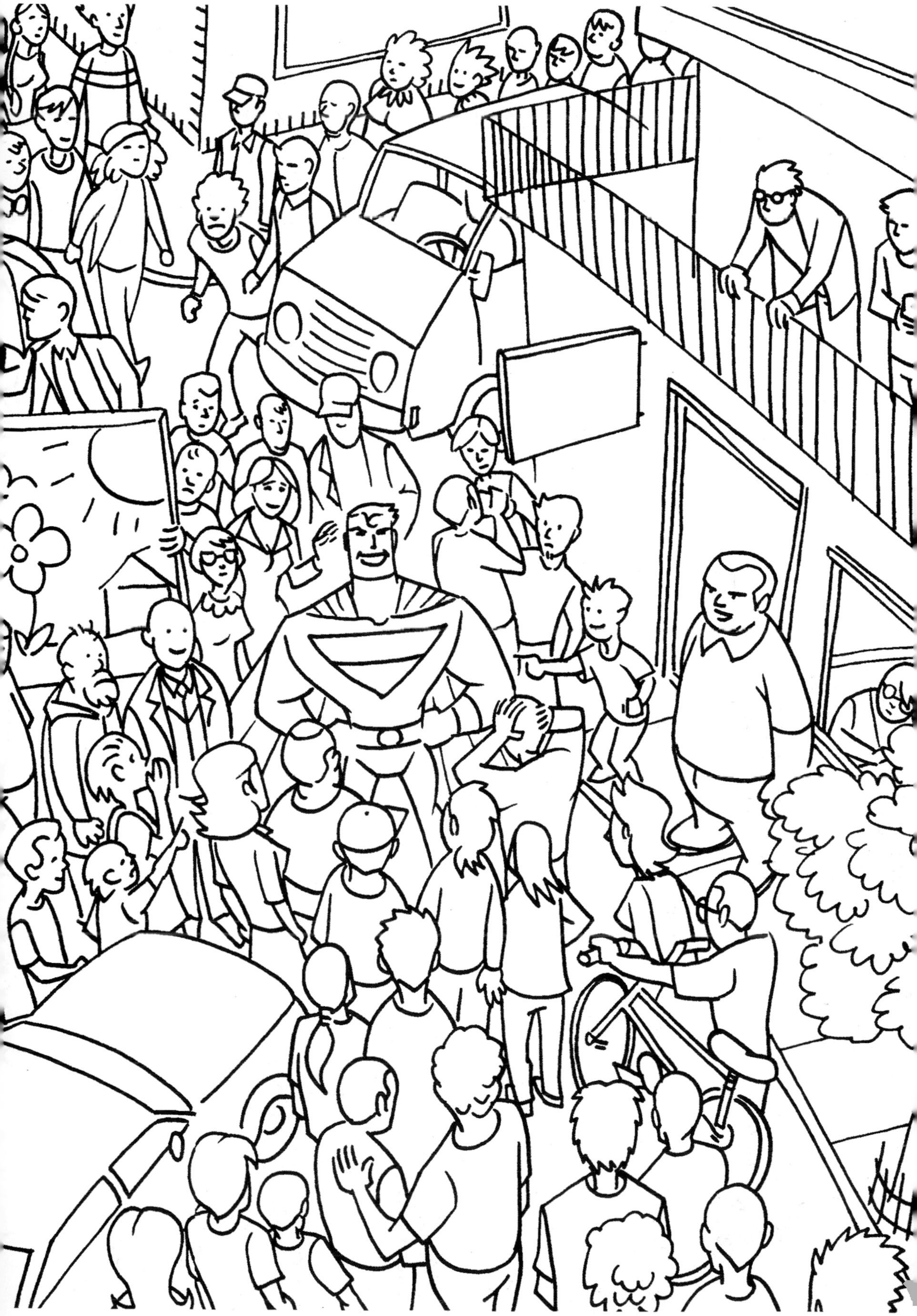

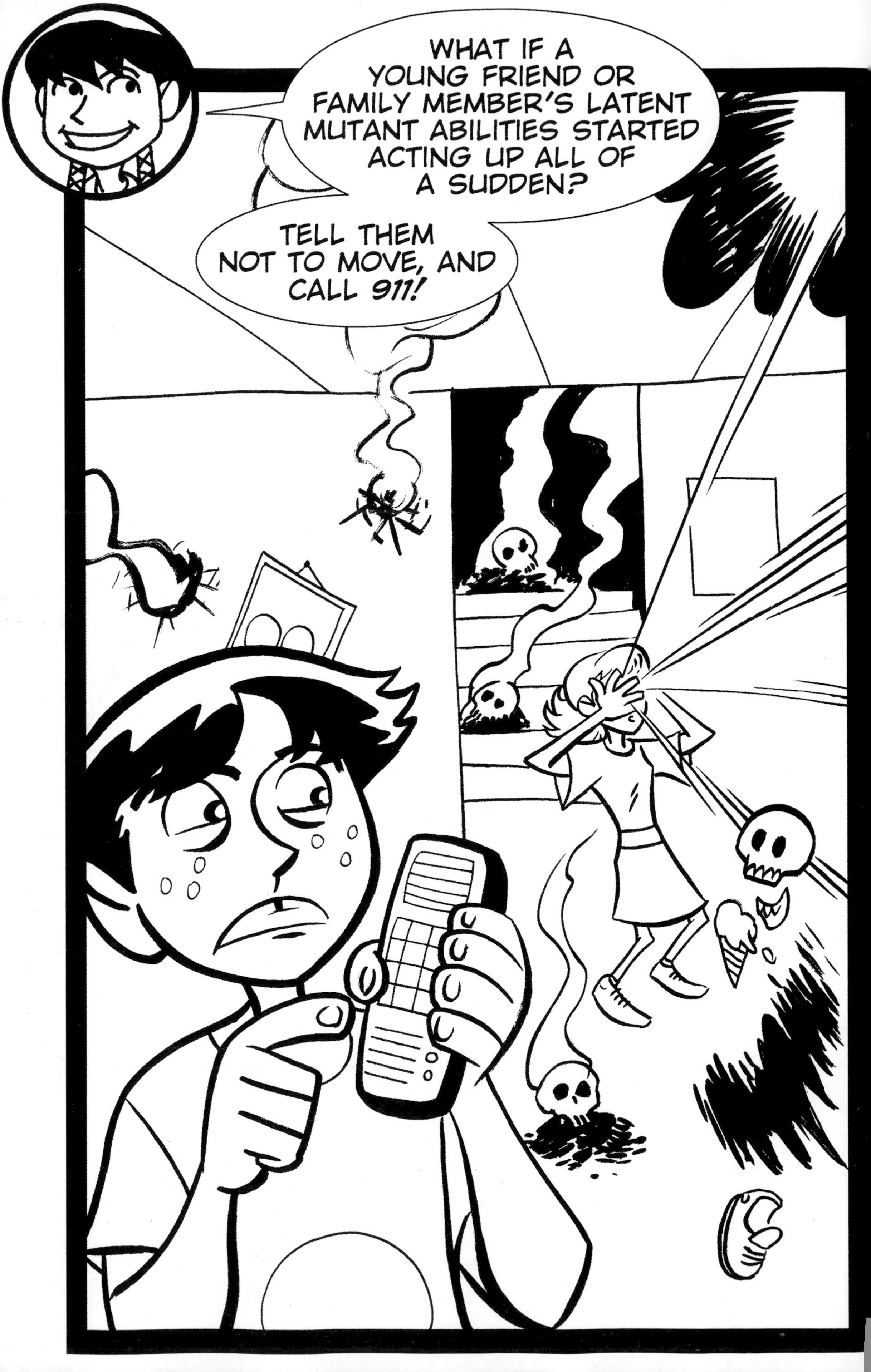
WHAT IF A YOUNG FRIEND OR FAMILY MEMBER'S LATENT MUTANT ABILITIES STARTED ACTING UP ALL OF A SUDDEN?
TELL THEM NOT TO MOVE, AND CALL 911!

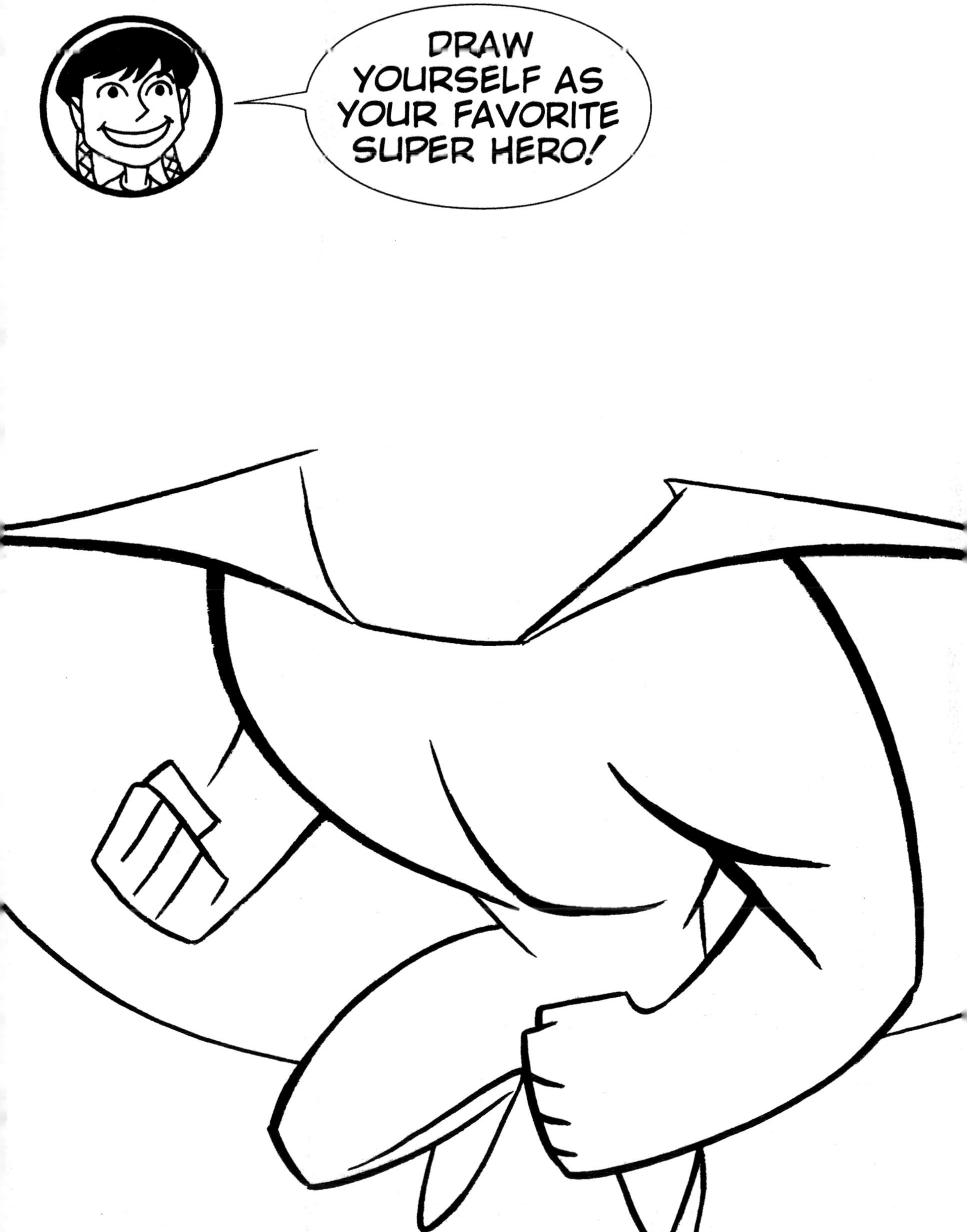
DRAW YOURSELF AS YOUR FAVORITE SUPER HERO!

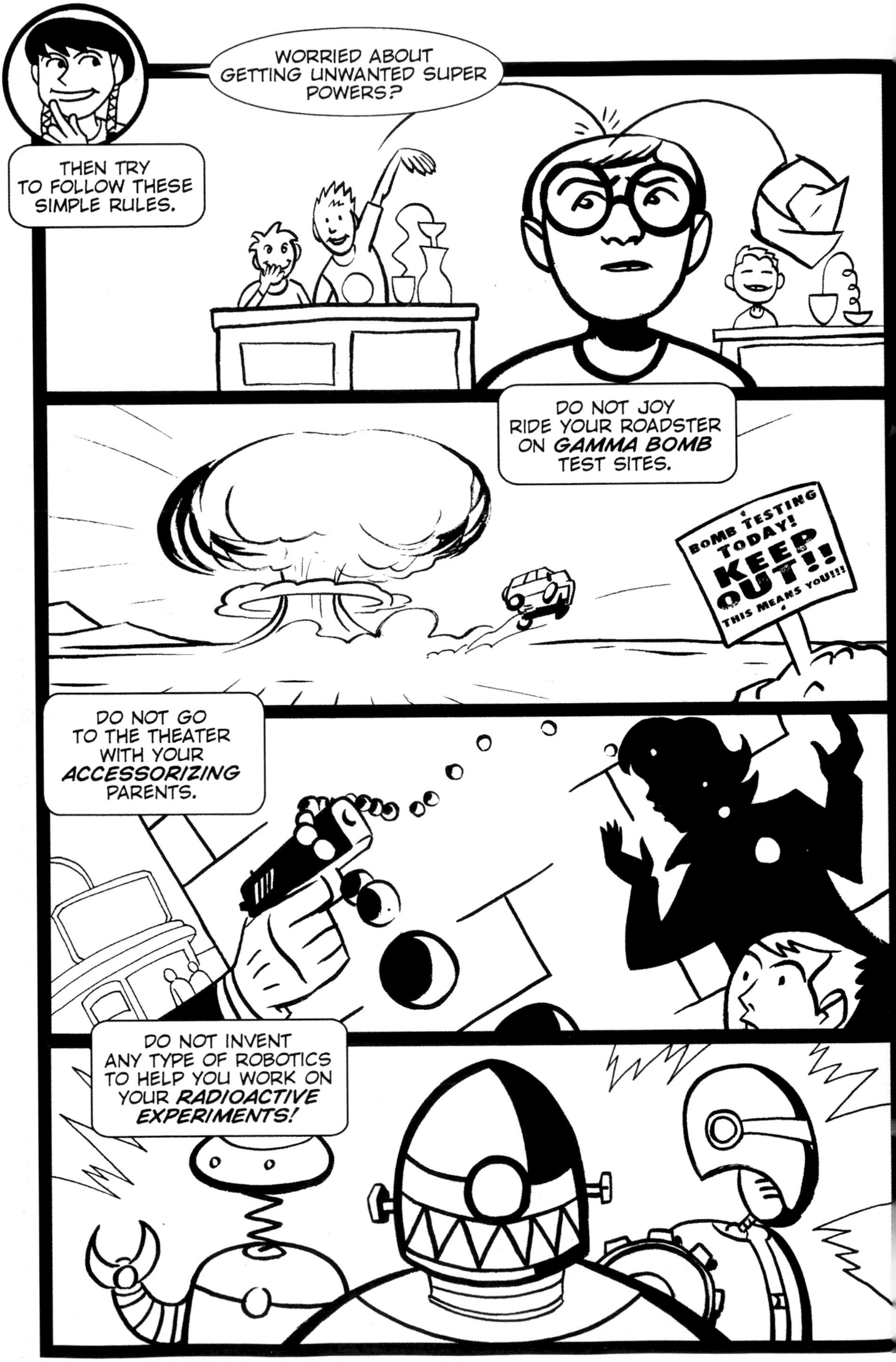
WORRIED ABOUT GETTING UNWANTED SUPER POWERS?
THEN TRY TO FOLLOW THESE SIMPLE RULES.
DO NOT JOY RIDE YOUR ROADSTER ON *GAMMA BOMB* TEST SITES.
BOMB TESTING TODAY! KEEP OUT!! THIS MEANS YOU!!!
DO NOT GO TO THE THEATER WITH YOUR *ACCESSORIZING* PARENTS.
DO NOT INVENT ANY TYPE OF ROBOTICS TO HELP YOU WORK ON YOUR *RADIOACTIVE EXPERIMENTS!*

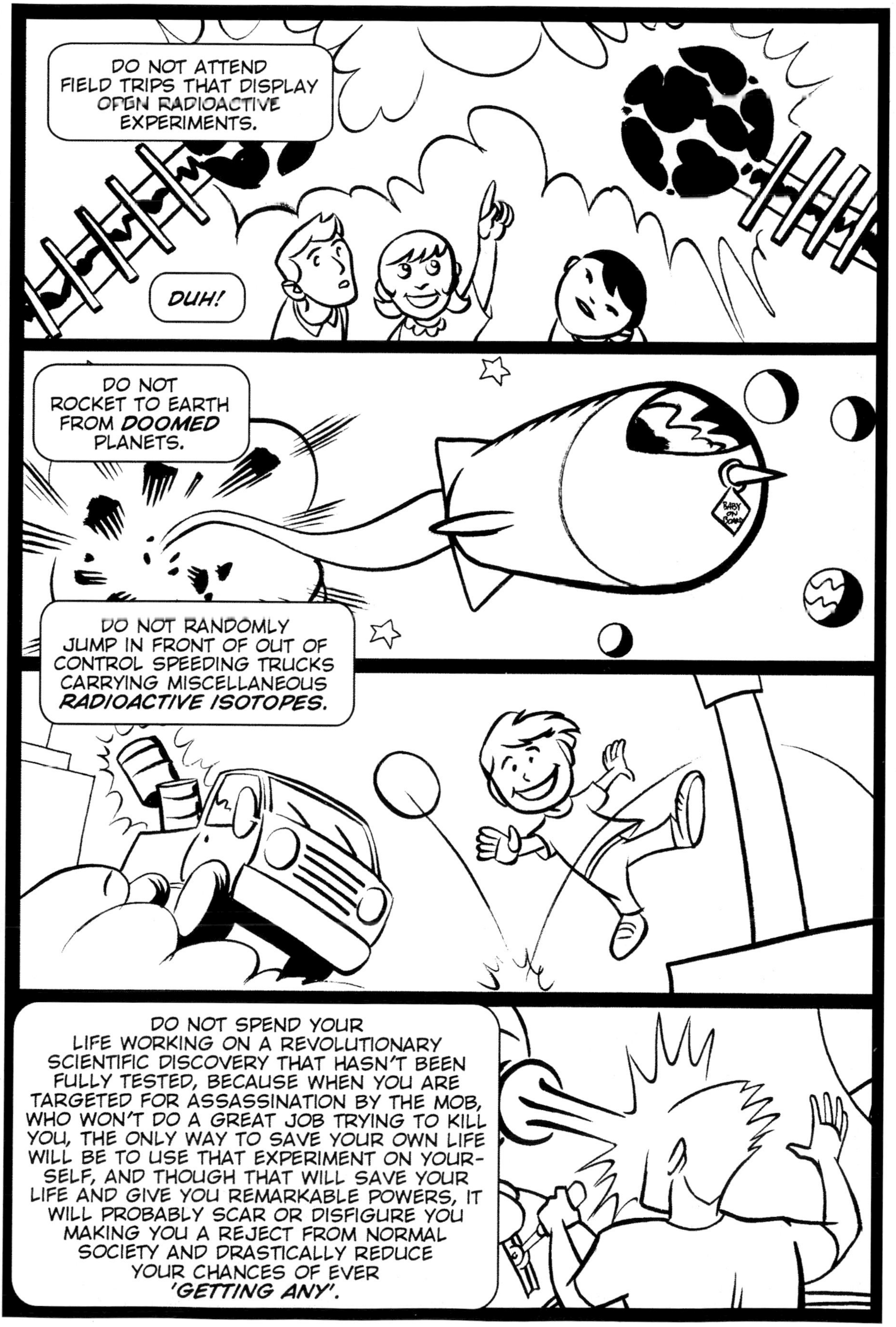

DO NOT ATTEND FIELD TRIPS THAT DISPLAY OPEN RADIOACTIVE EXPERIMENTS.
DUH!
DO NOT ROCKET TO EARTH FROM *DOOMED* PLANETS.
BABY ON BOARD
DO NOT RANDOMLY JUMP IN FRONT OF OUT OF CONTROL SPEEDING TRUCKS CARRYING MISCELLANEOUS *RADIOACTIVE ISOTOPES.*
DO NOT SPEND YOUR LIFE WORKING ON A REVOLUTIONARY SCIENTIFIC DISCOVERY THAT HASN'T BEEN FULLY TESTED, BECAUSE WHEN YOU ARE TARGETED FOR ASSASSINATION BY THE MOB, WHO WON'T DO A GREAT JOB TRYING TO KILL YOU, THE ONLY WAY TO SAVE YOUR OWN LIFE WILL BE TO USE THAT EXPERIMENT ON YOUR-SELF, AND THOUGH THAT WILL SAVE YOUR LIFE AND GIVE YOU REMARKABLE POWERS, IT WILL PROBABLY SCAR OR DISFIGURE YOU MAKING YOU A REJECT FROM NORMAL SOCIETY AND DRASTICALLY REDUCE YOUR CHANCES OF EVER *'GETTING ANY'.*

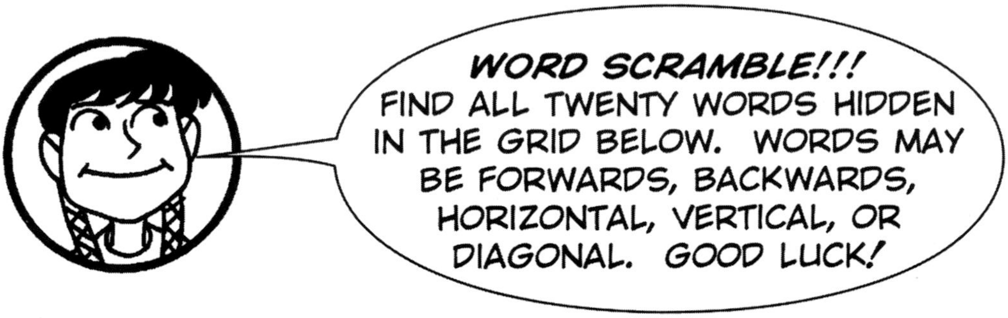

WORD SCRAMBLE!!!
FIND ALL TWENTY WORDS HIDDEN
IN THE GRID BELOW. WORDS MAY
BE FORWARDS, BACKWARDS,
HORIZONTAL, VERTICAL, OR
DIAGONAL. GOOD LUCK!

WORDS TO FIND:

1. HERO
2. VILLAIN
3. HEMPSTEAD ACT
4. DRAINERS
5. TRIPHAMMER
6. ZORA
7. COSTUME
8. REWARD
9. RETRO GIRL
10. DIAMOND
11. REPORT
12. MANIAC
13. SAFETY
14. STRANGER
15. ALTER EGO
16. SECRET IDENTITY
17. POWERS
18. CHESHIRE
19. POLICE
20. DANGER

L	I	V	E	R	D	E	G	G	B	S	W	Q	X	Z	K	A	C	Y	U
R	C	O	P	A	D	S	H	T	R	O	P	E	R	L	U	M	B	J	S
I	M	Z	X	C	A	Q	I	F	D	O	E	N	I	T	B	I	T	D	J
G	N	V	O	W	A	D	C	R	E	G	N	A	D	R	V	D	D	O	B
O	A	V	X	W	E	I	U	Y	F	R	W	E	C	I	L	O	P	S	C
R	Q	B	N	N	O	R	E	D	E	C	I	V	Q	P	U	L	P	B	M
T	U	E	T	R	E	T	I	Y	N	U	I	O	A	H	P	A	S	D	G
E	A	I	S	P	X	P	B	H	D	T	D	L	J	A	N	E	T	N	R
R	T	S	O	Q	A	W	C	V	S	Z	T	O	R	M	V	N	G	E	A
Y	R	R	C	R	I	M	E	H	E	E	R	M	R	M	A	P	W	V	H
T	I	E	R	O	D	I	R	T	R	B	H	O	U	E	B	A	B	I	L
H	P	N	C	U	M	E	R	E	K	R	P	C	C	R	R	C	U	T	F
G	L	I	F	U	G	C	G	D	W	E	E	R	K	D	E	P	M	C	B
I	L	A	M	N	P	O	W	E	R	S	J	G	E	P	L	N	S	A	I
F	G	R	A	F	T	T	R	H	O	W	D	D	N	O	M	A	I	D	W
I	T	D	N	H	O	E	N	F	A	B	I	A	T	A	F	G	A	A	I
N	S	T	I	I	R	N	R	L	I	C	E	S	T	E	R	W	O	E	F
N	W	E	A	R	B	T	W	C	E	N	I	N	T	D	E	T	C	T	I
R	E	D	C	O	U	R	A	G	E	O	U	Y	B	R	S	U	S	S	P
E	E	R	C	A	L	I	F	R	M	S	L	I	E	S	T	I	C	P	E
X	P	V	I	L	L	A	I	N	U	I	A	P	W	L	I	D	C	M	I
O	U	S	I	D	O	E	L	I	T	C	O	U	A	S	T	H	G	E	G
U	I	K	R	R	E	D	F	O	S	R	X	J	R	U	M	P	E	H	D
O	V	E	E	R	T	H	L	A	O	Z	Y	B	E	R	O	W	N	S	D
O	G	H	G	P	A	O	C	P	C	S	A	R	O	Z	S	D	I	O	S

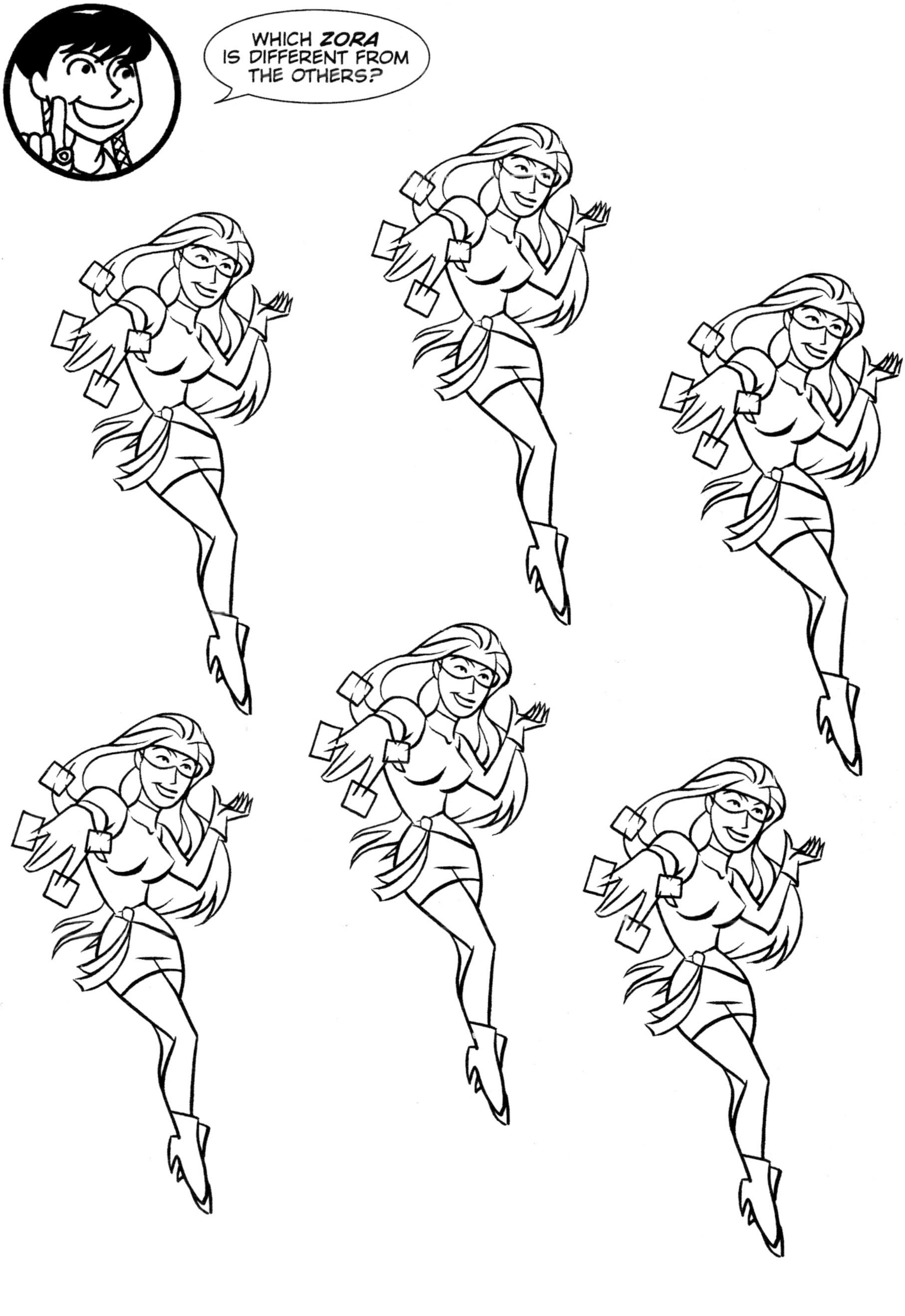
WHICH ZORA IS DIFFERENT FROM THE OTHERS?

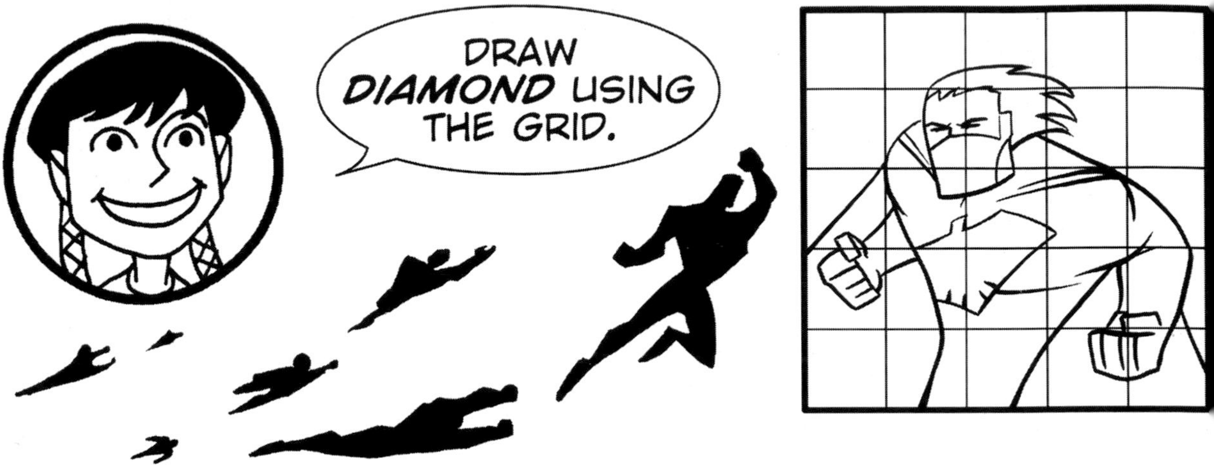
DRAW DIAMOND USING THE GRID.

USE COMMON SENSE AND
BE CAREFUL IN AN EMERGENCY.
SOMETIMES, SCARY THINGS HAPPEN.
IF YOU KNOW WHAT TO DO, HELP
IS JUST A PHONE CALL AWAY!

- TRY TO STAY VERY CALM.
- PICK UP THE PHONE AND DIAL 9-1-1.
- WHEN THE OPERATOR ANSWERS, SPEAK CLEARLY AND LOUD ENOUGH SO HE OR SHE CAN UNDERSTAND YOU.
- TELL THE OPERATOR THE NATURE OF THE EMERGENCY.
- ANSWER QUESTIONS, AND DON'T HANG UP UNTIL YOU ARE TOLD TO BY THE OPERATOR!

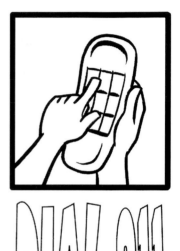

DIAL 911

BE READY TO GIVE THE OPERATOR THE FOLLOWING INFORMATION.

YOU CAN FILL THIS OUT AND KEEP IT HANDY IN CASE OF A REAL EMERGENCY!

MY NAME:

MY ADDRESS:

MY PHONE:

MY AGE:

WHAT'S THE NATURE OF THE EMERGENCY:

ARE SUPER-POWERED BEINGS INVOLVED:

911 MEANS *HELP* IS ON THE WAY!

SUPER HEROES

and what they do!

An EDUCATIONAL COLORING and ACTIVITY BOOK!!

image comics presents:

Compliments of the POLICE DEPARTMENT!!!

BRIAN MICHAEL BENDIS
director of public wording

MICHAEL AVON OEMING
chief of ink

PAT GARRAHY
sanitation supervisor

www.jinxworld.com

$1.50 U.S.
$2.25 Canada

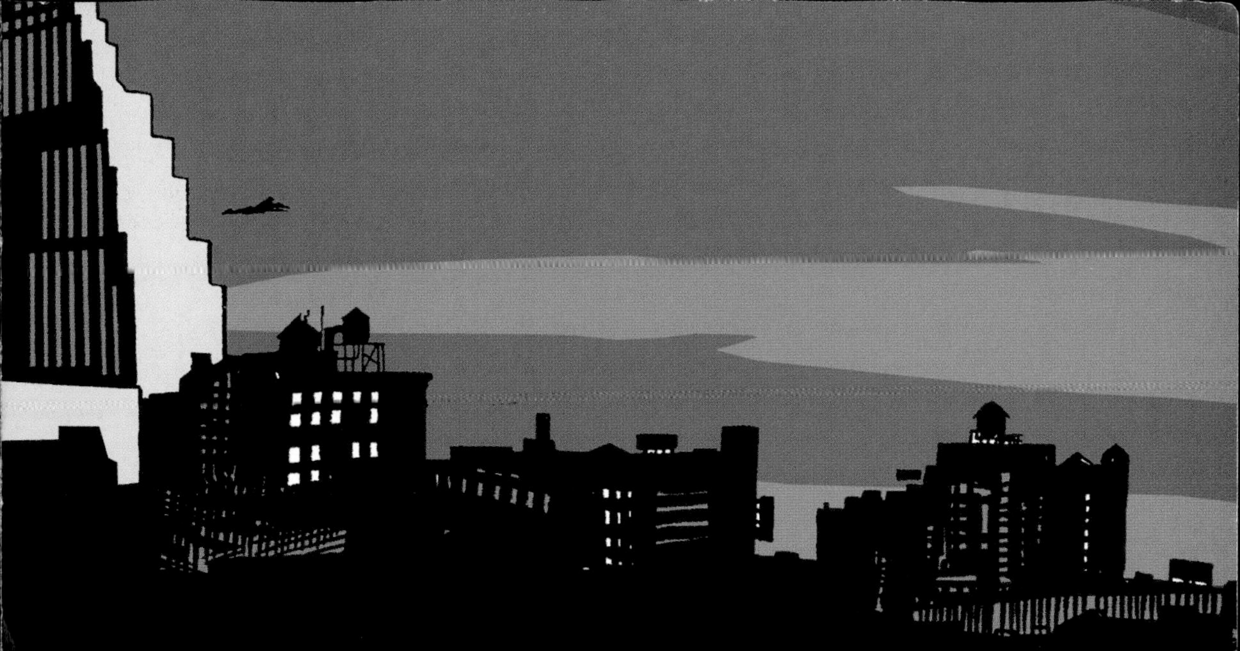

MALL OUTING

A.K.A. KEYS

THIS IS THE FIRST EVER
BENDIS/OEMING COLLABORATION

THIS FIRST APPEARED IN A
BOOK CALLED 'JINX: TRUE
CRIME CONFESSIONS.'
IT IS PRESENTED HERE FOR
POWERS COMPLETISTS AND
CURIOUSITY'S SAKE.

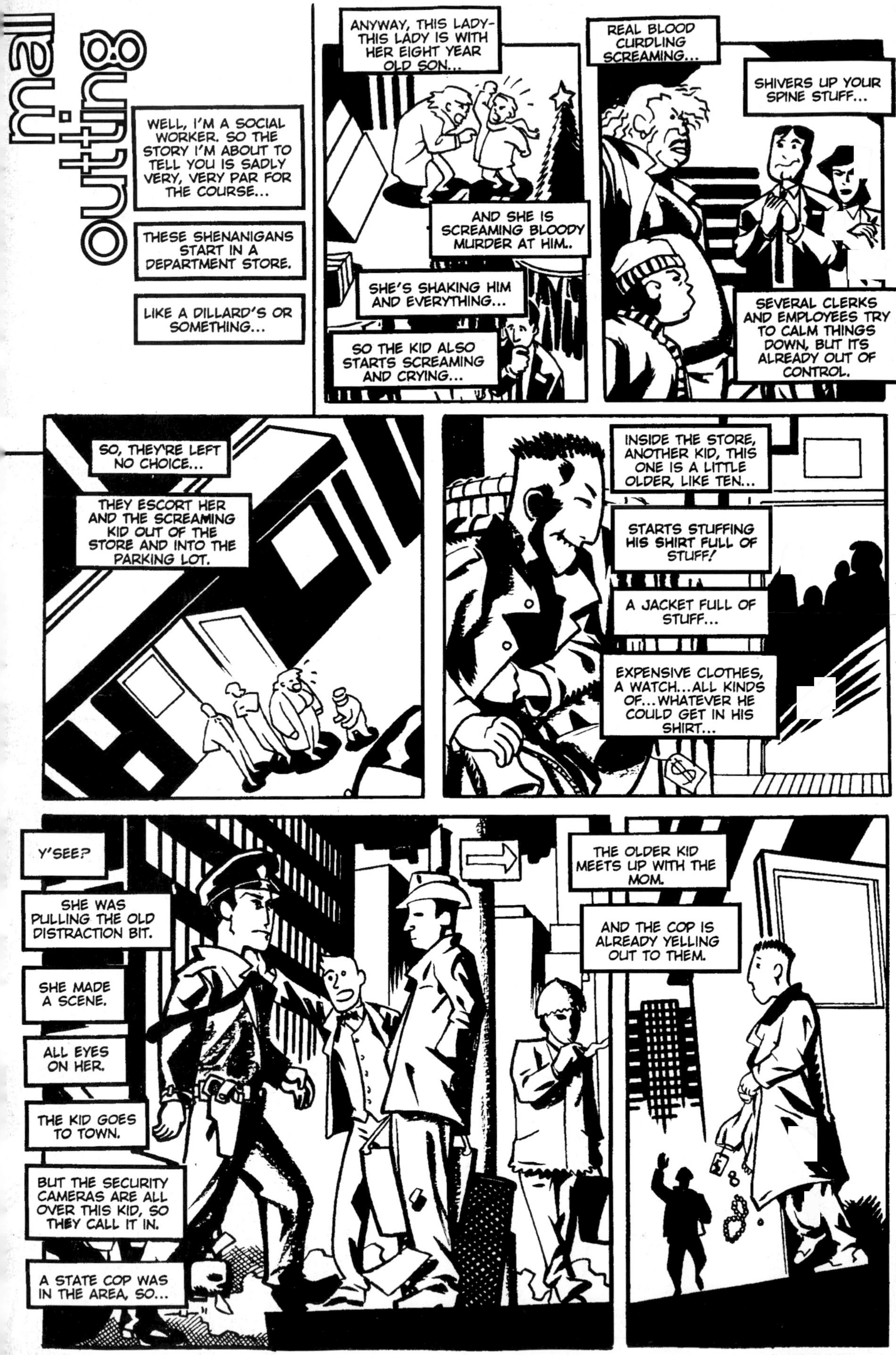
mall outing
WELL, I'M A SOCIAL WORKER. SO THE STORY I'M ABOUT TO TELL YOU IS SADLY VERY, VERY PAR FOR THE COURSE...
THESE SHENANIGANS START IN A DEPARTMENT STORE.
LIKE A DILLARD'S OR SOMETHING...
ANYWAY, THIS LADY- THIS LADY IS WITH HER EIGHT YEAR OLD SON...
AND SHE IS SCREAMING BLOODY MURDER AT HIM..
SHE'S SHAKING HIM AND EVERYTHING...
SO THE KID ALSO STARTS SCREAMING AND CRYING...
REAL BLOOD CURDLING SCREAMING...
SHIVERS UP YOUR SPINE STUFF...
SEVERAL CLERKS AND EMPLOYEES TRY TO CALM THINGS DOWN, BUT ITS ALREADY OUT OF CONTROL.
SO, THEY'RE LEFT NO CHOICE...
THEY ESCORT HER AND THE SCREAMING KID OUT OF THE STORE AND INTO THE PARKING LOT.
INSIDE THE STORE, ANOTHER KID, THIS ONE IS A LITTLE OLDER, LIKE TEN...
STARTS STUFFING HIS SHIRT FULL OF STUFF!
A JACKET FULL OF STUFF...
EXPENSIVE CLOTHES, A WATCH...ALL KINDS OF...WHATEVER HE COULD GET IN HIS SHIRT...
Y'SEE?
SHE WAS PULLING THE OLD DISTRACTION BIT.
SHE MADE A SCENE.
ALL EYES ON HER.
THE KID GOES TO TOWN.
BUT THE SECURITY CAMERAS ARE ALL OVER THIS KID, SO THEY CALL IT IN.
A STATE COP WAS IN THE AREA, SO...
THE OLDER KID MEETS UP WITH THE MOM.
AND THE COP IS ALREADY YELLING OUT TO THEM.

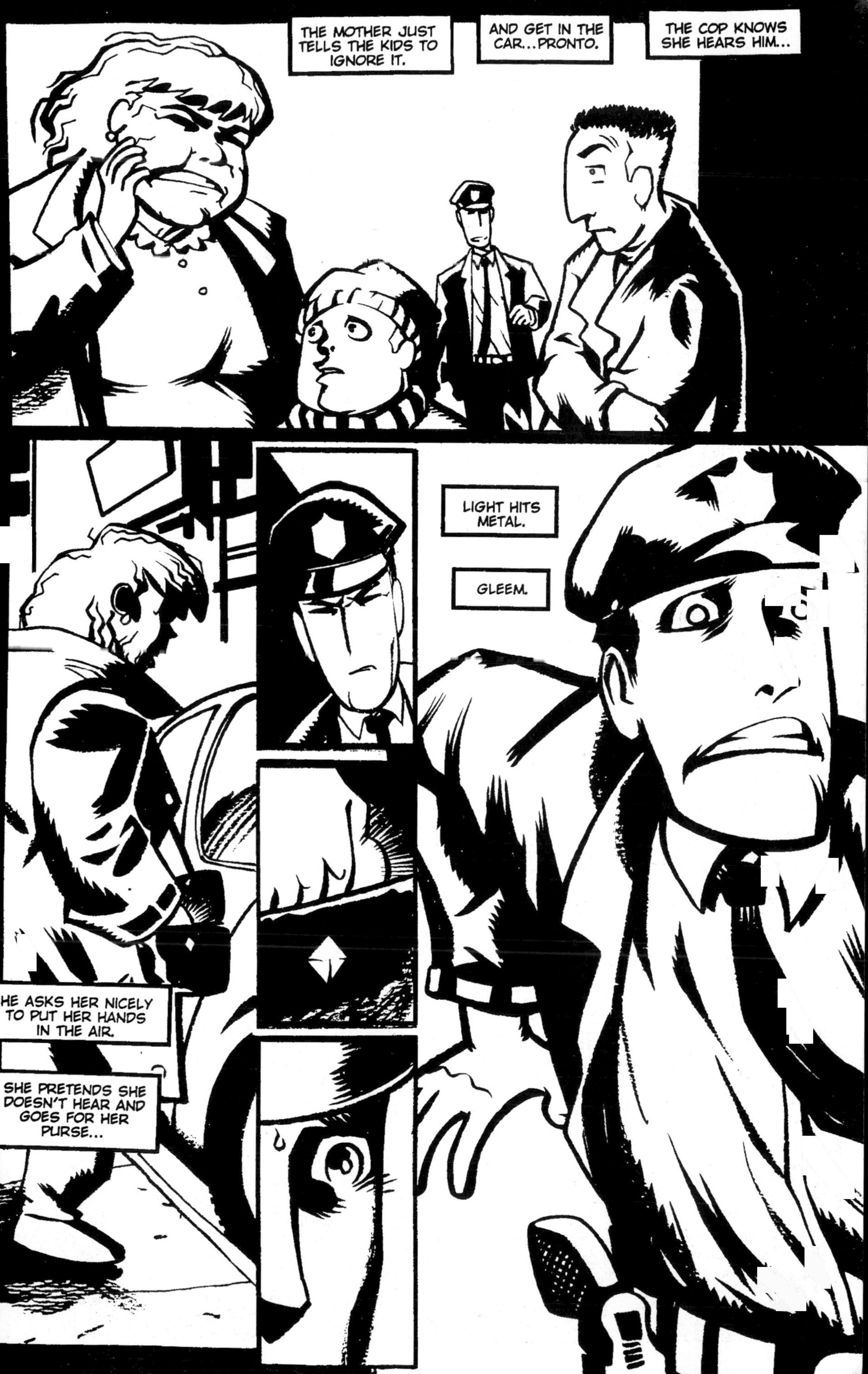
THE MOTHER JUST TELLS THE KIDS TO IGNORE IT.
AND GET IN THE CAR...PRONTO.
THE COP KNOWS SHE HEARS HIM...
HE ASKS HER NICELY TO PUT HER HANDS IN THE AIR.
SHE PRETENDS SHE DOESN'T HEAR AND GOES FOR HER PURSE...
LIGHT HITS METAL.
GLEEM.

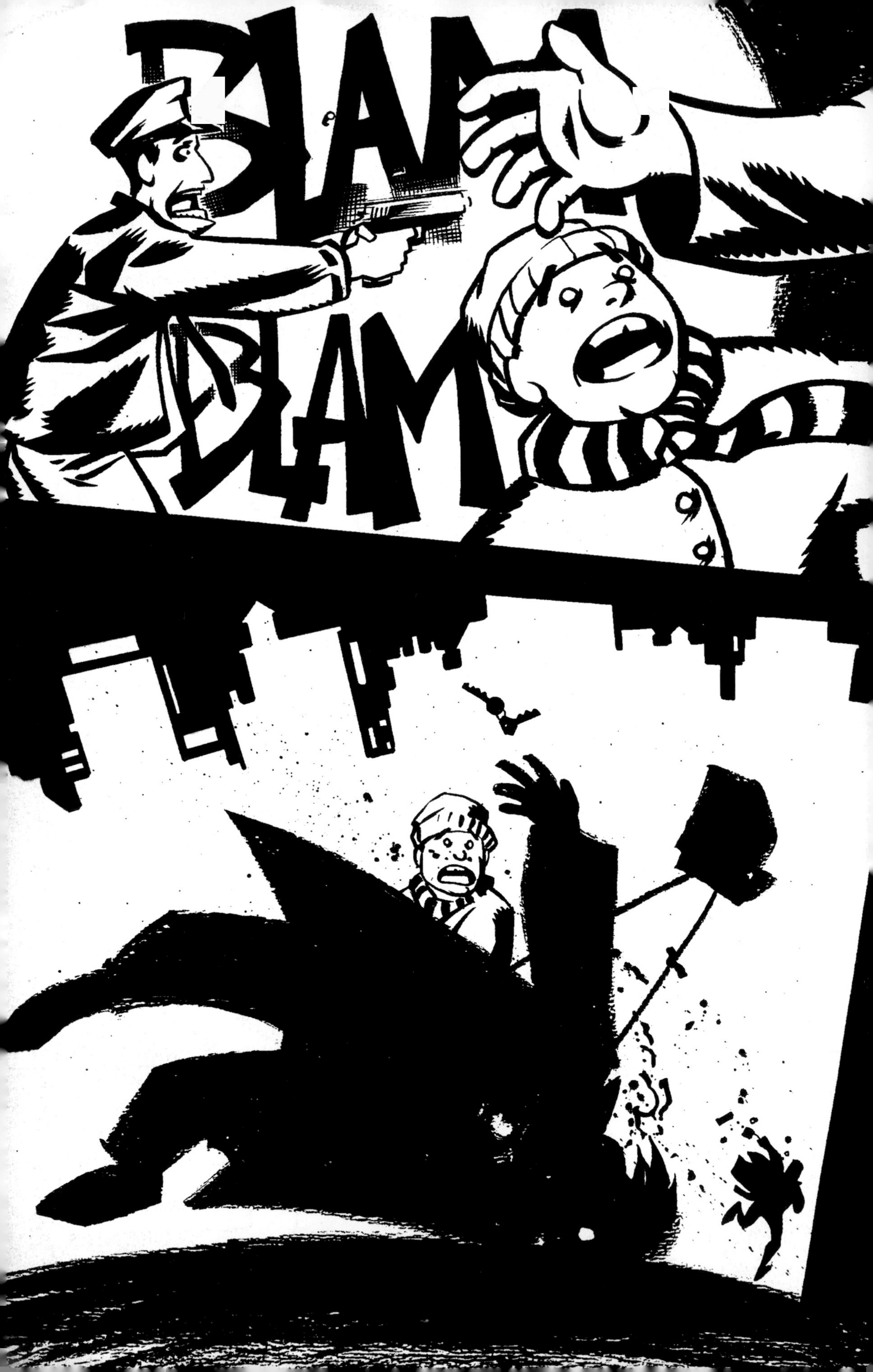
BLAM
BLAM

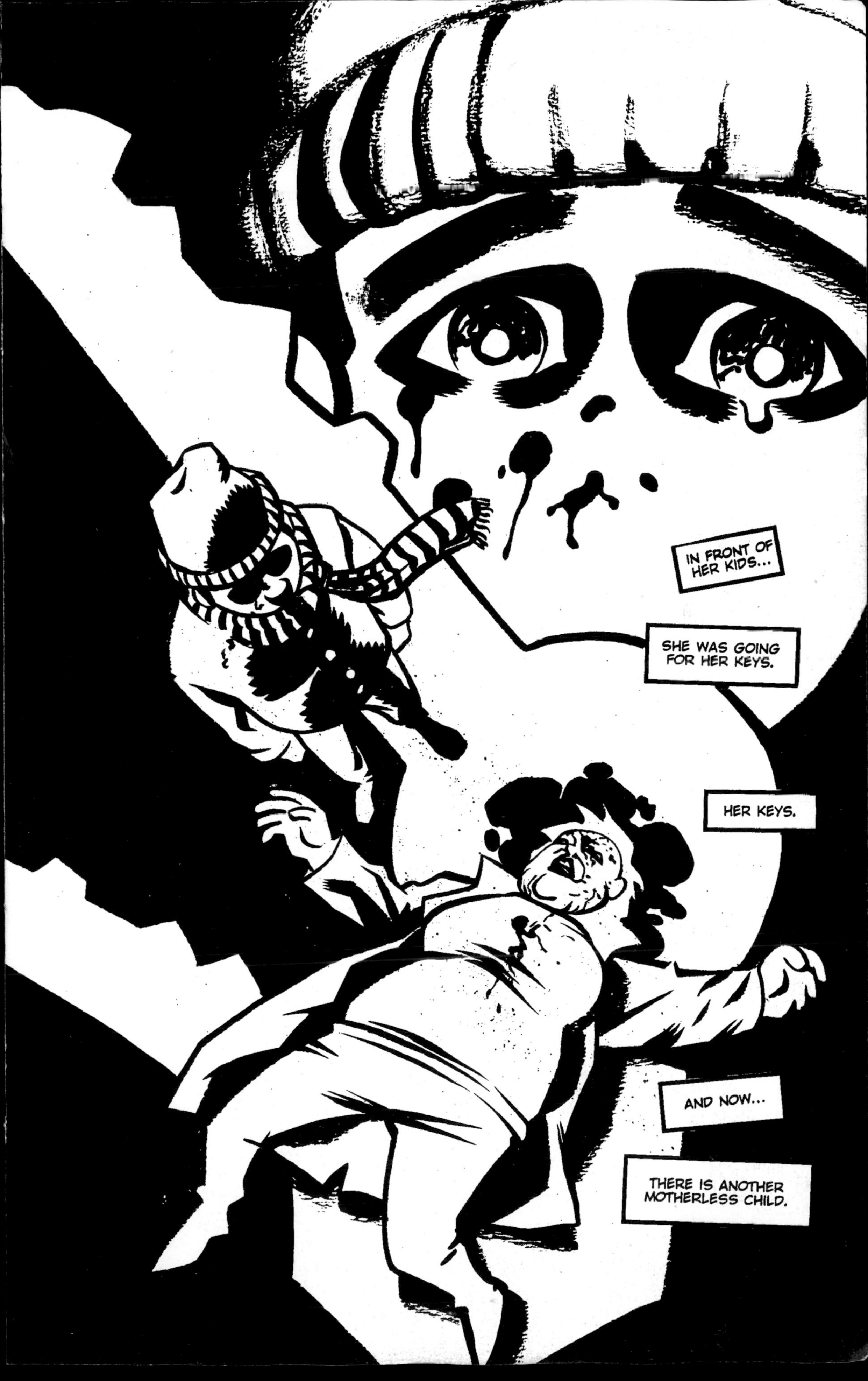
IN FRONT OF HER KIDS...
SHE WAS GOING FOR HER KEYS.
HER KEYS.
AND NOW...
THERE IS ANOTHER MOTHERLESS CHILD.

The following is a part of a very lengthy interview conducted by the rascals at heroreralm.com- for a complete transcript of the interview visit their site.

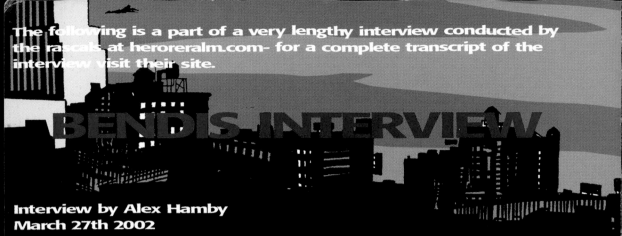

BENDIS INTERVIEW

Interview by Alex Hamby
March 27th 2002

Alex: I'm a big fan of Powers. Where did that idea come from?

Brian: It's hard to put a thing on it...

It was a mixture of Mike [Oeming] and me becoming better friends through the years. He'd always show David Mack and I these drawings he was doing. He started doing drawings in the Powers' style of Kabuki, Jinx and Goldfish because that's what we were working on at the time. They excite both of us but they excited me to such a degree that I couldn't even stand it. At the same time I started analyzing why it was that I never attempted to write a superhero comic but I loved them so much. I really loved the genre – and I realized that a lot of my generation of comic writers, if you weren't assigned on of the heroes, Dark Knight and Watchmen kind of screwed it up for us.

We were raised on the ultimate [not to use Ultimate without getting a royalty] superhero stories in Dark Knight and Watchmen. It's sort of like everything had been said. So, I just moved onto another genre where I thought I had something to say. Then here we come, years later, and I analyze what I like about the genre and what I would have to say about it. I started thinking about the VH1: Behind the Music look at superheroes. Then I started mashing together my love of crime-fiction, love of the police procedural – then I started thinking about what the police procedure would be for superheroes but really get into it.

I had just read Homicide, the book that the TV show is based on, which is an amazing procedural. Then Mike started doing drawings, then I told him the idea and then he started doing drawings based on the idea. Then BOOM you got the whole thing.

Then I read Janice Joplin's biography and for some reason that made it click. I can't tell you why.

Alex: Ah, you're a Janice Joplin fan. We've got something in common. How do your goals differ from Powers and all of your other work?

Brian: They don't. Anything with my name on it has the exact same goal, which is to craft a book that I would buy. That's the goal. My personal goals are very very high. Higher than anyone has got for me, be it my employers or my readers. If my name is on it – There are very few things in this world that you get to leave behind.

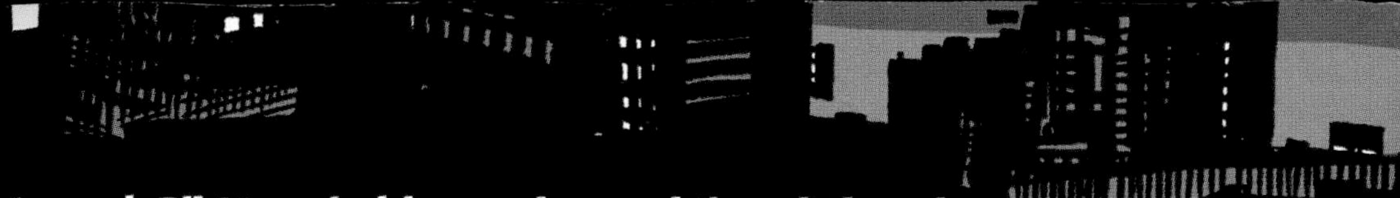

I just read Gil Kane's biography and I'm sitting there going, "You know what, man? There are very few things that will outlive you and comics will outlive me." Clearly we see that they will.

So, kick ass on them. At least make them something you would buy. People will like them, not like them, at least make sure that you will buy them. So, every decision I've made, jobs I take, that's the first test. Would I buy this book? Would I buy Daredevil with Alex Maleev drawing it? Hell yeah! Absolutely.

That's the goal.

As far as Powers is concerned, the only difference is that we get to kill everybody. We get to kill anyone we want whereas that is the one thing we wouldn't be able to do at Marvel. Marvel's not going to let me do a homicide book where I get to kill Captain America. So, we get to analyze the genre from that unique perspective.

Alex: You went through that whole starving artist thing.

Brian: Nine years of it thank you. [laughter]

Alex: You did a lot of stuff that people are retroactively talking about.

Brian: I don't care when they bought it as long as they bought it.

Alex: What do you think finally sparked the attention of Todd McFarlane and then Marvel?

Brian: Well, I actually know this. I was at Image and I had been there for many years before the founders even knew there was an Image central.

We all got comps. Todd was at Top Cow, saw the Goldfish trade and took it. He read it on the way home to Arizona. When he got back he said to Beau Smith, "Hey, find me this guy I think he's at Image." [Laughs]

He just really liked Goldfish, he really liked that kind of storytelling and he offered me a couple of projects. He goes, "I got two projects for you. One is a modern day Frankenstein..."

And I'm like, "Is this really Todd McFarlane on the phone?" It was really surreal, right?

"...it's about a giant monkey robot..." I don't want to do a giant monkey robot book.

Then he goes, "My other one's about two detectives." That sounds good! Then we started talking about Sam and Twitch and it was right up my alley. It wasn't a Spawn book and it was something I could do. That worked out real well.

Exactly at the same time, my friend David Mack started working at

Marvel Knights with Joe Quesada. I was absolutely in love with Marvel Knights, what it meant, what they were trying to do and how they were treating David. I think David slipped them a couple, I think Jinx — and I think Joe just loved Jinx. Loved my writing, not my drawing, which he made very clear.

He called me — you get the Marvel Knights call, which is, "If you came to Marvel what would you do?" And I laundry listed stories I've been writing in my head since I was eleven. We were going to do Nick Fury but that didn't work out. Then Daredevil became a scheduling mess and he asked if David and I would do Daredevil. I was like, "Er, yeah...ok."

That was a book I was actually scared of. It meant so much to me in my youth that I didn't know. But I had a story I had been working on for quite a while and to work with David also was very important to me. David and I have been best friends since we both got into comics and I wanted one time for us to do something worthy of that friendship. So, that was a very personal thing for me.

Then I literally handed in Daredevil scripts and that day Bill Jemas had plopped into Joe's office and said, "Gee, we've been working on this Ultimate Spider-Man but it's not coming together. Who would you hire?" And shockingly Joe said me. We took it from there.

Joe calls me and says, "You're going to get a call to start Spider-Man over again."

Alex: So, it happened all because you took on Daredevil?

Brian: If anything this says — and we're talking nine years into my comic book career this is happening — It's literally being in the right place at the right time. Finally one of my trades is on someone's desk at the right moment and finally I handed in a script and I was on someone's mind at the time when something I was qualified to do came around the pike.

I get this email everyday, every hour, that's like, "Help me. I can't break in."

I'm like, "Dude, I'm the last person to ask." I mean I Forest Gumped my way through this like no one's business. I am eager to be here and I am so happy but meanwhile I sent in 4,000 submissions between the age of 20 and 25 — I just stopped. I thought no one's interested. It's a lottery anyhow. Finally someone who could do something put me on a book like that.

It was fun and I didn't get fired right away, which I assumed was going to happen. So that was fun too.

I handed in a script for Ultimate two days after I got the gig. There was no Spider-Man, there's no costume. Either they're going to shit on this or they're going to love it. Thankfully they loved it or I would have been kill-feed me, you would have never heard my name again.

Alex: Here's the ego question: Do you think your taking the Marvel gig led to the company's regaining some of the momentum it had lost?

Brian: I think decisions like hiring people like myself, David, Paul Jenkins and Straczynski — there's a thought process there that I am very proud to be a part of. I am one of a few things that worked out pretty well. My goals are pure and so are those of my friends who I just mentioned. We all just want to make really good comics with a unique voice. People really wanted that.

David and I kinda joke that we had to wait till everyone else left comics before we got our shot. Everyone from the early nineties left. They made their money, or they didn't, and they left. We stayed because we were going to stay either way. I would have just made my black and white comics and I would have been fine. So, we finally got our shot because there was nobody else left to hire.

I don't think it's me but I think there's a decision making process that is very forward thinking. I like working for forward thinking people. I like it in comics, when I'm working on stuff outside of comics — I like it when people are thinking outside the box.

Alex: Here's a long one: Now that you are with Marvel doing Alias, Daredevil, Ultimate Spider-Man and you're producing a Spider-Man cartoon, are you an independent writer working for a mainstream company or a mainstream writer who happens to do an indy comic in the form or Powers?

Brian: I run a company and one of the services that I provide Marvel is a big client for. Jinxworld is a company and it produces Powers and out of there comes my work for Marvel.

It's really weird because I don't put labels on any of this stuff. I treat it all the same. Just because it has my name on it, it has to be treated as if it's the last book I am going to get to write. As if it is the only shot I am going to get at this. I give it everything I've got.

I don't care about all of this other stuff. What I care about is the fact that one of these books will be the first book that someone picks up — of mine or of comics.

Alex: Good answer.

Brian: I don't want it to suck. Even if you don't like it you can at least say it's an interesting decision process. It's not my cup of tea but at least I can see the people behind it gave it shot.

Alex: Now, with working on so many books, how do you manage to give them each a unique voice?

Brian: A) I don't drink. [Laughs] There are traps of this business that I've learned wisely from the generation before me.

I have always admired and respected the work of people who

produced a lot of work like Jack Kirby and John Romita. I think that them producing a lot of work made the work a lot better. I think that when they were using all of their steam, it wasn't the volume of the work that mattered it was the quality that mattered. I always aspired to be that kind of comic creator. On the same note, I don't want to be "Oh look he can write 50 titles". I have no interest in being that guy. It's just I can.

So, I don't drink and I don't play video games, which is the more horrible thing to happen to mainstream comics — the creation of Playstation. If they would take them away from comic creators you wouldn't even hear about a late book.

So, there's that and I am way way ahead of schedule. I am six months ahead on all of my books. That means whatever mood I'm in when I wake up, that's the book I'll write. There's no deadline emergency. If I wake up and I'm in a Daredevil mood — Usually when the book comes out and Alex [Maleev] and I are talking I am in a Daredevil mood, I'll write Daredevil because I'm in a mood to write it. I can be in a Powers mood for two solid weeks and write tons of it.

Alex: So, how long does it take you to turn out a book?

Brian: I don't know. Sometimes it takes a long time and sometimes you have a creative orgasm and it comes out of you. Not to be gross but sometimes it comes out of you. Don't you ever get to typing and, you know, it just builds and comes right out of you. I don't know, it's just very organic. When the organic thing's happening it's a lot of fun.

Sometimes I type something that ends up looking like an Alan Moore script. Then I go back on a day when I am less of a fanatic and I format it so it looks normal. [Laughs]

That's the thing. If you stay ahead of schedule deadline is not an issue. It's all pure. So, anytime I have to write something under a crunch, I always hate it. I just don't want that feeling. That's just spoiling myself but it works for me.

Alex: Let's switch gears. This will be where things turn a little bit. I read in the back of an issue of Powers where you spoke about continuity. It was a transcript from a convention where you spoke about continuity. Can you give me a couple highlights regarding your beliefs regarding continuity?

Brian: What did I say? [Laughs]

Alex: Alright, I'll tell you. I can't quote it verbatim, I'll just get the basic jist...

Brian: Yeah, fine.

Alex: Your idea regarding continuity was respect for creators who came before you; that you didn't want to contradict someone else's work.

Brian: Yeah.

Alex: So, you hold true to that statement?

Brian: Yeah, pretty much. That's not the only thing but yeah.

Alex: I would think that this comes from the fact that the comic industry, as a standard rule, treats itself like a mini-Hollywood.

Brian: Not really. It may be perceived that way by you but a lot of the people I know in comics don't treat it like the be all end all of human existence. They are so happy to be doing comics.

Alex: Errrr...

Brian: I know. There are people in this business but they come and go so quickly that they don't even count to me. They are making properties so they can sell them. That sort of stuff.

Alex: But there are people in the industry who still act like that. We've been in and around the industry since the 90's. There's still that fan perception of creators thinking they are above the fans.

Brian: Are you saying that there are comic creators who act above the fans?

Alex: Yes. There's a lot of them.

Brian: There are a few of them. I would call those people assholes. Let's refer to them as assholes and there are assholes everywhere. That's not just in comics. That's everywhere! You leave the house and you're going to bump into an asshole.

There are people, say you walk around the small press alley, and you find people who are acting like they are royalty deserving some sort of entitlement and they're shocked that you don't see it. They're just waiting for a mainstream break so they can be assholes to everyone. That guy is just waiting for a reason.

My thing is: I don't choose to view comics that way because there are so many people who don't act that way.

Alex: Can I ask you a question?

Brian: Yeah.

Alex: Based on the Internet, based on simply type written words on a screen, how is anyone supposed to make an accurate judgment call on anyone else?

Brian: Here's an idea: Just read the books and enjoy them.

END

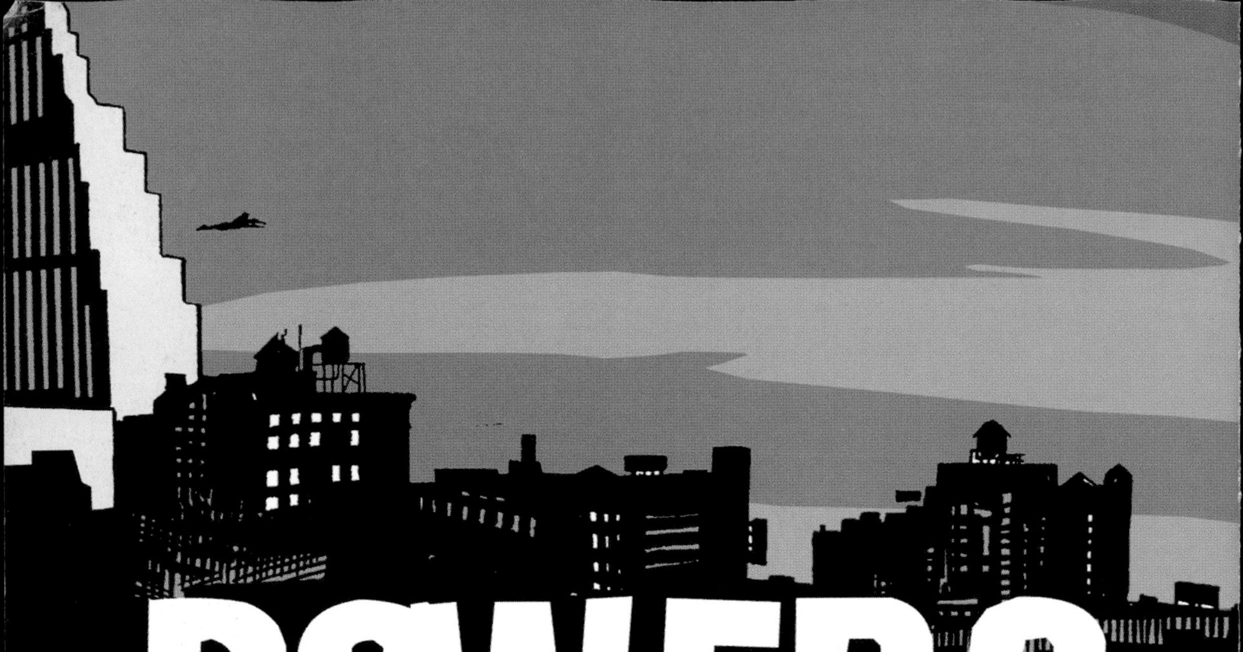

POWERS
COVER GALLERY AND SKETCHBOOK

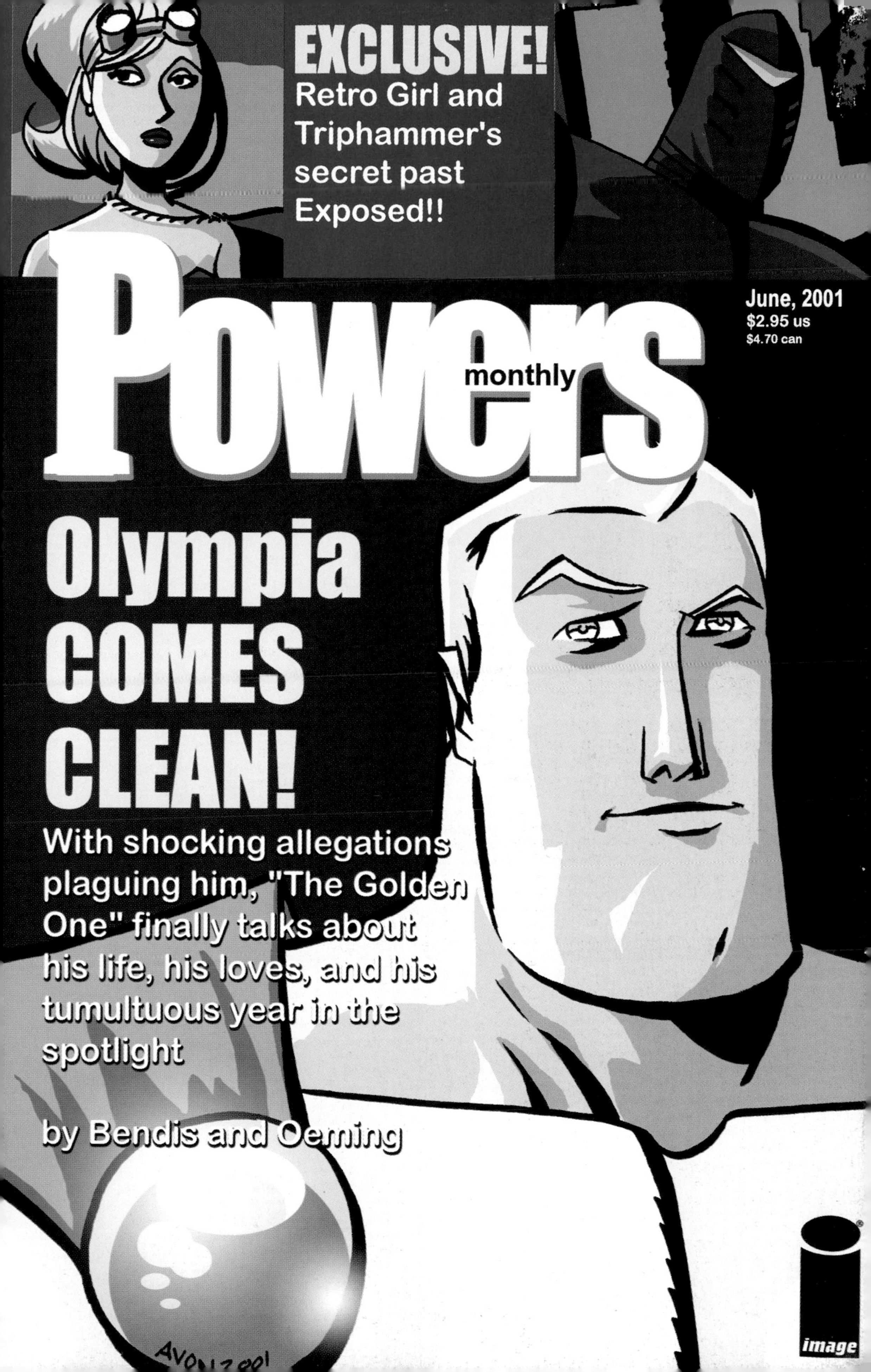
EXCLUSIVE!
Retro Girl and Triphammer's secret past Exposed!!
Powers monthly
June, 2001
$2.95 us
$4.70 can
Olympia COMES CLEAN!
With shocking allegations plaguing him, "The Golden One" finally talks about his life, his loves, and his tumultuous year in the spotlight
by Bendis and Oeming
image

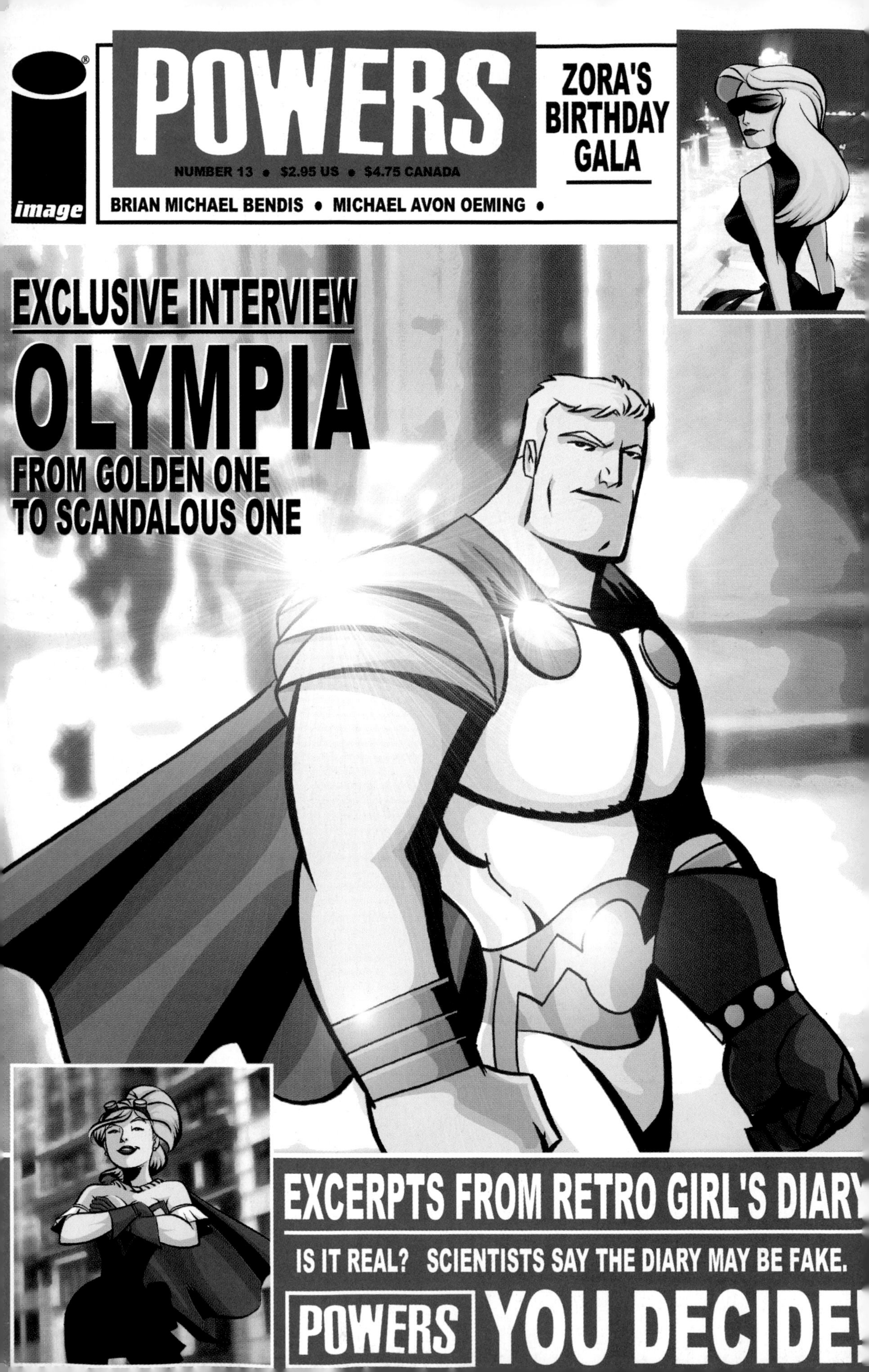
image
POWERS
NUMBER 13 • $2.95 US • $4.75 CANADA
BRIAN MICHAEL BENDIS • MICHAEL AVON OEMING •
ZORA'S BIRTHDAY GALA
EXCLUSIVE INTERVIEW
OLYMPIA
FROM GOLDEN ONE TO SCANDALOUS ONE
EXCERPTS FROM RETRO GIRL'S DIARY
IS IT REAL? SCIENTISTS SAY THE DIARY MAY BE FAKE.
POWERS
YOU DECIDE!

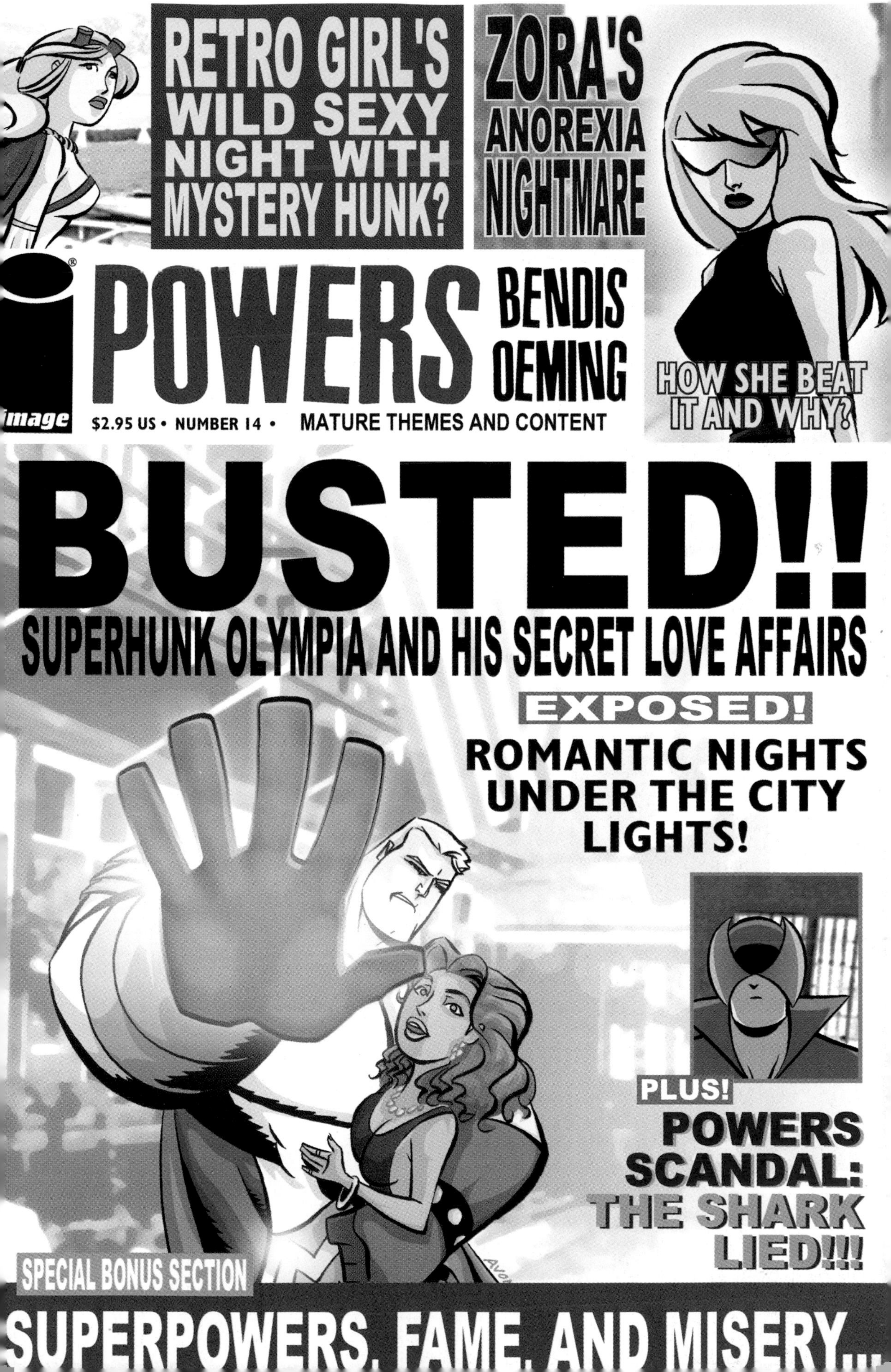
RETRO GIRL'S WILD SEXY NIGHT WITH MYSTERY HUNK?
ZORA'S ANOREXIA NIGHTMARE
image
POWERS
BENDIS OEMING
$2.95 US • NUMBER 14 • MATURE THEMES AND CONTENT
HOW SHE BEAT IT AND WHY?
BUSTED!!
SUPERHUNK OLYMPIA AND HIS SECRET LOVE AFFAIRS
EXPOSED!
ROMANTIC NIGHTS UNDER THE CITY LIGHTS!
PLUS!
POWERS SCANDAL: THE SHARK LIED!!!
SPECIAL BONUS SECTION
SUPERPOWERS. FAME. AND MISERY...

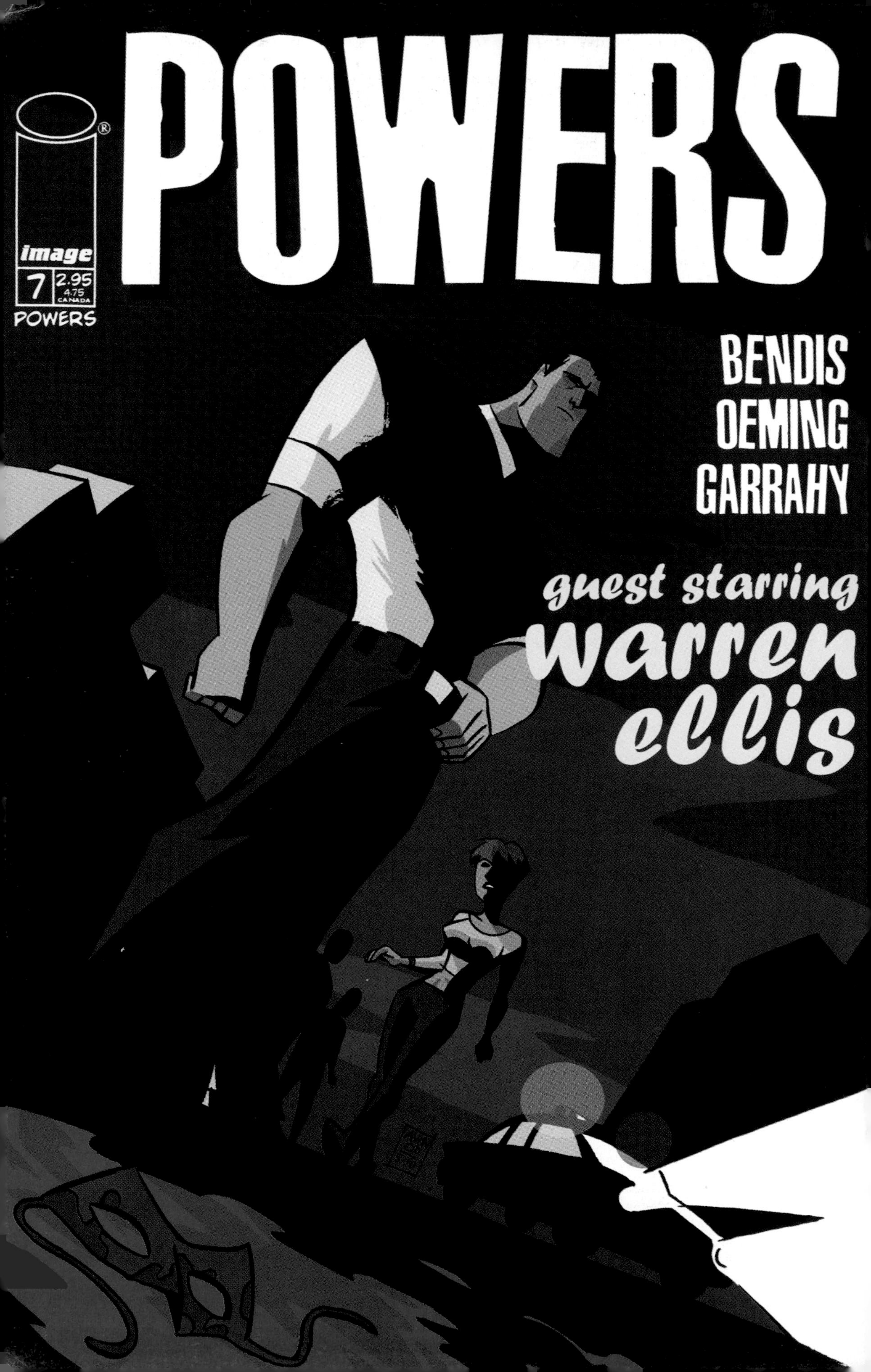
POWERS
image
7
2.95
4.75 CANADA
POWERS
BENDIS
OEMING
GARRAHY
guest starring
warren
ellis

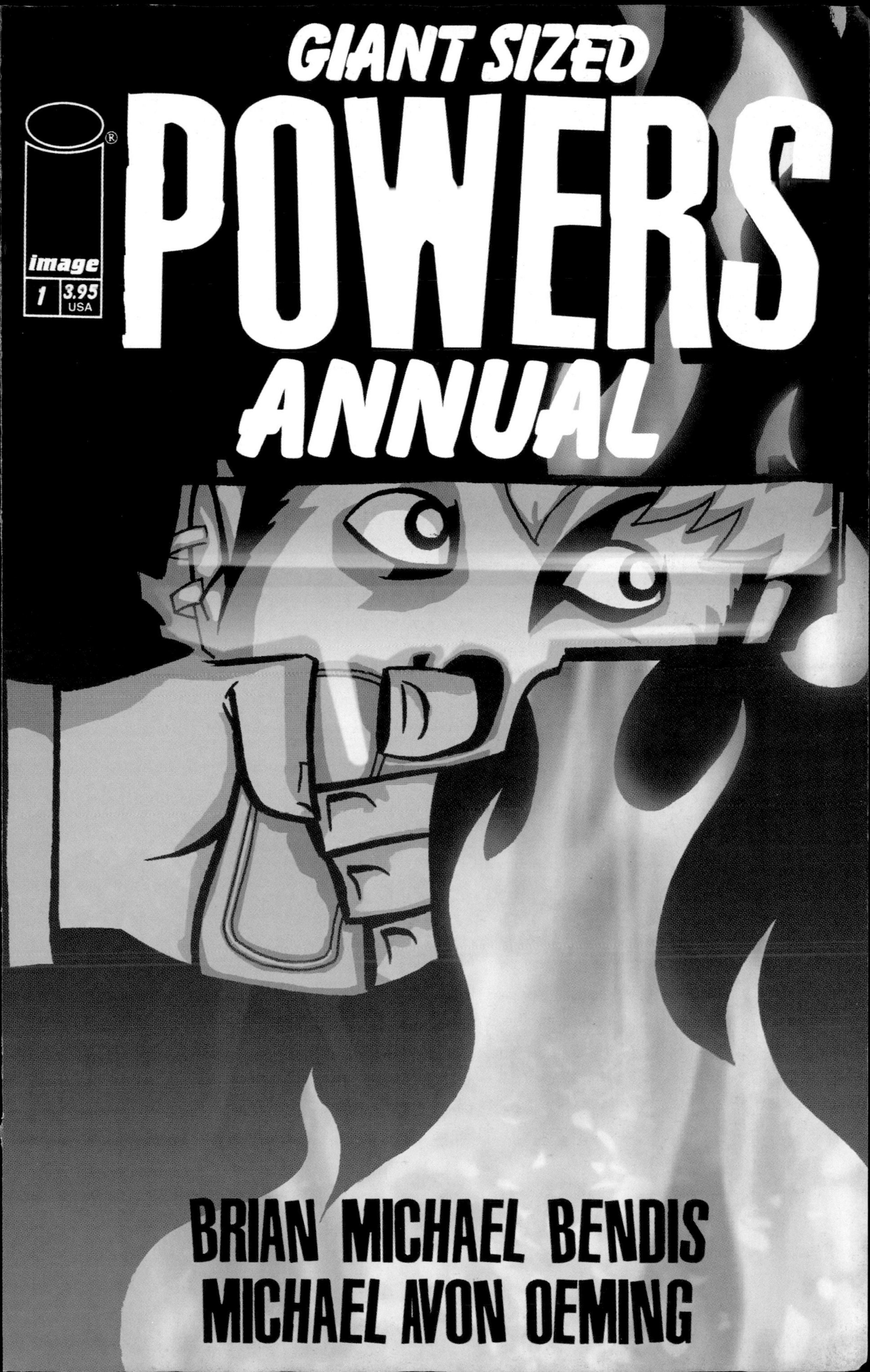
GIANT SIZED
POWERS
ANNUAL
image
1
3.95
USA
BRIAN MICHAEL BENDIS
MICHAEL AVON OEMING

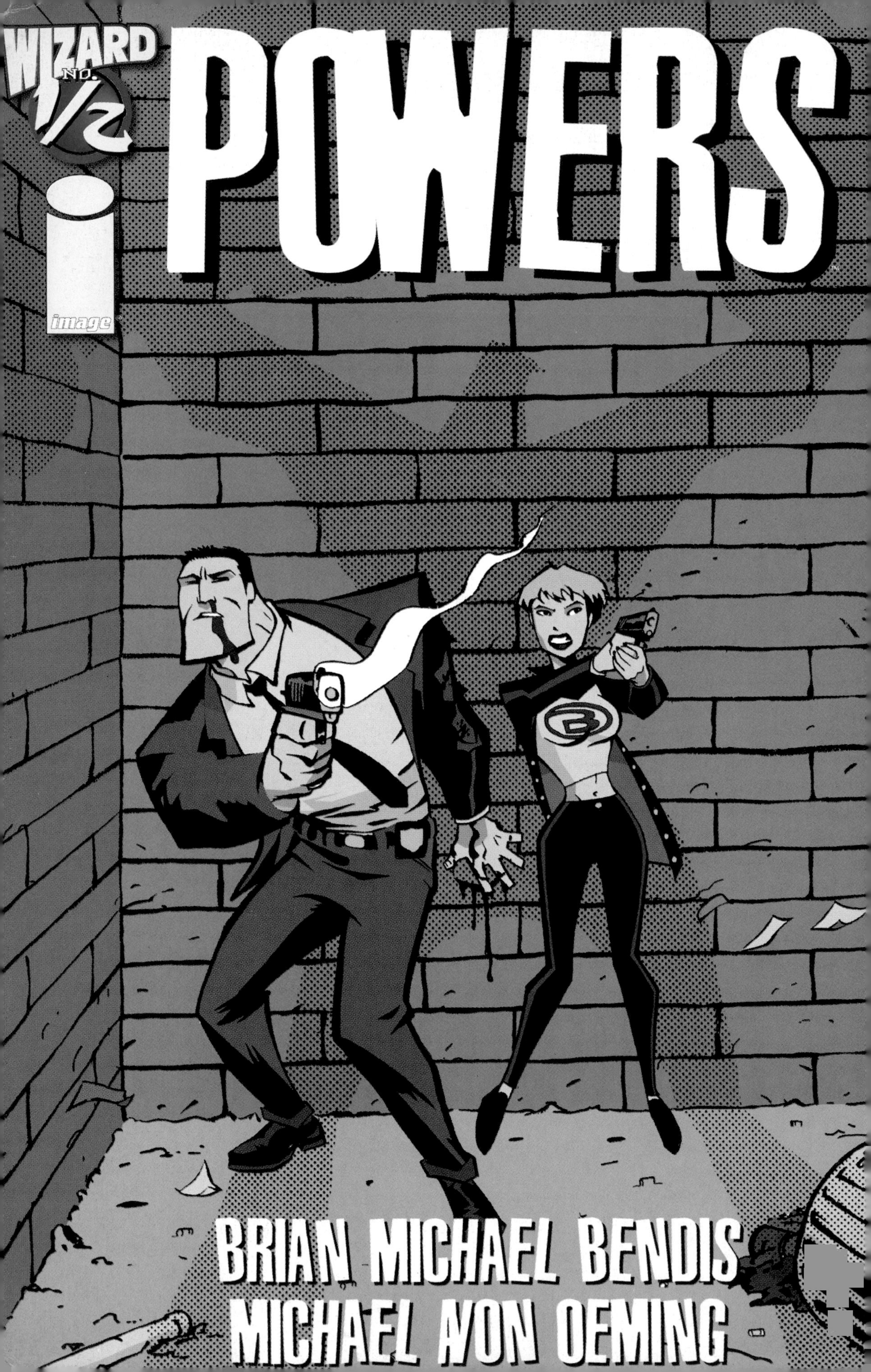
WIZARD
NO. 1/2
POWERS
image
BRIAN MICHAEL BENDIS
MICHAEL AVON OEMING

SKETCHES

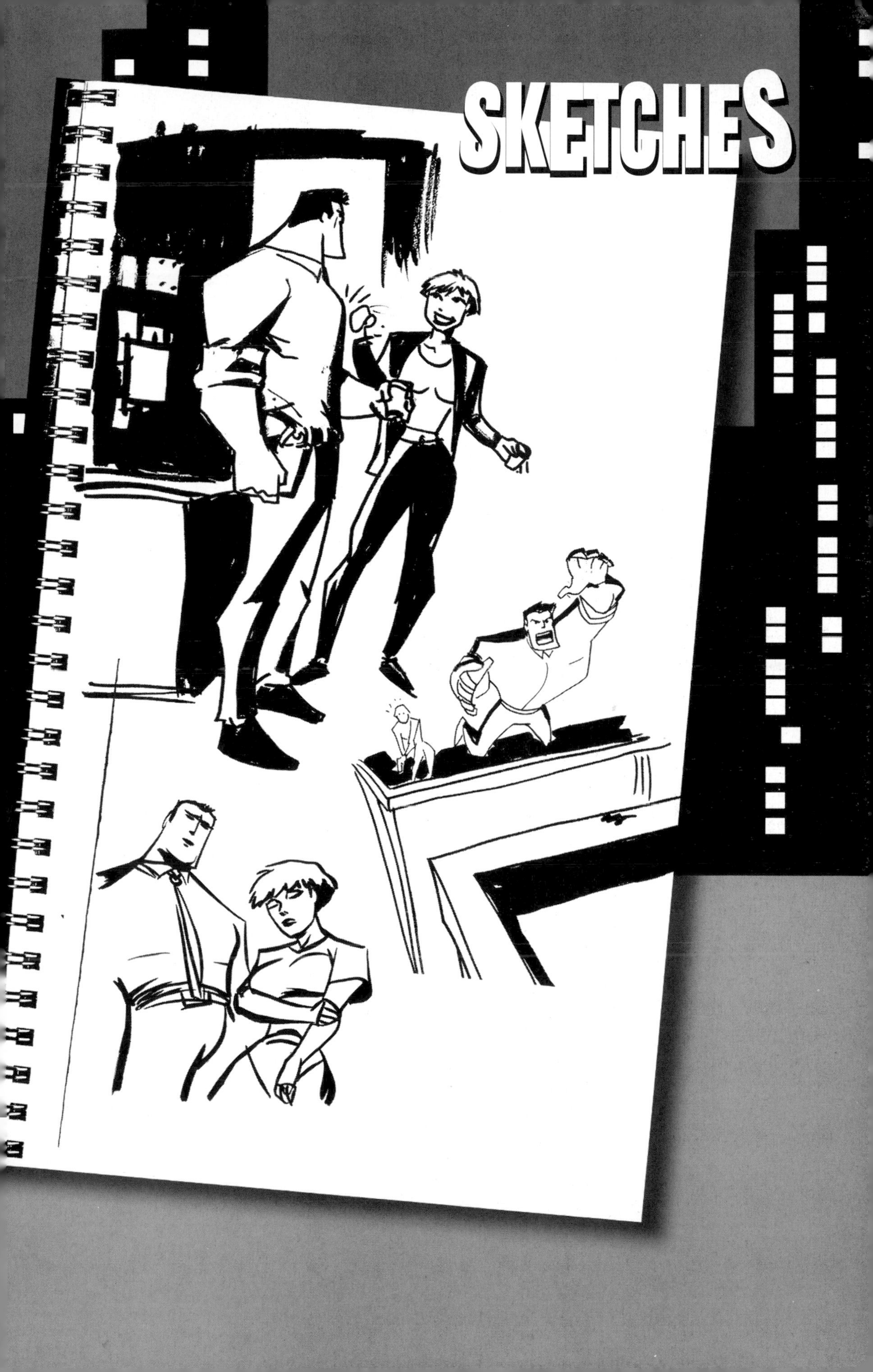

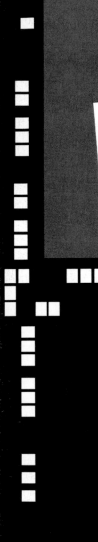

WE CAN TAKE ANY IMAGE + BREAK IT UP WITH SHARDS.
I'VE ALSO DONE A PATCH ON THE ONE WITH BIG-JAWED
WALKER + PILGRIM LOOKING OUT WINDOW —
ILL DO THAT MULTI-PANELED ONE TOO.
—m

NEWSPAPER SHOT.

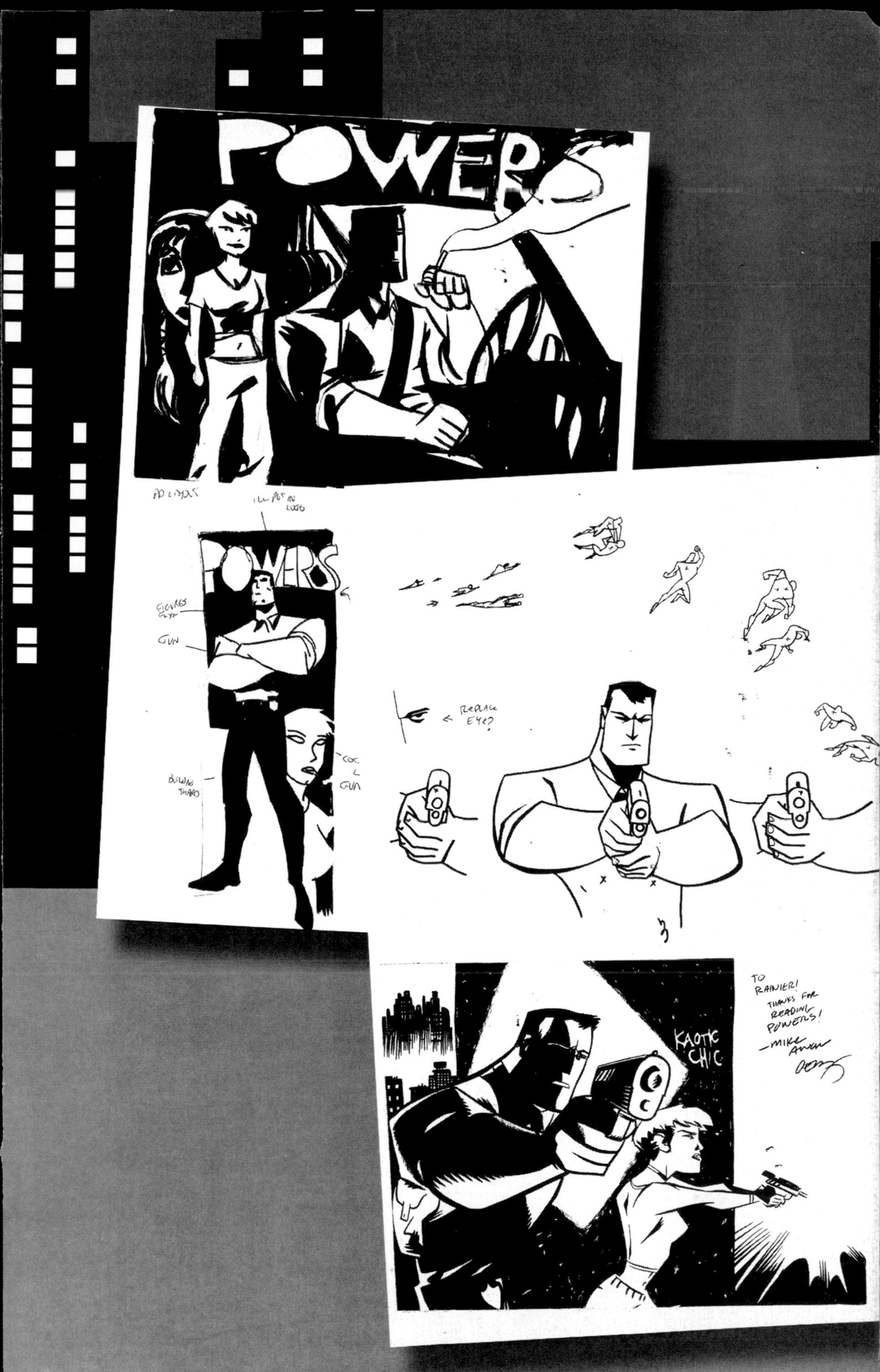
POWERS
AD LAYOUT
I'LL PUT IN LOGO
POWERS
FIGURES FLYIN
GUN
REPLACE EYE?
KAOTIC CHIC
TO RAINIER! THANKS FOR READING POWERS!
—MIKE AVON

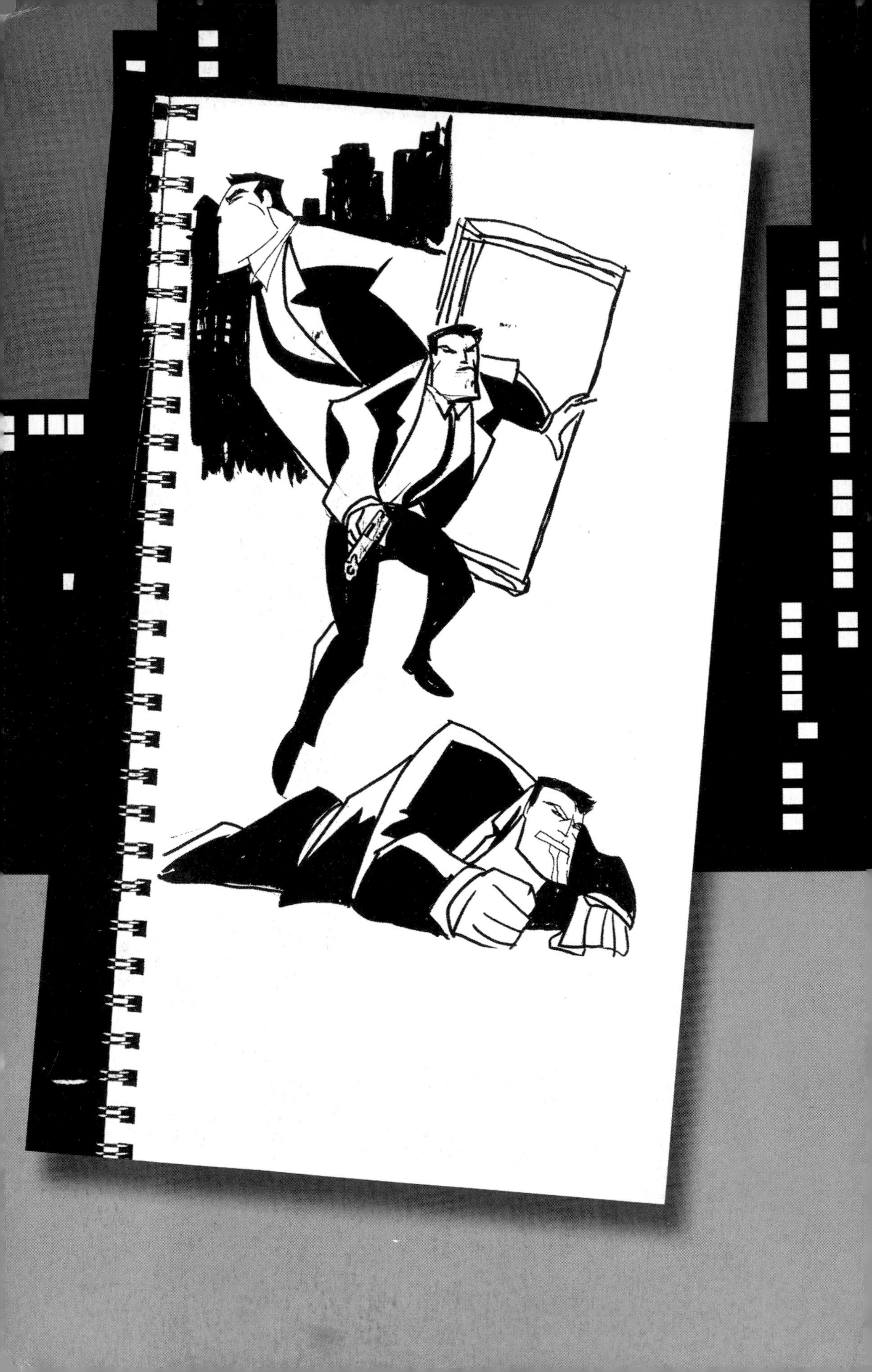

SKETCHES

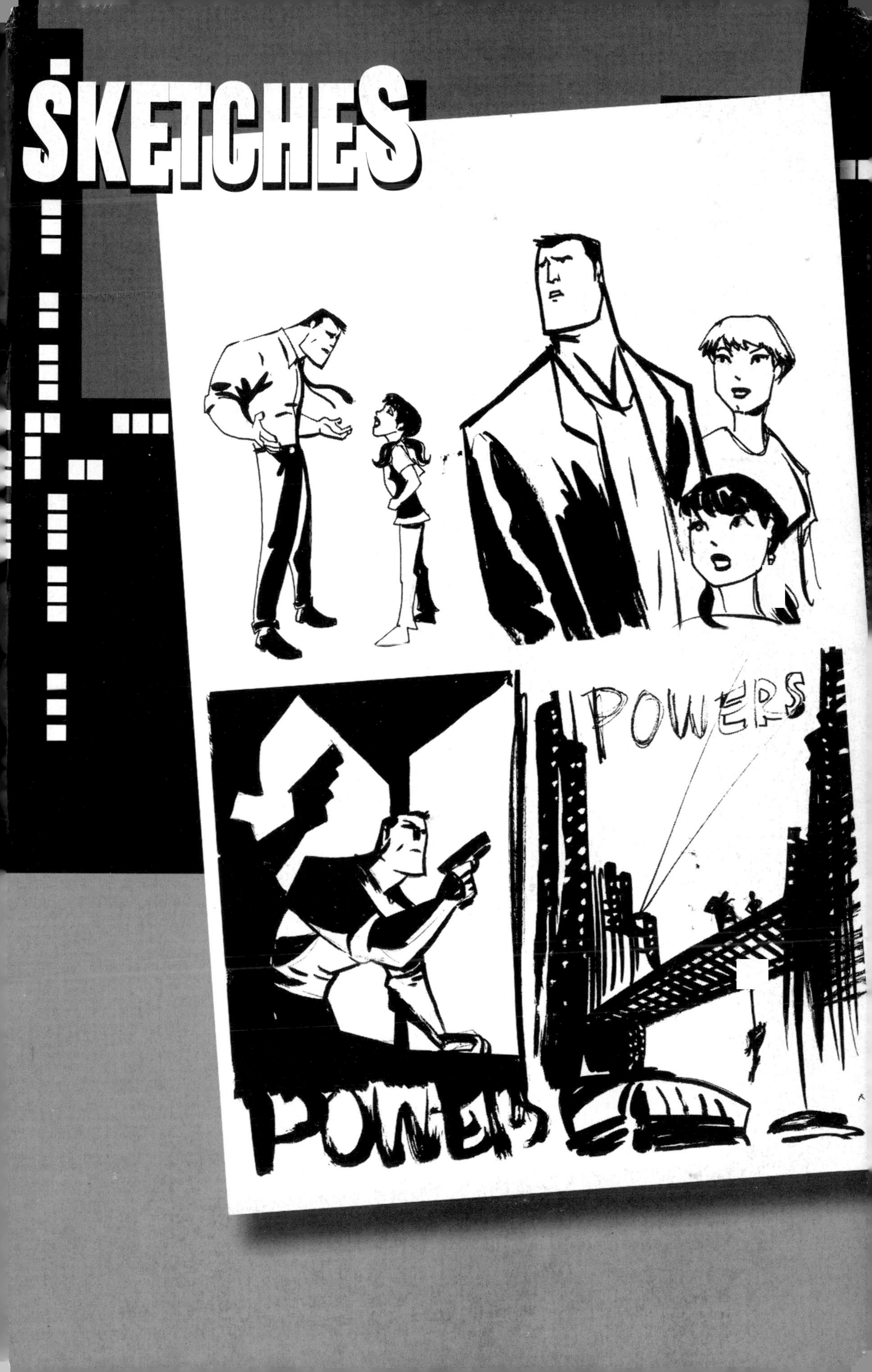
POWERS
POWERS